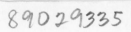

THE CREATIVE WRITER

The Creative Writer

Second Revised Edition

Edited by Aron M. Mathieu

WRITER'S DIGEST, CINCINNATI, OHIO 45210

Acknowledgements

Page 7: Photographs of the monastery at New Melleray by George Laycock. Page 12: Collage by Herb Beard. Page 71: From *Writing For Very Young Children,* by Claudia Lewis, Copyright 1954 by Bank Street College of Education, Reprinted by permission of Simon and Schuster, Inc. Page 118: From *The Realities Of Fiction,* by Nancy Hale, Copyright 1962 by Nancy Hale, Reprinted by permission of Little, Brown and Company. Page 125: From *Writers At Work: The Paris Review Interviews, Second Series,* Copyright 1963 by The Paris Review, Inc., Reprinted by permission of The Viking Press, Inc. Page 126: From *The Note-Book Of Anton Chekhov,* translated from the Russian by S. S. Koteliansky and Leonard Woolf, Copyright 1921 by B. W. Huebsch, Inc., Copyright 1949 by the translators, Reprinted by permission of The Viking Press, Inc. Page 129: From *The Elements Of Style,* by William Strunk, Jr., and E. B. White, Copyright 1959 by The MacMillan Co., Reprinted by permission of The MacMillan Co. Page 130: Photograph by Jacob Lofman from Pix. Page 201: From *The Greeting Card Writer's Handbook,* Copyright 1968 by H. Joseph Chadwick. Page 213: From *The Letters Of Thomas Wolfe,* edited by Elizabeth Nowell, Copyright 1956 by Edward C. Aswell. Page 214: Drawing by Diane Satterfield. Page 216: Copyright 1951 by Erskine Caldwell. Page 242: Copyright 1950 by William Saroyan, Condensed from *The Assyrian and Other Stories,* Reprinted by permission of Harcourt, Brace and Company, Inc. Page 274: From *The Summing Up,* Copyright 1938 by W. Somerset Maugham, Reprinted by permission of Doubleday & Co., Inc. Page 314: *A Decade Of American Poetry,* by Judson Jerome, Copyright 1968, *Saturday Review,* Inc., Reprinted by permission of *Saturday Review* and Judson Jerome. Page 320: Photograph by Victor Laredo. Copyright 1965 by *Writer's Digest,* Inc. Page 346: Photographs by Frederic B. Knoop. Pages 348-416: Copyright Aron M. Mathieu. Magazine layouts copyright Vogue. Mondrian adaptation by Don Ashcraft.

DESIGNED BY DON ASHCRAFT

Standard Book Number 911654-26-7
Library of Congress Card Number 68-56995
Printed in the United States of America

Foreword

The end papers of this edition of *The Creative Writer* offer some variations of the design you see on the cover. The artist who designed them, Barron Krody, took on a job similar to an editor who is asked to fill the interior of a magazine. Resolutely, he set out to fill the space. Some of his variations rise to wit and intellectuality—the sort of thing an editor seeks and rarely finds in his basket. Seeing these variations, and feeling that they made my day, reminded me of the day Harold Ross, after editing *The New Yorker* for twenty successful years, was reading a galley proof aloud to his editors. He completed half a galley, and, with the innocence that made him a legend, said: "Well, *now* we are beginning to get the kind of copy we want."

Each day in publishing brings its own special reward; sometimes the occasion is an "in" thing and only the insider thinks of it as a gift. One particular day in the publishing business that I often think of started out as one of the ordinary days. There was space to be filled, 80 pages of it, and like every editor, I hoped for something fine to turn up so we wouldn't have to use our least worst.

In the magazine business, you begin each month with a blank dummy. In just 30 days, your publication has to be edited, printed, and distributed all over the world. The pay? They give you another blank dummy and let you start over again.

Someone started the romantic notion that this sort of thing makes for a life-long attachment. There are people who, when they hear the words "printer's ink," instantly know "it gets into your blood." It does, too; the damn stuff has tar in it.

Everything was about the same at our shop on this particular

5

day. *Farm Quarterly,* our 75-cent quarterly for the top farmer, was running a little late. The cover paper was cut against the grain and wouldn't fold true and nobody could cut the extra words on a 15 pica caption so it came out 2 lines flush.

The editors of our photographic magazine were critically staring at Kodachromes in a light box, hoping that something would pop up that would "save the April issue."

At this point, a young free-lance writer by the name of Skippy Adelman, a bundle of wiry energy and dead-pan wit, wandered into our office.

A *Writer's Digest* staffer collared him and Skippy, being a free-lance writer, and the hour being noon, stopped to listen. The conversation went something like this:

"You're a writer, Skip. Come here and help us."

"I was just on my way to lunch . . . . ."

"Look, fella, we're thinking up ideas for prizes in our *Writer's Digest* short story contest. We've got all the usuals, but we want something special, something a writer really wants. What do you want, Skip?"

Adelman, who has the general appearance of a bantamweight champ, fixed a moody eye on what he apparently considered an opponent.

"Me, I'm a monastic fellow. All I want, is a cell, a loaf of bread and a cheese."

The editor said thanks, proceeded to compose the following memo:

Idea suggested by free-lance writer named Adelman for short story contest.

Consider this fellow's request. Lives in New York. Somewhere in the Village, 4th or 5th floor. Noisy, with streams of people going by on the ground floor. He sends out a manuscript. Comes back. Needs a rewrite. Can he hustle over for a conference? No ideas! Do it anyway. Cut 3,000 words down to 2,000. Put in an ancedote of 300 words but keep the whole thing to 2,000 words. No wonder this fellow wants to go to a monastery.

Peace and time to think. That's what he wants. Could we manage to give something like this in our

contest? A jug of wine, a loaf of bread and a monk's simple garment.

The boss editor got this memo. Mechanically, he corrected the spelling, the punctuation. He wrote a neat OK on the memo, and thoughtfully underlined it.

Far out in Dubuque, Iowa, the country telephone of the trappist monastery rang three longs and one short.

A voice said: "What do you want?" The phrase seemed abrupt rather than ecclesiastical. The *Writer's Digest* editor, worried but sincere, wondered how he should handle the conversation. Assailed by a vague doubt, he waved his secretary to an extension phone to record the conversation:

"Sir, to whom am I speaking? Is this my long distance call?"

"I don't know. I just picked up the phone."

"I mean who is this? Say, is this the trappist monastery?"

"Sure is. Why?"

"Sir, I have never spoken to a gentleman in a monastery before, and I don't know the proper way to address you. Do I say, 'Your holiness'?"

"Better save that for St. Peter."

"Ah, then, what may I call you Sir?"

"Call me Father Vincent. That's my name. Last name's Daly."

"D-a-l-e-y?"

7

"No. You're taking the Irish out of it. Drop the 'e'."

"Well, Father Vincent . . ." and the editor explained the nature of his call and the desire to award to some fortunate writer two weeks at the monastery, all expenses paid.

"We would like to reimburse you for the costs of putting up this guest. Would ten a day suffice?"

"My, no. A dollar a day is enough. Your free-lance writer may come any time. There's a nice guest house. I've lived in New York and I know just what those fellows are up against. He'd enjoy it here."

"Well, Father, we do want to reimburse you and we shall. Now may this writer enjoy any exercise in your retreat?"

"Say, if we see him standing around and we have an extra wheelbarrow, we'll let him put it to use."

"That will be novel, that is, after several days of meditation."

"This is a farm, you know. We work. No softies here. You ought to come out and see us. Do you good. The brothers have taken the vow of silence, you know."

"But the Abbott may speak to anyone?"

"Yes. Also the gate porter. What's this magazine, *Writer's Digest*? We know your *Farm Quarterly*."

The editor then explained *Writer's Digest* to Father Vincent Daly.

"Will you spell your monastery's name, please?"

"Sure thing. New Melleray. N for Nellie. Say, by the way, that prize goes to a man only. No women here. But any religion, any color."

The editor agreed and it was a deal.

That's the way it was, one late afternoon, during the 31 years I edited *Writer's Digest* and *The Writer's Year Book*. The New Melleray exploit didn't quite end there, however, for one of the editors thought it best to assure himself that there really was a trappist monastery near Dubuque and that a contest winner in our annual story contest would not only be able to get in, but out. He visited the good Fathers, and while there sent us a note along with the pleasant snapshots at the top of page 7. His note said: "The wine is old and red; the cheese cool and sharp; bed is firm. Will return."

The pleasures of publishing, I am sure, are romanticized, since the job is almost two-thirds administrative and the rest is detail slugging. A small amount of your time goes into creation, fun, excitement and the spirited animation that you expect from the bright people engaged in it. But that small amount of time is what binds you to the whole of it. You forget the day you spilled the rubber cement all over your pants and remember the trans-Atlantic call to Princess Xenophone in the Celebes. She spoke a tinkling French, and her soft langorous accent hung above the charts in your office, haunting you for days.

These incidents, and a flood of others, are there to remind me of the years, from 1929-60 that I edited *Writer's Digest* and *The Writer's Year Book.*

A few of the articles we published turned into what Arnold Gingrich calls "extra base hits," but you never knew in advance which one would do this. I kept an idea box and dropped into it the articles that had particularly pleased and helped our readers.

On being asked to create a book out of these selections, I made twenty copies of most of them and mailed these to experts in the particular field in which the article lay. About half the people answered, and they made numerous useful suggestions.

I incorporated the ones that seemed appropriate and sent the manuscripts to the original authors asking for either an OK or a re-write. A few articles in this book are originals, about a fourth are unchanged. The rest are in new clothes. That, in fine, is the story of this book. I hope some of the articles will stir a muse within you.—AMM

Contents

FICTION

NON-FICTION

CALL IT EXPERIENCE

INTO PRINT

MAN AGAINST WHITE SPACE

DRAWINGS BY HERB BEARD

Fiction

How I Plot A Novel

By Patricia McGerr

In July, I put a clean sheet of paper in my typewriter and tapped out these words:

> Ellen stirred uneasily in her bed. In a hazy suspension between waking and sleeping she had difficulty remembering where she was until, opening her eyes, she could see in the half light of dawn the familiar objects of her own room. Not fully roused from her dreaming, she moved her gaze from the cluttered dressing table to seek, as she so often did when she woke at an unusual hour, the smooth counterpane of the other twin bed. Only this morning it was not smooth. The spread was neatly folded at the foot, the blanket was pushed aside, nearly fallen to the floor, and the sheet half covered, half revealed a broad bare back. Oh, God! she thought. A man, not here! Not in the home of my children.
>
> The anguish of the thought brought her fully awake, and she knew at once where she was and all

14

the other things she had known when she went to bed. Her eyes climbed upward to the man's neck and hairline, above which the crisply curling black tangle was both strange and well known, as if she had brought the memory of it from the depth of her dreaming. This is Edward, she told herself. My husband. The father of my son and my daughter. He has a right to sleep in that bed, where for twelve years no man has lain. And because she was so unsure what rights he did now have, she repeated half aloud, "This is Edward. My husband."

Then I put the paper in a cardboard box and labeled the box "The Missing Years." Two years later, a novel with that title, opening with those words, arrived in the bookstores. The work procedures I followed in those two years were learned the hard way, through trial and error on six previous books. By setting them down here, I hope to provide a shortcut for you who are about to begin your first novel.

When I wrote the opening two paragraphs, I had my basic idea: write the story of a wife whose husband deserts her and, 12 years later, returns. Why he left, why he came back, what happened to her in his absence, what kind of people they were — these were things I had to find out by interrogating myself. Who else would know? My problem, like that of any novelist with a basic idea, was whether to go ahead and write the book, thinking it out as I went along. Or, should I delay the writing until I had solved every problem in advance?

I used the first method on my first book, "Pick Your Victim," because I didn't know there was any other. I thought of the idea on a Sunday, started to write it on Monday. I did have some stepping stones; a list of suggested chapters with working titles that summed each one up in two or three key words like "Beauty Contest," "Bertha Goes Overboard." But the careful outline work I failed to do in the beginning added up to much more work at the end. I had to rewrite it twice before publication.

At a writer's conference, I heard about outlines and, except for minor revisions, my initial draft was the final one for the next six books I sold. After trying various ratios, my best results came from dividing my time, roughly, 25 per cent for my outline and 75 per cent for writing.

"The Missing Years" took four months to outline and research. Four months before a third paragraph was added to the first two. By that time, my cardboard box was bulging with material.

I think a novelist's first step is to get a clear idea of the story he wants to tell, how much ground he needs to cover, what points he wants to make. A good novel should have not a moral exactly, but certainly it should have some significance. In my case, I had to decide what was to be the significance of this book and how best to get it across. For several weeks I sat and thought, lay in bed and thought, took long walks and thought. To pump-prime myself, I read dozens of books about marriage, broken homes, careers for women, everything even remotely related to my theme. I read them not so much for the facts they contained as for the ideas they stimulated in me. More useful even than reading was the talking. "What should a woman do when her husband walks out?" became my conversational gambit whenever I went out among people. The debates and discussions it started furnished fresh slants and provided an index of my novel's interest value.

At the end of this period I was ready to write the synopsis—a 5000-word summary of the main plot line. It made no attempt to arrange the story in sequence as it would appear in the book. Rather it was divided into general headings, with each aspect of the heroine's problem dealt with separately, even though they would overlap and dovetail in the final writing. One section, for instance, dealt with her economic progress, another with her emotional pressures, a third with her social embarrassments.

With my plot on paper, the next step was character. Of course I don't suggest that when you work up your characters you will stop thinking about your plot. It is more a matter of focusing on one while the other simmers in the background. In working up the characters, I do three separate jobs on each one: 1) straight biography; 2) physical description; and 3) psychological analysis.

No. 1 is a "Who's Who" type collection of the principal facts, dates and places in the character's life, including family background, education, jobs, marriages, military service, etc. No. 2 sets forth the details of height, weight, coloring and dress, with a special note on any idiosyncrasies, mannerisms and manifestations of nervousness or excitement. Both these are relatively brief and factual.

The third sketch is much longer, more comprehensive and by far the most important. I try to get down not only what kind of a person this is but also what made him that way. It is not enough to say a man is ambitious. I must also discover the early roots of his ambition and the goals toward which it is directed, as well as the ways in which it is shown. The more complex the character, the more difficult will be this part of the novelist's task — and the more imperative that it be properly done.

The most complicated character I ever dealt with was a man named Larry Rock in "Follow, As the Night." I had to make him capable of cold-blooded murder and yet able to hold the heroine's love and reader's sympathy. To accomplish this paradox it was necessary to go way back to his childhood and trace the pressures that had twisted his ego, made him at once vicious and lovable. I wrote reams about him that got into the book only by implication and suggestion — but this writing helped me to understand Larry and, more important, to pass this understanding along to the reader.

I like to write notes for my "idea box" that emphasize what I must accomplish to make my book come off. This clarifies my problem. In creating the husband in "The Missing Years," for instance, I wrote myself this warning: "My main problem is Ned. I can probably cope with Ellen. But the essential thing is to make Ned attractive not only to Ellen but to the reader. On the reader's abiliy to understand his pull hangs the story's whole motivation. And if the reader is to find him attractive, *so must I.* Hence, it is not enough to make him a charming weakling who may appeal to some women but not to me. There must be in him enough strength to appeal to everyone. How can I reconcile the qualities that attract with the qualities that make him capable of deserting a pregnant wife and child and then returning to them. I've got to make him behave like a thorough-going heel and yet not lose all reader sympathy. Can it be done? It must!"

For the effort that went into this characterization I felt rewarded by the verdict of the critics. What I was trying to do and how it was brought about was most fully expressed in *New York Herald-Tribune's* review: "Perhaps the best portrait is that of Ned Clement. In him Miss McGerr has created a completely recognizable individual. He has charm, he has an appetite and a flair for life; he rebels against the bit and rein. Marriage meant responsibilities and these he accepted but not at the price of snuffing out the spark of his vitality. To his wife, brought up in a conventional, affluent home, he was a gay companion, a tender lover but not a good provider, or, rather, not a steady one. As he himself ruefully put it, he continually let her down. 'You've got neat ideas,' he said. 'I don't know whether you brought them from home or got them out of books. And the trouble is, I'm not neat. I can't fit into any patterns. I'll work at it though, if it means so much to you.' "

My heroine was easier to handle since a deserted wife and mother is a natural for sympathy. I find a note of warning about her, however, this one dealing with the vital problem of reader identification. "The reader," I reminded myself, "must have a real emotional response to her problems, her love affairs, her children. The woman reader should be able to put herself in Ellen's place, to become involved in her troubles. The man reader must feel protective toward her. So while she must have faults, be somewhat to blame for the breakup, it must be always human weakness, never a shrewish temper. Since the story is told from her viewpoint, her own recognition of her faults can help hold sympathy."

Does this appear to give too much attention to the element of character? In my opinion, this cannot be overemphasized. If you know and understand them thoroughly, they will do much of your work for you. Much of your plot trouble will disappear because they — by reason of the kind of people they are — will react to circumstances in specific ways and thereby carry your plot forward.

A key scene in "The Missing Years" was that leading to the desertion. To make a man who is not a villain leave a wife pregnant and penniless is a tricky problem. Given a different couple, it might have been impossible. With Ned and Ellen, it evolved naturally. What I did was set his gambler's spirit in conflict with her craving for security and let them take it from there. It was in character for him to quit his job on a whim, equally in character for her to protest. The logic of his subsequent actions is summed up later in the book:

> With the complete picture now before her (thus ran Ellen's thought in retrospect), she could understand his leaving her, could see it as a kind of chain reaction in which each step made the next imperative so that once the motion had begun there could be no turning back. His intentions, when he drew the money from the bank, had been good if unwise. His reaction to losing it all could have been predicted. The one thing he could not do was take help from Ellen's mother. Rather than face this, he went away. And, having gone, each month he stayed made his returning more difficult. So many arguments had centered around her thrift versus his irresponsibility that he could well believe she placed security above all else, that until he could bring her this he had better stay away . . . He — being the kind of man he was, faced with a certain combination of circumstances — could hardly have chosen any other course.

There's one part in which Ellen steps momentarily out of character (under the dual pressure of a report of Ned's infidelity plus an unfair besmirching of her own reputation) to go off on a weekend with another man. With the trip barely under way, her native sense of virtue and conventionality reasserts itself and, since the man is an important contact, presents her with a serious problem. I stayed strictly on the sidelines. You got yourself into this, I told her, now let's see if you can wiggle out. I was quite proud of the way Ellen handled the situation.

If you are a writer who finds dialogue difficult to write, your real solution may lie in getting on more intimate terms with your characters. Once you know characters thoroughly, it's not so hard to make them talk. First, of course, you must have the actual "meat" of the scene clear in your mind — the information the dialogue is to convey, the action to which it must lead. But the words they use, the reasoning they follow, the way they express their ideas will, in each case, be inherent in the characters. If you've gotten inside your hero, you'll find yourself speaking his lines aloud, saying them first, then writing them down.

There are many ways, for instance, for a man to announce he's left a much-needed job. Ned, being Ned, puts it jauntily: "I quit — resigned — turned in my badge — whatever you want to call it. Me and the government of this sovereign state won't be keeping company any more." Again, his curtain speech, the line on which he slams the door, is not only typical of his casualness but takes a parting shot at her practicality: "So long. Don't wait up. You'll only waste the electricity."

When the dual jobs of plotting and characterization are done, you have finished a creative phase. The next steps are more mechanical. I find it practical to make three outlines. The first is chronological — a time chart showing each year covered by the novel. This lets me see at a glance where my characters are and what they are up to at a given time. It helps too to keep their ages straight, which is particularly important in the case of children. On the chart I also note significant events that occurred in the real world during each year in order to avoid such anachronisms as a too-lavish dinner table during food rationing.

The second outline might be called climactic, since it is based on the theory that a book needs dramatic peaks at reasonably regular intervals. It is useful to visualize the novel as a magazine serial, broken into four or five installments, with each one ending on a rising note. This outline can be very brief, like the five installment one for "The Missing Years":

    I.   Return, Marriage, Desertion
    II.   Life with Mother, On Own, First Man's Proposition
    III.   End of First Man, Juvenile Delinquency, Second Man's Proposal
    IV.   End of Second Man, Daughter's Fantasies, Third Man's Proposal
    V.   Return of Husband, Dilemma, Decision

Such an outline groups sections of the plot so that each part has action, interest and meaning, plus some element of suspense that will carry over to the next section.

The final outline is a chapter-by-chapter breakdown. It makes clear the particular function each chapter is to serve — how it forwards the plot, what it reveals about the characters, what light it throws on the novel's significance. The length of the summations depends on the complexity of the chapters. One of the few from "The Missing Years" that is short enough to quote goes like this:

CHAPTER TWO

This chapter will go back to their college days, establish their respective character and relationship leading up to their marriage. In this, it should be stressed that they are both very much in love — this must be well demonstrated here as a foundation for everything that comes later. Then will come her pregnancy, the scene with her mother, the gambling house. The primary purpose of this chapter is to get Ellen and Ned established as individuals and as a couple. Here must be shown what makes them close and what will later drive them apart. At the end of the chapter they can be confidently awaiting the birth of their first child, secure in their love and their roulette winnings.

So now, (Does it seem forever? It's been four months.), the note box is filled, the fun is over and the book has to be written. It may be personal eccentricity or detective-story training but I prefer to start with the last chapter. Once it is down *I know exactly where I am going* and am better able to find my way there. The end provides a guide to what must be explained, emphasized and suggested in the rest of the book. After the last chapter comes the first and, finally, the bridge between.

By the time I get to the body of the book I usually find that I have in my note box the big dramatic scenes — the ones in which people shout, shoot or make love. In writing Ellen's character sketch, I noted that she was dominated by a *grande dame*-type mother, and, very soon the explosive possibilities of a clash between this mother and Ned began to appear. In my idea box, I collected dialogue for Mama and Ned to throw at each other.

Later, I began to wonder how Mama's hatred for Ned would

make her treat his (and Ellen's) son. Before long I had a list of taunts and insinuations along the "like father, like son" line that later provided partial justification for the boy's windup in juvenile court.

That kind of seesawing — from formal notemaking to informal jotting — never stops. Ideas for dramatic action, snatches of dialogue, emotional highlights, psychological twists — these will flow freely through your mind while you are making your various outlines and sketches. Get them on paper while they're hot, even if it means interrupting your work a dozen times a day. The more interruptions, the better, for your goal is not a collection of outlines but a dramatic novel. And what a wonderful feeling, when you start the writing, to find the drama already there.

I began "The Missing Years" with the major scenes in almost finished form, minor ones in summary. In addition there were hundreds of oddments — notes to myself, keys to character and motivation, an occasional word or phrase for which I hoped to find use.

With all this material, I had to sort, assemble, select. Using a separate envelope for every chapter, I put into each the appropriate scenes and scraps. It was like a jigsaw puzzle. When I used up all my pieces, I had a completed picture. An important part is to make sure the cracks don't show — in other words, to make your transitions logical, your continuity smooth. The hardest writing, it's often said, makes the easiest reading. The end result of these elaborate preparations is to make it seem to the reader that the novel wrote itself.

A comprehensive list of book publishers begins on page 139. Consult the current edition of *Writer's Market* for a detailed listing of each publisher's requirements.

Plotting A Mystery Novel By The Question & Answer Method

By Harold Masur

Q.	Who shot him?	A.	Mary.
Q.	Who is Mary?	A.	His wife.
Q.	Why did she do it?	A.	She loves Bill.
Q.	Does Bill know?	A.	Hmmm, let me think . . .

We who make our living as mystery writers cannot afford to wait for inspiration. Two books a year may mean no more than $15,000 income. Six months dreaming cuts our revenue in half. We must start our own engine. Let us take a concrete example.

You want to write a mystery. This usually means someone will have to be murdered. A man decides to kill his wife.

Simple enough?

That is all we have. The bare fact of intent. Nothing else. Is it possible to extract a story from this? Under my method, you need nothing more than this to begin. Using what we will call the Question and Answer method, you will develop the idea differently from anyone else.

First, a pencil and paper. Ideas are transitory and must be permanently recorded. Do not trust your memory.

Having fixed the crime: *A man decides to kill his wife,* you start the mystery story plotting process by deciding why the crime was committed. Hence, our first question.

Why does the husband want to kill his wife?

Since each writer must tackle the problem from his own point of view, everyone's answers are different. Follow along with me for a choice of answers that quickly come to mind.

1. The wife is a shrew and he has begun to hate her.
2. She is rich and he wants to inherit her money.
3. He has fallen in love with another woman.

Three answers. By asking a single question, our imagination starts to function. Which answer shall we develop? We pause to consider, and we like them all. Fine, we will draw upon all three. Later, perhaps, we may discard one or more, or find a different motive altogether.

What progress have we made?

First, we have a motive for the murder. We have characterized the husband as a man of strong emotions, greedy, venal, a philanderer, capable of committing the ultimate crime. We have characterized the wife as an ill-tempered virago, dominating, vituperative, and probably stingy. In addition, we have added a third character, the other woman.

And our initial situation now has potential. We have a set of facts that are inherently explosive. Something is bound to happen. *The beauty of this method lies in the fact that each answer gives rise to a new set of questions.*

The system feeds itself.

Would your next question be this: Who is the other woman?

If so you might be tempted at this point to write down your own answers and compare them with mine. Or perhaps you just want to follow along. I wrote:

1. Someone he met on a business trip.
2. A friend of his wife.
3. The wife of a friend.
4. His secretary.

Arbitrarily, I will pick the secretary. What can we say about her?

Since the husband finds her attractive, I will assume that she is young and pretty. We can also assume that she is sympathetic to his problems and ingenuous enough to be misled.

But remember this. In the plotting process, you, the writer, are omnipotent. You can endow your characters with whatever traits you wish them to possess, so long as their traits are consistent with their actions. If you wish, you may conceive the secretary in an entirely different way. You may portray her as a calculating schemer, deliberately driving the husband to murder in the hope that he will marry her after inheriting his wife's money. If you do, your plot will take an entirely different course.

Now that we know the motive and three of the characters, how do we know who else is involved in the story? My question and answer method depends on this truth: *No human being lives in a vacuum.*

Take the secretary, for example. And again we rely on the Question and Answer Method. Does she live alone or with her family or with another girl? What friends does she have? Any admirers? We know that she is pretty. Pretty girls attract boy friends. Our secretary is no exception. One of these people, a boy friend of the secretary, whispers in my ear, "I want to become a member of the cast."

At this point most writers will feel a sudden sense of excitement. With this new character, the boy friend, a whole wave of fresh ideas come flooding in. The plotting process is beginning to gain momentum. Your imagination goes off on a dozen different tangents.

How can we involve the boy friend? Will he go to see the husband in order to remonstrate about his attentions to the secretary? Wait a minute. Maybe he finds the husband dead.

Maybe the wife learned about the secretary and in a jealous rage killed the husband. Is the boy friend accused of the crime by the police? Shall we, perhaps, write the story from his viewpoint, describing his effort to extricate himself? You're now on your own.

Originality will stem from your own individual approach, from fresh variations, from your ingenuity in devising new complications.

The hero of my own novels is a lawyer named Scott Jordan. I conceived him as an engaging chap who would not dodge peril, but who would joust against rogues and their cross-purposes with spirit, audacity, and humor. Having lived more or less intimately with him through a number of books, I had a close sense of identification. Imagine my surprise one day when I received a letter bearing the imprint: *Scott Jordan, Attorney-at-Law.* A real life lawyer, it appeared, had the same name as my hero.

Somewhere in this situation, I thought, there had to be a story. I could not shake the notion. Twisting it a bit, I wondered what would happen if my hero called his office one morning and a strange man answered the telephone. A man who had assumed the hero's name and identity.

I put the Question and Answer Method to work.

Who would take the hero's place and for what reason? My answers resulted in a book called "The Big Money." It was published by Simon & Schuster and became a Mystery Guild selection. It was on the lists of a European publisher and was reprinted by Dell. It is a practical demonstration of how a bare concept was developed and expanded into a full-length novel. I remember seeing an old movie about a poison pen letter that fell into the wrong hands. The idea of a character receiving a letter addressed to someone else intrigued me. I started asking questions and came up with a book called "Suddenly A Corpse."

If you cannot find a jumping off point at all, I have a suggestion that has worked for me on innumerable occasions. Most people read mystery novels simply for pleasure. They are content to go along merely for the ride, making no attempt to outwit the fictional sleuth. Forego that pleasure. Read a mystery and make a positive effort to unmask the villain and to determine before the denouement the reason for his misdeeds.

In all likelihood you will be dead wrong. But look what you will have accomplished in the meantime.

First, you now have a villain of your own. Second, you have probably cooked up a motive entirely different from the author's. And once you have a motive, half the battle is won. Motivation grows out of character, and no plot can be constructed from a sounder base.

In its simplest form, the suspense novel generally involves a sympathetic character in a portentious situation fraught with *imminent* personal danger. The villain may or may not be known. His identity is not the chief problem. The question here is, *will the protagonist be saved?* And to a lesser extent, how? As the situation deteriorates, *reader identification should be so strong* that he finds the suspense almost insupportable.

The Sub-Plot

What about red herrings?

Most full-length novels require some sub-plot action. For this purpose you will need one or more innocent suspects. If the suspect has something to hide, a prison record for example, his suspicious behavior will divert the reader's attention away from the culprit. Here is an example:

It is night and your hero is unable to sleep. He is standing at the window, gazing into the moonlight. Suddenly the figure of a girl standing along the garden path becomes visible. Her arm makes a throwing motion and something splashes into the lily pond.

When she leaves, the hero goes down and retrieves the object. It turns out to be the murder weapon. Later, he questions the girl. Her answers are conflicting and evasive. Naturally, she becomes a suspect.

This is mechanical contrivance. We have deliberately arranged the sequence of events to give the reader this impression. After doubt and misunderstanding, the hero unearths the facts. The girl, finding the gun in her brother's room, and not knowing it has been planted there, mistakenly suspects him of guilt. Hence, her efforts to protect him.

In this way, your innocent suspect adds to the mystification and creates additional action. The suspect also serves another function. In an effort to clear himself, he, or she, may give the hero valuable insights and information about the other characters in the story.

Because tangible clues have been done to death, I concentrate on behavior clues. Give your villain character traits that will ultimately lead to his downfall. Here is an example of what I mean:

Your hero visits one of the characters, casually noting the appointments in her living room, the half empty bottle of rare bourbon, cigarette butts in a tray, an original Lautrec. She tells him that she is alone, no one has been to see her for several days.

Then, much later, when the reader has forgotten these details, your hero learns that she is a compulsive housekeeper and a non-smoker. He recalls the cigarette butts. Was she lying? Someone may have visited her. The clues, you see, are linked to the character's personal habits.

Giving the clue on one page and its application on another is a trick of the trade. Only the most sharp-eyed reader is apt to spot it.

Other tricks of the trade:

Give the clue before the crime occurs. Seldom will the reader associate one with the other. He is not alert until a murder is committed. You notice I say "murder." In rare instances a lesser crime will suffice.

Present the clue during a moment of tense action. The reader's attention will be distracted, just as a magician waves a wand with his right hand to keep you from noticing what he is doing with his left.

Bury the clue among several items of a similar type, such as the contents of a purse or a desk.

John Dickson Carr, also known as Carter Dickson, creator of Dr. Gideon Fell and Sir Henry Mirrivale, and one of the giants in the field, told me to write every truth as though it were a lie and every lie as though it were the truth.

The reader must feel a bond of sympathy for your characters. He must *care* what happens to them. He must experience the same emotions, share their excitement, their fears, their concupiscence.

And there are techniques specifically designed to accomplish this purpose, such as the technique of identification which you work consciously and deliberately by choosing those traits it is natural for a reader to identify.

Thus, a male reader will readily identify with a hero who is handsome, courageous and resourceful. A female reader identifies with a heroine who is attractive, bright, appealing. These are qualities which the average person feels he possesses or would like to possess.

As your story progresses, your hero should become more deeply involved, his problems more complex, the danger that confronts him more menacing. The professional author plays out his line, keeping the reader constantly on the hook.

Lee Wright, former editor of the Inner Sanctum Mysteries for Simon & Schuster, and now with Random House, says that every known fact can be made doubtful. The resulting uncertainty will increase suspense. On several occasions she has asked me to make doubtful the status of a character whom I had established as a friend of the hero. Each time this suggestion was followed it improved the plot.

In the creative fever generated by the actual composition, new ideas constantly emerge, seemingly from nowhere. Nail them down at once in black and white. If the characters take hold on their own, breaking out of the rigid confines of plot, let them do it.

A full-length mystery is a big project and it is easy to forget certain items. I make a list of everything that has to be explained or clarified, and, after it is done, I cross it off.

I keep a name chart handy with a thumbnail description of every character. This saves the tedious chore of checking back through a mass of manuscript to recall the color of someone's eyes.

Similarly, whenever you mention a date, the make of a car, the name of a hotel, the caliber of a gun, write it down. You'd be surprised how easily one forgets these details. In his fine novel, "Passing Strange," Richard Sale mentioned the fact that a baby boy was born. At the end he described it as a girl. Nobody in the publisher's office noticed this error, but 467 readers did and wrote in about it.

It is impossible to calculate the number of people who read mystery novels.

Mystery writers have their own trade association: Mystery Writers of America, Hotel Seville, 29th & Madison Ave., New York, 10016.

The demand for new mystery novels shows no letup in Hollywood, and the suspense field is a bright welcoming world for writers who are attracted by this market.

The following publishers issue mysteries.

Ace Books
1120 Ave. of the Americas
New York, N.Y. 10036

Avon Books
959 8th Ave.
New York, N.Y. 10019

Curtis Books
355 Lexington
New York, N.Y. 10017

Dell Publishing Co.
750 Third Ave.
New York, N.Y. 10017

Dodd, Mead & Co.
79 Madison Ave.
New York, N.Y. 10016

Doubleday & Co., Inc.
277 Park Ave.
New York, N.Y. 10017

E. P. Dutton & Co., Inc.
201 Park Ave. S.
New York, N.Y. 10003

Fawcett World Library
1 Astor Place
New York, N.Y. 10036

Farrar, Straus & Giroux
19 Union Square, West
New York, N.Y. 10003

Harcourt Brace Jovanovich
757 Third Ave.
New York, N.Y. 10017

Harper & Row, Publishers
10 E. 53rd St.
New York, N.Y. 10022

Lancer Books
1560 Broadway
New York, N.Y. 10036

J. B. Lippincott Co.
E. Washington Sq.
Philadelphia, Pa. 19105

Little, Brown and Company
34 Beacon St.
Boston, Mass. 02016

Lothrup, Lee & Shepherd Co., Inc.
105 Madison Ave.
New York, N.Y. 10016

McGraw-Hill Book Co.
1221 Ave. of the Americas
New York, N.Y. 10020

William Morrow & Co., Inc.
425 Park Ave. S.
New York, N.Y. 10016

Paperback Library
315 Park Ave. S.
New York, N.Y. 10010

Pyramid Publications, Inc.
919 Third Ave.
New York, N.Y. 10022

Random House, Inc.
201 E. 50th St.
New York, N.Y. 10022

Charles Scribner's Sons
597 Fifth Ave.
New York, N.Y. 10017

The Viking Press, Inc.
625 Madison Ave.
New York, N.Y. 10022

Walker Book Co.
720 5th Ave.
New York, N.Y. 10019

8 Steps To Professional Writing

By Jean Owen Giovannoni

The moment you come right out in the open with the words *Basic Technique* you are likely to find yourself with your back against the wall, an apple on your head. Arrows and pot-shots notwithstanding, I am convinced that there are gifted writers who fritter away creative years without bothering to take a careful, *common-sense* look at basic technique as it relates to their own writing.

Here, then, are some of the elements of basic story technique. They were used by Scheherazade to keep King Shahriar from slicing off her head, and they are utilized in every Walt Disney production to insure high box office receipts. You will find them in Homer's narratives, Shakespearean drama and in your own stories when you see them in print:

1. A Story Must Have a Theme

A few years ago I went to Los Angeles to have a chat with Lilian Kastendike, then *Redbook's* fiction editor and talent scout. She was on a trip to the West Coast for the purpose of flushing out some potential material for *Redbook's* full-length feature novels. I was anxious to talk to her because I happened to have a novel nesting in my noggin that I was eager to have flushed. For several days before the interview I rehearsed the brilliant answers I would give to questions she might ask about the story.

Which would have been fine, had it not been for one miscalculation. Miss Kastendike didn't ask any of the questions I anticipated. She said, "Now, first of all, let's talk over the *theme* of your novel."

Theme? Theme? I tried and drew a blank. "Just tell me in one sentence," Miss Kastendike said, "what you are trying to *say* in your story."

I groped for words. A week later, still groping, I was assuring myself that my novel was too big, too complex, too full of subtle overtones and undertones ever to be wrapped up in a neat little package and tied with a single sentence. But no matter how often my ego swatted at it, Miss Kastendike's question continued to buzz. Every time I finished reading a story I found myself asking, "What was the story trying to *say*?" And I discovered that every story I was reading—frivolous or thought-provoking, humorous or serious—pointed up some basic, time-tested truth! Invariably I could dredge up an old one-sentence adage or quotation to fit the case . . . things like: *To thine own self be true* or *No man is an island* . . . or *It matters not if you lost or won but how you played the game* . . . truisms are seldom quoted these days for fear people will think they are being put down . . . yet truisms like these contain sentiment that everyone with a brain in his head knows, deep down, to be as valid today as they were when Polk was President.

I began going back over my own story-history, and I discovered that everyone that had sold had carried a theme without my realizing it while many of my rejects did not. And I finally learned that a theme is not something you wind, ribbon-like, around the *outside* of a story. In a good story, the theme is the very reason for the story's being written.

I scrapped the coreless novel I was working on and reached into my Partially Written files for a story that I had worked on from time to time for several years but had never been able to finish because the plot kept coming unglued. I asked myself what the story was trying to say and I came up with the Biblical quotation: *Love seeketh not its own.*

2. Your Characters Must Be Believable

Don't struggle to find "different" character types. Non-writers are always pointing to some queer, odd-ball person and saying, "Now, there would be a good character for a story." And he might be. *But not until you are able to depict him as a screwball who possesses the same thoughts and emotions as yourself and the ordinary, everyday, run-of-the-mill people around you.* For until a reader can identify a character through his own similar emotions, he isn't going to be interested . . . and neither will editors.

Think your characters through before you start your story. Get acquainted with them. Wait until you know how they would act in every situation, whether it happens to be a situation that will occur in the story or not. The thing that motivates your story is the characters' reaction to the conflict. Putting a character down on paper prematurely, may result in an unconvincing cardboard figure.

3. The Elements of Strong Conflict Must Be Present

Books on writing technique say there are three types of conflict: Man against Man, Man against Nature, Man against Himself. And they are right. Unless your protagonist is pitted against one of these three forces you may have an incident, not a story. And never mind what your Aunt Gertrude says about your work deserving publication because of your beautiful descriptions of sunsets. Aunt Gertrude isn't an editor.

There are degrees of conflict. Having a character involved in a *mild* brush-up with Nature, or with his own soul is likely to bring an editorial comment such as "Too slight."

Amateur writers have a tendency to pull their conflict-punches. It's much simpler (and easier writing) to give a female character a desire for a new dress than to have her determined to save her floundering marriage.

Selling writers pit their hero or heroine against something vital. Then they step up the conflict even further by giving the protagonist a personality handicap that makes it harder for him to win. Take, for example, the problem of the wife who wants to save her marriage. The experienced writer doesn't give her a worn-out bag for a rival. No, sir. He puts her up against an attractive siren equipped with warm hands, a cold heart and a big bank account. This is rough on our heroine because she already has an inferiority complex and the one thing she simply *cannot* bear to contemplate is a showdown with her rival. So the writer forthwith sets about putting her, as quickly as possible, in a position where she must decide to face up to the other woman or risk losing her man. And what happens? The reader decides that, by George, he'll just tag along to see how that brave little thing makes out when she tries to spit in that hussy's eye!

4. Suspense

It's not very hard to thrust a character into a situation that will pique the reader's interest—it's something else to be able to *hold* that interest for the next seventeen pages. Basic techniques suggest that you do it this way:

Once the conflict has been established in the opening para- graphs of the story, feed the reader the antecedent action (the events that brought about the conflict) as briefly as possible. If your material will permit it, try writing it without flashbacks. If this can't be done without moving your first conflict to page three, try using "spot" flashbacks—brief passages inserted where you need them throughout the story. If you find you *must* resort to one longish flashback, keep paring at it until you haven't one unnecessary word.

If you have the reader wondering whether or not the problem is going to be solved, you have a good "plain mincemeat" type of suspense, and some stories must settle for this. You can lace mince- meat with rum-and-brandy if you can work it so that you have the reader wondering if the problem will be solved in time! A lovers' quarrel is more ominous if the hero leaves tomorrow for a three- year job in South America.

I once wrote a magazine-length novel about four women stuck in a stalled elevator. I thought I had it as full of suspense as I could possibly get it merely by having the reader wondering if each of the women was going to get out in time to solve her own emo- tional problem. After the story was published, and it was too late for me to do anything about it, the television rights were purchased for a one-hour dramatic play. What did those script writers do but *add* to my conflict? By use of dialogue and occasional shots of a fraying cable the viewer was informed that the machinery had better be fixed in an hour or the passengers would crash to their death. Those capped molars in my mouth are the result of my sitting for an hour in front of my TV set grinding my teeth with chagrin because I hadn't thought of it first!

5. A Story Should Include a Dark Moment

Picture a steep hill. A man is struggling to reach the top. He is almost there; he can practically feel himself standing on the wind-swept summit. Suddenly a rock breaks loose on the path. It knocks him off balance and he rolls helplessly down the hill. He picks himself up. Bruised and shaken, he is discouraged. He knows he must try again to get to the top but right now he doesn't know where he is going to get the *oomph* to make the climb.

This is his dark moment.

Every good story has one.

6. Coincidence Must Not Be Misused

At a writers' conference a few years ago Richard Stern cleared up for me, once and for all, any questions about the proper use of coincidences. You can use all the coincidence you like to get your characters together for their first meeting or to ensnare them in a conflict. It's in getting them *out* of their difficulties that you must have a care.

Let us return to our hill climber.

Wrong use of coincidence: Just as our hero is wondering how he is ever going to make the climb, a car driven by a kindly soul pulls up alongside. "Hop in, friend," says the driver. "I'll give you a lift to the top."

Right use of coincidence: Just as our hero is wondering how he is ever going to make the climb, a car driven by a nearsighted drunk comes careening around the corner. It rams into our hill-climber and goes speeding on. As our hero picks himself up, he knows he not only is faced with his original problem of getting up the hill but *now* must do so with a *broken leg.*

7. The Opening Paragraphs Should Be Complete

The first few paragraphs of a story should provide an unobtrusive backdrop *setting* so that your characters won't float in space. In the opening paragraphs of a short story introduce the main *characters* with enough physical description to permit the reader to have a pretty fair idea of age, sex, general build, and whether or not the character is a Good Guy or a Bad Guy.

Set the *mood*—i.e., give the reader a chance to adjust his emotional antenna to receive the type of story you have written—serious, humorous, suspenseful, nostalgic, or whatever.

Establish the *viewpoint* so that the reader will know whose story this is going to be. Through whose eyes are the events seen?

Give the reader at least a hint of *conflict*—enough to make him curious to find out what's going to happen next.

Persuade the reader to make an *emotional investment*.

One fish may be like another as far as you are concerned—until one happens to nibble on a live you've baited. The moment you make any kind of an investment, however small, your interest is heightened. Detached interest isn't enough: the reader should *feel* something.

The only way I know how to get all or most of these elements into your opening page or page and a half is to write and to re-write.

8. *The Denouement Must Be Satisfying*

It was another writer who impressed upon me the importance of giving the reader an emotionally satisfying ending. If your protagonist has been struggling across the hot desert, then at the end don't let him just see the oasis . . . let the reader share a gulp or two of cool water with him. If you've written a love story, don't make the couple (and your reader) settle for any of this glance-across-a-crowded-room nonsense. Get rid of the rest of the characters and let the kids go into a real clinch. A curtain-of-privacy doesn't belong at any window of today's story.

When you have whittled each rule of technique down to its primary purpose, you discover that it is designed to help you shift your focus away from yourself and direct it outward to the reader.

The moment that you can look within yourself and know that your main goal is to write for the reader is the moment that you cross over the amateur-line.

AN APPEALING

CHARACTER

Strives Against

GREAT ODDS

To Attain A

WORTHWHILE

 GOAL

This sign is stapled on the wall over my old desk. Each time I sit down to write my eyes see it. The sign is over twenty years old, printed on paper now yellow with age. This formula has helped me sell a thousand short stories and novelets and one hundred books.

—Lee Floren

The Basic Plot Of Fiction

By Richard Deming

As a professional magazine writer, I have visited with the editors of some forty different magazines and discussed fiction technique with them.

Excluding taboo themes and unusable lengths, which are errors in marketing rather than in technique, most of these editors agree that a frequent reason for rejection is the author's failure to follow the basic framework of narrative fiction.

Sometimes called "the basic plot of fiction," this framework has been publicized so often, it's startling that all writers aren't thoroughly familiar with it. Even old pros occasionally forget their early training and turn out scripts lacking elements of the basic framework.

The basic framework of narrative fiction consists of 3 elements:

(1) Character: you must create a main character, or group of characters, of sufficient interest so the reader *cares* what happens to him or them. Your hero may be an angel or a devil, or anything in between. And the emotion aroused may be admiration, amusement, dislike, fear, hate, sympathy or anything else you

wish. When your main character arouses *some kind* of definite emotion in the reader, you're going forward right from the start.

(2) Conflict: having created your main character, you must present him with a problem or a series of problems to solve. The problem may be a purely external one, such as a chase. It may be an internal problem, such as a wrestling with conscience, or it may be a combination of both.

The magnitude of your character's problem is unimportant. It may vary from something as seemingly trival as a housewife wondering what to prepare for dinner when her husband brings the boss home, to having your hero in a predicament where his decisions can either prevent or cause World War III. What is important is the relationship of the problem to the main character. To him it must be a vital problem and when the reader as well as the character *feels* and *believes* it is vital, you've got the reader's interest.

A good way to test whether or not you have created an adequate problem is to ask yourself what the hero's plight would be if he failed to solve it. If his situation wouldn't be much changed, you'd better reconsider your problem.

(3) Resolution: at the story's end, the problem or problems you have set up are resolved in a manner acceptable to the reader. This needs come about through definite action on the main character's part. Neither fate, coincidence, God nor the devil is an adequate substitute.

You may apply this basic framework: character, conflict and resolution, against any great work of fiction ever written, and it will fit. All published authors, from Ernest Hemingway to published hacks, use it. It is an integral part of narrative fiction.

Yet day after day authors, both beginners and pros, louse up otherwise well-written scripts by neglecting this basic framework.

Sometimes it's the first element they miss on. The author has style, but is so enamored of his writing that he neglects his main character. In reading the script, the editor can't induce any interest in this character, consequently doesn't care what happens to him, and doesn't even finish the story.

Frequently it's the second element the author leaves out. The oldest standard plot is Boy-meets-girl, boy-loses-girl, boy-wins-girl.

Can you pick up a slick magazine without finding it at least once? You'd think even novice writers could do it in their sleep. Yet daily editors reject otherwise well-written love stories because their authors forgot the middle. The plots go simply: Boy-meets-girl, boy-wins-girl.

No conflict, no story.

Authors who think in intellectual terms will often create a story problem vital to themselves instead of to the main character. But it isn't the author's relationship to the problem that's important; it's your main character's relationship to it that makes the reader care.

The Character's Concern Over the Story Problem

A problem which would be completely trivial to the majority of readers may be made vital to your main character. Let's say your heroine is a teen-age girl who wants to be invited to the high-school junior prom. Her problems are who will date her? Will she be able to hold him in conversation? Will her dress impress the other girls? Will the stag line cut in, or leave her date stuck with her all night?

Perhaps you have written this story for *Harper's Bazaar* whose readership consists largely of mature and sophisticated women. To most of them this situation would be no problem if they were confronted with it personally, for they are socially assured people who have attended hundreds of dances and parties. But if you have managed to interest them in your teen-age character, her emotions will become theirs and they'll suffer right along with her over problems which wouldn't even faze them if they were their own.

Yet, a larger problem concerning world events which fails to arouse the main character would fail to arouse the reader's concern.

Try It On For Size

Let's build a plot. For our main character we'll take a daring young stock-market speculator who is regarded as a boy genius of Wall Street. He clashes with a multi-million-dollar cartel over control of a corporation. By various means our hero manages to raise a million dollars on credit with which to fight the cartel, and he and his opposition both undertake a series of speculative manuevers in the stock market in an effort to gain control of the corporation in question.

It is obvious that this problem can be resolved in only two ways: either our hero triumphs and gains great wealth, or he loses his borrowed millions and is ruined. The outcome of the struggle is vitally important to him.

Now let's take exactly the same plot, same characters, same stock-market fight, and add one more factor. Let's allow our hero to have a bank account of twenty million dollars before the fight starts.

See how something which would be a problem of gigantic proportions to the average reader, if he personally were confronted with it, now becomes minor in relationship to your main character? The potential gain or loss of a million dollars would excite almost anyone who personally faced the problem. But you can't expect a reader to get very excited over the possibility that your boy genius of Wall Street may have to struggle along on nineteen million if things go against him.

The commonest way in which writers fail to resolve their stories acceptably is by having the resolution stem from some utterly outside source, or from coincidence, instead of from within the main character. For instance, your hero is surrounded by Indians, his plight is hopeless, then suddenly the cavalry arrives.

But instead of feeling relieved, the reader is only going to feel irritated if the hero depends on an act of God instead of on his own initiative. The least the author could do in this case is have the hero, by some ingenious method, signal the cavalry about his plight and therefore be personally responsible for its last-minute arrival.

Let's take a situation where your main character is engaged to one girl, then finds himself in love with another. His problem is to break the news to his fiancee and obtain his freedom. But just as he works himself up to the ordeal, she saves him the trouble by telling him she's in love with another man and wants her freedom.

If, in this situation, you had your hero deliberately introduce his fiancee to a noted wolf, then encourage a romance between them so that the fiancee falls in love with the wolf and lets the hero off the hook, you have a story opening. But if he merely stands still and lets things happen to him, you have merely an anecdote.

Occasionally you will see published stories of excellent merit which deliberately omit one of these three basic elements of fiction.

The "notion" story, which is merely a provocative speculation dreamed up by an author, frequently skips characterization completely because it is the idea which carries the story. The last such story I did was based on the notion that under given circumstances a psychopathic killer could get away with repeated legal murder. I could have made it a fact article, because the sole interest of the piece was the "notion." But I chose to make it fiction and it was picked up for publication in the anthology, Best Detective Stories Of The Year.

But why ride your bicycle no-hands first? Almost all published fiction follows the basic framework of character, conflict and resolution.

For fun, you can experiment.

Characterization

Start with the journalism W's. For example: Who? An older woman who is lonely. When? It is morning. What? She is writing a letter; a poison pen letter. Why? She wants to play God but she is on the wrong side; she is committing a wrong to correct a wrong. She takes a break for a cup of tea. Give indications about her character by her gestures and her movements with the cup and the kettle, and how she walks about the room going to the window to peek out, again and again. Back to the letter. To sign or not to sign? When you decide what kind of a person she is writing to, then you determine what the wrong is. The important thing is the way the letter is phrased. On the surface the reader can believe that she is convinced that what she is doing is good, but under the surface, it is a piece of unimaginable cruelty. Above all, avoid falling into a farce.

Determine on your style at the beginning. Don't begin with a dear old lady and wait until the end to give the vicious impact all at once. The first word of the story must imply the last word. The first few phrases *and* the last line give you her indecision about whether to sign or not. "I think you ought to know this sort of thing is going on . . ." wander off . . . "You won't remember me but . . . You didn't notice me but . . . Never been one to cause disaster . . ."

Making the letter an "I take my pen in hand" old-fashioned flowery style, you will need to be careful if you want to make her vicious, for comedy endears characters to you.

Decide what triggered her off. It must be deeply emotional. Suppose she has a nephew and is writing to his girl. You must make her the only one of this kind in the whole world. She has a strong resentment. She must act as though she were smashing a doll. Her actions could tell this. She snips off a leaf from a plant. She could close a window and have it break, but—no—this would be too violent. She could break her pen by bearing down on it, *hard*. Perhaps the cup of tea is not to her taste and she could pour it out distastefully into the kitchen sink. Or perhaps the cup is chipped or does not match the saucer; she could replace it or throw it away. . . .

She doesn't want the girl in the family. She is not suited. She decides to sign, "Your obedient servant—."

You must figure out everything about all of your characters; enough to fill a novel so every word shows what kind of characters they are. You should associate a certain set of words with each character, and make lists of opposite characteristics of opposing characters. . . . Your words have to work *for* you. Don't use a word that means approximately the same thing. Be exact.

—*Shirley Jackson*

Writing For True Story

By Ann Finlayson

Have you submitted a story to *True Story* (or any confession magazine) expecting to get the full, free-lance price, and received instead a letter offering to buy it at a reduced, "plot germ" rate —to be rewritten by someone else? If so, you were not being victimized because you haven't got a "big name" (there are no by-lines at all in the confessions). You simply did not write your story as well as it could be written, in the opinion of the editors. And, chances are, the errors are the same as those made by other writers.

I ought to know. I'm the "someone else." For eight years, I was associate editor and staff rewriter on *True Story*, and since then have been writing for the magazine on a free-lance basis.

The writing errors that downgrade confession stories are fairly standard, occurring again and again. Since *True Story* is always happy—perhaps ecstatic is the word I really want—to pounce on anyone who not only has an ear for a story but the talent to write it, I'd like to list these errors and show how to correct them. Believe me, it's easier, quicker, and cheaper for editors to buy stories that do *not* need re-writing.

45

The following are points at which most new writers need help:

1. Theming

Most beginner confession writing troubles stem from the belief that a theme is synonymous with a "moral." To meet this notion, they create tales of adventure and sin and tack on "I should not have done it," at the end.

A theme is much more than a moral and it is just as necessary for a *McCall's* or *Harper* story as it is for *True Story*. *Gone With the Wind* had a theme—the hard, shallow flirt, feminine but unwomanly—who wound her ruthless way through the lives of her friends and lovers alike in search of a security she didn't recognize when she possessed it. This theme is woven into the heroine's character, into her actions, into the plot and outcome of her story. Usually it's a flaw in the heroine's make-up that sets her wrong at every crossroad in her life till tragedy clears her eyes and makes her see herself clearly. Such a "crossroad" in the heroine's life may appear small or be a temporary thing *for her*. It must not be small or temporary *for the story*.

Each turning point of the story should be tied to the theme, and if possible, the reader should be aware of the lesson before the heroine is.

Every story, article and book you read has a theme—that is, a point. But not every story has a moral—that is, moral in the Aesopian sense of a lesson to be learned from the characters' failings. Confession stories have both theme and moral—*and they must be interrelated.*

Theme must be woven into the heroine's character, into her actions, into the plot and outcome of her story. There's no point in writing twenty-five pages of rambling adventure, having the heroine seduced on page twenty-six, and on page twenty-seven attempt to pass off as the theme: "I shouldn't have let Johnny have his way with me." Theme starts on page one. Theme is present at every crossroad in the story, at every scene. Theme ties the story together and results in a moral.

How do you know if your story has a theme? Ask yourself, "What is my story about?" How do you know if it has a moral? Ask yourself, "What does my story mean?" And try to answer each question in one short sentence. If you can't, go back and rewrite.

The best themes are the simple ones, human and easily recognizable—like: It takes two to ruin a marriage; you always pay for your sins in one way or another; when you sacrifice something for another, greater happiness will come to you.

2. *Characterization*

This is the backbone of all writing; if you can create character, you can write. The people who inhabit lower-grade stories are nothing but names tacked onto cardboard figures that might just as well be tagged Rufe, the Mean Father, Slade, the Slick Gambler, Gramps, the Gruff But Lovable Old Character. They're like a pack of Old Maid cards, and they don't come from real life. Human beings are not so easily tagged; they are individuals, with habits, ways of reacting to situations, ideas that belong to them alone. Let your characters become individuals, and they'll be memorable.

Once you have an individual in mind, you have to get him across. A beginner will write, "My father was mean and ruthless; I hated him." That mean and ruthless father will be just that to the reader if you quote savage words he uses to the heroine; if you picture him hypocritically mouthing prayers over the child he's whipped half to death, if you write a scene in which he beats a mule till the blood runs from its mouth.

Characterization, to be complete, must be continuous. The addle-pated mother must talk drivel to the end, the kind and understanding husband does not lapse into senseless beratings of wife; our mean father cannot suddenly, *without motivation,* be reasonable.

The basis for any character change that occurs in stories must be built into the character from the beginning. Once you have an individual in mind, you get him across with action, dialogue and reaction. Here's how we show a wishy-washy mother:

> I knew the minute Mother walked into my room that Dad had ordered her to forbid me to see Ralph again. (Reaction—she knows her mother only too well.) She puttered around nervously, not looking at me, and ended up at the window, where she stood gazing out. Action—stalling betrays Mother's embarrassment.) "Dear," she said over her shoulder, "dear, there's something—well, your father and I talked it over, and

—you see—" (Dialogue—Mother shows that she is unable to come right out with an unfair order.) Inwardly, I was groaning. Why couldn't Mother stand up to him just for once? (Reaction again.)

As you build a character, you want to be reasonable and consistent. In fiction, certain deeds are unforgivable. You can redeem a brute, for instance, if you can show sufficiently terrible pressures that made him that way. But you can't redeem someone who's cautiously and carefully mean—that's a built-in defect. Don't try to stretch character changes too far. If your plot demands that a kind person do a mean thing, either: a) motivate the deed very, very well; b) change the whole character to fit the one deed; or c) change your plot.

3. *Motivation*

Beginners would do well to stick to lovable people. Your readers are interested in people they can identify with, and who wants to identify with a bitch?

The problem in a confession story is to show how basically decent persons get into these messes. The heroine must have full and sympathetic—though perhaps mistaken—motives for her deeds. For instance, in "Paid to Have His Baby," the heroine accepts a large sum of money to bear a child for a millionaire and his over-adoption-age wife. She can't do this just because she's tired of living in Levittown or longs to join the Colonial Dames. But she can get away with it if she's a widow with a child of her own who needs expensive medical care; and even so, she's got to repent long and hard at the end. When the heroine sins, she does so without malice aforethought, but with reasons that seem right to her at the time.

True Story's central characters come from work-shirt backgrounds. *True Story* tells writers this over and over. But still they come in—the stories about professional men and women with smart, sophisticated jobs, stories with social-climbing themes, stories about women whose problems are concerned with whether or not their husbands can think up sufficiently clever advertising slogans, stories laid in college. The editor buys true stories laid in a working class background, with the husband a machinist or a radio repairman or a welder; with the wife a homemaker. This woman's wants and ambitions are small ones. A steady job with regular pay is all she requires of her husband—that and fidelity. For her children she asks only nourishment and safety.

Each one of you knows many stories of universal application that can be translated into *True Story* terms. Perhaps your best friend is having trouble with her daughter who wants to join a socially unacceptable college sorority; you can put this in *True Story* terms by making the sorority a high school one and instead of social unacceptability, give it a rowdy reputation.

The only exception to the work-shirt rule is where the white-collarness is necessary to the story—where, for instance, the hero *must* be a doctor or a teacher; this doesn't happen often, though, so watch it. If you cannot identify yourself with a lower middle class background, you shouldn't be trying this field.

Though *True Story* has often been accused of making up the things that happen in its stories, this is unjust; the incidents are almost always real ones. We do invent motivations, however, simply because we can't print stories in which a heroine sells herself just to satisfy a whim or to get into café society. Such a character is either incredible to the reader or too shallow.

In line with motivation, I would like to pause a moment to talk about *True Story's* readers, because they live in a world where attitudes and ideals—and consequently motives—are different from yours. It is a difference of social status. A typical reader is twenty-one or two, married, the mother of three children (they marry young), a good plain cook, and a conscientious housewife. Her husband (and this is true of her father, brothers, in-laws, and friends) is a skilled worker of some kind, earns over $5000 a year, is justifiably proud of his accomplishments, and wears the pants in the family. They have no sense of inferiority about their status. They do not consider it a disgrace to work with their hands—they think everybody does (except for a few "rich" people perhaps, people like doctors and lawyers). They call themselves "just an ordinary couple," and they're right about it, because they constitute the majority of our population. To them, "being educated" means having a high-school or trade-school diploma. They do not scorn college education—they have simply not thought of it for themselves. They are not social climbers. If money is needed for a sick child or a laid-up husband, they have a few abstract scruples. They have limited ambitions. They love their children, but seek nothing for them beyond "happiness." They are not much interested in house décor or in other people's opinions or "world unrest." The family—husband and children, plus parents, siblings, and in-laws—constitutes their world. They are warm and emotional people. When they quarrel, they yell. When they are touched, they weep. And when they read, they choose *True Story*, because "it's so real . . . it's about people just like me. . . ."

You have to motivate your characters so that they will be real to this young woman and her husband. You have to make them behave as if they belonged to her world, thinking and acting in the same ways and for the same reasons that she does.

4. Scening

Inexperienced writers have a way of spending wordage on unimportant parts of their stories. As an example, here's a partial plot: Girl, adopted by rather strict couple, has always felt they don't love her. Although they dislike the reckless boy she dates, they have given her permission to go to the prom with him, provided he gets her home by a certain hour; boy and girl promise, but in the excitement, they forget and are late; she and parents quarrel, and in a fit of self-pity, she runs away. A beginner handled it like this: First ten pages devoted to talk between boy, girl, and their crowd about the coming dance, with a casual, two-sentence aside referring to parents' harshness and girl's feelings; second ten pages devoted to dressing up for, going to, enjoying, and returning from dance; on page twenty-one, girl has quarrel with parents, runs away, goes to Big City, gets a job, finds a room, and meets villain; pages twenty-two to thirty devoted to first date with villain, etc.

This kind of thing springs from laziness and embarrassment. It's easy to fill a page about dances and clothes and teen-age banter; it's not so easy to write about feelings, about quarrels, about terrifying decisions—you sit at the typewriter and get shy. *But it's the hard parts that make a story.*

A scene in a story is like a scene in a play. In other words, a scene is where the dialogue is. Every crucial point in a story needs a scene—the discovery of adultery, the moment when courage fails, the worm turning, the beginning of the end. Narrative is used only to tie the scenes together, cover time, relate introspection. In the above example, for instance, the dialogue needs to be in the part where the story is told.

Try removing the narrative from your story, reading it with just the scenes. Do you still know what's going on? If not, toss out some of that wurble-wurble about sunsets and coppery-tinted hair and the new dress covered with little gold spangles that made your waistline look so small—and write the *story*.

The purpose of the scenes is to move to a climax. When two characters—or a character and a group of characters—have been in conflict throughout a story, they must come to a showdown *on stage*. Otherwise, the reader feels cheated. Take our adopted youngster who has run off to the Big City and gotten into such terrible trouble with the villain; her parents come after her, find her, and—since she now realizes the truth—bring her home with better understanding existing between them. A beginner would probably say, "We had a talk, and I saw where I'd been wrong." But that won't do. Parents and girl must confront each other *on stage*, say what's in their hearts, and have it out face to face, each side stating its case.

5. *Cliches*

Most writers think of clichés as phrases: "Teeth like pearls," "a nip in the air." That's trite writing, all right, but a minor problem. The clichés that make it necessary to rewrite a story—and hence to buy it cheap—are clichés in the writer's thinking. Cliché characterization, for instance (all bookkeepers are timid, all cops are Irish, all spies are sinister, all ministers are clear-eyed).

Before you write down speech, action, introspection, stop and think. How would a real human being, stuck in my character's situation, react? Not a TV heroine, not Joan Crawford, not a slick-fiction glamour-girl, but a perfectly ordinary woman. How would I feel? *Really* feel? Project yourself into the situation. Shut your eyes and feel it out with your skin. The school dreamboat, the boy I've been yearning over for weeks and weeks, is actually here speaking to me. How do I feel? Am I tongue-tied? Do I giggle nervously and start babbling? Or perhaps, because of something that happened to me a few moments before, I'm suddenly cool and poised. Out of your memories, out of your observation of people, you will draw the answer.

Writing is hard work. Any time it comes easy, suspect it: did that last phrase pop up out of nowhere? Did I hear it on television last night? Am I slipping into an easy solution of this problem? Is this the way it would happen in real life — or only in a soap opera? . . . The villain pulls a gun. But do ordinary people carry guns? Even villainous ordinary people? All right then, he takes a poke at the hero. But does even that happen very often? What do angry work-shirt men really do? For *True Story,* you have to write it the way it really happens.

6. *Writing*

Use short, straightforward sentences, but don't let it get choppy. Write simply. A long sentence can be easy to read if it has no ambiguity. There's a rhythm to prose just as there's a rhythm to verse. If you're stuck for a simple way to write something, try saying it out loud as if someone were in the room with you and you were telling him the story.

You'll find that stories and articles move forward much more satisfactorily if each paragraph gets its own point across.

You can use a little typography to help you get your effects— dashes, italics, exclams. *The American Scholar* and *The Atlantic* frown on this, but it's all right in the confessions. Used too frequently, these devices lose their effectiveness.

Write emotionally. *True Story* heroines take everything big. Use strong words, vivid words, verbs, concrete nouns, adjectives and adverbs that are specific. Use your vocabulary to describe feelings, not scenery.

Be cautious about verbs of direct address. *I said, I cried, I told him,* are your stand-bys, and occasionally you can vary these with adverbs or fuller-explanation verbs like *I offered, I urged, I suggested.* But go easy on the fancy ones — *gritted, rasped, exulted, gasped, exclaimed,* etc. — and on the violent ones — *screamed, shrieked, moaned, groaned,* etc. (No more than one scream per scene is my rule of thumb.) In a two-party conversation, you often need no verb at all after the first exchange, and you can always substitute a piece of action for the verb in identifying the speaker. (He dropped the book. "What did you say?")

Write the way your heroine would write. If she's excitable, she'll write rapidly, semi-coherently. If she's warm, she'll write with compassion about other characters. If she's distracted, half out of her mind over her troubles, that should creep into the writing, too. This is one way you characterize your heroine. She gives herself away in the way she tells her story.

The quicker you sink your hooks into the reader, the better. So, get your story off the ground in the first paragraph — first sentence if possible. And no matter what you've been told in a writing course, it's better to do this with action than with dialogue. (No: "Does this place always have to be a mess?" I cried, slamming the door. Yes: I slammed the door and glared around resentfully at our seedy railroad apartment.) Dialogue is half meaningless until it's explained, while action carries its own explanation with it, its own setting.

7. Miscellaneous Don'ts

Avoid hospital endings. They're convenient when you're plotting, but not all of us are lucky enough to have an accident just when we need it to solve our problems. Stories themed around alcoholism and dope addiction, are usually dreary.

Be accurate about factual material. If you don't know what happens when someone has a heart attack or gets arrested, either find out or don't write about it.

The supply of writers is way below the demand. There aren't enough good writers in the world. There aren't even enough mediocre writers in the world. Pick a field, study it technically, and set to work. If *True Story* interests you, buy the current issue, borrow the previous one, and read each story. Outline the plot of each story in 100 words or less. Write the theme in a sentence. Write the moral in a sentence. Study your findings.

Try to locate some devoted readers of *True Story*. There are several million so this is not hard. Ask them which stories they liked in these two issues and why. Think over what you've learned from interviewing, analyzing and outlining. Then set up a story problem and check it with what you have learned. Now you are a writer at work.

Modern Romances

By Albert Delacorte

I flew down to Norman, Oklahoma (paid my own way), and gave a talk on romance writing.

If this sounds casual, it wasn't. I worked on it at home for a week. I worked on it from midnight, the night I arrived, until seven the next morning.

Because of the many "firsts" it embodied, it created a crazy stir. Women crowded around this wobbly, unshaven editor as if I were Paul Newman. They wanted copies. They stuffed my pockets and briefcase with manuscripts and I apologized that I hadn't worn an apron, so I could catch the overflow. One lady said, "I'm a court stenographer and I'll type up your notes for you." And that's the origin of this version.

The premise of my talk to my workshop audience (and it applies equally to the larger audience of this book) was that, as professionals, you all certainly know how to write. You all have that creative spark. But are you aware of the criteria by which we romance magazine editors judge your stories?

It was to provide these criteria, that my talk was offered.

The Editor's Tools

How can an editor confirm his own judgement? How can he establish a policy? He can begin with his monthly circulation figures. But if he tried to build his policy on these wayward statistics he'd zigzag so much that trying to sell him a story would be like trying to shoot down a drunk duck with a .22.

Circulation in any given month can go down because your West Coast freight car got side-tracked in Minnesota, or because the magazine buyer for a big supermarket chain with 3,000 newsstands decided he didn't like your book — or for the simple reason that it's a brutally humid, hot month—(and your competition isn't selling either). Circulation can go up because the readers go for the girl on the cover — or perhaps for the blurb on the cover — and you never know whether it was the girl or the blurb or the combination.

Only long-term circulation trends, carefully compared with competitive trends give the editor any information. But then, it's often too late for repair; you may need a new model.

Well, what about reader mail? If you know how to handle it, it has its uses — but if you're careless with it, it blows your head off.

Here's a case history. *Modern Romances* published a confession story by an alcoholic. Now I hope that not more than one per cent of our readers are alcoholics. But as we all know, one thousand alcoholics can make a lot of racket. Our story was dramatic. It was inspirational. And so this single confession pulled more mail than any twenty stories.

Well, if you're a careless editor, you immediately take off on a binge of alcoholic narrators — and wake up six months later with a circulation hangover.

Reader mail isn't *the* pulse of *the* magazine. It's *a* pulse beat of *a* reader. And, the heavy fan mail didn't prevent the story from rating near the bottom of our nationwide monthly reader poll — which is roughly where every story about a drunk rates.

We have learned that when a reader reports on a single story, she usually speaks only for herself. But we have also learned that when she reports on why she has the confession magazine reading habit, she frequently speaks for *all* confession readers!

On the level of *why do I read your magazine,* there is an eerie and litany-like unanimity that gives a confessions editor cues he dare not ignore.

Only the monthly hard labor of running 3000 reader ballots through our IBM machines gives us a verdict on each individual story. And even this reader poll verdict simply tells us how well the story was accepted . . . but not why. Statistical ratings aren't *reasons.*

A couple of years ago we published a story called "For Those Who Love God." No story before and no story since has equaled its nation wide poll rating. It was a story narrated by the husband of a fine, sensitive, devout young woman dying by inches of cancer. As she lay dying, the husband's faith in God crumbled. Paradoxically, her death, the purity, and the courage of it, gave her husband a profound transfusion of his wife's love of God.

As I said, that was and is our number one story. Why? The male narrator's soul-destroying grief and bitterness? The cancer angle? The wife's courage? The triumph of faith? The fact that the story made the reader cry? Or all of these elements in concert? As far as the poll returns told us, mum is the word. Readers merely said, "It held our interest." But we think we know why they liked it.

Our Editorial Theory

When Henry Malmgreen, our editor, came to work for us, he had a couple of convictions . . . from which he couldn't be budged. He believed that a confessions story couldn't do its job unless the reader could stop being the reader and literally become the narrator.

His other conviction was that just as people suffering from tired blood take Geritol, so people suffering from tired emotions buy confessions magazines. Henry gave first preference to stories that allowed readers to experience the big, purgative emotions.

Cram sessions with the reader mail helped Henry along. The handwriting, the stationery, the grammar convinced him that he was going to be catering to a lower class audience . . . the people whose door is never darkened by the *Ladies' Home Journal.* Secondly, he could see that even if the people who scrawled these letters on used wrapping paper wanted thrills, *they also wanted a balancing of moral accounts.*

Finally, he could see that they desperately wanted to believe the confessions loyalty oath: every story true. It was obvious they couldn't like a story unless they believed it.

In summary, Henry recognized that 100% reader identification and big emotions could be achieved only within the lower class, moral, every-story-true framework.

At the same time, it began to dawn on him — as it has dawned on many another confessions editor — that it takes discipline to make every story meet this need. On the editorial plane, discipline means this: every story has to have a theme. The theme has to be so manifest that the editor can put it in a paragraph so as to better evaluate it.

What Writers Need to Know

At this point you have a complete picture of our theory and tools. But you must also have a lot of questions. I'm going to enumerate questions I think you *ought* to ask.

With what kinds of narrator is the reader best able to identify? What are *the* big purgative emotions the confessions reader wants to experience? How can they be created?

Granted that the confessions reader needs to believe that every story is true, how does the confessions writer achieve this appearance of truth? Why are morality and faith in God such important conditions? What about dirty confessions magazines — and there *are* some?

Is emotional sensation the basic reason for the fact that almost half a billion confessions magazines have been bought over a period of forty years? Or do they serve some profounder purpose? When we say that *every* story must have a theme, does this mean every story must have a moral — like one of Aesop's fables?

Well, let's go back now to the first question. What kinds of narrator are accepted? I only wish our readers were as single-voiced about all their attitudes as they are about this one! They want an attractive narrator. We have published and, believe me, regretted stories like "I Was Too Fat." Some readers will identify intensively with the problem of the ugly duckling. But from sad experience, we editors have learned that most readers do not.

The narrator must be active. The narrator must cause the major event of the story. Therein lies part of the significance of the phrase; sin, suffer and repent. For if the narrator is more sinned against than sinning, she is passive.

A reader identifying with a narrator is compensating for personality assets she does not have and for frustrations she *does* have. She wants the narrator to be the person she, the reader, would *like* to be!

Remember this last sentence, and the confession stories you write will snap into focus. Avoid alkies, junkies and nymphos.

Just ask *yourself*. Would you *like* to be any of these?

To sum up: Don't send us stories about spineless, jelly-fish, dish-rag narrators. Readers who are this kind of person want the chance to identify with a strong narrator who fights back, who gives them respite from their own weakness. Respite and a glimmer of hope.

Let your narrator suffer the torments of the damned. But make sure she fights back, make sure she grows in the process. The satisfaction derived from the conflict is in proportion to the odds against which the narrator fights.

Will the female reader accept a male narrator? I have a hunch that the female reader will inevitably identify with the story's feminine figure. Even so, if the male narrator is a *loving* figure — and, in the process of the reader's identification, she experiences male *tenderness* — yes, she will accept the story in spite of male narration. But let the narrator be a rough, tough guy who exploits his women, the readers turn thumbs down.

And what about the social category of the narrator? If to identify means to stop being you and to become someone else . . . how can a girl stop being a waitress and start being a debutante? Confessions readers are not looking for *phony* escape. They dream best within their emotional ken.

I realize this presents writers with a mean dilemma. We have to think-our-way, feel-our-way into the soul of a lower class narrator. It isn't easy — but if we fail, our story fails too.

To a lesser degree we have another dilemma. A writer's age is roughly from the middle twenties to the fifties and up. And yet our biggest *demand* is for teen narrators. Reason: An older reader can remember nostalgically and identify successfully with a teen narrator. But a teen narrator has no patience with the problems and dreams of older people.

Only a fifth of our stories have teen narrators, yet half of our highest rating stories are teen oriented! As a confession writer, if you increase your teen output *successfully,* you increase your sales — and not just your sales to us — but to most confessions magazines.

Let me ask some rhetorical questions about narrators. What about stupid narrators? What about cold narrators? What about amoral narrators? You know the answers. And yet our mails are flooded with narrators who don't seem to have all their marbles. The reader doesn't *want* to be smarter than the narrator. As soon as she can look down her nose at the narrator, she withdraws from the identification relationship. The dream is shattered.

How about "I Was A Frigid Wife?" You can answer that now. Confession magazines want stories about women — and men too — who can give love . . . not stories about narrators who take negative pleasure in withholding it.

Those Big Purgative Emotions

Right now, I want to talk about those big, purgative emotions I promised to name and define for you.

The other day, I read about a fascinating rocket the army's just bought. It nullifies gravity. Strap it on your back, and you can literally run as fast as a race horse or jump twice as high as the world's champion high jumper. Reading about it, I suddenly realized what a burden gravity is.

To the confessions reader, the realities of her daily existence are like gravity, binding her, containing her vital emotions, giving her few opportunities to express anger or even admit to it — to feel and express love. The confessions story is *her* outlet.

A confessions story in which anxiety prevails, in which small, ugly fears proliferate is destined to have a poor rating on our reader poll. How about the themes of our low rating stories? Here are a few: A story about a woman who gets into the hands of a loan shark — who keeps abreast of her debts by incurring new ones — until finally the situation explodes; a story about a woman whose husband, still in his forties, becomes sexually impotent; a story about a woman who supplements her husband's income by dress-making and who finally recognizes that she has become a slave to her family.

What do these low rating stories have in common? Were they badly written, badly constructed? They weren't. Their flaw was that the dominant emotional stuff of each of them was anxiety and frustration. And since it is precisely anxiety and frustration from which the reader is seeking release, she necessarily rejects them in a story.

So the most popular stories are those that avoid the neurotic, domesticated, hypertensive emotions. They cater instead to those that are beautiful and those that are damned . . . to the emotions that our readers are deprived of and guard against.

Vicariously, safely and indeed therapeutically our reader's erupt with murderous indignation. They succumb to the death-wish that broods over so many of us. They imbibe the salty, purgative waters of grief. They are lifted to great heights of love of God. Their sense of guilt is exorcised by uncommon punishment and suffering. They love and they are loved profoundly, and sometimes the love is stained red. For violence and the lower class reader are not strangers to each other.

So now, I've got to the heart of the matter — the big purgative emotions. As far as the ones I'm going to discuss are concerned, they could be counted on the fingers of one hand by Three-Finger Brown. Love, anger and sorrow. What dials can the writer manipulate to turn the volume up? What about fear, terror?

Why didn't I list fear with the big three? Simply because while manipulation of fear contributes to suspense, it's not one of the staples readers identify with *Modern Romances*. In that case, what about suffering? I'd say no. I distinguish between emotional *eruptions* (e.g., sudden awareness of being loved; flare-up of anger; surrender to sorrow) — and emotional *states* such as suffering — which can be quite monotonous, prolonged and make for heavy reading. It's the eruptions that jolt the readers. And if these eruptions occur frequently and intensively enough, your story is strong.

Keep Your Narrators Love Starved

Although we demand a strong love element in every story, we do *not* limit you to boy-girl or man-woman love. In five of our fifteen highest rating stories, man-woman love was either secondary or missing altogether.

The gift of love can come from a sibling, a parent, a friend. It can even come from a group. Let me tell you about a story called "They Prayed My Son Back to Life." A young woman, inconsolably bitter about the imminent death of her two-year old son, rejects her neighbors' proffers of sympathy. She rudely questions the sincerity of her minister's attempt to give her religious solace. But all these good people huddle together one rainy morning and kneel in prayer on the little patch of grass and weeds in front of her house. And now a miracle takes place. The incurable child is cured. This, in capsule, is the action of our second highest rating story. What is the love source? God? Well, it's His miracle. And we are awed. But actually it's the affection which the group extends to the narrator that stirs us.

The good confessions stories are the ones that nourish us with that sensation of being meaningful to another person . . . or even, as above, to a community. And it's best of all if this awareness of being meaningful to another person can be a sudden thing, a revelation, a moment of truth. As I said before — emotional *eruptions* are more dramatic than emotional states.

Well, let's get into literary technique. How do we make the reader *care* about the narrator's love? *Privation is the answer.* We build the importance of the narrator's love by either depriving her of it or threatening it. So ask yourself quite cold-bloodedly: Have I starved the narrator for love? Does she suffer enough for the lack of it, so that when it comes, the gift of love will be of great moment? Have I thought through the devices through which her longing is expressed? Certainly unless both the privation and pre-occupation with it have been established, the gift of love will be less moving when it comes.

If privation makes the receiving of love more meaningful, what makes the *giving* of love more moving? Once again there's a one word answer: Sacrifice! So ask yourself: "By what act or acts does the giver of love express it? Is that act a sacrifice?" Why do you suppose we fixed the script so that it was raining the morning "They Prayed My Son To Life?" Would the scene have been as moving on a bright, balmy day?

In our confession story the narrator glances out of the window expecting to see nothing but the bleakness she feels — and there are the people she has driven away praying for her son — returning love for hate.

As you re-read a confession story you wrote, ask yourself: is there any scene in the story where the reader must cry because the narrator either gives or receives love? And you know what the motto of the confession editors is: no love — no sale!

If love is so important — what about sex? You are as aware as I of the popular stereotype of the confessions magazine: "Sex and seduction."

Is it true? To a careless observer leafing through a confessions magazine there's a lot of merit to such a remark. Our narrators are frequently involved in sexual perils. Rape stories — stories of enforced prostitution occur with a frequency out of proportion to their incidence in real life, But, in general, the sex events in our stories come under the heading of suffering and debasement and not sex. Significantly, appraisal by a careful observer scarcely ever results in disapproval.

Why is it that a professional and religiously motivated censor sees no prurience where a self-appointed censor claims to be shocked? The contradiction evaporates when you apply a simple criterion to the sex passages in our type of magazine: Do these passages create libidinous thought and desires? The religious censors, who rarely blacklist any of the better confessions magazines, don't think so. Could you imagine for a moment that if we printed lustful passages we could escape the issue by issue vigilance of the various dedicated and thoroughgoing censorship bodies—especially the religious ones?

We Sorrow Only for Those We Love

Sorrow is a way of expressing love, and readers like to cry because when they are crying, they are loving.

There's no doubt that *any* confessions story that gets readers to cry is a good one, and if they sob, it's a great one. Sacred though tears are, you as writers and we as editors have to consider them clinically. The tears in a story don't usually just happen. They're planned.

Maybe you'd like to see the editorial mind at work, and I'm going to tell you briefly about a story Henry Malmgreen and I replotted. "Any Man Can Have Me" is about a teen-age runaway from a convent school. She falls into the hands of white slavers. Ultimately, she is rescued by a young man who is more or less shoved into her life in the course of a high school fraternity initiation. In the original version, the boy rescues the girl successfully, and the writer indicates the usual happy ending. In our revised version, the boy dies.

Our decision was a gamble. Sure the readers would have liked the original version in which she married the boy. But perhaps, we reasoned, if he died, the sorrow would give the story values a happy ending could never provide.

The raw material of the sorrow then was the death of the narrator's boy friend. How could we eke every last tear out of it? Step one was to build the boy maximally. The finer he was, the greater would be the shock of his death. We gave him spiritual dimension in the girl's eyes. We sealed off any chance of escape for the girl. We gave the girl nothing to want, nothing to dream of but the boy. We made sure the readers knew that the boy understood fully the odds against him, so that he became all hero and not part fool.

And now we were ready for the death scene itself. Should the boy die slowly or quickly? Offstage — or in the narrator's arms? Should he be hurt internally, or should he bleed? The emotional success or failure of the scene depended on these problems being posed and on their being resolved with action that would make the final passion of this boy ineffably moving.

In other words, when we reached the boy's death, we mounted an assault on our readers' emotions.

This process, the calculating appraisal of the emotional potential of the high points of your story — this conscious warping of story line to emotional considerations — is the only road I know to successful exploitation of emotion. Use your *head* to get at your readers' hearts.

Anger, the Third Emotion

Anger, indignation and related explosive emotions, all hark back, as you know, to a conflict situation. A conflict situation in which

Dear Editor!

I enjoy reading your good story's. Some of them is really a knock out. All of them are good. But some is just more interested. **The Story God Make me brave.** It gave me more faith because I am afraid to have a baby. because I don't want it brought up to know hard ship like I did. But now I can make it because I have more faith. I was a delinquent girl & forced my Guy to marry me. But now I think it will work out. I am not afraid anymore. I still live in a army town. Which is an air force Base. My husband trust me. he is still in service. I will have my baby.

Example of reader mail from Modern Romances showing how reader identifies herself with narrator and writes to express good wishes for her.

the opponents are equals can be merely competitive. Shift the balance of power — and one becomes the underdog. Add injustice — and indignation appears. Add physical violence and retaliation in kind can be expected. As for reader identification — underdogs of the world don't need to be *told* to unite.

What are the variables which the nimble writer can manipulate? Well, for one, there is the righteousness of the narrator's cause. Obviously, the silver cord of identification is strained if the reader mutters to herself: "She only got what was coming to her!" But if the narrator's cause is just, immediately the reader is a fellow traveler. The second variable follows from the first. Anger, of course, varies in direct proportion to the grossness of the offense, the tyranny, the physical violence, if any. Pour it on. Within the bounds of credibility and the inner consistency of the malefactor, the sky's the limit. Be sure the "villain" is a person who can be *expected* to violate the narrator's rights grossly . . . or else that the narrator can forgivably read meanness into well-intentioned behavior. I qualify because I don't want to leave the impression that I am issuing a clarion call for old-fashioned villains.

Ask this of yourself: Are the wrongs perpetrated against my narrator of sufficient stature? Do they pile high and beyond endurance? Is the narrator's reaction just — or will she lose reader sympathy? And finally is my narrator's retaliation commensurate with the offense?

Pile the Agony High

Time after time, our polls confirm that other things being equal, the more acute the suffering, the more total the degradation of the narrator — the more warmly the readers receive the story.

Because our courageous narrators triumph over degradation, and love triumphs over privation, finer stories are tireless dynamos of hope.

Violence of emotion is a goal in successful confession writing. *Profound* love — *violent* indignation — *abysmal* suffering — *agonizing* grief.

But only when identification occurs can the overpowering emotions be felt.

So *belief* is the bedrock. Tragedy, skepticism and humor aren't very far apart. As soon as doubt or sophistication colors the reader's

Mr. Henry P. Malmgreen:

Have just read "Confession on the Raw" and I thrild to see such frank testimony written. I pray that Mary will find happiness and that her mistake will be put behind her. For the blame is not hers intirally but her parents. If more parents would love and guide and above all understand our youngsters more. If more faith and religion was exercise in each home, and more love lavished on each child our teen-ager would be a lot less likely to be out looking for a thrild yet perhaps if that mom & dad had been home at night this child would be safe and free of carring such a heavy burden on her shoulders. May God bless and watch over Mary and every boy and girl that today through no falt of their own fine their way out to our streets each night. You may print this if you disire my name and all. (Excuse my spelling I am not a good speller.)

Example of Modern Romances reader mail showing how the magazine plays a useful part in the reader's life.

attitude — the tragic becomes droll.

We talk about "our reader" as if there were one person typical of all 8,000,000. But obviously they are 8,000,000 individuals. Each of these women has her own threshold of disbelief — the point at which she loses faith and says to herself, "This story can't be true." When we buy stories beyond this reader's threshold of credibility — we've lost her. Give us enough stories that *do* generate belief, and we have a reader who'll never kick the habit.

How does the confessions writer achieve the all-important appearance of Truth? Well, you'd get the answers in any good short-story course, and I'm afraid I have neither the time nor the training to give you even a *short* short-story course here. But, once again, here are some telling questions with which to test your stories.

How well do I know my narrator? Do I know the street where she lives? Or the factory she works in? If I don't, can I find out?

Have I selected a narrator who's real to me and who can be real to my readers, not an oddball, not too high on the social ladder, not a transparent steal from a too recent newspaper headline?

Is my narrator's behavior always consistent? Am I sure that *every* thought she thinks, every emotion she feels, every action she takes is the thought, the emotion, the action that's inevitable — she being the person she is? Editors are alert for the chameleon narrator who changes in personality to oblige the plot. Remember that a plot has to be limited by the personality of the narrator — and not the other way around.

Are the guts of my story told by a succession of vivid scenes—or is it unfortunately mostly narrative — and therefore just a synopsis? Readers believe and are moved only by what they *see* — and not by what they're told. The identification process doesn't even begin until your first scene. Naturally, open with a scene if you possibly can.

Ask yourself this: Is my story long enough to do the job that needs to be done to establish people that will be believed, to re-enforce the impact of their personalities by showing how they act and react in a series of scenes, to permit an ending that's really an ending — not a surrender. Other things equal, long confessions stories are stories; short ones are synopses.

Listen to what our reader poll has to say on this subject. The average poll rating of all our stories is about 75. No story of 4,000 words or under has ever achieved so much as a 50 rating, and our short-shorts have dipped all the way down into the 20's. In other words, out of every hundred readers twenty liked them! What the heck, we pay by the *word*. We like to save money, but not by starving story values. Story values need Lebensraum. What self-respecting narrator can sin, suffer and repent in the strait-jacket of 3000 words — or even 5000 words?

One last, bridging observation on the subject of belief. Most of us, and especially confessions readers, believe what we *need* to believe. We perish — spiritually at least — if we lose faith in what we need to believe. That's why there are churches. And, no disrespect intended, that's why there are confessions magazines.

Do you recall that I suggested earlier that you might be wondering — is emotional sensation the basic, rock-bottom reason for the fact that half a billion confessions magazines have been read two billion times over the past forty years? Or do they serve some even rock-bottomer purpose?

The answer is yes, they do serve a profounder purpose. And the reason, though it deals with profundity, is a simple one. Man is a goal-directed creature. Force him to act without a goal, and he may go through the motions. But the savor is gone. Carry the process a giant step further. Make him live his whole life without a goal, and once again, if he is strong, like the Neanderthal man, he can go through the motions. He will subsist. But he will not live.

The confessions reader will have no part of this grey universe. Only belief makes the dangerous and often tragic world she lives in safe. Through belief, Death the nullifier, is transformed from an end to a mystic beginning. This belief she must have. She turns to any person or institution or magazine that affirms it dramatically.

Our story "For Those Who Love God" did this job. It stands first on our list of top stories — and it will stay where it is until another story delivers the same message better.

Confessions magazines have a function. Our finer stories give love to the loveless, hot tears to the dry-eyed. But we go beyond feeding the hungry. We affirm beliefs which the ugliness of some lives controverts. In their letters, our readers say, in effect, "Tell us these truths are self-evident." And, reaching them through their emotions, we tell them over and over that order, forgiveness, retribution, penance and, above all, love and God are real. And so after forty years, confessions magazines still prosper — and will until another medium is born which can give these troubled souls the same affirmation better.

No Place for Smut

Let's consider for a minute the sex-thrill confessions magazines. These magazines come and go not because they are banned, but because by titillating the reader with spicy stories, and by thus confounding the verities the reader *wants* to believe they ultimately burden her with a guilt that leads to angry rejection of the magazine.

If we have eyes to read our mail with, hearts to feel with, heads to think with, polls to measure with, we don't need censors. For the exacting process of editing the magazine our readers need and live by, leaves no place for smut.

Can You Commit Your Theme to Writing?

I have often mentioned *theme*. What *is* a theme? It is a statement of the emotional, moral and didactic values of a story and the means by which they will be achieved.

Before you start a story, commit your theme to writing. Simply forcing yourself to face your theme, or your lack of it, will call attention to the unsuspected potential of your story . . . or perhaps, unfortunately, to its unsuspected bankruptcy. Will your theme convert into a story that makes readers cry and love and hate? Will it permit you to say anything positive about those verities I've invoked? If not, let it mellow.

No one can be completely objective. But you should know more about the watermarks the editor wants to see when he holds your story to the light. You know you must stress credibility; that your story must have a clear and present theme; an active, likeable, lower class narrator; that it must compel those eruptive, purgative emotions; that, finally, it must pay more than lip service to the moral verities.

I have described all the ingredients of a confessions story except talent. If I could define *that,* I'd be writing those wonderful stories we expect from you myself.

Modern Romances, published by Dell, is one of 30 confession magazines. No other single group of magazines buys as much or pays as well.

Dauntless Books, Inc.
17 W. 44 St.
New York, N. Y. 10036
Publishers of: *Confidential Confessions, Daring Romances, Exciting Confessions, Revealing Romances, Secret Romances,* and *Secrets*

Dell Publishing Co.
750 Third Ave.
New York, N. Y. 10017
Publishers of: *Modern Romances*

Ideal Publishing Co.
295 Madison Ave.
New York, N. Y. 10017
Publishers of: *Intimate Story* and *Personal Romances*

Bronze Thrills Group
1220 Harding St.
Fort Worth, Texas 76102
Publishers of: *Bronze Thrills, Hep, Jive, Soul Confessions.*

KMR Publications
21 W. 26 St.
New York, N. Y. 10010
Publishers of: *My Love Secret Confession, Real Romances, Real Story* and *Uncensored Confessions*

Macfadden-Bartell Corp., Publisher
205 E. 42 St.
New York, N. Y. 10017
Publishers of: *True Confessions, True Experience, True Love, True Romance* and *True Story*

Magazine Management
625 Madison Ave.
New York, N.Y. 10022
Publishers of: *My Confession, My Romance, Intimate Secrets, Secret Story* and *True Secrets*

Sterling Group, Inc.
315 Park Ave. S.
New York, N. Y. 10010
Publishers of: *Modern Love Stories* and *Real Confessions*

Writing For Young Children

By Claudia Lewis

"How do people feel when they are grown up? Do they feel tall and fat? Do they feel all finished?"

No doubt about it. Children know how they feel, inside and out, from their toenails to their teeth. This child's comment strikes upon our blunt ears like a language from another time and place.

It is a children's language, and a writer's language, because it springs from lively sensory perception and is, for that reason, fresh.

In his early encounters with our adult speech he is bewildered by metaphors. Ask him, "Did you have difficulty this morning?" and he may answer, "No. I had an egg." Comment upon what sharp eyes he has, and you may only disturb him. "My eyes don't have points on them!"

He puts the world together for himself, bit by bit, touching, reaching; an explorer with his own hands. "Suede feels like liver." "When your foot's asleep it feels like cracker crumbs." He comes racing in from watching a parade: "I saw a man with a big, big drum, from his knees up to his neck!" His *eyes* measure the world around him. He has not yet taken over those wooden

71

rulers we try to foist upon him. "The bread in the toaster just stays bread," he tells us, as he tries to explain that the electricity is not working at his house. And with simple, honest acknowledgment of what it feels like, in his young responsive body, to stand in the presence of new-fallen snow, he reports: "How nice it looked, and so I lay down in it."

Secret wish of us all, but how we cast it from us. No more lying in deep snow to test the weight. No. The snow is "beautiful." Let it go at that.

When you begin writing for children, tear off those top layers of yours. Take some experience that was vivid to you—pleasant or frightening—anything that had strong sensations connected with it. Now forget these adjectives that I have just used, "pleasant"—"frightening," these nondescript borrowed words. What really happened to you? And by "you" I mean the breathing, balance-loving body of you with its two movable legs and arms, its emotion-registering stomach, its need of warmth and dread of cold, its marvelous perceiving eyes.

Try a familiar summer vacation experience like lying in the sun on the beach. Keep the words close to the sun and sand as you felt them:

> *"I spread my towel on the dry, deep and hot sand and stretch out on my stomach. I feel the sand move and seep under me. I feel the sun reach down to find me. It slowly heats every part of my body until I think I feel myself turning brown at the edges. The sun heats my body until the strength crawls out of my arms through my fingers and out of my legs through my toes."

Or take a common thing like gardening:

> "I made rows with my fingers, letting the earth cover my hands and get under my nails. Soon my hands feel very dry, as though the skin is being pulled tightly toward my wrist."

———

*Exercises used as examples were written by students in the Language Arts courses at Bank St. College of Education. They are presented not as models to be copied, nor as illustrations of expert use of language, but rather as examples of first steps a beginning writer or story teller can take for himself.

Writing For Young Children

We have become too used to our skin. Yet when someone says, "See here, remember that feeling at the wrist," then the dormant past stirs in us. It is through our wrists and hands, our eyes and ears—through our tallness and fatness, if you will—that we find our way to juvenile story vitality.

Out of the child's reservoir of sensory responsiveness come rushing up the words that move with the rhythm of his thought; bumping, swinging words. How does the choppy sea go? Why, "wibbly, woobly, dabbly, dubbly, bibbly," of course. And the child dances this as he speaks it.

Kipling spoke this language of imagery and sound, and children do not forget the "great grey-green greasy Limpopo River, all set about with fever-trees." They go back again and again to the story teller who talks with the tumbling words. "In the High and Far-Off Times the Elephant, O Best Beloved, had no trunk."

They go back to Kenneth Grahame, for the sake of the little Mole who "scraped and scratched and scrabbled and scrooged" till he popped up into the sunlight.

The youngest ones recognize their language with delight in the refrain of *The Little Engine That Could*: "I think I can, I think I can, I think I can." They are drawn back to the old folk tales, too, by the power of the rhythmical repeated words: "No, no, by the hair of my chinny chin chin," . . . "Very well, then, I will, said the Little Red Hen, and she did" . . . "I am the gingerbread man, I am I am" . . .

Whenever the writer can make us *feel* the hot sun on our backs, whenever he can *strike* rhythmical clinks, snaps, thumps, from the black print letters, children will listen, and will return to listen again.

Is there nothing more to it? Is this *all* children want?

They want a great deal more. A story that offers only images—sound without content—is scarcely a story at all. And a distinction must be made between what the 3-year-old wants and what the 8-year-old wants.

How do children do it?

Age 3:

"This high hill makes my legs feel like bending."

Age 6:

SONG OF THE RIVER

Oh my heavy load,
My heavy load,
I cannot hold,
I cannot hold.
When the wind blows,
Waves go over me.
I shiver,
I'm cold.
It ripples so, it itches me.

Age 7:

SPRING

(Dictated by a group of children)

Flowers are blooming in spring, and the trees and the birds. Grass grows green. Butterflies are in the air. Trees are growing, and potatoes and carrots and lettuce and celery and onions and beets. Children are playing in the nice sunshiny day. The sun shines on the brooks. We begin to eat strawberries for breakfast, and raspberries. The farmer begins to drive out the cows and the horses and the sheep and the chickens. All fruit begins to blossom, all fruit blossoms that there are. Pears begin to grow. Nearly every night I go over to the bay to see the boats sailing. The trees get sort of flower leaves. You pick them off and take them home. Little birdies drink of the spring. Children rollerskate in the park. I take pictures through the trees. Morning glories grow and blossom. The daisies begin to bloom, and roses and violets.

Age 8:

THE BRIDGE

The bridge is a long arm and he stretches his long arm way across the river and I think it is beautiful. The cars go bumpty, bumpty, bump and the street cars go over it. And his fingers just touch the other side, and his back must ache sometimes, but he never

lets go for he knows that it would hurt. So he never
lets go and he looks down under him and he sees the
boats go under him and at night he goes to sleep.
And pretty soon a boat comes and the bridge has to
wake up. And the boat goes toot-toot-tooting and that
is the way his life goes.

Age 9:

MORNING AIR

Sometimes I go out of doors before breakfast. In
the early morning, the air is fresher than further on
in the day. You can smell pine trees, box hedges, and
flowers. When I go in, breakfast smells so good!

The 3-year-old, climbing his high hill, has not learned to say
that it "tires" his legs. In his simple statement of what actually
happens to him lies the key to his mind.

The 6-year-old, writing so vividly of the river, becomes a river.
He does not stand on the shore and watch, detached, like a recording machine. He *is* the river, sensing its weight and movement.
His skin is alive to it. And in the same way the child who describes
the bridge is not vacantly describing. He reaches, with the bridge.
Eyesight is not yet cut off from body sight. What Louis Danz
said of the artist might well be said of the child: "The eyes are
merely holes for the body to feel through."

The 9-year-old, writing of the morning air, scarcely relies upon
his eyes at all. He lets the fresh morning air come through to us
on the sense of smell.

Elizabeth Enright, writing in "Thimble Summer" of a little farm
girl's trip to the "cold room" to get the milk and butter on a hot
day, shows us the room as the child sees it:

"It was still and dim down there. A spigot dripped
into the pool of water where the milk cans and stone
butter crock were sunk. Garnet put a square of butter
on the plate she had brought. She knelt down and
plunged both her arms into the water. It was cloudy
with spilled milk but icy cold. She could feel coolness
spreading through all her veins and a little shiver
ran over her."

Make contact with your joints and bones. What is coldness like?
"My legs are cotton, my toes hard icy rocks . . . "

Awe, Peace, Freedom, Power . . .

Words like these are hard to get away from. We use them as
thoughtlessly and as commonly as the pennies cluttering up our
purses. But there is a way to get beneath them, as a child would.
Take an easily imagined situation: You are standing on skis
at the top of a snowy slope in mountain country. No one else
is with you . . . Now, talk to us of power, awe, peace, freedom:

"I grow tall and taller; to the roots of my hair I
grow until my arms are nine miles wide and my throat
is a shouting canyon."

"The hill is a large white sheet of paper that no
one has written on. My ski prints are like writing on
it, but I do not feel sure I am allowed to write on it."

"My pores opened and the air flowed through my
head as if it were cheesecloth."

Words and sounds are savoured in the mouths of children as
though they were lollypops; they are turned, twisted, smoothed,
rounded, toyed with, smacked, sipped: "Herschel, Herschel," mur-
mers a four-year-old, as his friend walks by, "Herschel, Hushel,
Hush my baby, Hushel, Herschel."

Even a two-year-old knows when she has struck a good phrase.
Never mind what the adults mean when they use it:

Yiks, tie my shoe
Yiks, tie my shoe
Yiks, tie my shoe
and a half!

To children who cannot read, the sounds they hear are all
symbols, hinting of the unknown worlds circling their universe. Is
there a symbol for color? Another for a number? A five-year-old
can combine them in a single incantation, and why not? They
turn upon a single axle, a three-rimmed wheel:

Red and yellow and purple and blue
And red and another yellow,
And green and orange and three blacks,

And three pinks, and one pink, and three browns,
And brown three brown,
And white eighteen turquoise,
And three another pink,
And dark navy-blue three,
And eighteen pink threes,
Black pink three,
Two four three,
Six eight nine,
Ten three eight,
Five three Y,
Five Y Z,
A—L—K
A ten three,
Six eight ten,
Eleven, twelve, thirteen,
Eighteen fourteen fifteen,
Seventeen, sixteen, eighteen.

Incantation is the stuff of childhood. The ritual words of games and ceremonies and celebrations have magic meanings; "Aunty-over!" "Run, Sheep, Run!" "Allee-allee-oxen-free!" These enigmatic play cries of children resound in the cups of the summer sky, over the little towns of the east, the little towns of the west. Chants, signals, symbols. They absolve, seal, protect. No question why.

The adult, looking back years later, wonders, "Was it really 'ante-over'? Was it really 'All-ye all-ye outs in free'? What did it mean. 'Heavy heavy hangs over thy head'? Why did we say to the ladybug, 'Fly away home, your house is on fire, and your children will burn'?"

Children do not ask. The accept what is given to them, and carry their magic keyrings about with them as naturally as they carry jackknives and marbles: Open Sesame! April Fool! Finders Keepers! Holders! Starlight, starbright, first star I've seen tonight . . . Eeny Meeny Miney Mo . . . Inty Minty Tippity Fig . . .

Incantation can magnetize a story. Children like to hear it just as they like to listen to the sound of an egg beater whipping up a deep bowl of cream, or the sound of a lawnmower cutting the summer grass. They have taken the nursery rhymes to themselves for the sake of the deedle-deedle-dumplings; the hickory-dickory-docks; the muffets and tuffets; the wee-willie-winkies; simons and piemans—all meaningless, except to the ear.

It is partly this: a "stick stuck" is a stuck stick, as a "caught twig" could never be.

A B C Exercises

How do you write for young children? First of all, try a *listening* exercise. Listen to all the "vowels" and "consonants" in the radiator; listen to the hollow clacking of the children's blocks; or to the rushing of the rain on the windows; and if you want to please the children themselves, listen even to the clap and plop of egg yolks when you stir a cake.

Get the words down, in any form, as they come. If no form that you know of seems right, invent a new one. If no word that you know of seems right, put one together out of the sounds it should have. You are in the child's territory now.

A four-year-old boy stands at the top of the playground slide. To the world beneath he announces:

> You know,
> I'm not a boy,
> I'm not a girl,
> I'm not a lady
>   and
> I'm not a man
> I'm not the sky
>   and
> I'm not the sand
> I'm really
>   ICE
>   and
>   soon
>   I'll
>   turn
>   into
>   water!
> And down he slides!

To the boy, it is a game. To us, watching from the world

beneath, it is visible poetry, thought translated into form. Through repetition, contrast, and suspense, we are led to the climax, where the metaphor bursts upon us and leaves us staring in surprise.

The little boy is acting out a new discovery. Ha! Ice melting is like me sliding down the slide. I see! This is the world! It has boys in it, and girls, and ladies and men, and a sky up above and sand below—and I, I, though I'm really a boy, can make myself like ICE!

He is investigating the nature of things. Standing there on the top of the slide, he gets his bearings. What he discovers is something to shout about, to celebrate. And because he is only four years old, his thoughts touch singly upon each point he surveys. He cannot gather his observations into a generalization. He must enumerate, contrast, and repeat. "This is not this, or this, or this. It is THAT!" Furthermore, to him, repetition is the natural language of celebration; contrast and suspense are the language of discovery.

In a spontaneous way, the announcement from the slide shapes itself into a design. At age three it may amount to no more than:

> I'm sitting by you
> And you're sitting by me.
> I have a book,
> You have a book,
> We're looking at books together!

> Today is today,
> Tomorrow is tomorrow.
> Today is Friday,
> Tomorrow is Saturday,
>   and my daddy is going to see me.

Every story—whether for the four-year-old or the child of school age—is, in its own way, a drama. The writer for the youngest children frames his drama on a toy stage, as it were. We follow his characters, one by one, in *all* their exits and entrances; we hear *each* word that is spoken. Each movement is shown.

We are not left to assume what might have been spoken, as we are in the dramas for older children; we are not asked to fill in gaps between Acts, from our knowledge of universals; we are not presented with a complexity of scenes set forth upon a revolving stage. Instead, the small scurryings down among the grass blades are revealed, in their minutiae; through a magnifying glass, the scene is blown to life size.

The Little Red Hen returns to her grain of wheat for the cutting, the grinding, the baking. As she returns, we go with her. These journeyings are not summarized, not disposed of as a single episode in the life of the Little Red Hen.

Likewise, we hear, each time, the repeated words of the duck, the cat, the dog: "Not I," "Not I," "Not I."

The movement of this kind of patterned story, in short, builds up into a design. The child can almost put out his hands and trace its symmetry. It is right for the concrete world he lives in; it is a structure he can understand, and one that he can delight in. Let's recall an old favorite:

THE LITTLE RED HEN

One day the Little Red Hen was scratching in the farmyard when she found a grain of wheat.

"Who will plant this grain of wheat?" said she.

"Not I," said the duck.

"Not I," said the cat.

"Not I," said the dog.

"Very well then," said the Little Red Hen, "I will."
    And she did.

After some time the wheat grew tall and ripe.

"Who will cut the wheat?" asked the Little Red Hen.

"Not I," said the duck.

"Not I," said the cat.

"Not I," said the dog.

"Very well then," said the Little Red Hen, "I will."
    And she did.

"Now," she said, "Who will take the wheat to the mill
    to have it ground into flour?"

"Not I," said the duck.

"Not I," said the cat.

"Not I," said the dog.

"Very well then," said the Little Red Hen. "I will."
    And she did.

When the wheat was ground into flour, she said,

"Who will make this flour into bread?"

"Not I," said the duck.

"Not I," said the cat.

"Not I," said the dog.

"Very well then," said the little Red Hen. "I will." And she did.

Soon she was taking from the oven a lovely loaf of bread.

"Who will eat the bread?" she said.

"I will," said the duck.

"I will," said the cat.

"I will," said the dog.

"Oh, no you won't!" said the Little Red Hen. "I found the grain of wheat. I planted the seed. I cut the ripe grain. I took it to the mill. I baked the bread. I shall eat it myself." And she did.

It would be possible, of course, to take the content of "The Little Red Hen" and shape it into an entirely different form, one that summarizes and condenses as it moves ahead:

One day the Little Red Hen found a grain of wheat when she was scratching in the farmyard. "Who will plant this wheat?" she called to the duck, the cat and the dog. Each of them answered "Not I," so the Little Red Hen planted it herself.

Soon the wheat was ready to cut and take to the mill for grinding. Again, the duck, the cat and the dog would have nothing to do with it, so the Little Red Hen cut the wheat and took it to the mill herself.

When she came back from the mill with her flour, she asked, "Who will make this flour into bread?" Again, the answer from the duck, the cat, and the dog: "Not I," "Not I," "Not I." So the Little Red Hen baked the bread herself.

When the lovely loaf came from the oven, the Little Red Hen asked, "Who will eat the bread?" The duck, the cat, and the dog were ready at once: "We will!"

"No you won't," said the Little Red Hen. "I did all the work. I shall eat the bread myself." And she did.

81

The writer who feels more at home with generalizations and condensations than he does with repetitions, enumerations and refrains, should probably address himself to children of school age—that is, children of roughly six or seven years and up. With this style, which permits complexities of plot, leaps in time and space, and subtle interactions of characters, enter Mary Poppins, Freddy the Pig, Pinocchio, Dr. Dolittle.

The old nursery favorite, "The Tale of Peter Rabbit," still selling well today, is written without a line of repetition. The story unfolds as a narrative, without any design except that provided by the action as it rolls up its dangers and suspense, small episode upon episode, until at last Peter makes his way to safety.

Beginning writers, in love with patterned story designs and the rhythmical refrains that sharpen them, sometimes make the mistake of loading them into stories for older children. The eight-or-nine-year-old will be impatient with story phrases such as "Jimmy had a bicycle, and every day he rode it up and down and around and around." If Jimmy is nine, and old enough for a bicycle, he won't be content with riding it "up and down and around and around." This is tricycle behavior. The nine-year-olds are eager to be off down the street on their bicycles, on the look-out for adventure.

We need only listen to a five-year-old talking to herself, as she paints at her easel, to be reminded of what "story" means to children:

> Once upon a time there was a teen-ager and his name was Jimmy, and he had a girl friend, and her name was Mary. He was waiting for his food 'cause he was waiting in a restaurant. And he was very mad. He was waiting 7 hours for his chop suey to come, and so then he got his chop suey after 9 more hours were over. Then it was time for him to go home. So he couldn't have no date with his girl friend. So when he came home it was 12 o'clock and he went to bed at 1 o'clock. And that day after he woke up everybody was yelling outside. They were saying, "Make way . . . make way . . . make way . . . for the beautiful princess!" He ran outside to see what all the excitement was. He finally saw that a princess was

coming to town so he said, "Princess, will you marry
me?" The princess said, "Yes, I'll marry you." So they
got married and lived happily ever after . . . BUT . . .
the other girl friend was very sad and this is a song
about the boy, the Princess and the girl . . .
This is a song of the beautiful princess and the boy
    and the other girl.
To never take another girl like the boy friend did.
Keep your own girl.
If she's mean don't take her.
Keep your own girl friend.
That's my lovable, lovable, lovable song.

Out of the trappings of this comic-strip fairy tale emerges the
intimation of a universal theme. The scene is set uncertainly,
somewhere between Chinatown and the royal high road, and the
characters slip in and out of their symbolic parts. The child author
feels her way through material that is almost too difficult for
her to handle, but there is no confusion in the underlying emotional reality. With the help of symbols and heightened language,
she flings out a footbridge for herself, to carry her toward the
knowledge of something she has sensed.

Children do not hesitate to walk straight up to emotional experience. They *ask* us for it. Give them no more than the skeleton
of a story of pity or courage or compassion, and they will rush
into it with their own emotions, as the tide rushes in and swirls
about the piles beneath the dock.

It is an interesting experience to turn back to some of the
stories that were landmarks in our own childhood. "The Fir Tree,"
by Hans Christian Andersen, for instance. For how many of us
does the very sound of these words stir up a residue of the old
emotional response? Yet if we go back to the story now, with the
hope of plunging deep into the old poignancy, we will be disappointed. The poignancy is not there. It was in us, who were
swelling to receive for the first time the knowledge of death, and
change, and loss.

Children bring emotions to stories. The author must meet them
with emotion. His stories will be charged with meaning for

children to the extent that he writes what is meaningful to himself. It is fruitless to stand aside, detachedly contemplating children and their interests and needs, and from that vantage point setting forth to try to please or, worse still, to "help" them.

The great author writes his books not "for children," but for and from the child in himself. Contact with children, in his daily life, may help him keep in touch with the childlike part of himself.

It can be taken for granted that children look for more than amusement alone in books, just as we do; that they ask us for stories that give them something to put their teeth into, something to draw strength from. Call it a "moral view," if you will. This is not to be confused with a "moral tag," or preaching, which is as strongly resented by children as we, ourselves, resent propaganda in literature. The difference is perhaps just this: The writer who preaches at children has removed himself from what he considers their world; the writer who opens up a "moral view" to children stands among them, and lifts them up to look through his own windows.

In the jealousy-over-a-new-baby story, for instance, the child reader may indeed identify himself with a character who is having troubles similar to his own, and there may be comfort in this, and in the glimpse it may give him of the universality of the problem. Sometimes, when teaching slips in, the *story* slips out.

The tonsil operation story is another case in point. It may indeed help a child who is going to the hospital, for instance, to become acquainted beforehand, through a "story" written just for this purpose, with the setting and the process, in order that his fear of the unknown may be mitigated. This is arming him with knowledge. Well and good.

But stopping at this point is stopping very short indeed. Why not arm him, also, with that particular kind of strength that flows from a *story?*

A child setting forth to the hospital could conceivably be better armed—if books are to be thought of as arming—with a story comparable to the beautiful and moving "Li Lun, Lad of Courage" by Treffinger, than with a battery of written facts about operating rooms, hospital beds, friendly nurses, and ice cream. Here, in Li Lun, is a child hero to identify with, who lives not in a two-dimensional world screened of fears and dread, but in one that leaves him alone on the very peak of difficulty, to find his way home through his courage.

This is not to make a plea for overlooking the power of facts, but rather to suggest that knowledge is barren if it does not include knowledge of ourselves, and our human potential.

Tempo

The best test of the tempo is to read one's manuscript aloud, particularly if it is a story for pre-school or young school age children, and destined for this kind of reading.

It is not hard to know if one becomes restless during the reading. It is sometimes a little harder to put one's finger on why, and where the remedy lies.

Lagging of the movement is sometimes due to weights in just those passages which, according to the sense of the story, should be made to move particularly rapidly. An example might be a story for pre-school children revolving around guessing, or hunting for surprises. The simple plot takes the child character from one wrong guess to another. Finally, at the end, he knows that the answer, or the surprise, lies at the top of the stairs. He starts up . . . If the writer, at this point, overloads him with thoughts that must be expressed in print, or with refrains to be sung—all of them taking much longer to read aloud than it takes a child to dash up a flight of stairs—he will be disregarding one of the most important tools that is at his disposal for creating the illusion of reality, and carrying his reader with him.

Children are impatient for the plot to begin; we capture their interest at once by the promise of adventure to come, or conflict, mystery, suspense, excitement. One of the writer's best exercises will be to study the opening paragraphs of the books that have won the solid approval of this age group—from "Mary Poppins" to "Heidi." In how many of them does the plot begin with an arrival or departure? This imitates life itself. Any one of us knows that on a journey we go forward into the unpredictable.

We come, in the end, to the point that was our springboard in the beginning. The source of both the meaningful theme and the vigorous phrase is in ourselves.

Big Ideas In Little Words

By Miriam E. Mason

Editors of juvenile books divide their lists into age groups, keeping in mind school grades as "the norm." Broadly speaking, there are three bases for juvenile books. (1) The Picture Book—for the child who cannot yet read or is no further than the first grade level. In these books, pictures are more important than words, and the text can be as short as 500-1,000 words. (2) The Young Reader book. Pictures are less important, vocabulary, while simple, is interesting and colorful, and plot can be more full-blown. Lengths range from 15,000-25,000. These books can be read by a bright youngster of six or may even be interesting to a slow reader aged 12. I write for this age group and my fan letters come from children whose ages range that far apart. (3) The junior high novel for children from 9 to 14. Here, the plot can be more complex--action and suspense play a greater role, and of course, the vocabulary is practically adult. Lengths run up to 50,000 words. After that comes the teen-age novel which differs little from the adult novel except in subjects and taboos.

Each juvenile book editor has his own vision of the market and his sights may either knock off or add a year or two from the age groupings I have given you.

To a juvenile book writer, checks and contracts are indeed satisfying but there is another type of mail which brings special delight. Those are the letters addressed in big, straggling handwriting, sometimes printing, sometimes careful script. They may come from one child, or from an entire class.

From New Jersey, a 9-year old boy writes:

"Dear Miriam E. Mason—For Book Week we are writing to our favorite authors. I picked you. . . . I liked your book Dan Beard. I liked the part of the book when Dan and Harvey went hunting for Indian charms and the part where he started the Lone Wolves, and when Rolla took the bow and arrows and was going to get the big turtle. . . . I liked your book because it *gave me the feeling* of the great outdoors and I like Indian Crafts, too. . . . I like books about Indians and pioneers."

To the children's book author who loves his work these letters mean more than any material success. The good children's book author wants to give joy through reading and these letters show the writer that he has fulfilled his aim.

They serve as a guide, too. You begin to see what you do the best, and in which way you give the most reading pleasure. They help to understand the audience.

Let me choose certain points from these letters which might aid the author who is just starting out. In the brief space of this article, one could not possibly say everything there is to be said, but one thing mastered will open many other doors of knowledge.

(1) VISUALIZE YOUR READER: My reader, for purposes of this discussion, is the child who has mastered the mechanics of reading and is now ready to read books for enjoyment. These books must not be mere exercises in word recognition, for word recognition is no longer a novelty. Now the words must take him somewhere and not just mark time.

As you develop an idea for a juvenile book, have a child in mind. Go to the library and watch your desired reader choose a book.

Visit a schoolroom. A fourth grade of nine and ten year olds is a median average for the group we are discussing. Notice children in their play, and talk to them. I find that many aspiring juvenile writers have no clear ideas about the children whom they hope to please. If they fail, it is because they are not writing a children's book at all. They are doing a whimsey, a recollection, a sermon, a word exercise, which has no real appeal to the child.

Children today are busy and hurried with activities they did not have two generations ago. Forty, or fifty years ago, golf, boating, tennis, riding, station wagon camping, and auto touring either did not exist or were for the rich. And there was no television to compete with a slow moving, moralizing book.

Look at the children running along the street and then at your manuscript. Does it have that quality which will entice those hurrying children to stay home and read?

(2) HAVE A STORY TO TELL. This may sound simple, but many aspiring writers have a character in mind, probably a pioneer or an animal. They have some cute little sentences, some rhymes, perhaps. But they have no real story, and by that I mean a story with conflict, growth and climax. This is as important in children's writing as in any other form of fiction.

Every juvenile editor will tell you that even the simplest picture book must have a story, in the sense of a beginning, middle and end. In the case of the beginning reader this is even more important. Something must happen all the time, and there must be a real climax.

Now, with your reader in mind, and your story at hand, how do you begin your juvenile book? From the suggestions based on the method I follow, you may develop your own, perhaps entirely different, plan.

I write out a brief condensation of the book, making it about 1,200 words long, giving the beginning, major scenes and climax of the story. This is much like an outline for a novel but much shorter, of course, because the final book is much shorter than a novel. The outline tells me whether or not I have a real story. In it there is no conversation, no description, and no fine writing—only essential story.

Here is an example of a condensation of "The Middle Sister," a book about 20,000 words long. The two paragraphs of my condensation, which follows, were expanded into a complete chapter of about one thousand words.

"One day Mrs. Glossbrenner sent Sara Samantha out to the apple hill to get apples for a dumpling. Uncle Romeo was coming for supper, and since he was a favorite relative, everybody in the family wished to help get ready for his visit.

"But Sara was timid and everything scared her: the greedy ducks, an old rat, the sniffling pig, and the mean old ram. She had to return without the apples."

The entire first section of the book was compressed into five short paragraphs. Expanded, they established the setting, introduced the leading characters, brought forward the project or quest which will motivate the whole book—i.e., the little girl's determination to win a lion's tooth charm which she thinks will make her brave.

Books for children in this reading group usually run from 15,000 to 20,000 words. When you are slanting for older children you can go up to 40,000.

I usually give one-sixth of the book to the climax and, naturally, put it at the end of the book.

Downbeat endings are taboo in children's books, because reading for children must be an affirmation of life, a joy, a growth. There can be sadness in the book, but never hopelessness. For me the climax must always be the final flowering of a desire, a problem, a wish, a project, a quest, or some significant effort which is introduced or fore-shadowed on the first page of the book.

The analyses of what I consider good juvenile stories show me that there are from five to six actions which lead to this final big scene, or climax. Each of these actions is lively and interesting in itself, but subordinate to the final one.

In a children's biography, for instance, the opening page should reveal the action or trait which will motivate the biographee's life, and will be revealed in his adult achievement. I try to have the first action in the story linked directly to the final achievement.

Thus, the story of "Dan Beard" opens with a very young boy

and his friend rising early one morning to go hunting "wood magic" in the nearby forest. Dan Beard grew up to be the founder of Boy Scouting in America and a tremendous climax in his life came when he was honored, on his ninetieth birthday, by an ovation from thousands of Boy Scouts. In this way, the opening, in which Dan sought to learn about natural things tied in with the climax in which scouts honored him for this achievement.

My juvenile biography of Audubon opens with the four-year-old boy watching the swallows return to North America, and with his longing to follow them there. When Audubon's book of bird paintings comes out, that longing has been fulfilled. Children are sticklers for clarity and order and logic. If your hero does something out of character they'll know it immediately.

"I like your books because they have big ideas in little words," a boy once said. This is the writer's reward for searching, choosing, discarding, experimenting with many words in order to find those which are most simple and most packed with meaning.

The book for the beginning reader should be simply told. Words employed to tell the story should be words which the child can understand. Sentences need to be short. There should be no fifteen or twenty line paragraphs.

Here are examples of the way I feel that simple words can be used to convey ideas:

The cat came from a hidden place.

You could say the cat came from under the barn, from behind a tree, etc. But the word *hidden* does it. A simple word, it adds to the mysterious personality of the cat.

In "Timothy"—the story of a dog from puppyhood to adulthood, the following paragraph tells of his first night away from his mother:

"He opened his eyes quickly. Where was his mother? Where were all his warm, pushing little brothers and sisters? He was all by himself in a great big strange dark place."

The question form of the sentence shows the doubt in the puppy's mind. The words "warm," "pushing" give the feel of the hungry litter of pups nursing the kind mother. His new place—a nice dog basket—was not great big, but seemed big because he was alone in it.

To Give a Feeling

"I liked your book because it gave me *a feeling,*" said the little boy in New Jersey. He states a basic principle. A good children's book should start with a feeling which the author wants to communicate.

Homesickness, tenderness for small and weak creatures, disappointment, the thrill of effort, humor, romance, the excitement of misfortune which may be overcome, the longing for approval, courage, family loyalty and unity—all these are potentials of *feeling.* Of course, you want to communicate the sort of emotion which the child will understand.

"What values shall we emphasize in our modern children's books?" was a question asked recently at a conference I attended. My personal answer to that is that *values* do not change though social background may. The author, in addition to the other things I have mentioned, should know what his own values are and should incorporate them honestly without preaching.

In my own books I stress the triumph of the humble, the acceptance of reality, the return to mother, the greatness of courage, the possibility of achievement. These sound like big philosophies for little books, but even a little book needs significance. I never talk down to my child readers or think they will fail to grasp the significance of the book. The child may not be able to state your philosophical purpose but it can help him to love the book.

"What are favorite subjects?" The answer to this question, I think, must be found in the author's own personality. He should write of what he likes. The author who can remember his own childhood is fortunate, because he can write for the child he was. All my books feature animals because I loved animals as a child and still do.

Children like stories of adventure, family fun and activity. Pioneer tales are perennially charming, but there, again, the beginning author must beware of the stereotyped, the covered-wagon, Indian tale. If you are going to choose subjects which have been written a thousand times, that is all right, but be sure that you do not roll along in the ruts of others. Have some original approach. In my book "Young Mr. Meeker" (Bobbs) I told a covered-wagon story. The trip to Oregon has been written countless times. But I told mine through the eyes of a month-old baby.

Smells, Tastes, Colors

Children love textures, tastes, smells, color, so I plan such sensory detail. But this has to be an integral part of the story; you don't stick an adjective in as every other word. In all my books I have lots about food, because I loved reading about food in my childhood. Take this passage from "Herman, The Brave Pig," to show what I mean:

"Aunt Vanilla was one of the finest cooks in the world and dearly loved to fix up delicious meals on her old iron cookstove.

"She began talking of the many good things which you could cook from a bag of corn meal. (This was when they passed a store which had a sale on meal.) There was mush, boiled and fried. There was pudding. There was bread. There were pancakes. There was porridge and corn meal soup."

A novel may be forgotten in a year. A good children's book should last for at least twelve years. Figure it out.

Mechanics

A few words on the mechanical side. The manuscript should be double spaced on a good quality white paper with inch margins all around; 300 words to the page.

I advise beginning writers to query a publisher before sending in a manuscript. Describe the story briefly and offer to submit it for consideration at the publisher's usual terms.

As a rule, the author does not need to assume responsibility for the illustrations. The publisher chooses the artist. Sometimes, if the artist has a high enough name, the contract is a joint one between publisher, author and artist; that is, royalties are divided between author and artist.

Most juvenile book publishers have a regular publishing agreement, and it is a fair one. Sales and money?

Book club selections, added 10,000 to the regular book store and library sales. Book club choices are sold at a reduced rate and the publisher and the author split the proceeds fifty-fifty—around $1,000 each on a 10,000 sale. From 3 to 4 thousand copies is about average sale for a first juvenile.

"Although there are not as many subsidiary sales to pick up in the juvenile field as in the adult, there are some. I have sold serial rights to juvenile magazines on two of my books for about $300 each. 'Boys Life' offered $400 for a 7,000-word excerpt from a biography written by me in collaboration with another author which Scribner's published.

"Juvenile book contracts usually give the author 10% royalties on the retail price for the 10,000 or 12,000 copies, and 12 1/2% thereafter. Advances vary. Mine have run from $300 to $700. All except one of my books are still in print, and that one brought in a trickle of royalties for three years before its demise."

Once the first book is out it is imperative to keep up the output. No publisher wants a one-book author, for the whole purpose of taking the risk on a first book is in the hope that the kids will ask their parents, teacher, librarian for another—by you.

There are about two hundred publishers of juvenile novels and non-fiction books, juvenile specialty and picture books. The name, address, and editorial requirements of each is in the current WRITER'S MARKET. Another good list is included in Literary Market Place, an annual paperback directory of book publishing that some metropolitan libraries purchase.

After securing the names and addresses of the juvenile publishers that interest you, write to a dozen and request a copy of the latest catalogue of their juvenile books. You are sure to learn some useful things about the nature of a juvenile book publisher's activities (number of juvenile titles published each year and their character) by examining their recent catalogue. Consulting this will help you gear your book, or your inquiry, to the juvenile publisher closest to your area of interest.

The Clock in the Copy

by Aron M. Mathieu

The funny thing about any piece of copy is that inside of it a clock is ticking away, and, when enough time passes, the copy shows its age. Some copy, however, is old before it is born. The writer who wrote it has his heart and his mind stuck in another day. As writers, can we recognize the mental approach that leads to this kind of copy so that we may do it differently?

With this question in mind, let's look at some pieces of fiction written in another era.

The first sample is from the pages of *Good Housekeeping*, published just after the turn of the century. There hadn't been a war for two generations and half of the nation lived in small towns or on farms. No car ran on the public highways; in fact, most of the highways were mud roads.

The author of this fragment is Isabella Helena Nordeck, a popular fiction writer of the day.

> Mrs. Marsden looked up from the telegram with a troubled face. "Agnes is very sick; I must go to her at once," she announced.
> "That is bad news," answered her husband; "of course you must go."
> "Yes, but"—in her nervousness she picked a biscuit to pieces;" I don't see how I can."
> "Why not? What is to hinder you?"
> "Oh, George, don't be so stupid! You know very well we are without a maid just now, and—"

"Well, there is Helen. What is the matter with Helen?"

Mrs. Marsden looked at her husband and sighed. "Do you expect Helen to go into the kitchen and cook?"

"Why not? You've done it often enough."

"Oh well, that's altogether different."

"No it isn't. When I married you, you knew how to cook and keep house, didn't you? The Lord knows how I would have prospered otherwise," he added in parentheses.

"Now look here, my dear," he went on, as he saw that she was about to continue the argument, "say no more about it, but pack up and get off. Leave the rest to me—we'll pull through all right. Let me see, there's a train leaves at 9:10; you've just time to dress; hurry up and I'll wait for you." Mr. Marsden was a man of action, and when he spoke in that way, his better half knew that expostulations would be in vain. Half an hour later husband and wife were on their way to the train. A note left on the uncleared breakfast table informed Helen of the state of affairs, winding up with the plea: "take good care of your father and brothers, my dear."

Well, is it dated, and if so, what dates it?

Naome Lewis, the present fiction editor of *Good Housekeeping,* looked over the story you just began and sent these comments.

"No one can fault Mrs. Nordeck for the dated detail: people sent telegrams only in emergencies (even in my day, a telegram always meant bad news); and everyone in town knew the schedule of the two- or three-trains-a-day railroad. These are all reflections of the time, and it's the kind of detail that is a form of shorthand for the reader—the reader understands immediately that Agnes must be seriously ill if the situation warrants a telegram. Where the author seems to fail in these introductory paragraphs is in her neglect of other important sign posts: Who is Agnes? Who is Helen? (And . . . who is Mrs. Marsden to call her husband stupid?)

"But, for the rest, it's mostly the limpness of the language that weighs heavily. In one sentence, there's the lovely juxtaposition of Mrs. Marsden being called "his better half"—a phrase that was approaching cliche status in the 1900's, and had kept all of its original jocular flavor, a real thigh-slapper of a few years before—combined with all the cumbersome "expostulations would be in vain."

"This is leaden language, and it pops up in currently written manuscripts all the time. In an account of my parents' wedding that appeared in the Deerfield (pop. 501) *Independent,* the item read: "The guests tripped the light fantastic until the wee hours of the morning." That news appeared in the 1920's, but I see variants of this today in manuscripts where the authors clearly thought it was a clever or fresh and sparkling way to convey their meaning.

"The common usage of thread-bare expressions makes me believe there really is a subconscious repository of shared language and memory. Every phrase we ever heard that seemed so right at the time (and that is how clichés got to be worn-out words: they *were* so right) is lodged in some old, neglected memory bank, ready to use with seeming inspiration when needed. I often defend the use of the cliché in our pages with the argument that a common expression, judiciously used, especially if it's been around since ancient Greece, says something most accurately in the smallest space to most people.

"But the majority of clichés elude that category. And drawing on old stories should not be the easy resort of the writer who hopes that he will say what he wants to say in the most meaningful way possible. A writer with such ambition should weed his writing carefully: the phrase that feels the most comfortable is probably not your own.

"Actually, I have such mixed feelings about that ambiguous gunnysack called the cliché that the whole idea leaves me saying, on the other hand . . . Clichés are part of the language; this is how we communicate with each other quickly. They are devices that transcend barriers. In a day when we have to deal with the terminology of every government bureau, the double negatives and circumlocutions of any candidate for office, the careful hedging and fudging of words on a news broadcast, well . . . isn't it nice to have old reliables like "sold out", "he's got his front feet in the trough", or "hand in the public till"? These are all Tea Pot Dome vintage; they seem to serve equally well today.

"In fairness to Mrs. Nordeck and the *Good Housekeeping*-of-the-past, I have to allow that—once you read the whole story—the author hasn't done too bad a job. "Father to the Rescue" is a moralistic tale. It says something about responsibility on all sides that wouldn't be a popular theme today, but was a likely one at the time, and I'm not at all certain but that it doesn't have something to say—granted that it were translated into a contemporary context—today."

One way, then, to date our story is to think in terms of literary clichés and to use many of them.

The Clock in the Copy

The unfixable way to date a story is to possess an attitude toward your characters and toward the world itself that is mired in another day. Does this mean a writer must not only be aware of his times but must also accept every new idea or new value that comes along? Of course not. If, for example, you favor political conservatism, your response should be as original and personal as William Buckley's rather than an echo of Warren Harding. Though you may agree with your ancestors, your readers should hear *your* voice, not Aunt Martha's.

We jump to the middle twenties for our next example. Freud and Joyce were being read in the colleges; women smoked cigarettes, wore knickers, voted and drank martinis in public; Hemingway was setting a new editorial style.

Ray Long's *Cosmopolitan* was the lively magazine of the period and here is how Royal Brown, whose fifty-cent-a-word rate brought cries of "Foul" from competing editors, opened a story in 1925:

They met, without benefit of clergy, of a June evening. Met, that is, in the sense that fate forced her to acknowledge that he existed and even to hold converse with him. Other times when they might have met they had passed without speaking: she—Ann Sylvester—at a decorous and restrained twenty miles an hour, looking as if butter would melt neither in her pretty mouth nor on the radiator of the little tin coupé she drove; he—Richard Duer—at his customary cocky thirty-five. Or even sixty-five.

No one could rebuke Dicky Duer for driving thirty-five. Or even sixty-five. But he, if he chose, could rebuke Ann for driving twenty-five. This was because Dicky was a member of the Massachusetts State Patrol and it is, presumably, the business of a state patrolman to go faster than anybody else has any business to go.

Anyway, that seemed to be Dicky's idea of it.

Ann detested him. Long before she even saw him—officially.

The corners of feminine eyes are ever so serviceable.

"He's got an awful crush on himself!" she decided.

As for Dicky he had, as both a state patrolman and a private citizen, a roving eye. The latter had noted Ann, as both a patrolman and an individual.

"Easy to look at," the individual had decided. "And quite aware of it." To which the patrolman, noting the way the little tin coupé suddenly slackened speed whenever he appeared, had added with a grin: "Clever, my dear—clever. But I'll get you yet!"

This particular June evening, however, Dicky and his motor-cycle were to be neither seen nor heard. Both it and Dicky were in ambush off the state road. Dicky's official explanation would have been that he was hoping to surprise a bootlegger. Actually he was smoking a surreptitious cigaret. This was a violation of rule number something or other and Dicky jolly well knew it. He remained unperturbed.

The quality of the night, he would have maintained, was excuse enough for his dereliction. It was a June night but not the sort of a June night that poets customarily celebrate. Poets adore moonlight; rain they ignore. It was raining. Emphatically. Dicky could not ignore it. "And I left my happy home for this!" he murmured.

Nevertheless, he wasn't sorry. He was free, white, and twenty-four. He had known what he was up against when he became a state patrolman. His father had put the case before him and his father was trained in the presentation of facts, being an able and well compensated corporation lawyer.

"And," Dicky's father had perorated. "there's the discipline. You've never been particularly amenable to discipline, you know, Richard."

"Probably just what I need," Dicky had retorted cheerfully.

How's that for a fiction lead that's nearly fifty years old? Look at the phrase "without benefit of clergy" in the opening line. This turn of the cliché gives the lead a rakish air; God only knows, the 1925 reader may have wondered, are we going to see two young people in private embrace in a park?

The three words in the 5th paragraph, "Ann detested him" come as neatly as anyone would want for an ideal "boy meets girl—boy loses girl—boy wins girl" lead. The phrase about being "free, white and twenty-four" dates the story for today, but fifty years ago it went unnoticed to most all of *Cosmo's* readers and the act of changing the number from twenty-one to twenty-four was enough to make it clever. The characters, at the end of the lead, are well set for a joust; he, the son of a corporation lawyer and just the right age for being a good catch and she, pretty, free, and a car owner to boot.

The characters aren't *real* in the sense that one of today's underground newspapers would define it and their general disposition to each other and to success in life makes the story the sort of fantasy-like tale that made people feel good just for the reading of it. So here is a superficial story, snugly fitted into its times. What does Junius Adams, today's fiction editor of *Cosmopolitan*, think of it? Says Mr. Adams:

"The story is dated in its language and in its clichés, but even more so in its attitudes. Today's *Cosmo* heroine does not go around pretending to herself that she detests attractive young men into whose arms she is obviously going to fall a few pages later. And neither is she described as a pretty little piece of feminine fluff—the way Ann Sylvester seems to come off, to me. Our women's lib-oriented readers would hate such a character. If we were to redo this story for the modern *Cosmo*, we might make the highway patrolman an out of work actor moonlighting as a cop or a boy working for his PhD. in criminology (rather than making him a good catch by giving him a rich father). The girl would be a career girl who thinks all cops are "pigs." And the couple would be apt to end up in bed. On occasion, we still use a story in which the characters are stereotypes, but they must be modern stereotypes. . . . "

It took a world war and a depression for real life conflicts to enter into the pages of magazine fiction. The boy and the girl that Royal Brown wrote about in *Cosmo* in 1925 were fantasies but the reader accepted the fantasy as part of the game plan of enjoying fiction. The depression altered some people's attitude toward what they wanted in fiction and the editorial response happened first in the avante garde magazines and then in *Harper's* and *The Atlantic*.

By the middle thirties, a story that denied the passing of William Howard Taft or Horatio Alger was old before it was born. It is this denial or unawareness of ideological change, rather than the currency of the language, that dates a story, and dates it in such a way that the editor can't fix it. Here is a fiction lead from *The Atlantic Monthly* writen by Edwin Corle and published in 1933. It is from his story "Amethyst:"

> The desert road curved through the rolling brown hills covered with Joshua trees and straightened itself out for the long, gradual drop into the sweltering little town of Baker. Old Man Thompson had been resting at Yucca Grove. When the shadows of the sagebrush and Joshuas told him that it was about four o'clock in the afternoon, he ambled to the road, adjusted his improvised knapsack, and walked slowly along the grease-soaked strip of hard surface known as the Arrowhead Trail, or U.S. Highway 91. He had sixteen miles of Mojave Desert between himself and Baker. But it was all down grade. Even if he had to walk the whole distance, he could make it in approximately three hours.
>
> Old Man Thompson was not exactly pleasant to look upon. He was tanned, and so dirty that it was difficult to differentiate betwen tan and dirt. He had a five-day stubble of gray beard. His clothes were soiled and torn, and smelled of sage and perspiration. Only his clear blue eyes were pleasant, and they twinkled in satisfaction as he plodded on, looking not at the road but at the broad vista of arid desert dropping away before him. Far on the horizon he could see a long white splotch. That was Soda Dry Lake.
>
> A car approached from the rear, and Thompson stopped and turned. He didn't expect to be picked up, but it might happen. Motorists rarely stopped for him. The car was a sedan. As it came on at a high rate of speed, Thompson saw that it contained two passengers—a man driving and a woman beside him.

Several passages in Mr. Corle's lead tell us that forty years have passed since he wrote it. Did you notice the phrasing: "so dirty that it was difficult to differentiate between tan and dirt"; and that his eyes "twinkled in satisfaction"; and a car "came on at a high rate of speed." This dates the copy but doesn't kill it. The good thing Mr. Corle did was to write in the here and now. For in 1933 when the jobless accounted for 15% of the working population and welfare didn't provide a refuge, Old Man Thompson could have been you. The desert road, the knapsack, the grease-soaked highway and the 16 mile walk are removed by only 8 years in time from Royal Brown's pretty young thing in her own sports coupé but more like 80 years in ideology. And the scene is even further away from the Marsdens who just naturally had a maid. You might say that the good thing about Mr. Corle's story is that it was alive and well when it was writen.

Let's try one more example, this time from a science fiction story that is relatively recent (1960), and see if the author delivered fresh goods. Theodore Sturgeon wrote it and *Fantasy and Science Fiction* published it under the title "The Man Who Lost The Sea."

Say you're a kid, and one dark night you're running along the cold sand with this helicopter in your hand, saying very fast witchy-witchy-witchy. You pass the sick man and he wants you to shove off with that thing. Maybe he thinks you're too old to play with toys. So you squat next to him in the sand and tell him it isn't a toy, it's a model. You tell him look here, here's something most people don't know about helicopters. You take a blade of the rotor in your fingers and show him how it can move in the hub, up and down a little, back and forth a little, and twist a little, to change pitch. You start to tell him how this flexibility does away with the gyroscopic effect, but he won't listen. He doesn't want to think about flying, about helicopters, or about you, and he most especially does not want explanations about anything by anybody. Not now. Now, he wants to think about the sea. So you go away.

The sick man is buried in the cold sand with only his head and his left arm showing. He is dressed in a pressure suit and looks like a man from Mars. Built into his left sleeve is a combination time piece and pressure gauge, the gauge with a luminous blue indicator which makes no sense, the clock hands luminous red. He can hear the pounding of surf and the soft swift pulse of his pumps. One time long ago when he was swimming he went too deep and stayed down too long and came up too fast, and when he came to it was like this: they said, "Don't move, boy. You've got the bends. Don't even *try* to move." He had tried anyway. It hurt. So now, this time, he lies in the sand without moving, without trying.

Edward Ferman, who bought the story, has this to say about it:

"Some people have the notion that science fiction does not require particular awareness or response to the times in which the story is written.

I would say this is not true. The main business of science fiction is to extrapolate technological, social, philosophical trends and to dramatize them in such a way that the reader will be willing to suspend disbelief. It would be hard to be convincing about the future if the writer were not sharply tuned in to what is going on now.

Sturgeon delivered fresh goods. For one thing, he *sees* everything that he writes down: colors, shapes, and in addition here, sounds. I don't mean to say that he sets a scene in his mind's eye and describes everything; no, instead of that, he *selectively describes* what is necessary for the story.

For another, he has felt free to be flexible with style, when it is compatible with the situation. Alternating between second and third person narrative may seem unusual, but it is right for the story, since it later becomes apparent that the kid and the sick man are the same person.

Well, where do these samples leave us?

We have just read four story leads and saw that although they were dated by vernacular or topical situations, as well as by attitudes of the time, they were with it when they were written.

How can we make sure that what we write is equally tuned in? How can we prevent our material from being dead before it's born? We begin by knowing what's going on in the minds of people.

II

Since the early 1960's, many of us have changed our attitudes toward fundamental things. What are these changes in attitude? The answer is important to free lance writers. Through awareness of these changes, a piece of copy is fresh when it is written.

Here is a check list of some changes in our attitudes. You will know of several more, some of them more important to you than those listed.

The issue is not to get every last one of them into a story, or even half of them. But somewhere along the line, as your characters meet, speak, fight, make up, make love, take action, dream or despair, they need an awareness of several of the following, *plus* their personal, bouncy response.

No editor demands that you *agree* with the mores of the seventies. Your characters are asked only to recognize that they exist: to sound yea or nay in their own terms rather than expressing themselves in a quote of what people used to say.

Here are some changes during the past 12 years that you may wish to recognize in your writing.

1. The sexual revolution. At more than one hundred colleges, the dorms are co-ed on alternate floors, or alternate suites on the same floor. At University of Michigan, a university approved rooming house experimented with room mates consisting of a boy and a girl and two girls and one boy. Suburban movie houses show "R" rated films, the scenes of which were beyond comprehension in a family theater as little as 25 years ago. The no-bra dress, the pill, the porno book stores that outnumber regular book stores in numerous cities, the topless waitress, the demand for equal rights by homos and lesbians, the offers of free contraceptive advice to all comers and the abortion laws in New York State which will surely travel to other states are all part of the sexual revolution. So is the nice young unmarried couple who live next door.

How does *your* character feel about these new mores and who in your story feels differently and why?

2. Affluence is everywhere. Meanwhile, poor people number into millions. To many of the young, the straight world of affluent people is made up of individuals who are trapped in games they aren't aware of. They use their energies to reach for a better motor car, a bigger home, fancier decor. Some of the young say they see this clearly and in their life style, they reject materialism. Materialism, they say, knocks the socks off character. One polarized version of materialism is drifting and crashing, standing around waiting to see what will turn up. The young are replete with characters who have yet to see themselves as clearly as they see the wheeler-dealer. They await an author to hold up a mirror so that they may see . . . what is it you want them to see?

3. Drugs. "Fifty per cent of our serious crimes (robbery, assault, murder) are drug related," said the prosecutor of Hamilton County, an industrial county with a million population in Southwest Ohio. In this county, the history of heroin arrests shows a blank page in 1955. Drug arrests at that time were made mostly for forging prescriptions for paregoric. Today, drug addicts are multiplied by 100. They are after hard drugs and they turn to crime to support the habit. How did it happen so fast? The prosecutor's office does not know. Federal figures suggest it is the same in other industrial counties. As drug use increased, the attitude of people toward legislation about drug usage has changed. The sweetish cinnamon-like smell of grass drifts across the school yard to Flamingo Park

and on to the beaches. Are we to live with this and concentrate on reforming the heroin user and incarcerating the pusher? There is today a social drug user (grass) just as there is a social drinker. Must you story mention this? No. Need you be aware of it? Yes. Why be aware of it if you aren't going to have a drug-using character? Because the knowledge of it and your response is part of the complexion of your work.

4. Permissiveness on the part of parents toward their young is extensive. In my acquaintance are two sets of parents whose children live on subsistence farms, with an unmarried mate. Part of the support comes from the parent, in one case, and from a trust fund in the other. In each case, the children negated their father's way of life; one father being a real estate broker; the other a department store buyer. One father thinks this is great, and admires his child. The other father doesn't know what to do about it and continues to mail a support check. Both children deny the way of life of their parents whose lifetime job, they say, blotted up their energies and thrashed their spirituality and made their whole life into a kind of art-form for amassing possessions. "Where is the beauty in this?" they inquire. Are you writing a story whose characters are in this situation and whose vigorous response is a fresh statement?

5. Welfare is a way of life on the part of millions, and among the most cynical people are welfare workers themselves. People receiving welfare are increasing in number and so is the amount they receive. Are they unworthy?

Did you hear that happy cry? A young bleeding heart has just accepted a job in the welfare office. Want to make house calls with her to verify claims? Should a welfare client enter your story or article? No. Then why bother about it? It's like milking the cow with mastitis. One drop of blood in the milk pail changes the color of the milk, ever so slightly, but perceptibly. Has welfare changed you life? Do you sense the change and do you want your reaction to be in the story? If not, why the reticence? You might write down the answer and examine it next month.

6. People have always worn costumes and the pages of old magazines show what they were like. Today's costumes make the streets look as though you wandered into a Halloween ball. An awareness of dress can be a fun thing and add some dash to your copy.

7. Negroes demonstrated that hostility and aggressiveness get certain results. In many sections of all cities, whites may not comfortably walk after dark. These sections are larger and more numerous than they were 15 years ago. The invisible man is after you. Contain him! Is that your point of view? Or, do you believe the aggressiveness some negroes do show is a small part of what it should be on the basis of society's treatment? What that black should really do, your character says. . . .

8. It turns out that we are the endangered species. In the early thirties, in the Talk of the Town department of *The New Yorker*, a cheerful little item listed the increasing number of smoke stacks belching black smoke as the New Haven Railroad cars rolled from Connecticut to Manhattan. Things were finally looking up again. Today, the same smoke stacks, belching the same smoke, send outraged citizens to their telephones to call the pollution control department. Our environment has become hostile to us. We pollute everything we touch whether it be the air waves or city intersections. How does this affect a character? How does it affect you?

9. It looked like a good investment to separate Vietnam as South Korea has been separated. In that way, Communism (remember the fellow who wanted to push us into our grave?) could be contained and our defense perimeter increased. The protective steel ring around America would be made larger, more secure. Who could argue against this? The argument against it came from citizens who used the streets to make their own foreign policy. Run to Canada, burn your draft card, go AWOL to Sweden. A hell of a way to run a country. Is that what your character thinks? How could a writer's stance on Indo-China affect a fictioneer?

No single story wants or needs mention of all these items, nor are all the significant ones listed.

You may want to examine your own response to some of the items just offered. Remember, no editor demands that you agree or disagree with the young man who ran away to Canada. Editors ask only that your response be original because it comes from your awareness of the whole, and that the language you use is equally your own and not borrowed phrasing of a yesterday reaction.

How about an example that does just this? The one we have selected was written for a school publication and then selected by

The Clock in the Copy

Whit Burnett as one of the best stories of the year. The title is "We've All Been Saved," the author is Sara McAulay and here are the opening paragraphs:

> Karl and Miriam's bed is in the very center of the room, and when they aren't in it it's covered with a rug that Miriam insists is genuine Persian. Karl doesn't know why she's so sure; there isn't enough pile left on it for him to tell what color it used to be. But Miriam took it to a man who once was an assistant curator at a museum somewhere and he told her that it was a real find. Those were his very words, Miriam says, whenever Karl starts to argue with her.
>
> He sits alone on the Real Find, and Miriam sits on a claret-colored cushion at his feet, so that she can gaze up at him. Her friends, when they come over, sit on cushions too—there are no chairs—and listen to every word Karl says. They nod solemnly whenever he pauses. Go on, they say. Karl racks his brain to think of something he can say that might interest them. They nod solemnly. Go on, they say.
>
> The walls of the room are white. The ceiling is orange, the wide floorboards painted black and red. Several lamps, hidden behind potted plants, cast patterns on the wall and ceiling and on Miriam's things which she has heaped in the corners and under the sink.
>
> When Miriam goes out she takes a good-sized wicker basket with her, and she fills it with things that other people don't want. Things too large for the basket she slings over her shoulder. The Real Find came home with her that way, as did more than half of a high chair, a road sign, and a huge gilt picture frame. They're piled against the wall now, and Miriam dusts them when she thinks about it.
>
> Props, she says. I bring them home for you, Karl. You can use them in your films.
>
> Karl tells himself that she's only trying to help, and then he goes into his studio and closes the door.
>
> His studio must have been a nursery at one time. A peeling teddy-bear applique still grins from one wall. Karl has been meaning to do something about that bear for a year, but once he's in the room with the door closed against the booming stereo and the excited talk of Miriam's friends he becomes so interested in whatever film he's working on that he forgets everything else. It's always a shock to him to look up from his splicer and see the bear simpering at him, its right ear flaking off.

The author of this story knew the time of day. The setting, the characters, their lifestyle are with it. How about the author's personal response? Is it original or secondhand goods? Ask yourself, could Aunt Martha have written this story in these words?

It takes a careful eye to spot the delicate way Sara McAulay loads the dice against her characters—she doesn't tell you what she thinks, she makes you see and hear them her way.

Look at something you've written lately. What time does the clock in your copy show?

I Sold It!

By Millie McWhirter

It was the editors at the *Saturday Evening Post, Ladies' Home Journal,* and *Collier's* who helped me to make my first story sale. That story was called "A Loaf of Bread and Thou," and was published after many revisions, in the June issue of *Good Housekeeping.*

I am, of course, extremely grateful to *Good Housekeeping.*

My idea for this first story, like so many of those that followed, came from a kind of "free wheeling" exercise, in which I just sit down at the typewriter and begin writing whatever comes into my mind. I don't recommend this as a fool-proof way of getting ideas, but there are days when I'm absolutely stuck for something to write about. It seems better to sit down and write something, anything, than to wait around for the perfect idea. For me, this was one of those days.

I'd just had a letter from my mother in Tennessee, in which she told me of the engagement of one of my school chums. I suppose it's always true that mothers want their daughters to get married, but it seems especially true in the South. You often hear people speak of a girl's getting "married off."

So that day I was thinking of this and when I sat down to my typewriter, I wrote:

> "Mother came into the kitchen and set down the groceries and said, 'Well, it looks as if they're going to get Jane married off.' Then she turned and looked at me, and I knew what she was thinking. She was wondering when *I* might get married off."

Now these lines never appeared in the finished story, but they served as my springboard. I stopped and looked at those lines and thought *here's an idea*. Here's a problem. Here's a girl whose family is worried because she isn't married. But why should they be so worried, so anxious?

Well, suppose they have four daughters, and they feel that the oldest should be married first. So let's make the heroine of our story the eldest of four daughters. Also, though the younger ones are pretty and golden-haired, our heroine has hair that is, in her own words, "short and dark and has no more body than John Brown." And though she wants to love and be loved, she doesn't believe in subterfuge. She feels more at home in blue jeans than in her sisters' starched petticoats. But her family insists that she'll never get a man that way.

And then let's make the problem a little worse. Suppose they live in a small town where there aren't many men? So when a nice, eligible man does come along, the family is even more anxious that she look pretty and feminine and flirtatious.

It took me a while to figure how she was going to meet this man, and finally I decided that the father has a grocery store and our heroine likes helping in that store. Then one day, our hero comes through town selling a new bread made from his own formula. The father is not in the store, just Edie, our heroine, and when she sees Chris, our hero, she feels herself go soft all over, "like butter left on the counter." She gives him an order for his bread, but unfortunately she orders more than this small store can sell. This I intended as a complication.

The father discovers her error, but he, too, likes this young man and he wants Edie to make a good impression. So he doesn't cancel the order. The family likes him, too, and asks him to Sunday dinner. Then they dress Edie in frills, imply that she thinks "blue jeans are

107

just some kind of Texas wildflower," that she has cooked the crusty fried chicken, that she'd be the perfect wife. Edie loves the man, loves her family, and so, for a few weeks, she goes along with this subterfuge. She is torn between desire to tell Chris the truth, and fear of losing him.

The denouement comes when Chris finally tells Edie that he won't be seeing her for a while because he has to move on to another territory where he hopes to sell larger orders. When the father learns of this, he doubles his order with Chris in the hopes of keeping him near. But this is too much for Edie. She finally tells Chris that her father is going broke from all that bread that is actually stacked in the back of the store, that she isn't a good cook, and in fact, isn't perfect at all. She decides to tell the truth, even at the risk of losing his love.

Now Chris tells Edie that he was going away in hopes of becoming good enough for Edie, that he isn't perfect either, and was afraid that she was too perfect for him. He tells Edie that he thinks she's just perfect for *him*!

This, then, was my story, and I began mailing it out to the magazines.

One of the editors wrote: "Your plot development is too slight to make it a possibility for us. The complications are amusing but too mild."

I didn't know what to do with the story. I continued mailing it out. Then one day the story was returned from the *Saturday Evening Post*. But with it was a two-page letter from the editors. The letter read:

> "Several of us have now read 'A Loaf of Bread and Thou' and found it appealing and very readable. Unhappily, it has not made the grade here as it is, but because it has so much warmth, and, to quote one editor directly, 'nice writing, fresh style,' we would like to pass along the reactions of the staff for what they might be worth to you.
>
> "First, the bread situation seems too extreme, and we feel that it can be modified a bit without hurting the story.
>
> "The main criticism, however, is that the denoue-

ment is too tame—your heroine, Edie, really doesn't *do* anything.

"Edie's family is trying to establish three things: that she has a business head, that she can cook, and that she is completely feminine. Granted that she is none of these things, but we think there ought to be something definite that she *is*, something they don't want Chris to know. Our suggestion would be that she is an ex-tomboy and mechanically inclined. Then, when she's on the picnic with Chris and he has told her, truthfully, that he has a larger territory and isn't sure how soon he can get back to Centerville, Edie can feel that it's just a gentle brush-off and that all is lost. Consequently, when they have trouble with the car, she decides that, since she's lost him anyhow, she might as well be herself and fix the car, thereby letting him know that she isn't the helplessly feminine and fragile creature she was trying to pretend to be. Edie could then go home, thinking she had lost out entirely, now that he knew the awful truth about her, and climb into her dungarees, and start washing her hair. Then, of course, Chris would appear and find her like that and tell her he's been interested all along, and that her mechanical ability which her family was trying to hide from him is just one more endearing quality of hers.

"You see, there is no necessity for his being so shy. You have described him as an attractive young man who, in all probability, is smart and on-the-ball about girls, business, and so on. He could have an inkling of what her family is up to, be amused and intrigued, still like Edie but just be taking his time about letting her know it. After all, the story is Edie's, and just because she thinks she's getting the brush-off doesn't say that he's not interested. She is unsure of herself because of her family's conviction about what it takes to get a man.

"This also makes it easier to modify the bread situation, because if you somehow convey the idea that Chris is aware of what is going on, you wouldn't have to have the father doubling his order to keep Chris from moving to a larger territory. Certainly he could notice when he came to the store each week that they were over-stocked, or he would see it stacked up at the house, particularly the day of the picnic.

"So much depends on the doing that we cannot promise anything, but if you would like to try a revision along these lines, we'll be glad to give it a hopeful reading."

This was the first real encouragement I'd ever received from editors, and it was a strange, unbelievable, wonderful thing that editors at the *Saturday Evening Post* had actually sat down together and read my story and given it such careful thought. My story had gone in "cold," into the slush pile, and this has always been proof to me, and should be to all hopeful writers, that each story is read and is considered.

I remembered having heard writers discuss rewriting a story to an editor's specifications.

"A story belongs to its author," one writer had said, "and if he changes it to suit someone else, he's prostituting!"

I am an humble soul, and usually I feel that if someone fails to get the point of my story, then it's possibly *I* who have failed to put my point across. And now, I re-read the *Post's* suggestion that I failed to make my main character a definite personality and I suspected they were right. When they suggested that I make Edie an ex-tomboy whose family insisted that she'd never get a man by admitting that she was mechanically inclined, she became more alive for me.

So, together, Edie and I set out on that long, hard road of revision.

The story was told by Edie, and was written in the first person. It opened like this:

> My mom, my pop, and my three younger sisters have always said that silence may be golden but it certainly has no glitter and it is absolutely no way to get

a man. They said that in this day of nylon stockings and uplift bras and home permanents, the competition is keen and the girl who gets herself noticed is the one who toots her own horn. They shook their heads and insisted that I should never go around admitting that I am just an average-looking, mechanically inclined twenty-year-old girl. Men were liable to agree with me and go off in search of someone who claimed to be Lana Turner's stand-in.

I added phrases to show that Edie is a tomboy. Such as: "But I'll admit anytime that I can fix a leaky faucet or a plugged-up carburetor, and, given a screwdriver and a monkey-wrench, I could probably tap the blood out of a turnip." This planted the denouement when Edie does fix the carburetor on Chris' car.

Because you can't just *tell* a reader what kind of person your character is, you must *show* your character in action. So I added a brief scene that takes place when Edie and Chris are in the grocery store together. And Edie tells us:

That was the time Chris picked up a potato and tossed it at me. I caught it and hurled it back, high and hard.

"Hey, look at Bob Feller!", he laughed, and threw it back across the counter.

But in that instant I caught the worried look from Marie, and I let the next potato crash into the shelves of canned tomatoes.

I did take the *Post's* suggestion that I modify the fact that Edie had ordered so much bread that it was stacked in the back of the store and in the pantry at home. I had the entire family helping to sell the bread, and had Pop advertise the bread to such an extent that he didn't have enough money to advertise his other products, so they do sell the bread, but Edie realizes that it is still costing her father too much to carry such a large order.

I completed the revision and mailed it off to the *Post*. I held my breath and spent all the money the *Post* was going to pay me for this wonderful story!

It's a good thing I spent the money only in my mind.

In a short time, I received a letter bearing the *Post* return address.

It was a small envelope, not large enough to contain my story. I just looked at the envelope a while before I dared open it. Finally, I opened it. There was no check inside. There was a letter. It read:

"Dear Miss McWhirter:

"*A Loaf of Bread and Thou* still has not gone over here, we are sorry to say. Although the feminine reaction to it was extremely favorable, the final decision went against it on the grounds that Edie wasn't convincing. With this in mind, we passed it along to the *Ladies' Home Journal*, since we thought it might be more appropriate for a woman's magazine."

As you probably know, the *Ladies' Home Journal* is published by the same company as the *Post*, and so the editors had taken it over to the *Journal*. Now I ask you, could anything be kinder than an act such as this? I had never sold a line. I knew no editors, had no "pull."

I'll admit that even now there are days when I tell myself that editors are just callous people who will publish only those stories by their friends and relatives. But then I remember how hard these editors worked to try to help an unknown writer, and I remember that an editor doesn't care whether you have a "name" or not. What he cares about is whether you have a *story!*

The day I received this letter from the *Post* I was, of course, saddened that they had rejected my "baby." But I looked forward to receiving the promised letter from the *Journal*.

The letter which I received was written by Anne Einselen, the editor in charge of the *Journal's* "unsolicited" manuscripts. Her letter read:

"Dear Miss McWhirter:

"As you probably know by this time, the *Saturday Evening Post* editors sent your 'A Loaf of Bread and Thou' up to us, because the girls on the *Post* were so enthusiastic and thought possibly a woman's magazine would be the place for the story.

"I remember reading the story about a year ago, in its original version, and liking it."

(Writers please note: I had sent my story to the *Journal* a year previously, and they had returned it. But Miss Einselen had read it then, and had remembered it. Amazing? Don't ever let anybody tell you that your unsolicited manuscripts aren't read!)

To go on with the letter now:

> "However, even in its new dress, I think it lacks some conviction, and so do most of the *Journal* staff readers. For one thing, there ought to be a twinkle in Chris' eyes (an intimation that he's wise to Edie.) For another, it's too long and a lot too much stress is laid on the family's help. A bit of sharp cutting, and more personality to Chris, then; and perhaps a switch to third-person telling. It it always much easier to handle romance by third person, we think.
>
> "We do think you will want to rework it. Whether you choose to submit it to the *Post* or to us is your decision, though it does seem more slanted for a female audience."

Now the sad truth of the matter is that, in the final analysis, my story was not bought by the *Journal*. Does anyone ever claim that the writing business isn't fraught with disappointment, with heart-break?

Once again, I set out to rewrite.

I worked on Chris' characterization, trying to show that he was, as the *Journal* suggested, "wise to Edie." I put in a scene where Edie first sees Chris in the grocery store, and Edie says:

> "He was looking down at me and I had the feeling that he was smiling, for though his mouth was serious, his eyes seemed to know something that his mouth had not yet caught on to."

And later, when her family has Chris to dinner and are telling him what a good cook she is, Edie says: "But his eyes had that look again, as if they knew more than his mouth would admit."

Then, near the end of the story when Edie fixes the carburetor on Chris' car, she thinks: "I had thought that Chris would act surprised at least. But it was even worse than that. He did not seem impressed one way or the other. He only said, 'Feeling better?' . . ."

Now when the denouement comes and Edie confesses that she

isn't a feminine, fragile creature, Chris says: "I know. I tried to find the words to tell you. Now you've made it easier for me to tell you . . . I had a theory that when a girl like you will let herself be buttoned into a pinafore or talked out of being herself, she might be playing for keeps. It might be the real thing with her, just as it is with me." . . .

Finally, I finished the revision. I mailed it back to the *Journal*. Day after day, I stood by the window, watching for the postman. The day arrived when he brought me an envelope from the *Journal*. It was a large envelope, large enough to contain my story.

They were returning the story, along with a letter in which they said that they were sorry, they were as disappointed as I, but the story was still not "convincing."

During this time, I was mailing out so many stories that it kept me busy running to the postoffice, and I thought it would be helpful to have an agent.

I mailed an agent several stories, along with the letters of encouragement from editors. She wrote back that she liked my work, felt I was close to becoming professional, that she would accept me.

She started sending my stories around. The story, *"A Loaf of Bread and Thou,"* went to *Collier's,* who liked the story *but* . . .

Here's the letter that the agent wrote to me:

> *Collier's* has expressed a mild sort of interest in *"A Loaf of Bread."* In case you feel like taking another crack at it, on the off-chance of a sale to *Collier's,* they've made the following specific suggestions:
>
> The plot itself is slim and predictable. The people, though stock, are nice to read about. The story needs cutting and tightening, so that the few incidents and scenes stand out more sharply and give some essence of the dramatic. Also, the young man is pale. He's pleasant, but he needs to be more emphatic. In short: we think this a genial piece of work which needs highlighting.

At this point, I had done so much work on this particular story that now I couldn't decide whether to rewrite once more, burn the whole thing, or go out and shoot myself! But since I'd put so many hours into that story, I felt that surely I could put a few more.

Now *Collier's* wanted high-lighting. How on earth could I do that? Once again, I reread that story, trying to pretend someone else had written it. I saw that I had been too wordy, that the opening was too long. Some cutting could come there. So the opening of what was to be the final draft of the story began like this:

> My three sisters are always shaking their heads at me, and it's quite a sight. It's like seeing golden wheat fields waving in the sun. But in this family of golden-haired girls, I am the oldest, and my hair is short and dark and has no more body than John Brown. And I am quite a trial to my sisters and to Mom and Pop.

In the earlier versions, I had written an entire paragraph describing how hard the family worked to sell Chris' bread. I compressed all of that into one sentence: "The rest of the week was just a nightmare of the whole family trying to sell Milk 'n Honey Bread."

One of the complaints from Collier's was that the "young man was pale." I decided to try to make the dialogue spoken by Chris more clever. Chris first speaks in the scene where he comes to the house and Edie walks out onto the front porch to greet him.

The earlier version of the story read like this:

> "How do you do?", I said.
>
> Chris closed his hand over mine, more as if he were holding it than shaking it. "I'm fine," he said, "how are you?" And he smiled at me, crinkling his eyes a little.
>
> I couldn't for the life of me think how I was.

Now in this rewrite, that scene read like this:

> "How do you do?" I said.
>
> Chris closed his hand over mine, more as if he were holding it than shaking it. "Best I can," he said, "how do you?" And when he smiled, there were little wrinkles around his eyes.
>
> "I couldn't for the life of me think how I do."

In the scene where Chris sits in the living room and the mother asks him to stay for supper, the earlier version was:

> "Mr. Kelly," Mom said, "we were just setting the table and I'd like to put on an extra place if you . . ."

Chris made polite remarks about not wanting to put her to any trouble, but that odor of fried chicken was drifting in from the kitchen, and nobody can resist my mom's fried chicken. So we all started for the dining room.

Now in the new rewrite, that scene read:

"Mom said, 'We were just setting the table, Mr. Kelly, and I happen to have plenty of fried chicken for you.'

Chris shook his head: "Shouldn't think of it," he said, and he grinned. "Because if I think of it . . ."

Mom smiled brightly. "Well, come right in," she said, and he came.

I went through the story word for word and cut every excess adjective. It's surprising how many words you can cut out that way. If this is too painful a process for you, you can always write those beautiful phrases on a card and keep them in your file as I do, for future use.

Finally, I knew that the story was as good as I could possibly write it. Maybe it still was not good enough (but I could do no more). I mailed it back to my agent. The agent liked my revision, and hoped *Collier's* would.

Collier's didn't.

If this is beginning to sound repetitious to you, think of what it was doing to *me*!

Collier's said that they did think the revision was an improvement on the story, but that it did not seem suited to their audience.

My agent felt, as the *Post* editors had, that this story was better for a woman's magazine. She sent it to *Good Housekeeping*.

In a few days, I received a letter. "I'm happy to say," she wrote, "that *Good Housekeeping* loves 'A Loaf of Bread and Thou,' and they are buying it!"

And now all that work, all that heartbreak, all that frustration was worth it! *I had made my first sale.* I had hit a top magazine. Somehow I expected flags to fly, banks to close, people to dance in the streets. Well, only *I* danced in the streets, but then only I knew how long and hard and tedious was my road to recognition in the writing world.

I Sold It!

Good Housekeeping published my story in their June issue and mentioned me on their Editorial Page under the title "*Local Girl Makes Good.*" They wrote: "This issue of *Good Housekeeping* is expected to create quite a flurry in one small town in Tennessee, because it contains the maiden effort of Millie McWhirter. "*A Loaf of Bread and Thou*" is Miss McWhirter's first published story, and Miss McWhirter is the first writer from her town to get in print. This is naturally going to provide a new topic of conversation for the members of the McDowell Club, and the people around the post office.

"Naturally, we're proud to be in on this event, and we hope everybody in Tennessee is going to like this story as much as we do."

Yes, my dream had come true. But in working to make the dream come true, I'd realized something else, too. I found that people do want to help you, that editors in particular always want to lend a helping hand if you'll help them to do it. *Good Housekeeping* was as pleased to find a new writer to publish as I was to be that writer. Since that time, they have published several of my stories.

As a postscript to this article, may I add that when the story was published, it was seen by the *Post* editor who had worked with me on that first revision. She took the time to sit down and write to me.

"Dear Miss McWhirter:" (she wrote).

"Just got a look at the June *Good Housekeeping* and was very happy to see your story, "*A Loaf of Bread and Thou*" in its pages. Congratulations, and I'm only sorry that we couldn't buy it for the *Post*.

"With best wishes . . ."

And if this article on revision has become an article about editors, too, then that's the way I intended it. If all this sounds like a love letter to the publishing world, it *is*!

A Note On Feeling

By Nancy Hale

One of the things that appears most difficult to put across about the art of writing fiction is concerned with this point: that creative writing, unlike criticism, is not analytic in its methods, but synthetic. Creative writing does not take feelings apart, it puts them together. This seems to me a simple enough concept, yet again and again in speaking of it one is met by kindly, intelligent, but uncomprehending faces.

In the beginning the writer has a *feeling*. The writer, actually, is one who goes around in a state which has been described as skinlessness. This is the "state of open susceptibility" which Elizabeth Bowen speaks of. It is a state of being hardly to be dignified by the name of love; it is, even, distantly akin to far less reputable states. Supersensitivity, touchiness, liability to take everything personally are some forms subjectivity takes in people unequipped to do something with it, people who fluctuate between the sterile alternatives of inferior and superior; who are not artists, to use the broader term. The writer is, precisely, one who does know what to do with his subjectivity. In this state, which can be as well of exaltation as of gloom, objects along his day's path—sights, sounds, smells, a taste, touch—impinge upon his fragile sentience and reach painful or thrilling fingers into the depth of his being.

A Note On Feeling

The earliest recollection I have of needing to write anything is of when I was about eight, sitting on the back steps of our house after a rain, staring out at the swamp that was purple with loosestrife and joe-pye weed. A cat came skulking out of the long wet grass and wove its way past the steps, rubbing its sides against the rough boards. I couldn't bear it. After a while I went back into the house, and in my journal—my "Diary. Private. Keep Out!" which had hitherto been filled only with accounts of meetings of the Four Queens Club and of swimming at Lake Pearl—I began, "As I was sitting on the back steps today, a cat came skulking out of the long wet grass. . . ."

Feeling is so essential in the writing of fiction as to be like charity in First Corinthians: if the writer hasn't got it, he is nothing. The reason for this may be that feeling for fiction—or indeed for anything else— is the same as belief in it. If the writer doesn't believe in his own fictions he is certainly not going to persuade the reader to believe in all that imitation grass, bogus activity, and imaginary conversation. If he does have feeling for his fictions, if he masters tricks of conveying his feeling without too much interfering with it, a light will go up on the scene he has set, the blindfold will be snatched from his readers' eyes, and, purring with delight, they will set themselves to the willing suspension of disbelief.

I have never felt that the literal taking of notes by a writer went very far in creating characters that came alive. A writer in New Hampshire was telling me how he makes careful notes of every interesting event or person or scene that comes his way and then transfers the scribbled notes by typing them out on file cards. Next he inserts the cards into their proper places in a file-case and, he said, he has five of these file-cases already filled with notes on every aspect of life. He has really pinned experience down. But I must confess I have more confidence in Mr. Faulkner's system of running along after characters who originated in his imagination and writing down what *they* say. It may not be so neat, but it is much more like being a writer. The writer who files his notes has everything put away safely where he can find it again, but Mr. Faulkner has feeling for his characters— and, need I add, it profiteth him.

Feeling, not emotion. Similar to the people who don't believe in fiction, who can't seem to grasp that a writer can "make it all up," are the people who insist on using the word "feeling" interchangeably with the word "emotion," as if they were of the same quality. They are certainly allied; but feeling, as I am speaking of it here, is neither hate, fear, anger, nor desire; it is a method of perceiving. It is concerned with secrets, with hiding-places, with inventions, with phantasy; with imaginary people and imaginary conversations. I remember once finding myself alone at dinner in a New York club, tired after a long day, looking about the roomful of men and women, for the most part elderly, and being slowly filled with an enormous delight, not in them as real people, but in them as characters. It could hardly have been called love—I knew nobody present—it was more an ecstasy of examining those idiosyncratic old faces, mentally caressing their withered arms, admiring their necklaces and their tortoise-shell crosses on chains, their black satin dresses, their too-soft white hair, their pink scalps, their old fingers loaded with diamond rings, the glittering crystal of their pince-nez; a side-comb about to tumble here, a spot of gravy upon a starched shirt-front there; an ambassadorial mustache, a hairdo of looped-up gray scallops above an intellectual brow, a mink cape thrown back over a chair, a gray woolen dress wholly unsuitable for dining; a copy of Plato laid by the plate of one solitary diner, a scarlet brocade purse beside the plate of another; an important frown, an experienced laugh; frowsty old eyebrows lifted knowingly, an air of firm, forthright address delivered with no nonsense, tinklingly sweet tones, a voice overheard saying, "My dear . . .," another voice that whined, " 'Her-bert,' I told him, 'that just won't do!' " They were so marvelous. I was full of joy. This may have been partly feeling for life, but it was mostly feeling for fiction.

Feeling's function is to inform its possessor of what things mean to him. Unlike emotion, which is not a conscious function at all, it gropes, touches, caresses, explores; although it is so wholly absorbed in the meanings of things, it is thing-centered, not, like emotion, self-centered. Emotion inundates, like that thunderous dam-water; but it is feeling's whole nature to discriminate, to select. Feeling plays with the scene—and perhaps this is the safest definition of all for the kind of feeling a writer needs: a feeling for play with the materials of experience.

At . . . [a] lecture of John Knowles' . . . he was asked why writers view critics as their enemies. (One arch questioner put it, "Mr. Knowles, you will concede, I presume, that the well-disposed critic can be the writer's friend?") The speaker replied that the trouble is,

A Note On Feeling

critics are so much more intelligent than writers, writers can't really understand them. There was some dissatisfied shifting about seats at this. Yet it is true that fiction simply cannot proceed from the intellect —a fact known to the wisest old editors, who, in making suggestions for change, try to soothe their author's feelings rather than to challenge their minds. For some time it has been fashionable to salaam before intellect and all its doings, and most people today either lead with the intellect or play like they are doing so. There are some things the intellect cannot do, however, and one of them is, unaided, to write a good story. A friend of mine, one of the dozen best short story writers in the country, told me she learned how to write short stories from being in love, at different times, with two men who wrote short stories. Not that they told her much. It just came off on her.

The novelist Rosamond Lehman writes, "I am surprised when writers have perfectly clear ideas for what they are going to write, and I find it dismaying, for more reasons than one, to have the projected contents related to me, at length and in rational sequence. I would be more encouraged by such an answer—given in rather a hostile and depressed way—as: (It is about some people.) And if the author could bear to pursue the subject, and mention any of the images and symbols haunting his mind—if he spoke; for instance, of a fin turning in a waste of waters, of the echo in the caves, of an empty house shuttered under dust sheets, of an April fall of snow, of music from the fair at night, of the burnt-out shell of a country house, of that woman seen for a moment from a bus-top, brushing her hair before the glass—I should feel that something was afoot." Something would indeed be afoot, for all this is the stuff of feeling (which clothes itself, at least in fiction, with symbols and snatches of vision.

Often, moreover, the writer himself—hostile, even frightened, adrift among today's sea of critical minds—tends to identify with the critical aproach, which is not at all the same thing as developing the ability to think. So the writer becomes not a critic but an apostate artist. The writer is not incapable of thought, any more than the critic is incapable of feeling; some critics evidence very deep feeling indeed. But the critic's feeling is for finished works of art, not for the imaginary stuff of art (else, perhaps, they would be not critics but writers). For a natural writer to strain to emulate the critic's approach is an expense of spirit in a waste of shame; it is a selling of his birthright. The writer normally lives on feelings, intuitions, and symbols, a state of mind difficult to make believable in real life to even the kindliest critical intelligence. His art consists of the overcoming of this barrier by a supreme act of transference. If he fails in his task, he may become one of those artists who claim to despise the intellect and all its works. But this is no victory, for only false pride despises its opposite.

It is as though once upon a time there was a forest, which was approached at opposite sides by two brothers. The older brother came up to the forest, examined its appearance meticulously from various angles, peered into it, drew out a notebook, and set down some notes in which he commented on the forest's vast extent, overgrown condition, and likelihood of containing snakes. He then walked away, having understood the forest. The younger brother approached the forest and, his fancy at once captured by the sight of a lichen growing on the silver-gilt bark of a birch tree just inside, plunged into the woods and in no time at all was lost. Treading on treacherous and swampy ground, hemmed in on every side by bristling primeval tree-trunks, threatened by poisonous serpents that hung from the branches of the trees, too far inside to call for help, it took every particle of ingenuity he possessed to figure out the way to get back again. At last, however, he did emerge, and with quite a story to tell. It is so with the writer, faced by experience.

This parable is of course misleading, because the older brother, the critic, is viewing the experience of real facts, real finished forests and books, when he takes his notes. For his writing brother, moreover, the perils of the forest exist largely in his own imagination. The tree-trunks were, possibly, papier-màché; the snakes, rubber hose; the critic brother would never have allowed himself to become so panicky. Yet that is the way the writer is. He needs every bit of technical wisdom—tricks of telling, organization of method—he can summon if he is to rescue himself from his experience, if he is to persuade anybody else of what happened to him. His thinking self is thus employed in the service of his feeling self, and not, as with his critic brother, in soberly viewing outer reality—whether real life or real books—and coming to conclusions about it.

Form and technique are the salvation of those who, like the writer, feel threatened with inundation by the forces released by experience. They constitute the artist's kind of thinking. A similar salvation used to be the technique of draftmanship to the painter's art, or the technique of manners in society—which used, in fact, to be called "good form." For some, there are the forms of a lifetime's habits, or the ritual forms of the church. The writer, unable to find satisfaction in any order he can discover in or impose upon life, creates his own forms, something to put his experience in. The writer needs form because he cannot contain himself.

"At the end of his writing day," William Maxwell says in his essay on the tricks of writing fiction, "the writer, looking green with fatigue —also from not having shaved—emerges from his narrative dream at last, with something in his hand he wants somebody to listen to. His wife will have to stop what she is doing and think of a card; or be sawed in half again and again until the act is letter-perfect. And when the writer is in bed with the light out, he tosses. Far from dropping off to sleep he thinks of something, and the light beside his bed goes on, long enough for him to write down five words that may or may not mean a great deal to him in the morning. The light may go on and off several times before his steady breathing indicates that he is asleep. And while he is asleep he may dream—he may dream that he had a dream, in which the whole meaning of what he is trying to say is brilliantly revealed to him. Just so the dog asleep on the hearth-rug dreams; you can see, by the faint jerking movement of his four legs, that he is after a rabbit. The writer's rabbit is the truth—about life, about human character, about himself and therefore by extension, it is to be hoped, about other people. He is convinced that all this is knowable, can be described, can be recorded, by a person sufficiently dedicated to describing and recording; can be caught in a net of narration."

Yet, all rabbits aside, is it really the truth the writer is after, in his imagining, in his play? The writer, as easily intimidated as he is exalted by words, finds, if he thinks about it, that the word "truth" becomes monolithic, formidable. Is that really what he was trying to convey about his dear trove of sea-shells, his handful of wildflowers from the wood, his private joke? Truth? Possibly if he were Tolstoi . . . But let me quote one more excerpt, this time from Hemingway's short story. "The Three Day Blow." The two adolescent boys, drinking whisky before the fire, have become quite tight. They have been talking about literature:

"Gentlemen," Bill said, "I give you Chesterton and Walpole."
"Exactly, gentlemen," Nick said.

They drank. Bill filled up the glasses again.

"You were very wise, Wemedge," Bill said.

"What do you mean?" asked Nick.

"To bust off that Marge business," Bill said.

"I guess so," said Nick.

'It was the only thing to do. If you hadn't, by now you'd be back working, trying to get enough money to get married."

Nick said nothing.

"Once a man's married he's absolutely bitched," Bill went on. "He hasn't got anything more. Nothing. Not a damn thing. He's done for. You've seen the guys that get married."

Nick said nothing.

"You can tell them," Bill said. "They get this sort of fat, married look. They're done for."

"Sure," said Nick.

"You came out of it damned well," Bill said. "Now she can marry somebody of her own sort and settle down and be happy. You can't mix oil and water, and you can't mix that sort of thing, any more than if I'd marry Ida that works for the Strattons. She'd probably like it, too."

Nick said nothing. The liquor had all died out of him and left him alone. Bill wasn't there. He wasn't sitting in front of the fire, or going fishing tomorrow with Bill and his dad, or anything. He wasn't drunk. It was all gone. All he knew was that he had once had Marjorie and that he had lost her.

That is pure feeling, all right, laid bare before our eyes. It is feeling being revealed by the ultimate in prestidigitation—the art of communicating meaning in terms utterly artless. Hemingway thought that particular trick up for himself; all the best tricks are the ones writers have invented for themselves out of their need. Although it is certainly truth that Hemingway is communicating in this passage, it is neither monolithic nor formidable. It is just something worth trying to say. It is just true.

The Writer's Craft

I copy what I admire. I pinch . . . I read not only for pleasure, but as a journey-man, and where I see a good effect I study it, and try to reproduce it. So that I am probably the biggest thief imaginable . . . *Panic Spring* . . . seemed to me dreadful, because it was an anthology, you see, with five pages of Huxley, three pages of Aldington, two pages of Robert Graves, and so on—in fact all the writers I admire. But they didn't influence me. I pinched effects, I was learning the game. Like an actor will study a senior character and learn an effect of make-up or a particular slouchy walk for a role he's not thought of himself. He doesn't regard that as being particularly influenced by the actor, but as a trick of the trade which he owes it to himself to pick up.

—Lawrence Durrell

Leaves From A Writer's Notebook

By Anton Chekhov

There's nothing more pernicious on earth than a rascally liberal paper.

To dine, drink champagne, make a racket, and deliver speeches about national consciousness, the conscience of the people, freedom, and such things, while slaves in tail-coats are running around your tables, veritable serfs, and your coachmen wait outside in the street, in the bitter cold--that is lying to the Holy Ghost.

A little queen in exile—is the actress who imagines herself great; uneducated and a bit vulgar.

An example of clerical boorishness. At a dinner party the critic Protopopov came up to M. Kovalevsky, clinked glasses and said: "I drink to science, so long as it does no harm to the people."

A man, who, to judge from his appearance, loves nothing but sausages and sauerkraut.

A pregnant woman with short arms and a long neck, like a kangaroo.

A serious phlegmatic doctor fell in love with a girl who danced very well, and, to please her, he started to learn mazurka.

A large fat barmaid—a cross between a pig and a white sturgeon.

A certain captain taught his daughter the art of fortification.

But bears his riches like a cross.

Really decent people are only to be found amongst men who have definite, either conservative or radical, convictions; so-called moderate men are much inclined to rewards, commissions, orders, promotions.

Glancing at a plump, appetizing woman: "It is not a woman, it is a full moon."

From her face one would imagine that under her stays she has got gills.

A woman is fascinated not by art, but by the noise made by those who have to do with art.

N. and Z. are intimate friends, but when they meet in society, they at once make fun of one another—out of shyness.

N. rings at the door of an actress; he is nervous, his heart beats, at the critical moment he gets into a panic and runs away; the maid opens the door and sees nobody. He returns, rings again—but has not the courage to go in. In the end the porter comes out and gives him a thrashing.

In a play: In the middle of a serious conversation he says to his little son: "Button up your trousers."

If you wish to become an optimist and understand life, stop believing what people say and write, observe and discover for yourself.

He was proud of his peasant origin, he was even haughty about it.

Son: "Today I believe is Thursday."
Mother: "What?"
Son: "Thursday! I ought to take a bath."

Mother: "What?"
Son: "Bath!"

When an actor has money, he doesn't send letters but telegrams.

He loved the sort of literature which did not upset him, Schiller, Homer, etc.

In a letter: "A Russian abroad, if not a spy, is a fool."

And she began to engage in prostitution, got used to sleeping on the bed, while her aunt, fallen into poverty, used to lie on the little carpet by her side and jumped up each time the bell rang; when they left, she would say mindingly, with a pathetic grimace: "Something for the chamber-maid." And they would tip her sixpence.

A young man made a million marks, lay down on them, and shot himself.

Everyone has something to hide.

They are honest and truthful so long as it is unnecessary.

A careful and honest writer does not need to worry about style. As he becomes proficient in the use of the language, his style will emerge, because he himself will emerge, and when this happens he will find it increasingly easy to break through the barriers that separate him from other minds, other hearts—which is, of course, the purpose of writing, as well as its principal reward. Fortunately, the act of composition, or creation, disciplines the mind; writing is one way to go about thinking, and the practice and habit of writing not only drain the mind but supply it, too.

—E. B. WHITE

Alone and engrossed, the First Reader sits and reads. It is his hopeful eye that first sees the incoming new novel. The "first reader" above can prove himself one way, by discovering novels that will sell. To an author, the sale of a first book means two or three thousand dollars, maybe ten on the outside. To the "first reader," discovering one such author a month means an expressway to one of New York's most sought after jobs. editor-in-chief of a major publishing house. To miss a find may mean the reader's job. To unearth a booming best seller is his every moment's goal. This man looks upon you as his bread and butter.

Non-fiction

If we are not concerned with ideas, if we make no effort to tell right from wrong, however mixed up the two may be, we are lost.

Like most of us, I have placed my stuff wherever I was able to, and I would be a hypocrite to condemn the pulps or the "true" papers. But I believe that any writer who is worth his salt will take each piece of work seriously and remember that he is writing for something more than a check figured at one or three or ten cents a word. Before everything else, he is writing for human beings. He need not ever lead his reader to a moral judgment, but he must always remember that words are an expression of life and can never be separated from it.

A good many critics have noted that we are in a fair way in this country to breeding a generation of mindless writers. The emphasis on reporting, both in journalism and in fiction, has made a talent for organizing facts an acceptable literary substitute for hard thinking. And that is not all to the bad, for the American genius for basing theory on fact rather than twisting fact to suit theory, pragmatism in other words, has often saved us from the errors led to by an overdose of high-flown theory. To be good writers we must have both knowledge and ideas, and ideals, and for both we must have the respect of a good priest for his altar and his cloth.

—Richard H. Rovere

New Markets For
Non-Fiction Books

By Dora Albert

The letter from Prentice-Hall, Inc., was a complete surprise. Although I've been writing for national magazines for about 25 years, this was the first time a national book publisher had approached me.

An associate editor of the Business Books department of Prentice-Hall read my article, "How To Make Up Your Mind," in the January-February issue of *Your Life*. "We are very interested in manuscripts on self-help," the editor wrote.

"Ideally, these self-help books assist the reader formulate a positive, step-by-step program, detailing for him, in common sense order, what he must do so that he can better face the difficulties confronting him in his daily life. Is there anything that you might have in mind that would fit into this category?"

Naturally, I wrote thanking him for his interest, and suggesting briefly several subjects in the self-help field that appealed to me.

The response was quick and gratifying. Prentice-Hall, Inc., liked my suggestion, "How To Improve Your Luck." The editors suggested that I prepare an outline on this subject.

I then discovered that a rival publisher had brought out a book on the identical subject a few years previously. Of course, I mentioned this to Prentice-Hall and we agreed to abandon the subject. I never again was slack in researching a subject to see whether it had been treated before, and how long ago, and by what angle. Now I had to think up a new subject.

My subconscious mind must have been working on the problem, for shortly afterwards an idea did occur to me that became the theme of the first non-fiction book I ever wrote. In due course (it took me about 15 months to write the book) it was accepted by Prentice-Hall, and was published under the title I originally gave it, "You're Better Than You Think."

Now at this point you might very well say: "That lucky so-and-so. She hammers out an article for *Your Life*, and is approached by one of the better publishing houses in the United States. What in the world has that got to do with me? Am I supposed to turn out dozens of articles each year for magazines, in the hope that 25 years from now a publisher will ask me for ideas for a book?"

Of course not. Any writer seriously interested in writing a non-fiction book can find out, by studying *Writer's Digest* and the current catalogues of the big publishing houses, what type of book interests each house. Book publishers are as individual in their requirements as magazines, and therefore their policies should be studied just as carefully. You can also learn about their policies by studying book announcements and advertisements in *Publisher's Weekly* and *The Book Buyer's Guide*, which are available at most libraries. You'll soon find that certain publishers are consistent leaders in specific fields in which they specialize. One publishing house may specialize in religious books; another in metaphysical books.

Aside from knowing that Prentice-Hall, Inc., was interested in a particular type of self-help book, I was on my own. I had to sell the specific idea for a book that I wanted to write; I had to outline it, research it, and, of course, write it.

How To Launch A Non-Fiction Book

Considering the vast amount of work that goes into the writing of a non-fiction book, most writers cannot afford to go ahead and prepare such a book without a definite assurance of interest and a contract from a reputable publisher. To get this, they will have to go over the same steps as I did.

Here they are:

(1) After selecting a publisher who is outstanding in a field in which you are interested, suggest your idea in this field. Describe that idea in a one or two-page letter, just as you would if you were querying an editor about a magazine article. If you are unknown to the publisher, include in your letter enough about your background to show you are qualified to write the book.

To sell my own idea I wrote: "A great many successful men have said that most people have abilities they seldom use; most of us just scratch the surface of what we could do. Chapter headings might be along the lines of: You're More Attractive Than You Think . . . You're Smarter Than You Think . . . You Have Lots More Ability . . . You're Healthier . . . You Can Do Almost Anything . . . How to Conquer an Inferiority Complex. The book, 'You're Better Than You Think,' would prove not only that most of us under-estimate ourselves, but tell how to reappraise and make the most of ourselves in every direction: our attractiveness, our abilities, our spiritual happiness, etc."

(2) Be prepared to submit a detailed outline on the book, if a publisher shows any interest in your query letter.

This outline should tell, chapter by chapter, what ground you expect to cover.

In my own case, I spent a month of intensive research on my subject—basically, the conquest of inferiority feelings—and then proceeded to prepare my outline.

When you have completed your outline, with two carbon copies, send the outline and one carbon copy to the publisher. This will enable two editors at the publishing house to read the outline simultaneously, and you may get a faster reaction that way. When you indicate, on your outline, the wordage you intend to invest in each chapter the editor can see and really know how the writer plans to put emphasis.

My outline for "You're Better Than You Think" was 18 double-spaced pages.

This outline was returned to me with several comments, and the request that I prepare a sample chapter. If the publishers liked my sample chapter, they would offer me a contract.

In my outline, I used some movie stars as examples. I've been interviewing movie stars for years; am thoroughly familiar with their stories; met almost every big star you can think of while doing a series, "The Role I Liked Best," which I handled for the *Saturday Evening Post.* It would have required very little research for me to use the movie star examples, with which I was so familiar. But, to fit the business book markets which the editor of Prentice-Hall had in mind, it was necessary to delete all the references to movie stars. "Substitute, instead, references to big-time business leaders," I was told.

(3) Be ready to write one or two sample chapters at the publisher's request.

The sample chapter doesn't have to be your first chapter. It can be a chapter about which you feel most enthusiastic, or have the most material.

Although I had discarded the idea of doing an entire book on the subject of luck, I wrote my sample chapter on it. It appears in the book as Chapter 10—"You're As Lucky As You Think You Are."

After reading the sample chapter, Prentice-Hall, Inc., decided to offer a contract for the publication of the book. If you don't know much about book contracts, let an agent handle final negotiations. An agent handled my contract.

II

While writing chapters on which my research has been completed, I continue, in other hours of the day, to research chapters yet to be written.

As you write, you become extremely alert for any authentic information that will fit into your book.

For instance, knowing that I would do a chapter on "You'll Live Longer Than You Think," I made it a point to attend a lecture at the first Cavalcade of Health and Medical Progress in Los Angeles, where I heard Dr. George W. Ainlay, Sr. talk on the subject of how to enjoy life more as we grow older. I took careful notes; then quoted him in my own chapter.

In order to do this, I submitted my quotes to him, with a letter asking for his authorization for their use in the book. Pertinent points made in lectures are often extremely useful to non-fiction writers, but should not be used without permission of the lecturer.

I called up publicity agents I knew, and told them that I was interested in interviewing successful businessmen on various subjects covered in my book. As a result, I was able to interview some of their clients, men like the late Alfred N. Steele, at that time chairman of the board of Pepsi-Cola; Paul Smith, president and owner of Republic Van and Storage; Olive Salembier, president of the Specification Packaging Corporation, and many others. Working through the publicity agent, you get time set aside for you that otherwise might be much harder to obtain.

A friend told me of a very fine psychiatrist and neurologist and quoted some of the brilliant remarks he made in talking with friends. We both agreed that if I could get this man to give me an interview on how to conquer fears and worries, it would be an asset to the book.

Before I went to see him, I read much of the popular literature on the subject. He analyzed and demolished some of the rules commonly given for conquering fear—then he gave me his own methods. The result was Chapter 16, which my publishers and I both considered one of the strongest chapters in the book.

All the material I gathered through interviews, library research, newspaper clippings, and lectures went into a four-drawer legal file. I used the usual legal-sized folders; each had its own heading—Attractiveness, Ability, Faith, Health, etc. I also had a miscellaneous file for each letter of the alphabet, as I found it convenient to place my typed notes on interviews in the miscellaneous file that started with the last name of the person interviewed.

I believe in sending individual chapters to your publisher as they are completed if the publisher is willing. This kind of "sharing" gives the author the feeling of being on a team.

Personally, I am too timid to write an entire book without getting an editorial opinion of portions of it as I go along. In a non-fiction book, once you get off base, you can easily end up in left field. So I was very pleased when Prentice-Hall agreed to read individual chapters, as they were completed, for their comments.

Most editors of non-fiction books will work this way with you.

You can send them three or four chapters at a time; and they will return these chapters to you with detailed suggestions. Prentice-Hall, Inc., used pink slips attached to the manuscript. If I made a statement that the editor felt needed illustrating, a pink slip would call for a specific anecdote. If I told an anecdote they considered unconvincing, a pink slip would say so.

In connection with a mention of Nick the Greek, I had assumed that every one of my readers would know that he is a famous gambler. I was reminded, "Never overestimate the reader's knowledge or underestimate his intelligence."

The safe and really routine procedure when quoting various authorities is to get a letter of permission for each quotation or close paraphrase that you plan to use. You don't have to carry this to extremes in the case of short quotes, but actually you upgrade your book when you do this. Often the authority, when he sees the quote, in the context in which you plan to use it, will alter it to suit your book.

If you are quoting from an already published book, get permission from the copyright owner.

You need to prepare yourself to revise at the publisher's request. My contract called for a book of 90,000 words. A few months before the book was completed, I was told that shorter books were selling better, and asked to keep my final manuscript down to 80,000 words.

Although you have a contract, the publisher usually has the privilege of accepting or rejecting the final manuscript. Your contract may call for a cash advance for you and set your royalty terms. It may also bind the publisher to produce the book within a given time after he receives a satisfactory manuscript. He will not agree blind, to publish your first version. If it isn't satisfactory, he may ask for revisions.

However, if his editors have seen the various chapters as they were written and commented favorably on them, the chances are that your book will be accepted and published on schedule.

My own good news came in the form of a letter telling me that everyone who had read "You're Better Than You Think" liked it, and that the verdict was favorable. Furthermore, the publisher asked if I would consider doing another book for Prentice-Hall.

"Consider" it? I was extremely flattered! After some preliminary correspondence, the publishers and I agreed that a promising subject for a self-help book would be how to handle and conquer the emotional fatigue or "beat" feeling that is so prevalent in our times. The contract for "Stop Feeling Tired and Start Living" was signed shortly after I had completed the first three steps shown above. The book was published in August 1959, sold well from the start, and was syndicated all over the country by the Times Mirror Syndicate.

Later I signed a contract with Prentice-Hall for a third book, How To Cash In On Your Abilities. This time the contract was signed after the completion of a satisfactory outline and I wasn't asked to show a sample chapter first.

If you have a book idea and wish to choose a publisher, here are the names and addresses of some of the better known publishers of books. To get a reasonable idea of the subject interests of these publishers consult the *Trade List Annual* (R. R. Bowker) at your local library. This is simply a bound collection of publishers' trade order lists. You may also write the publisher for his current catalogue.

Abelard-Schuman Limited
257 Park Avenue S.
New York, N.Y. 10010

Abingdon Press
201 Eighth Avenue S.
Nashville, Tenn. 37202

Academic Press, Inc.
111 Fifth Avenue
New York, N.Y. 10003

Ace Books
1120 Avenue of the Americas
New York, N.Y. 10036

American Elsevier Publishing Co., Inc.
52 Vanderbilt Avenue
New York, N.Y. 10017

Appleton-Century-Crofts
440 Park Avenue S.
New York, N.Y. 10016

Arco Publishing Co., Inc.
219 Park Avenue S.
New York, N.Y. 10003

Avon Books
959 Eighth Avenue
New York, N.Y. 10019

Ballantine Books, Inc.
101 Fifth Avenue
New York, N.Y. 10003

Bantam Books, Inc.
666 Fifth Avenue
New York, N.Y. 10019

Barnes & Noble Books
10 E. 53rd Street
New York, N.Y. 10022

Basic Books, Inc., Publishers
10 E. 53rd Street
New York, N.Y. 10022

Beacon Press
25 Beacon Street
Boston, Mass. 02108

Belmont-Tower Books, Inc.
185 Madison Avenue
New York, N.Y. 10016

Berkley Publishing Corporation
200 Madison Avenue
New York, N.Y. 10016

Bobbs-Merrill Co., Inc.
4300 W. 62 Street
Indianapolis, Ind. 46268

Thomas Bouregy & Co., Inc.
22 E. 60 Street
New York, N.Y. 10022

Broadman Press
127 Ninth Avenue N.
Nashville, Tenn. 37234

William C. Brown Company
135 S. Locust Street
Dubuque, Iowa 52001

Cahners Books
89 Franklin Street
Boston, Mass. 02110

Chilton Book Company
401 Walnut Street
Philadelphia, Pa. 19106

Thomas Y. Crowell Company
666 Fifth Avenue
New York, N.Y. 10019

Crowell Collier and MacMillan, Inc.
866 Third Avenue
New York, N.Y. 10022

Dell Publishing Co., Inc.
750 Third Avenue
New York, N.Y. 10017

Diplomatic Press
11 W. 42nd Street
New York, N.Y. 10036

Dodd, Mead & Co.
79 Madison Avenue
New York, N.Y. 10016

Doubleday & Company, Inc.
277 Park Avenue
New York, N.Y. 10017

E. P. Dutton & Co., Inc.
201 Park Avenue S.
New York, N.Y. 10003

Wm. B. Eerdmans Publishing Co.
255 Jefferson Avenue S.E.
Grand Rapids, Mich. 49502

Farrar, Straus & Giroux, Inc.
19 Union Square W.
New York, N.Y. 10003

Fawcett World Library
1 Astor Place
New York, N.Y. 10036

Frederick Fell, Inc.
386 Park Avenue S.
New York, N.Y. 10016

Funk & Wagnalls, Inc.
53 E. 77 Street
New York, N.Y. 10021

General Learning Corporation
250 James Street
Morristown, N.J. 07960

Gordon & Breach
440 Park Avenue S.
New York, N.Y. 10016

Grosset & Dunlap, Inc.
51 Madison Avenue
New York, N.Y. 10010

Grove Press
53 E 11th Street
New York, N.Y. 10003

Harcourt Brace Jovanovich, Inc.
757 Third Avenue
New York, N.Y. 10017

Harper & Row, Publishers
10 E. 53rd Street
New York, N.Y. 10022

Harvard University Press
79 Garden Street
Cambridge, Mass. 02138

Hastings House
10 E. 40th Street
New York, N.Y. 10016

Hawthorn Books, Inc.
70 Fifth Avenue
New York, N.Y. 10011

Hillary House Publishers
303 Park Avenue S.
New York, N.Y. 10010

Holt, Rinehart & Winston, Inc.
383 Madison Avenue
New York, N.Y. 10017

Houghton Mifflin Company
2 Park Street
Boston, Mass. 02107

Humanities Press, Inc.
303 Park Avenue S.
New York, N.Y. 10010

Indiana University Press
Tenth & Morton Streets
Bloomington, Ind. 47401

Richard D. Irwin, Inc.
1818 Ridge Road
Homewood, Ill. 60430

Jonathan David Publishers, Inc.
68-22 Eliot Avenue
Middle Village, N.Y. 11379

Alfred A. Knopf, Inc.
201 E. 50th Street
New York, N.Y. 10022

Lancer Books, Inc.
1560 Broadway
New York, N.Y. 10036

J. B. Lippincott Co.
E. Washington Square
Philadelphia, Pa. 19105

Little, Brown and Company
34 Beacon Stret
Boston, Mass. 02106

McGraw-Hill Book Co.
1221 Avenue of the Americas
New York, N.Y. 10020

David McKay Co., Inc.
750 Third Avenue
New York, N.Y. 10017

The MacMillan Company
866 Third Avenue
New York, N.Y. 10022

Meredith Corporation
1716 Locust Street
Des Moines, Iowa 50336

Charles E. Merrill Publishing Co.
1300 Alum Creek Drive
Columbus, Ohio 43216

Julian Messner
1 W. 39 Street
Nw York, N.Y. 10018

Monarch Press
630 Fifth Avenue
New York, N.Y. 10020

William Morrow & Co., Inc.
105 Madison Avenue
New York, N.Y. 10016

New American Library Inc.
1301 Avenue of the Americas
New York, N.Y. 10019

W. W. Norton & Company, inc.
55 Fifth Avenue
New York, N.Y. 10003

Oxford University Press
200 Madison Avenue
New York, N.Y. 10016

Paperback Library
315 Park Avenue S.
New York, N..Y. 10010

Penguin Books Inc.
7110 Ambassador Road
Baltimore, Md. 21207

Pergamon Press, Inc.
Maxwelll House
Fairview Park
Elmsford, N..Y. 10523

Playboy Press
919 N. Michigan Avenue
Chicago, Ill. 60611

Pocket Books
630 Fifth Avenue
New York, N.Y. 10020

Popular Library
355 Lexington Avenue
New York, N.Y. 10017

Praeger Publishers, Inc.
111 Fourth Avenue
New York, N.Y. 10003

Prentice-Hall, Inc.
Englewood Cliffs, N.J. 07632

G. P. Putnam's Sons
200 Madison Avenue
New York, N.Y. 10016

Pyramid Communications, Inc.
919 Third Avenue
New York, N.Y. 10022

Random House, Inc.
201 E. 50th Street
New York, N.Y. 10022

Fleming H. Revell Company
Old Tappan, N.J. 07675

Rodale Press
Book Division
33 E. Minor Street
Emmaus, Pa. 18049

The Ronald Press Company
79 Madison Avenue
New York, N.Y. 10016

Scholastic Book Services
50 W. 44 Street
New York, N.Y. 10036

Scott, Foresman and Company
1900 E. Lake Avenue
Glenview, Ill. 60025

Charles Scribner's Sons
597 Fifth Avenue
New York, N.Y. 10017

Sheed & Ward, Inc.
64 University Place
New York, N.Y. 10003

Simon & Schuster, Inc.
630 Fifth Avenue
New York, N.Y. 10020

Springer-Verlag New York Inc.
175 Fifth Avenue
New York, N.Y.. 10010

Stackpole Books
Cameron & Kelker Streets
Harrisburg, Pa. 17105

Taplinger Publishing Co., Inc.
200 Park Avenue S.
New York, N. Y. 10003

Charles C. Thomas, Publisher
301-27 E. Lawrence Avenue
Springfield, Ill. 62703

Transatlantic Arts, Inc.
North Village Green
Levittown, N.Y. 11756

Tri-Ocean Books
62 Townsend Street
San Francisco, Calif. 94107

Charles E. Tuttle Co., Inc.
28 S. Main Street
Rutland, Vt. 05701

Twayne Publishers, Inc.
31 Union Square W.
New York, N.Y. 10003

Frederick Ungar Publishing Co., Inc.
250 Park Avenue S.
New York, N.Y. 10003

University of California Press
2223 Fulton Street
Berkeley, Calif. 94720

University of Chicago Press
5801 Ellis Avenue
Chicago, Ill. 60637

Van Nostrand, Reinhold Company
450 W. 33 Street
New York, N.Y. 10001

The Viking Press, Inc.
625 Madison Avenue
New York, N..Y. 10022

Wadsworth Publishing Co. Inc.
Belmont, Calif. 94002

Franklin Watts, Inc.
845 Third Avenue
New York, N.Y. 10022

The Westminster Press
Witherspoon Building
Philadelphia, Pa. 19107

John Wiley & Sons, Inc.
605 Third Avenue
New York, N.Y. 10016

The Williams & Wilkins Co.
428 E. Preston Street
Baltimore, Md. 21202

World Publishing Company
110 E. 59 Street
New York, N.Y. 10022

Yale University Press
149 York Street
New Haven, Conn. 06511

Zondervan Publishing House
1415 Lake Drive S.E.
Grand Rapids, Mich. 49506

I Make $20,000 A Year Writing For Trade Journals

By Robert Latimer

If an epitaph is to be engraved on my tombstone, it should read simply: "Here Lies Robert A. Latimer — who wrote 'Extra Fitting Rooms Increase Corset Sales'."

Finding a corset buyer who has actually stepped up profits by a device of his own making, or a tire dealer who has solved a common merchandising problem, is the story of my life. It's the story of 24 years of writing for trade-papers which covers everything from embalming to rockets.

To me this has been a good, productive life. Productive in a dependable income, in travel through the entire nation, and in the satisfaction of seeing 95 per cent of my output sold. The last ten years I sold 90 articles per month; 1,000-3,000 word pieces illustrated with photographs which I shot myself. I average $25 per article — and I get four or five such checks every day.

My net return of $15,000 to $20,000 per year isn't unusual for trade paper journalists. It has led me into owning an airplane, a completely equipped rolling office, and $2,500 worth of photographic equipment. But mostly, it takes a sense of humor!

I Make $20,000 A Year

Take my own blundering entry into tradepaper corresponding for example. This was at East High School, Denver, during 1936. I was the editor of the school paper's news section, and was assigned to write a feature story on the junior branch of Franklin D. Roosevelt's mighty WPA program. The National Youth Administration was finding part-time jobs for needy students.

Somewhere along the line, a plan was worked out whereby half a dozen students worked a few hours a week in the stationery department of The May Company, Denver department store, drawing both pay and scholastic points toward graduation. A bit nervously, I interviewed the department buyer, assembled the facts, and typed out 900 words on the program.

I sent the piece to *Department Store Economist Magazine* in New York just to see what they would say. Editor C. K. McDermut, Jr., thought it was a free-lance contribution, and okayed a check for $15. Fifteen dollars then looked like $150 now, and, in joyfully exhibiting my check to my classmates, I knew that I had found a profession.

I suspected there were other magazines needing this sort of on-the-scene coverage, and so I made a pest of myself, begging for back-issue tradepapers in every sort of business in Denver. I found more than fifty of them in six months of searching. In the end, I made the decision to toss away my comic books and read instead the entire contents of a different business publication every night before going to bed. I've been doing the same thing ever since, and feel it's the only practical means of understanding an editor's needs and subject treatment.

Another basic decision which I've followed ever since was that "if the subject is worth a query, it is worth a story." I pecked out each story and sent it in with nothing more than my name and address. I found that short manuscripts would stick, providing they were written around one single idea, simple and to the point.

I looked for unusual merchandising stunts which other businessmen in the same field could put to use. For example, I found that a bakery store hired a drug store window trimmer to improve their displays on his day off. That story brought my first $25 check from *Baker's Weekly*.

I shuddered when an editor wrote asking for a photo. Even

in those days, commercial photographers asked $4 for an 8x10 shot, while business paper publishers offered an unrealistic $2 photo payment. (Many still ignore photographic cost in story payment.) There were instances when a story brought a check for $5 when the photographer's bill was $5.10!

Finishing high school put me in position to become a fulltime tradepaper correspondent, since family economics ruled out college. To discipline myself, I broke the month down into four weekly periods, and listed week by week the publications for which I intended to write. This produced a schedule based on simple chronology — doing up all of the department store publications in the same week downtown, all of the plumbers, appliance dealers, super markets, and out-lying interviews the next week, etc. Adhering tightly to this schedule, producing one story per month for this editor, one per week for another, made me a "regular" contributor almost from the first. Editors appreciate steady production timed to their own deadlines, I found.

In the second year, accumulating old copies of trade publications at every opportunity, I built my string to 90, and was faithfully shooting in a story per schedule listing to each publisher.

What was my biggest help at the start? The simple collecting and reading of so many tradepapers showed me the two essentials in this field—building up a backlog of idea material for future months, and the impetus which diversification gave my own thinking.

Good ideas never die. For instance, when tape recorders were brand new, I did a story on how a Denver camera shop was merchandising them; 1,000 words and two photos. Back it came from *Photo Dealer* with the statement, "Our readers don't handle them." Five years later, every camera retailer was displaying tape recorders, and the original ideas in the story were sound enough to sell this story for $45 to *Photo Dealer Magazine*. A 1,200-word piece on how to train Christmas extras for jewelry-store operation didn't make the grade during the war—but, ten years later when jewelers recognized courtesy and efficiency, it sold. My theory is that all material built on good ideas is timeless, and will always retain some value in the files.

No two publishers are alike. One wants terse newspaper styling, another the case-history type of article. The solution, I found, was to open a copy of the pertinent magazine alongside my typewriter, and ape the lead feature in writing my own contribution. This was excellent training, and taught me to "tell the story in condensed form in the first sentence"—elaborating with the details in the rest of the manuscript. *If the editor can grasp what the entire story covers in one glance at the lead, the yarn is half sold.* This holds true for 90 per cent of the 300 business publications for which I write regularly.

Example—"Reinforcing the floors of his new hardware store with six inches of Mastipave concrete so that fork lift trucks can roll right to the display shelving with heavy merchandise has saved $400 a month in store operating costs for Ladd's, lumber and hardware dealers in Pueblo, Colorado."

That's a long sentence, but it will sell a business paper editor at a glance. (Later he will break up the sentence which is all right with me!) From there on, I write the piece the way the editor obviously likes it, as proven by his current issue.

In the beginning I wasted much of my time in writing stories of great depth which covered the subject's entire operation. Then I learned that the easiest salable trade journal article covers *one subject* and *one subject only.* If a dealer has set up a system for charging 25 cents for home deliveries, the story should dwell on why he conceived the idea, how he applied it, the reactions of his customers, and the effect on his profits. A brief background of the business is allowable—and that may be chopped.

I try to visualize the trade paper's reader and unearth what he would want to know. I put myself in the reader's shoes and ask: "What do I want out of this story?"

II

Interviewing then, as now, is a matter of forcing myself to make the approach. Here's a seed store with a window full of ant palaces. Has the owner sold a lot of them? Any trouble keeping the ants alive? How much did he spend for a newspaper ad? Did he try to sell them to his tropical fish customers? Result, 550 words on "Novelty Appeal Will Sell Anteriums to Aquarium Owners." This might go to *Seedsmen's Digest* if I shoot a picture of the window.

Here's a chain store super market. Someone has set up a roll of chicken wire in the center of a table display, and filled it with peanuts, so that as some are scooped away at the bottom, more tumble by gravity to the bottom. A sign offers "Fresh Roasted Peanuts in the Hull, 29c lb." This display creates "impulse buying" and is a cinch to sell to any of the food merchandising publications. How many bags of peanuts did it sell in a week? Does it encourage customers shopping in the store to enjoy a sample peanut? Did the hulls cause too much dirt? One clear picture of this setup and 350 words of copy will bring a check for $7.50 to $10 from *Progressive Grocer*.

Last stop on the street is a shoe repair shop. The owner is wrapping repaired shoes in cellophane instead of opaque wrapping paper. (He can find the correct shoes easier when the customer loses his repair ticket.) Also, he rubs a shine on each pair before returning them to the owners. How much does the cellophane overwrap and shine cost per pair? Is the shine added to the repair charge? What is patron reaction? Are more pairs of shoes repaired per month since the program began? This is a progressive shoe repairman, and the story is worth 1,000 words and at least two pictures. Perhaps *Master Shoe Rebuilder* would consider it.

That's a typical morning. It should take around two hours on the dictating machine to wrap it up or five hours on the typewriter.

After my subject has allowed himself to be photographed, vouchsafed the information, and shooed me away, I consider my job three quarters done. But, before the article can be sold, it *must* be submitted for approval. Even a 100-word short on how a window display helped the sales of Kleenex in a surgical supply store can rub someone the wrong way. The subject will often be carried away with enthusiasm and divulge facts which he will deny later. This is particularly true where the article mentions costs, profits, salaries, commission payments or other "money facts." It isn't pleasant when the subject flatly orders the story killed after reading it over; but it's better than branding yourself a Benedict Arnold with the editor who uses the piece. I have thrown thousands of dollars worth of first-class copy in the wastebasket because the subject got cold feet when he read his words in black and white.

In doing a story on a Salt Lake City super market, for example,

I Make $20,000 A Year

I was invited to take a ride and look at a magnificent new 35,000-square-foot store just about to be completed. I was impressed enough to write four articles on various phases of this new store, including a piece on its complex refrigeration system. To meet a deadline, I didn't take the time to have this article approved. I had taken it for granted that the store belonged to the super market owner who had escorted me into it. When the article was published, however, there were angry wires and letters from several sources; all pointing out that I had identified the store with the wrong super market chain altogether. As matters developed, the super market owner had been speaking as a prideful citizen, rather than an owner, in showing me the huge new store, in which he had no more interest than as a member of the community! I fully expected the hatchet to fall from the magazine that had bought the article, but, in view of 20 years of writing for it without an error, I was let off this incredible blunder.

Best procedure is to bring the manuscript back to the source in person. He is less likely to become critical if the writer is right there. Mailing it to the subject brings up the danger of the manuscript being lost or thumbs-downed by a publicity-shy partner. Once the meat is cut out of the story, it is difficult to get it back.

In general, the owner who has built up his own business is the most cooperative story subject. He has the pride of accomplishment. The worst subjects are department store buyers, who fear losing their jobs if they divulge anything useful about their merchandising or management methods. Almost as bad at the other end of the scale are advertising managers who spout generalities on promotions, but say nothing useful whatever. Most of them appear to know only the clichés and none of the fundamentals. I'd rather interview a hardware retailer on how he sells power lawn mowers on credit without materially increasing his own capital investment than to ask a department store advertising manager whether active demonstrations of can openers will boost sales turnover. Most big stores—department stores, furniture stores, variety stores, etc.—have some sort of shadowy "policy" which nobody understands, but which buttons their lips. Consequently, I'll go to the top man first, and save myself aggravating evasion and delay from underlings.

To grease the wheels for a successful interview bring a copy of the publication concerned along—preferably with one of your own bylined articles in it. I carry an attractive brief case full of sample copies with the interviews I have written. When I had no published samples in the specific field I used the actual typed stories I had written for other trade papers as a sample of my ability.

III

Five years after I started, I converted over from typing my own manuscripts to dictating them to a secretary. I bought a Dictaphone, hired a housewife who was an ex-secretary to do the typing, and settled down to learn the altogether unfamiliar science of dictating.

At first, my copy had no continuity and my secretary proved to need a lot of help with spelling. Manuscripts I planned as 1,000 words turned out to be 2,500 words when typed. Now, I seldom touch a typewriter myself, and own three tape recorders. One is in the family automobile, which is my rolling office, equipped with inverters which turn 12-volt battery power into 110-volt alternating current. The second recorder is a midget which I can carry in my pocket to record convention talks, difficult figures, etc., on the spot. Another, operating through an induction coil on my office telephone, makes it possible to record long distance or local calls, and put the instructions on tape rather than frantically scribbling story instructions or notes. I can dictate 3,000 words per day while driving from one story source to another. At least 75 per cent of the total output is dictated in the car, parked or rolling.

From 1946 to 1955 were halcyon days for a trade-paper writer. Even with all of the advantages of dictation and two full-time typists, I couldn't keep up with the demand of articles, news, and pictures. Still peeved at the high expense of commercial photography, I bought a Speed Graphic, with all accessories, and began shooting my own pictures. I wasted more than $500 worth of film, flash bulbs, and finishing costs before I could make presentable photographs. Even now, using strobe lights, the dependable and lightweight Rolleiflex camera, I'm a barely acceptable photographer. Photography is part art, part point of view and part technique and I've never mastered the three at one and the same time. I built a photo laboratory in my basement and processed my own pictures. I learned that even a *Life* photographer shoots scores of negatives for one good picture, and I do the same. Using up a 12-exposure roll of film for one good shot only costs around 50 cents—and it averts a letter from a disappointed editor who states grimly: "It's a good story—but the art is terrible."

The ability to make photos is a *must* in business paper writing. Not only does it hold photo cost to the point that a profit can be earned, but it wins assignments. Entering a store draped with cameras and lights automatically identifies a reporter, and does away with a lot of time-wasting preliminaries in getting the interview started. I wear my camera like a badge, even when I have no intention of illustrating the article I'm seeking.

Editors were telling me, "Too much Denver!" The time had come for traveling. I visited St. Joseph, Missouri; Rapid City, South Dakota; Decatur, Illinois; Biloxi, Mississippi; Montgomery, Alabama; and similar cities which I knew were almost unrepresented in the trade press. On such trips, I put together notes representing a minimum of $200 worth of copy per day, doggedly carrying out one interview after another. Then, returning to the office, I holed up until all of the material was dictated. The long miles and wasted time were a problem until I decided to capitalize on my Air Force training and buy an airplane. I have owned four airplanes since, which permit me to reach almost any city in my area and return on the same day. A tiny motor scooter fits into my current plane, and lets me get into town fast—independent of cabs, buses, or automobile rentals. For 90 per cent of my articles, I follow the problem-solving formula I learned as an Air Force officer during World War II. This is set up as follows:

1. The problem.
2. List the possible solutions.
3. Analyze the solutions.
4. Apply solution chosen.
5. Reaction.
6. Final results.

That will cover everything from how a paint dealer is going to meet heavy price competition to the methods used by a service station to sell more fan belts. Liberally sprinkled with quotations, an occasional bit of humor, and good, clear 8x10 photos which illustrate the points, this system is practically foolproof.

Not that I mean to suggest that every article for every trade paper should follow a hide-bound format. The editor who has built up a hard-hitting, thoroughly respected journal in his narrow field will welcome the fresh approach, dramatized story-telling and interpretive photography. This "fresh approach" may increase your payment and earn a complimentary, welcoming letter from the editor. But it may cut down your per cent of sale for scripts written because once you get off the beaten formula, it's like offering fresh, choice, thinly sliced, butter browned mushrooms and eggs in a hamburger joint.

Things are changing in the trade press. For one thing, the quality of business papers has steadily been upped. This means that the free lancer must put more preparation into fact gathering, more skill in preparation, and better pictures. In the last five years, I've written less and been paid more.

This brings us to an important point. It is normal to find three trade papers covering the same market. For example, in the profitable office-supply field there are *Office Appliances, Office Products Dealer* and *Business Forms Reporter,* all three good, solid markets for merchandising, management, and promotion stories. In the liquefied petroleum gas bracket there are *LP Gas,* and *NLPGA Times.* And for every major national trade paper, there are as many "regionals," which cover areas of 10 to 14 states. *Hardware Retailer,* for example, is a national paper, while *Southern Hardware* covers the southeastern states, *Hardware World* the 14 western sates, *Hardware Trade* the upper central northern area and *Hardware Merchandising* the Canadian provinces.

Thus, the writer can often mail a piece to several trade papers until one of them buys it. You don't mail copies simultaneously but wait until your manuscript is bought or rejected before considering what to do with the remains. After the first reject, I check page one to see if it is neat and often re-write the lead.

Tip For The Energetic Beginner

Provided you are sincere and willing to do research, there is a wonderful way to find out why the editor may have rejected the story.

Take one of your articles to several merchants in the identical field for which your article was written. Ask them to read it! Although the men you show it to are merchants, not editors, and even though they are not experts at communicating to you what they feel, and may not bring their greatest personal effort to bear on your story, you can expect some choice constructive remarks if you can press without being pesty.

Perhaps your article was written for a magazine read by printing salesmen and told a novel way to sell printing. One of these salesmen to whom you would show the article might say:

"I don't understand how the salesman in your story showed his idea to this printing buyer. Can't you get a picture of it? If the salesman mailed the idea to the printing buyer by letter, what did his letter say? You mention he used 3 follow-ups. What did they say? Did this salesman try this idea on only one printing buyer or on many? How many? How many bought printing? How much did the idea cost to produce and who paid for it—the salesman or his company? And I'd like to know just how a salesman like this operates: does he work on salary or straight commission? What's his commission?"

With this sort of questioning comment, your story quickly comes into sharper focus. Then you get more facts, re-write and sell it.

The writer is at the editor's mercy in the matter of payment. I resolved during my first years that I would never grumble over the size of a check. I have labored as strenuously to produce an article for $15 as one which paid $150. The editor alone can decide what a story is worth, and he is inclined to cut off any free-lancer who gripes at the size of his check. All things even out in time, and even the thinnest regional publication will come up with a healthy check now and then. Most trade papers pay "on publication," which may mean this year, next year or never. It does no good to write asking for payment—the story may come back.

My philosophy has been to complete a heavy schedule of writing every week, add up the checks which have accumulated during the month, and call the result my "salary." In September, I work for my May income next year, and I can insure it only by maintaining the backlog which produces all checks. Write the article, mail it, and forget it until the check arrives. Sooner or later the editor will clean out his files, and either return the piece or use it.

I have been using two effective gimmicks to identify myself to editors. First, I use color on my envelopes, copy paper and credit identification on the ms. Even the most myopic eyes will recognize my submission when it arrives in a bright yellow envelope, or he sees the copy typed on pale yellow, almost white, bond sheets. For further identification, I use a rubber stamp, with my name in lower case, address in upper case letters. The stamp pad is red, contrasting well with the paper. Although editors characteristically ask for white bond paper, none has even objected to this use of color packaging—and they know who it's from on sight.

I never do bench work! It is tempting to write a piece full of good, practical ideas which isn't tied to an actual story source. This is "boiler plate"—and it will come right back. Every story of mine is produced from an interview, sprinkled with quotes, and backed with pictures.

What the editor wants in return for his money is a *correspondent*—someone on whom he can depend for well-written, factual articles, clearly illustrated with 8x10 photographs, and needing as little editing as possible. Then he'll write the check with a happy smile.

Criticism of Four Typical Trade Journal Leads

Example of a Good Lead

"It isn't necessary to cut prices to sell 250 power mowers a years, but a good service department is," according to J. M. Preach, owner of Preach Hardware Company in Phoenix, Arizona.

Mr. Preach sold 250 units, both gasoline and electric powered, during 1959, by planting an attractive lawn to the left of his suburban hardware store, and "letting the customer mow away to sell himself." His salesmen also show customers a big service department, equipped with plenty of power tools and replacement parts, to convince his customers that perhaps it isn't so wise to buy a bargain price power mower at a super market or chain drug store which gives no service guarantee.

This is a good lead because it strikes at a problem common to every dealer—the necessity of cutting prices to sell power mowers. The writing is not inspired but the idea is good.

A Second Good Lead

Chicago—Investing $1,000 in the purchase of six oversize 2-wheel trailers, and mounting 250,000 BTU propane-fired furnaces on them has opened the road to an extra $25,000 per year in home-heating volume for Howard Frehling, heating and air conditioning.

Because any passenger car or truck can haul the trailer right up to any home where canvas ducts can pipe heat into any window, Frehling can remodel heating plants in the coldest winter temperatures. The portable heating plants keep the family warm while the old furnace is removed and a new one installed.

Before he rigged up these "rolling furnaces" Frehling's winter volume sagged alarmingly. Now, he keeps a crew busy year around.

This lead is an example of how to use hard-cash figures in the first paragraph to show that $1,000 invested brought $25,000 more volume. Then there is the novelty "gimmick" of mounting furnaces on wheels. American businessmen love sales gimmicks and will always stop to read about any which apply to their own fields. Last, to widen the application of the idea, the lead indicates that this operation can be carried out with a passenger car such as the reader owns. The lead fails to indicate whether the additional $25,000 volume was profitable, and, if so what was the net.

A Mediocre Lead

Offering cold sufferers "everything needed to alleviate the situation" in one package at $5.95 was a clever merchandising stunt which attracted much additional attention and many extra sales in the prescription department of Martin's Pharmacy in Birmingham, Alabama, last year.

The site was a counter in the rear of the store where manager Fred L. Bixler set up a sign and a row of sample packages containing antihistamines, cough syrup, nose drops and vitamins. The sign pointed out "Cold Sufferers—Here's Your Aids in One Package." Sales people in the store watched for customers complaining of colds or obviously suffering from them, and pointed out this display.

While this lead does go right to the point, it isn't necessary to tell the reader that this is a "clever merchandising stunt" inasmuch as he will decide that for himself in reading the piece. The phrase "many extra sales" is somewhat childish in these days of cold facts. The sentences are too long. There isn't one word that shines.

A Lead That Needs Improvement

One of the most unusual fountain merchandising programs in the history of the Western industry has paid dividends to the tune of an $80,000 per year volume from a 10-stool soda fountain at Michelle's, in Colorado Springs, Colorado.

John Micholpolus, Colorado Springs restauranteur, has parlayed a combination of extreme high quality in sundae ingredients plus a sense of humor into a soda fountain which is a "must" for the tens of thousands of tourists who flock into the Colorado resort city each summer, as well as a favorite spot for local Colorado Springs residents. Operating a combination of a tea room, soda fountain and a confectionery, Micholpolus three years ago invested $35,000 in remodeling a thoroughly unattractive retail shop building into a downtown exclusive restaurant and candy shop, with the soda fountain in the center as the "spark plug" for the entire operation.

"One of the most unusual" is a trite crutch to begin an approach. The piece doesn't get off the ground until the second page, and only an excellent set of photos made it sell. Unless the editor is willing to read further to determine *why* the soda fountain did an $80,000 volume this article would be rejected.

Free lance writers have a choice of hundreds of trade papers and house organs now willing to buy their material. Some of these are weeklies; others monthlies, a few dailies. To list the editorial requirements of each would require a book; in fact about 200 pages of "The Writer's Market" is devoted to the editorial requirements of these journals.

Following are about one hundred names and addresses of leading trade journals that buy free lance material. Each of these has two to twelve competitors in its own field. To get going, write a note to several of these trade journals, in fields where you have some knowledge, and ask for two back issues. It wouldn't hurt to enclose fifty cents as some trade journals are "thick as a brick" and the postage for two back copies is an item.

After you read one or two back issues, and get an idea for an article for that particular magazine, call upon a half dozen people in that trade in your vicinity who might be subscribers. Explain your article idea and see how they react.

This will give you a "for real" approach in writing your first trade journal article.

Adult Bible Teacher
6401 The Paseo
Kansas City, MO 64131

Advertising and Sales Promotion
740 N. Rush Street
Chicago, IL 60611

Airport World
Air Rights Building
7315 Wisconsin Avenue
Washington, DC 20014

American Dairy Review
575 Madison Avenue
New York, NY 10022

American Drycleaner
500 N. Dearborn Street
Chicago, IL 60610

American Family Physician
Volker Boulevard at Brookside
Kansas City, MO 64112

American Laundry Digest
500 N.. Dearborn Street
Chicago, IL 60610

American Paint and Wallcoverings
   Dealer
2911 Washington Avenue
St. Louis, MO 63103

American Paper Merchant
200 S. Prospect Avenue
Park Ridge, IL 60068

American School Board Journal
National School Boards Association
State National Bank Plaza
Evanston, IL 60201

The Antiques Dealer
1115 Clifton Avenue
Clifton, NJ 07013

Automotive News
965 E. Jefferson
Detroit, MI 48207

Auto Trim News
129 Broadway
Lynbrook, NY 11563

Beer Wholesaler
Islip, NY 11751

Boating Industry
205 E. 42nd Street
New York, NY 10017

The Bowling Proprietor
375 W. Higgins Road
Hoffman Estates, IL 60172

Brick and Clay Record
5 S. Wabash Avenue
Chicago, IL 60603

Broadcast Engineering
1014 Wyandotte
Kansas City, MO 64105

Buildings Magazine
427 Sixth Avenue S.E.
Cedar Rapids, IA 52406

Business Insurance
740 N. Rush Stret
Chicago, IL 60611

Business Screen
757 Third Ave
New York, NY 10017

Campground and RV Park Management
319 Miller Avenue
Mill Valley, CA 94941

Canadian Doctor
Gardenvale 800
Quebec, Canada

Canadian Forest Industries
1450 Don Mills Road
Don Mills, Ont., Canada

Canadian Transportation and Distribu-
   ion Management
1450 Don Mills Road
Don Mills, Ont., Canada

Catering Executive Newsletter
P.O. Box 788
Lynbrook, NY 11563

Chain Saw Industry and Power Equip-
   ment Dealer
Louisiana Bank Building
Box 1703
Shreveport, LA 71166

China Glass and Tablewares
1115 Clifton Avenue
Clifton, NJ 07013

College Store Executive
211 Broadway
Lynbrook, NY 11563

Construction Equipment Operation
and Maintenance
220 Higley Building
Cedar Rapids, IA 52401

Consulting Engineer
217 Wayne Street
St. Joseph, MI 49085

Drug Topics
550 Kinderkamack Road
Oradell, NJ 07649

Drycleaning World
750 3rd Avenue
New York, NY 10017

Earnshaw's Infants, Girls, Boyswear
Review
393 Seventh Avenue
New York, NY 10001

Electric Light and Power
Cahners Building
221 Columbus Avenue
Boston, MA 02116

Electrical Contractor
700 O.F.C. Building
Washington, DC 20036

Farm Building News
610 N. Water
Milwaukee, WI 53203

Feed Industry Review
152 W. Wisconsin Avenue
Milwaukee, WI 53203

Fire Chief Magazine
625 N. Michigan Avenue
Chicago, IL 60611

Florist (formerly FTD News)
900 West Lafayette
Detroit, MI 48226

Foundry Magazine
Penton Plaza
Cleveland, OH 44114

Freezer Provisioning and Portion
Control
25 S. Bemiston Avenue
St. Louis, MO 63105

Furniture & Furnishings
1450 Don Mills Road
Don Mills, Ont., Canada

Fur Trade Journal
Bewley, Ont., Canada

Gas Appliance Merchandising
1 East First Street
Duluth, MN 55802

Grain Age
152 W. Wisconsin Avenue
Milwaukee, WI 53203

Handbags & Accessories Magazine
80 Lincoln Avenue
Stamford, CT 06904

Hardware Age
56th and Chestnut Streets
Philadelphia, PA 19139

Harvard Business Review
Soldiers Field
Boston, MA 02163

Heating and Plumbing Merchandiser
P.O. Box 343
E. Paterson, NJ 07407

Heavy Duty Trucking
P.O. Box W
Newport Beach, CA 92663

Hosiery and Underwear
757 Third Avenue
New York, NY 10017

The Independent Banker
Box 267
Sauk Centre, MN 56378

Industrial Arts and Vocational
Education
22 W. Putnam
Greenwich, CT 06830

Trade Journal Markets

Industrial Machinery News
P.O. Box 727
Dearborn, MI 48121

Industrial Photography
750 Third Avenue
New York, NY 10017

Jeweler's Circular-Keystone
One Decker Square
Bala-Cynwyd, PA 19004

Juvenile Merchandising
Empire State Building, Suite 4719
350 Fifth Avenue
New York, NY 10001

Leather and Shoes
10 High Street
Boston, MA 02110

Maintenance Supplies
101 W. 31st Street
New York, NY 10001

Medical Lab
750 Third Avenue
New York, NY 10017

Modern Jeweler
15 W. 10th Street
Kansas City, MO 64105

Modern Packaging
1221 Avenue of the Americans
New York, NY 10020

Modern Machine Shop
600 Main Street
Cincinnati, OH 45202

Modern Steel Construction
American Institute of Steel
   Construction
101 Park Avenue
New York, NY 10017

Municipal South
Box 88
Greenville, SC 29602

National Hardwood Magazine
P.O. Box 18436
Memphis, TN 38118

The National Public Accountant
1717 Pennsylvania Avenue, N.W.,
   Suite 1200
Washington, DC 20006

Naval Engineers Journal
Suite 807, Continental Building
1012 14th Street N.W.
Washington, DC 20005

Nursing Outlook
10 Columbus Circle
New York, NY 10019

Ocean Industry
Box 2608
Houston, TX 77001

Office Products
Hitchcock Building
Wheaton, IL 60187

Offshore
3333 West Alabama
Houston, TX 77024

Paperboard Packaging
777 Third Avenue
New York, NY 10017

Pest Control
9800 Detroit Avenue
Cleveland, OH 44102

Petroleum Marketer (formerly Petroleum & TBA Marketer)
636 First Avenue
West Haven, CT 06516

Physician's Management
26 Sixth Street
Ridgeway Center
Stamford, CT 06905

Plastics Technology
630 Third Avenue
New York, NY 10017

Pollution Engineering
1301 S. Grove
Barrington, IL 60010

Printing Magazine
475 Kinderkamack Road
Oradell, NJ 07649

Progressive Grocer
708 Third Avenue
New York, NY 10017

Sales Management
630 Third Avenue
New York, NY 10017

Southern Pulp and Paper Manufacturer
75 Third Street N.W.
Atlanta, GA 30308

Specialty Bakers Voice
299 Broadway
New York, NY 10007

The Student Store
735 Spring Street, N.W.
Atlanta, GA 30308

Tobacco Reporter
424 Commerical Square
Cincinnati, OH 45202

Today's Secretary
1221 Avenue of the Americas
New York, NY 10020

Water Well Journal
P.O. Box 29168
Columbus, OH 43229

Weeds, Trees and Turf Magazine
9800 Detroit Avenue
Cleveland, OH 44102

The Welding Distributor
Box 128
Morton Grove, IL 60053

Western Milk and Ice Cream News
15 Sir Francis Drake Boulevard East
Greenbrae, CA 94904

Western Outfitter
5314 Bingle Road
Houston, TX 77018

Western Paint Review
1833 W. 8th Street
Los Angeles, CA 90057

World Dredging and Marine
    Construction
P.O. Box 269
San Pedro, CA 90733

Murder Is My Business

by Hal D. Steward

One of the first rules for a good true fact detective story is that it must have mystery in it. Because of this, every murder case is not a potential article for you. There must be a lapse of time between the murder and the arrest of the killer if you are to have material for a salable story.

This rules out all cases, and they are in the majority, where the murderer is apprehended almost immediately after he commits his crime.

With this essential rule established, let's set up a hypothetical murder case and then approach it the way a true detective story writer would. Although the murder is not real, the techniques described are the ones I use.

You pick up your daily newspaper and there on page one is a headline: "Beauty Strangled by Unknown Killer." You learn a 24-year-old secretary has been found strangled to death in her apartment and that police have already questioned several suspects, but the murderer is still free.

While you are reading about the murder, so are several other freelance writers. You have no time to waste.

You grab your *Writer's Market* and turn to the "Detective Magazine" section. You decide on a magazine you think will want the story when the murderer has been caught.

Once you decide on your potential market, you go to your typewriter and bang out a query to the editor to be sent either by telegram or air mail:

> "Margie Smart, 24, a private secretary, was found strangled to death in her apartment at 2:10 a.m., Saturday, Dec. 5. Body was discovered by landlady. Numerous suspects so far questioned by police, but no arrest has been made. Photographs available of victim, murder scene and police officers assigned to case. Are you interested in my doing story on speculation when solved?"

You have now taken the first key step in writing a true fact detective story—the attempt to find an interested editor. Unsolicited articles in the fact detective field are virtually unwanted by editors. If the editor you have queried does not have a regular contributor in your area, and if he thinks the crime has the elements he wants, you may get the go-ahead to do the piece on speculation.

But, at this point, you don't have a complete story—you won't have until the murderer is caught. You begin now to clip all news stories on the murder as they are published in your area's daily newspapers. Each news story gives you more facts about the crime, about the victim's background and about the police investigation.

Days, perhaps weeks, pass. Your folder on the case is becoming fat with news clippings.

Then the news story you have been waiting for is published. The headline reads: "Murder Suspect Confesses to Strangling Beauty."

The editor you queried has given you the go-ahead. He has staked out the story for you and will buy it if it meets his standards. You know that to meet these standards your story must have four major ingredients: it must be true, it must have accurate facts, it must be a good detective story, and it must be interesting.

The murderer has been caught, so now you begin your serious research.

Don't try writing the story the easy way—just using newsclippings for your information. It won't work. Furthermore, how can you be certain all the facts in all the news stories are accurate? You can't. So, you must do your digging.

Your first step in this direction is to personally talk with the homicide detective in charge of the murder investigation. His name has been in the news clippings, so you know who he is. You telephone police headquarters, and when the operator there answers, you ask for him by name. He comes on the line. Your conversation with him goes something like this:

"Sergeant Smith, this is John Pratt, a freelance magazine writer. I have an assignment from TRUE FACT DETECTIVE MAGAZINE to do a story on the Margie Smart murder you investigated. When would it be convenient for me to come down and talk with you about it?"

Police officers, generally, are cooperative with writers. The homicide detective sergeant will probably tell you:

"Well, Mr. Pratt, I'll be busy the rest of the day, how about coming in tomorrow at 10 a.m.? I can talk with you about the case then."

When you arrive for your appointment, Sergeant Smith may have already prepared himself by collecting together all the case files. He may let you take notes directly from the reports in the files, or he may use the files to refresh his memory in answering your questions.

What do you need to know from the homicide detective? Get the answers to these questions:

1. Who discovered the body, what was the precise discovery time, and what were the circumstances surrounding the discovery? How and by whom was the crime reported? Who was the first police officer at the crime scene, what does his report say he found when he arrived?

2. When did the homicide detective in charge of the case arrive? What did he find on arrival? What did the crime scene, in his own words, look like?

3. What were the first steps the detective took upon his arrival. Was there any physical evidence present that might have indicated a suspect. If so, what was it?

4. What was the coroner's report on the body and the cause of death?

5. How was the first suspect tracked down? What did the suspect say in answer to police questions?

6. How many suspects were tracked down and questioned in the case? Who were they? How did they become involved as suspects? How did they account for their movements and whereabouts at the estimated time of the murder? Fictitious names will be used for these in the story. The suspects will help build suspense and describe the detective work done on the case.

7. Can I see a copy of the murderer's confession so I can make verbatim notes from it?

The homicide detective sergeant may provide you with all this information. If he does, you are ahead in your research. If he does not, you have more digging to do.

Your next source is the newspaper reporters who covered the murder story for their newspapers. They frequently have more details of the crime than were included in their published stories. These reporters usually will cooperate with another writer, so don't be bashful in asking their help.

If your county uses the Grand Jury system, ask the county clerk to permit you to see a transcript of the case as presented to the jury by the district attorney. The transcript will include testimony of police officers, a copy of the confession, plus details of other evidence collected against the suspected killer.

By this time your research includes news clippings, notes from your interview with homicide detective, notes from the reports of police officers on the case, evidence submitted by the district attorney to the Grand Jury, and notes from your interviews with reporters who covered the murder story.

Along the way, you have inquired of police and the librarians of the local newspapers what photographs can be made available to you to illustrate your story. These are vital and no true fact detective story will sell without them. You make a list of available photographs so it can be submitted to the editor with your finished manuscript. He will decide later and let you know which ones he wants.

You are ready to begin writing your story. How do you start?

If you do as I do, you will take all the information you have, put it in chronological order, and type it out. Don't worry at this point about a lead, description, and planted clues. An idea for a lead may come while you're doing this chore. If it does, jot it down. But, first of all, get the case, detail by detail, in chronological order. Your chronological draft must run at least 20 double-spaced, typewritten pages. You want a completed manuscript of 5,000 to 6,000 words, about 20 to 25 double-spaced typewritten pages.

Your chronological draft is completed. Now start work on your lead. How about this one for our hypothetical murder case:

"Margie Smart was 24, a beautiful brunette, and a girl who had everything to live for. She was employed as the private secretary to an important business executive and was known to enjoy her work. Her private affairs had never held the slightest scent of scandal. Who would want to snuff out her young life?

"It was a balmy Southern California morning when Homicide Detective Sergeant Jack Smith stood thoughtfully and asked himself that question.

"Near his feet was the sprawled body of Margie Smart, the victim of a strangler's cruel hands."

You're off. The next few paragraphs tell the reader who found the murdered girl and how the murder was reported, when it was reported, what the first police officer on the scene found, and so forth.

The lead you first put down may not be the one you finally use. But put down anything to get started; you can come back later and polish or change the lead, if necessary. The important thing is to start writing.

Remember—and this is a must—good conversation is important to true fact detective stories. The people you are writing about must talk throughout the story. Use plenty of direct quotes. The sentences should be short, but at the same time carry along the story action.

You will have to create some of the quotes in line with the action. This does not mean you have to stray from the facts because you are making up words for the persons in your story to speak.

These examples of how conversation can be interjected into a story were taken from my article "West Coast's No. 1 Murder Mystery" in TRUE DETECTIVE MAGAZINE:

"The child's body evidently was dropped into the ditch and was covered with mud and bits of brush by recent rains," District Attorney Keller said as he surveyed the scene. This conversation gives information as well as moves the story along.

"Mrs. Castro de Hernandez told police, 'I visited National City with my young son about three or four months ago. While we were there we went to Kimball Park. My boy wandered away into a wooded section of the park and I went to look for him. That was when I came upon Mary Lou Olson in the company of a young man who appeared about 25.' " This dialogue also provides information and the direct quotes make the facts seem more authentic.

Your story must include conversation between police officers working on the case, between detectives and the suspects they are questioning, and between detectives and witnesses who provide information about the victim and possible suspects.

Keep your story in chronological order. Carry your reader along with the homicide detective investigating the case. When the detective discovers a clue, tell the reader what it is, but don't slow down the story's pace by pointing out its importance.

Clues as well as false leads should be sprinkled throughout your story to keep up reader interest. You can't hold back an important clue and then suddenly at the end of the story spring it on the reader. That's not fair, and the reader will resent it.

Build up suspects along the way in your story. Tell how they were located, what put the police onto their trail, what they said when questioned by detectives, and why they were finally cleared of suspicion. (*Fictitious names must be used for suspects except the actual murderer.*)

It is important you stop every now and then in your story and give the reader a breathing spell. You can do this with paragraphs that briefly recap what has occurred in the story up to this point, or by recounting the number of suspects so far taken into custody and questioned. I do this about every 500 words or so.

True fact detective story readers are interested in good detective work. They want to know the methods and techniques used to solve a murder. So, you must constantly weave such information throughout your story.

Describe the homicide detective in charge of the case as well as the principal suspects. Readers like to know what they look like; their height and weight, the color of their eyes and hair, and their manner of speaking.

Throw in some brief biographical facts on your principal homicide detective. Tell how many years he has been a detective, mention a well-known case he may have worked on in the past, and so forth.

It is important, too, to describe in detail the scene of the crime. Tell exactly where the body was found, in what position, and describe the physical surroundings. Your readers want these facts.

Unless there is a confession or an indictment with strong physical evidence to support it, true fact detective magazine editors shy away from current murder cases. They must heed the law of libel and avoid it. If a suspect pleads innocent to murder, you may have to wait for a guilty verdict before you begin writing your story. Your editor will make this decision for you.

If you do hold off until a guilty verdict is in, you may want to write a trial story—some have high drama. Such a story tells the details of the murder, detective work, and courtroom drama through testimony presented.

This, for example, is how my article "How A San Diego TV Station Cracked A Homicide Riddle" began in the April issue of TRUE DETECTIVE Magazine:

"To prepare his case against the three defendants, Prosecutor Bruce Iredale had worked harder than usual. This in itself was unusual because Iredale is known as one of the hardest working prosecutors in the district attorney's office of San Diego County, California.

"But Iredale knew the extra work he devoted to the case's preparation was necessary. One of the three defendants he was to prosecute was one of the most violent men he had ever encountered in his years as a prosecutor. Iredale knew public safety demanded the man's conviction for first-degree murder, robbery and conspiracy to commit robbery with his two companions."

Your facts for trial stories can be obtained from the transcript of the murder trial. Newspaper reporters who cover the county courthouse also can be of help on these.

Don't worry about the title to your story. Use the best one that comes to mind. Frequently the editor will change it.

Once you master the true fact detective magazine writing technique and learn the kind of murder stories the editors want, you will be on your way to a steady flow of checks.

Following are some of the better-known fact detective magazines:

Confidential Detective Cases
235 Park Ave. S.
New York, N. Y. 10003

Crime Detective Cases
235 Park Ave. S.
New York, N. Y. 10003

Detective Cases
1440 St. Catherine St. W.
Montreal 107, Quebec, Canada

Detective Dragnet
1440 St. Catherine St. W.
Montreal 107, Quebec, Canada

Detective Files
1440 St. Catherine St. W.
Montreal 107, Quebec, Canada

Front Page Detective
800 Third Ave.
New York, N. Y. 10017

Inside Detective
800 Third Ave.
New York, N. Y. 10017

Master Detective
235 Park Ave. S.
New York, N. Y. 10003

Official Detective Stories
235 Park Ave. S.
New York, N. Y. 10003

Startling Detective
1515 Broadway
New York, N. Y. 10036

True Detective
1440 St. Catherine St. West
Montreal, Que., Canada

True Police Cases
1440 St. Catherine St. West
Montreal, Que., Canada

How To Be a Small Town Stringer

By Reinhart Wessing

Today, in several hundred small towns, there is an open field for the "stringer" or local correspondent who will keep his regional paper supplied with items about his local community.

As a State editor, I employed forty part-time, free-lance writers in outlying communities. Other State editors, in the 1700 daily newspapers across the country, have their stringers who supply local items from small towns in the newspaper's circulation area.

"Stringer" is an old newspaper term based on the fact that the local correspondent's copy is strung together, measured, and then paid for by the inch. My stringers made from $20 to $40 a week.

Who can be a stringer? Almost anyone—housewives, school teachers, professional men, full-time writers. You needn't be a Pulitzer Prize winner, nor is a college education necessary. Stringing can be something as unliterary as getting the facts and just calling them in to your editor.

The Editor of the *Arizona Republic* says:

> Among the half a hundred Arizona Republic correspondents, we have to fight constantly for full attention to our deadlines. We ask all our correspondents to telephone us on any major thing

the moment it happens. Depending on the event and the correspondent, we direct them from there.

A little trick I adopted from an old-time staff reporter has resulted in some top stories. This is forcing them personally to ask the principals of every case what their age is. Sometimes we don't get the age—but the personal contact means more accuracy in the story itself and often leads us to a story that other papers, radio stations and even the wire services miss completely. It can be "Well, that accident was funny. You see today was my birthday . . ." or "Every year on (this date) something awful has happened to me . . ."

Truthfulness, diligence and alertness are the qualities that mean most. Skill in writing is less important.

Our best correspondent is Jean Duffy, Page, Ariz. A woman who a year ago had never written a newspaper article. She isn't long on writing, but she is a top fact-getter and photographer. She's a housewife and mother of a college-age girl.

As a stringer, you promptly acquaint yourself with all local officials, such as sheriff, chief of police or constable, mayor or village president, school board officials, courthouse clerks, and the secretaries of civic and social clubs, pastors of churches, and of course the undertakers. "A good stringer," says Hal Schellkopf, of the *Columbus Dispatch*, "should call the sheriff, chief of police or constable every morning and not depend on them to call him!"

News can break any hour of the day, any day of the week, so being a stringer is like being a fireman; you're never off duty. Stringers say this gives pace and zest to their life.

Some stringers are afraid that along with their regular daily duties, either as breadwinners or homemakers they will not have time to cover such things as city or village council and school board meetings. It is not necessary to attend all of them personally, provided you have attended enough of them to know what they are like and who's who. You can get the story the next morning by calling the recording secretary, or any other member of the board whose word can be considered reliable. They are usually willing to tell you what went on. To ask the right questions, you have to know what forces are behind the development of the news. It is this knowledge that makes a good stringer so valuable. One State editor on a large Midwestern daily says, "My best stringers work on county weeklies where they have access to news. I tell my stringers to plug for pictures. I pay $5 flat for them and they tend to put the town in the news when there is no news worthy of a story."

Here are some things to consider when deciding what is news.

If your city or village council decides that your town ought to float a bond issue to finance new lights in the business district, everyone will—or at least should—want to know about it, because eventually it is they, the taxpayers, who will pay for the new lights. Your community will expect the paper to carry the full story so it can keep abreast of the arguments pro and con, and know how to vote when the referendum is held. It is your job as a reporter to see that the paper gets the full and complete story.

If your PTA and school board decides that one of your schools needs an addition or is obsolete and should be replaced, the community must have the full and complete story so it knows how to vote on that referendum.

Youth club activities which provide young people with recreation and the opportunity to develop leadership are news, because they strengthen the moral framework of your community.

Church activities are newsworthy because they deal with the spiritual life of a community. Every church has organizations for men, women, and young people, which carry on various community and charitable projects.

The activities of your local clubs are newsworthy when they are of community-wide interest. Many of them carry on projects for charitable institutions, youth programs, or sponsor scholarships.

Here's a quote from an experienced stringer:

> I string for two papers in the far west, averaging about $40 a week. Luckily my two papers have different circulation areas so I send the same features and news to both.
>
> I illustrate everything I submit except, naturally, telephoned spot news. Editors like pictures of people doing things, and not more than five in a group. They will use photos which are sharp, in focus, and close in to the subject. Fill-in flash should be used for face shadows in outdoor pictures.
>
> Life is never dull because in this job one deals mainly with people, all kinds. I never do a feature story about a person without, at the same time, gaining a new friend.
>
> I have always been frightened of heights but I will do anything (almost!) for a picture, so I have flown in a tiny plane with

the door removed to photograph a parachute jumper, almost falling out myself because my seat belt was unfastened the better to manipulate my camera; I have climbed to the little platform at the very end of a telephone lineman's service truck ladder to shoot a street scene; and gone down 700 feet into a canyon in a truck bed dangling from a cable hook, the only woman among a group of three governors, the Secretary of the Interior, other dignitaries and some fifty reporters.

Here are some quotes from editors on what kind of stories they buy from stringers:

> Any *news* story from the stringer's community—fire, automobiles in which there are fatalities, acts of heroism, deaths of prominent people—are used regularly. Good feature stories are always wanted. New farming techniques, unusual hobbies, success stories, interviews, inventions, etc., can all be used.

Large, metropolitan dailies using wire services often differ slightly in their requirement. Writes Lee Olson of the *Denver Post*:

> Stories bought from stringers fall into the general classifications of news and features. The former doesn't bulk large on our payroll because we depend heavily on the wire service for news. Features, accompanied by pictures whenever possible, are valuable because there is no adequate source, exclusive of our own staff members, for such regional material. Features we have bought include such items as people with interesting hobbies, life at a high altitude cattle camp, cattle and sheep roundups, irrigation developments, etc.

Most State editors point out that they do not want to see routine items like meetings of the Chamber of Commerce, or stories which have a strong promotional slant for some firm or product. Casual social items are a red flag in front of most editors' eyes, and yet many stringers make the mistake of sending these in. They are probably trying to please some friends or business acquaintances.

Here's an example:

> Mr. and Mrs. Alex Picke were the dinner guests to their neighbors, Mr. and Mrs. Robert Smith. Mrs. Smith served a delicious beef roast, which was eaten by candlelight. A bouquet of huge yellow chrysanthemums decorated the table. After dinner the couples played cards and reminisced.

This may be all right for the village weekly, but it will never do for a daily. It is bewildering for editors to receive material like this and then find that some important story was not sent in.

For instance. One morning I received nothing but dribble from one stringer. In the afternoon I received a tip that a large bond issue was being proposed in that town to build a new water system. A referendum approving the first $80,000 worth of bonds was to be voted on in three days. I called the stringer. Not only was the tip right, but she knew the whole story. She hadn't sent it in because she didn't know whether I would use it. Again I say, please send everything in and let your editor decide if it's news. I did give her a bonus for the complete story she had. But it could have been two or three times as much if she had sent it in sooner.

When you gather material for your stories you should keep in mind the journalists' five "W's" and "H". The five "W's" are these: what, who, why, when, where; and the "H" is how? If you will try to find the answer to all these whenever you do a story, you will not end up with a thin, down-at-the-heel report. Sometimes when people give you a report of a meeting they won't answer all these questions. That's where you show your mettle as a reporter; you ask for the information they left out. If you are turned down, you keep trying. If you can't or won't ferret, then back to housekeeping or your job.

Many a story comes to the editor's desk with one or more points unanswered. He calls the stringer and asks him for it. If the stringer says he doesn't know because he wasn't given that information, the editor cannot accept the excuse. It's the stringer's job as a reporter to find out.

A story has to have meat on the bones. You can't sell a skeleton.

If the story leaves doubts or questions in the reader's mind, chances are your editor will toss it in file 13. Which means the little effort you did spend to get the story was wasted. Unused material is not returned.

Another matter to watch is such a seemingly minor point as people's names. It is very important to spell names correctly. If there are two Robert Smiths in town, the middle initial, which is likely to be different, should be inserted.

You can also save yourself and your editor some time by writing out in full the names of organizations and clubs when you refer to them the first time. If you send in a story about a TMTM Club, probably only you and the members of the club know what the initials stand for. Your editor will shoot the copy back to you with a circle around TMTM and the words, "Who dat?"

When I interviewed a prospect for my newspaper, I paid close attention to his grammar. If he spoke with bad grammar, chances were he'ed write the same. That was my cue to move on to the next possibility because it would take too much time to rewrite his copy. Other editors don't feel as strongly on this matter.

I always liked a stringer who knew how to keep his distance from the town gossip. A gossiper can get his editor into a lot of hot water by sponging hearsay. Also my stringer had to have a reputation for honesty above all else, and be well liked in the community. I knew such a person would get the necessary cooperation from everyone in the community. Age doesn't matter too much. I took anyone if he had the qualities I was looking for.

At one time I had a high school senior on my staff—but that was the exception rather than the rule, as well as a stringer who was in her seventies and still going strong, after being with the paper almost 20 years.

Paul S. Plumer, Managing Editor, *The Kennebec Journal*, Augusta, Me., writes:

> A stringer must have the willingness to work hard, mix with people, take an interest in public events, accept the task of reporting routine unimportant news along with the more glamorous assignments. We tell them anyone who can write a letter can master the writing side of the trade.

How do you get your story to the editor? Most of the time it goes by mail, and that's why it is doubly important to have it fresh since you lose a day in transit. Your copy should be typed, of course, and as clean-looking as possible.

There are some things your editor will want you to telephone to him collect. All editors want you to call in accidents, fires, crimes and obituaries. Get all the details and all the correct names. People in your town will be watching the evening paper for the full story. The better job you do on these stories, the bigger your bonus.

Stringers are usually paid by the column inch for material of theirs that is published. There are exceptions where a paper will pay a flat monthly salary no matter how much you send in. But most papers pay from 15 to 20 cents a column inch. Which means that if you send in a story 10 inches long and your paper pays 20 cents an inch, you make two dollars. If that story happens to be a fire, an exceptionally good report of the village council meeting, you'll probably be given a bonus of anywhere from one to five dollars. So it's possible to net six dollars with one good story.

Most papers pay once a month. Some of them will tabulate your lineage and bonuses for you by recording it from day to day. Others will make you keep a "string". These will require you to clip your stories every day and paste them on sheets of paper with the date it appeared written alongside each story. At the end of the month you send in this "string". Your editor will measure your string and verify your total inches and add a bonus for outstanding jobs.

Here's how one of my stringers earned her money:

In a town of about 300, she covered a $12,000 tavern fire last month. The building next door started to burn and was heavily damaged by smoke and water. The stringer phoned in the complete story. The story ran about eight inches—$1.20 at 15 cents an inch. The regular bonus for calling in a fire was 50 cents. But her story was very complete, with the estimate of damages, names of people involved, time of fire, how many fire departments were there to fight the blaze, who owned both buildings, and so on, so I gave her a $5 bonus. The story netted her $6.70.

Editors, who need stringers, will go out and beat the bushes for them, but every editor I asked said they give first attention to those who approach them. It shows enterprise. Many stringers come to us recommended from one who is leaving the paper for some personal reason. One paper in southern Illinois with 90 stringers hires four to six new ones each year because of turnover. People move, take new jobs, die. Often it's a good idea to send in a trial submission, on a story you think is news. That plus a good letter will surely get you an interview.

Here then is how I would apply for a job as stringer if I lived in Oscal, Nebraska, and it was within 40 miles of two daily newspapers both of which have circulation in the immediate farm communities around Oscal. First, I would read the two dailies for a month and clip all stories about my community.

Then I would list the stories that happened in my community

in the past month that one or both dailies missed.

Perhaps each daily missed 8 stories. I would write three of these stories complete, and either take them to the State Editor or mail him something like this:

> To the State Editor:
> I am applying for a job as a stringer in Oscal, Nebraska. Clipped to this letter are the stories you published in the last 30 days with an Oscal date line. I believe you missed these 8 stories.
> (then list each one with a very brief description)
> I have written up 3 of these for you. May I have the job?
>> Sincerely,
>> Jack Jones

You'll find that once an editor is interested in employing you, he'll help develop you on the job. News is these people's livelihood, and they will give much time and effort for a good man (or woman).

Mary K. Winslow of *The Bellevue Gazette,* Bellevue, Ohio gives an operational insight into her own work and her last paragraph shows we are sisters under the skin:

> We pay a $5 bonus for on-the-spot reporting, or for a hot tip. Many times this has given us the jump on an accident simply because a reporter phoned in to inform us, and we promptly dispatch a staff photographer-reporter.
> We call stringers together three times per year and go over news they've submitted. It's surprising what they learn from one another and what we learn from them.
> I put my life on the line when I suggested getting rid of some of our neighborhood-gossip stringers we had, some who'd been on the job 20 years. You need only to have changed the names of the people in their stories—otherwise, the reports were the same. Sometimes we use display advertisements in our Help Wanted Columns to secure stringers and this produces some very adept people who have no idea we're in need of help. We request that our stringers list things they know about; also items that are forthcoming in their area and this often produces new ideas for features we can assign them. Often they wouldn't have thought the newspaper could use something on the very subject they know best. I do work on the Great American novel from time to time—doesn't every editor? Guess the thing I couldn't stand is some other editor telling me how bad my work really is after I spend my days telling others what's good, bad and pure rubbish.

Joe Gluvna, Jr., editor of the *Chronicle-Telegram* at Elyria, Ohio talks about the general rate of payment increase to stringers.

> Our biggest problem for several years had been length of stories. That was solved six years ago, when we junked the inch-rate pay-

ment and installed our own. We pay a flat rate of $4 per meeting and $3 per story resulting from the meeting. For example, a stringer attends town council, and writes three separate stories. She gets $4 for attending the meeting plus $9 ($3 for each story), totalling $13. We spend less time in the office unscrambling one, lengthy story about a meeting into separate stories, and it teaches a stringer that a story does not have to be long to be worth more money. These rates are minimums, incidentally.

It is much easier for us to tack together two or three separate stories into a story, rather than separating them.

Good stringers are hard to find. The good ones average as much as $100 a week; the occasional worker earns as little as $2 a month.

Most stringers here have routine beats. They regularly cover council, school board, board of public affairs, or whatever is the important governmental body. The gravy, as far as stringers are concerned, is the writing of features and taking of photos. We use photos, a lot of them, and if a stringer is good with a camera, there's extra money to be made. Our Sunday edition is packed with features, and we also have a magazine section on Sunday so features are always in demand. The rule of thumb is to check with us on a feature before writing it.

We cover about 1800 square miles, much of it in the rural area of Lorain County. Farmers do not call us and tell us what they are doing, so we depend on rural stringers to let us in on the news. Rural police departments seem to distrust that voice on the other end of the telephone line. Thus the personal contact of a stringer who generally knows the police chief, is a great aid. We do not care for the old country copy here. "Mr. and Mrs. Suggins went to Cleveland to shop," or "entertained friends" is taboo. Stanley, Tupper Ware, or any other "parties" are also out.

Metros often upset the small communities by their handling of a story because the only time the small town gets coverage is when council has a donnybrook, someone murders someone else, schools close due to financial trouble, or anything "hot".

We cover the "hot" news, but also cover what leads up to that news—before it gets in the metros.

We use the code-a-phone method to get stringer's news in the paper. A stringer covers a council meeting, then calls a special telephone to reach our code-a-phone (essentially, a tape recorder). The stories are transcribed by a typist who works from 10 p.m. until the wee hours, and the copy is ready for the state editor at 6:30 a.m. It is a MUST that stories be code-a-phoned in the same night as the meeting is held. Some correspondents who have worked for weeklies have a hard time getting used to the pace in a daily newspaper.

Stringers are under instruction to phone in newstips or breaking news. Many's the time we have gotten our first break on a serious accident due to a stringer's phone call.

A good stringer is a useful citizen and a very real part of every small-town paper.

How To Syndicate
Your Own Column

Before me is the annual *Syndicate Directory* of *Editor & Publisher*. In it is a list of syndicates who offer twenty-four hundred different features to any newspaper, house organ or magazine who cares to buy them. Some of these features were created and sold by their authors by the method I am going to describe.

Syndicated features deal with all manner of subjects such as: Family Finance, Chess and Checkers, Books, Etiquette, Fashions and Beauty, Boating, Fiction, Graphology, Health, Religion, Agriculture, Household Decorating, Photography, Horoscope, to name a few. The variety demonstrates the full-bodied range of material that editors buy.

To get the heady scent of what's going on, I would advise a writer interested in selling a syndicated feature to secure this Syndicate Directory of *Editor and Publisher**, which describes, classifies every feature now being sold, and gives the name and address of each syndicate. This is useful whether the writer wishes to syndicate his own column, and keep all of the profits, or sell his column on royalty, to one of the several hundred national syndicates.

---

* Available from metropolitan libraries or send $2 to Editor & Publisher, 850 Third Avenue, New York, New York 10022.

There are two good reasons for starting your own syndicate (1) if you build up thirty paying newspapers as your clients you have attractive bait for an established syndicate, (2) you learn a lot by starting a syndicate of your own.

With the above mentioned *Syndicate Directory* before him, a writer knows exactly what competition awaits him. Let us assume you want to write an automotive feature. You consult this *Syndicate Directory* and immediately see that there are already 22 automobile features on the market neatly classified for your inspection. These include Car Crazy, Inside Auto Racing, Ray Carr Talks Cars, Teenage Driving Tips and The Driver's Seat.

If your own automobile feature does not compete directly with these, and if your idea is not too specialized (Fender Repair), you are ready to proceed. Simply by reading a classified list of syndicated material now available to editors, you may perceive an editorial hole you can fill.

If you find several syndicated features similar to the idea you had in mind, write the syndicate owning these features and get several samples of each. Possibly you can do better. Or possibly they are well done, but in this particular case the reader interest in such a syndicate may be so fertile that there is room in the field for another. This is a big country and there are 1,800 daily newspapers and 3,000 weeklies all buying syndicated material.

Thus, the *Syndicate Directory* of *Editor & Publisher* lets you make a common sense, inexpensive survey and feel the pulse beat of a gigantic industry.

I am now assuming that you have (1) selected a field (automotive, recipes, etc.) which you intend to enter; (2) investigated what daily or weekly columns are currently offered in this field; (3) learned whether your chosen field is popular with editors. For instance, there are two columns on chess, thirty-six about children and more than a hundred about women.

Which is best — to enter a crowded field with tremendous mass interest or to be a loner? That's why you have that little room with the table, the chair, the sofa and all those pencils. Only you can supply the answer.

After settling on *the kind of feature* you wish to produce, and with some grasp of the market, you are ready to write and sell it. Let's move on by answering two questions:

Do you live near a small town?

Do you know a small town newspaper reporter?

If the answer is yes to both questions you are ahead; but if the answer is no, you have no great handicap. Let's assume it is "yes." Write six samples of the syndicated feature you wish to sell. If the column is titled "Let's Talk About Dogs Today," and you plan a daily column about dogs, their ills, how to teach them tricks, how to feed and care for them, how to know them better, the personal rewards of owning dogs, why dogs become mean, advantages of each breed, etc., then write six samples. Type each separately on 8½ x 11 white bond paper.

How long should the column be? Rene Cappon, Supervising Editor of AP Newsfeatures, says: "Newspaper space is at a steadily greater premium, and the writer who can hold his column to 400 or even 350 words, on the average, stands a better chance. The shorter ones are harder to write, but by and large, brevity gives you an edge."

If your column is daily, mark on the first one *"Use Monday,"* on the second one *"Use Tuesday,"* etc. If your column is weekly, write on the first one *"Use first week."* and on the second *"Use second week."* On the top right corner of each page place your name, address, and title of column.

Now if you have a friend on a small town paper of about 5 to 10 thousand paid circulation, ask him to give your six sample columns to the editor with the following line of talk:

"My friend Jonathan Edwards of Parsonville is a pretty good writer. He has written a column and wants us to publish it. He intends to syndicate it himself and is offering it to us daily (weekly) free for a month (three months) to get it going. I read the column and like it. And by the way, if we run Edward's column he'll be glad to do any stringer work in Parsonville that we may need. Could we give the boy a break? I think he's got the stuff."

This, briefly, is the general sales talk your friend should give the editor of a small town paper near you to give your column its birth. If he succeeds, you're STARTED.

What if he fails, or you do not know a small town newspaper staffer? In that case, select some small town daily paper near you with a circulation in the neighborhood of seven thousand. Prepare samples of your work as explained previously, and mail them to a nearby newspaper in good editorial standing.

Write the editor a letter something like this, after first getting his correct full name:

"Mr. John Clarke Fullore
Yonkerstown Gazette
Yonkerstown, Ala.

Dear Mr. Fullore:

Enclosed with this letter are six complete samples of my daily feature 'Let's Talk About Dogs Today.' These samples offer you a good idea of the quality of my work. The interest in dogs, you know, is not confined to any one class of people, and I believe most of your readers like dogs and enjoy reading about them.

" 'Let's Talk About Dogs Today' is offered to you free for 12 consecutive insertions. I will prepare 6 more (in addition to the 6 enclosed) and send them to you 48 hours after your request. They will also be offered gratis.

"The reason I am offering these to you free is because I want to get my syndicated feature started. If your readers like 'Let's Talk About Dogs Today' and write you letters commending this new feature, I trust you will decide to continue it.

"As you helped me start, I will offer 'Let's Talk About Dogs Today' to you at that time, at a most reasonable rate—$2.00 a day, with exclusive rights within your active circulation territory. Possibly, later, you will care to write me a letter commenting on 'Let's Talk About Dogs Today' to help me sell it to other papers in nonconflicting circulation territories.

"Thanks for any attention you will give my column.

Sincerely,
Jonathan B. Edwards"

Type your column double spaced. Use an original or a first class Xerox copy, not a carbon. A carbon is harder to read and is too impersonal for this experience. Do not ask the editor for any criticism suggestions. Take yourself seriously in your letter, and the editor will take you just as seriously.

In typing your letter to the editor, don't emphasize phrases in red ink or use underscoring. Be leery of putting words in capital letters. Don't inter-line with after thoughts. In the column itself, avoid indicating that you feel the need of type tricks to gain reader attention, such as bold face, italics, caps or unusual punctuation. Play it straight.

It is unlikely that the first editor to whom you offer your column will accept it. His budget may be so tight he can't afford $2.00 a day, after your promised free samples have run their course. Perhaps, his per cent of editorial matter compared to advertising is such that he is seeking to reduce the number of editorial inches so he can print fewer pages. Maybe he caught Hail Columbia that very morning for spending too much money editorially and won't look at a new script today. Possibly the editor has a personal prejudice on the very kind of column you sent him. Or, does it make him think of a competing column, costing a little more, that he prefers? Or maybe he tried a similar column and it failed. Keep paramount in your mind the fact that there are 1,200 daily newspapers and until a full dozen intelligent, responsible editors turn your idea down *flat*, you aren't licked. And if they do turn your idea down, and you are the kind of a writer who will succeed, you will start over again on a new idea for a column. If you're woozy after the eleventh rejection, remember that most of the great novelists the world has known, each had to write three or four novels before their first one was accepted. Put that alongside writing twelve letters and six sample columns.

I strongly advise getting three or four papers to carry your column free. This gets you STARTED. It lets you demonstrate to yourself that you can produce a column periodically *and* on time.

When the first editor accepts your column on a free basis, keep right after other papers (you may have to mail or call on forty) until you secure three or four newspapers that will carry your column regularly and free. After you have done that, you are now ready to start syndicating your column for pay.

Secure a copy of Standard Rate and Data's "Newspaper Data Section" which lists all daily newspapers, their circulation, staff members, and other data you will want. The cost is $5.00 from Standard Rate & Data, 5201 Old Orchard Road, Skokie, Ill. A large metropolitan advertising agency might loan you a recent issue. *Editor and Publisher* also issues a *Year Book* which sells for $10.00. This lists every U. S. newspaper, its circulation, staff, address. Using one of the newspaper directories in conjunction with a map will keep you from offering your column to newspapers whose circulations compete.

The circulation of newspapers is confined preponderantly to the city in which they are located. Thus 40 miles away from any small town newspaper, you may offer the same column to another newspaper. In the case of large newspapers with over 150,000 daily circulation, you will want to keep your customers about 75 miles apart.

With a good directory of newspapers before you, and a map so that you will not offer your column into conflicting territory, list 100 newspapers who are your prospective customers. Then compose a letter somewhat similar to one of the following two examples. The first example assumes you have not enjoyed the experience of a "free start" with several papers; the second assumes you have.

Letter A to 100 Editors
    J. V. Kane
    Managing Editor
    Boston Telegram
    Boston, Mass.
    Dear Mr. Kane:
    Enclosed are six samples of my daily newspaper feature "Laugh Before Breakfast," offered to morning newspapers only. When set in type, this column runs between three and four inches daily.
    The humor is bright, genially satirical and suits the circulation of a metropolitan morning paper. The price for six columns a week is $9.50. I supply a larger

Sunday column under the same title, two samples of which are enclosed. The price of this Sunday feature is $2.00.

The features enclosed begin Monday, January 8th. To order, use the enclosed stamped addressed return envelope. Bills are payable at the tenth of each succeeding month for material used during the past month. Your order protects you against sale of this feature to any newspaper within 75 miles of you; if you wish a larger protection area, prices are slightly higher. Your order is cancellable at any time.

To users of this feature we have several novel circulation building contests that tie in with the feature, "Laugh Before Breakfast." If you wish to make use of this, there is no charge.

Sincerely,

Jonathan B. Edwards

Regarding the last paragraph, it would be possible to offer several daily small prizes (the paper pays for these prizes) for the best tag lines sent to limericks, for the last line of a joke, for the best ending to a short funny story, for the best children's brightest saying, remark, etc. Such a contest feature lets your column do double duty, and it is mentioned here to show you how to be a merchandiser. First, the reader-mail from the contest proves to the editor that your column is popular; second, by getting wind of this and handling it the right way, you can milk the editor for a testimonial which will help you sell the column elsewhere. If the column pulls no contest answers, you get no testimonial, and may lose the paper as well. This is a game in which you, the author, are on stage all the time to entertain and inform . . . or get canned.

Your letter should be typed on a good bond. Use printed stationery. Head your stationery "The_____Newspaper Syndicate," with your address and phone under it. Five hundred sheets of such stationery with envelopes shouldn't cost more than $25 at your local printers. Typographically, it wants to be simple. Use a single type face such as Caslon or Bodoni and only 1 color. Using any kind of art but the best, which is rare and expensive, may ham it up. Use standard 8½ x 11 white paper. Your aim is quiet good taste. Each letter should be typed individually and whenever possible addressed to the managing editor by name.

The addressed, stamped return envelopes (use No. 10) that you enclose with your letter and sample columns should also be printed. The outside envelopes in which you enclose the material you are sending should be kraft and any convenient size. You need not have these printed, but write your return address in the upper corner. If the package is heavy, you may want to send it "Special Fourth Class Rate—Manuscipt" (14c for the first pound), including an extra 8c for the First Class covering letter. Enclosing a stamped addressed return envelope is a matter of choice. Using it adds to your expense and increases the number of replies. To start such a syndicate described here, which offers your wares to 100 newspapers, cost a little over $100.

Where else could you start a business with the possibilities of such good returns for such a sum? In any other business, your rent, show cases, insurance, license, taxes, window display — in other words, your immediate out-of-pocket expense before a customer steps into your store, would be well over the very small investment needed to launch a well done feature. No amount of financing can sell a bum feature. I suggest, therefore, that before making your investment you submit your feature to some able critic, to get an outsider's viewpoint on your work.

The critic you seek is not a friend but a pro. Be willing to pay for professional criticism. Try to reach a newspaper editorial executive with a good education. Since you're trafficking with this man's judgment, you want him to be informed on a great deal more than current events.

Parlaying a Free Column

Let us now move on to Letter B. You will remember that when we started out to sell our column, we offered it free to a few papers, in the hope that about four would accept. Your four free customers, if you get them, may also be nice enough (if you are diplomatic enough) to write you a letter, or permit you to quote them, like this:

How To Syndicate Your Own Column

"Dear Mr. Edwards:

We have received reader response from our readers on your column 'Let's Talk About Dogs' and are considering giving it more prominent position. It certainly hasn't hurt us in the sale of additional dog food and dog boarding advertising.

Sincerely,
Watchville Gazette"

You need a letter from each of your free customers complimenting the circulation building abilities of your column. That's why the editor buys your column, and therefore, that's what you have to prove it offers. After you have secured three or four such letters from your free customers, set yourself down and compose a sales letter to 100 non-competing newspaper editors.

Enclose with samples of your work, a return envelope, a personally typed letter to the editor and a sheet of your stationery on which has been duplicated the kind words of praise which your free customers have given you. As an alternate to copying the "puffs" on a single sheet of paper, you can multilith them, making 100 copies of each for under $4.00. Stapling together 4 such letters, as evidence of the value of your column, is impressive. And, since your free column has been printed, enclose proof sheets of it instead of typed copies. The newspapers that published it will let you have 100 proofs of each column for about 2c each. You need to ask for these right away or the type will be killed. The proof sheets give you a shade more stature.

Letter B to 100 Editors

Dear Mr._____:

Several newspapers with circulation problems somewhat identical to your own have used our column "Let's Talk About Dogs" with remarkably fine results. I am enclosing some excerpts (or actual letters) received from papers using our column. Also enclosed are six samples of "Let's Talk About Dogs." The price of this column for your paper is $2.00 a day.

(Then follow with parts of the letter given in Example A.)

How much should you charge for your column? This depends

on the circulation of the paper to which you are selling it, plus their ability to pay a good rate, (second paper in a poor town?) plus the amount of territory that is closed out for you if you sell them. Thus the daily column that takes five inches of space would cost the New York *Daily News* $20.00 a day, and some little weekly paper off in northern Michigan, only $1.00. A weekly column that would cost the *Chicago Tribune* $25.00 a week might be sold to a tiny newspaper in central Alabama for $1.00.

In Chicago, New York, Los Angeles or Boston, big name columns that have been snow balled up for some years, will bring $50.00 a day. Syndicate authors earning over $50,000 a year are not rare. But our concern is the average rate of the writer starting off with a new column.

For such a writer, a daily column should bring no less than $1.00 a day and not much more than $5.00 a day for a big metropolitan daily. This estimate is based on a column running about 500 words, or less. On a weekly column of the same length, the rates should not go under $2.00 and normally not over $10.00 If you write to 100 newspapers and your column is good, your letter intelligent, neat and professional, you should be able to sell 3 papers from that one mailing. You need 15 papers buying a daily column, plus 18 papers taking a weekly column to show you any kind of profit for your work. It is not difficult to build a good column that is offered at a modest price to 30 papers in three years' time. And that means an income of approximately $50.00 a day for a daily column plus $90.00 a week for a weekly column. Of this $400.00 a week, about two thirds is profit after you have 30 papers. But you have added business details to your creative hours. If, instead of creating your own syndicate, you sell it to an established national syndicate, you will receive from 40 to 60 per cent of the gross revenue, depending on merit, bargaining ability and the years you remain with the syndicate.

Some syndicates charge authors to launch their columns. At this point you consult your Better Business Bureau. Selling your column to an established syndicate is the easy out and the best; but creating your own syndicate is enormously instructive and gives you a "come back" if the established syndicates say "no." Authors start both ways.

How To Syndicate Your Own Column

The weekly column runs longer than the daily column and does not carry such timely copy. Daily copy should be at the newspaper's office *no less* than 8 days advance of publication; and weekly columns should be at the publisher's office three weeks in advance.

The samples of your column that you send to editors should be multilithed on plain white paper, size 8½ x 11 and double spaced and stapled together. The cost is about $4.00 per page for 100. Thus, to duplicate six different columns, each on a separate sheet of paper, costs $24.00 for 100 sets of six. I would not advise buying a duplicating machine until your column shows life in the way of sales. Here is an itemized list of your expenses:

Stamps for mailing a campaign to 100 newspapers	$ 24.00
Mulitilith 100 sets of 6 columns, or 6 sets of proofs	$ 24.00
Editor and Publisher's Year Book	$ 10.00
Editor and Publisher's Syndicate Section	$ 2.00
Printing 300 sheets of stationery (good bond)	$ 20.00
Printing — 300 return envelopes	$ 3.00
300 heavy envelopes for mailing out all material	$ 4.00
Critical opinion of your column	$ 10.00
Typing 100 letters	$ 22.75
	$119.75

After you mail your first 100 letters, you may wish to change the letter before sending more. Thus your first 100 is in the nature of a test. Less than 100 is not a fair or accurate test.

Some of the country papers are issued weekly or twice a week. A list of them appears in N. W. Ayer's *Directory of Newspapers and Periodicals.* To such papers, you could offer your weekly column if the local big Sunday paper says "no." Their pay rate is low.

There remains but one point to be covered: copyright. The title itself cannot be copyrighted. You can however, register a title with the Bureau of Patents at Washington, D.C. To do this you must go to considerable travail, fill out a number of forms, supply a drawing of your title on special paper drawn to a specific size. Along the way, a lawyer will collect $50.00. The cost of registration is about $35.00. Until your column gets going, I don't think it is worth the money. Common law, and priority of use in interstate commerce protects you whether or not your title is registered.

The title, *Writer's Digest*, for instance, is not registered. Yet, it has established priority of use in 50 states.

Someone, however, might register and own the title *Writer's Digest* by simply sending $35.00 to the U. S. Patent Office and complying with the red tape. But, if that person tried to *use* the title, however, in any way whatsoever, it would be a matter of days before his business was stopped by injunction.

Registration legally proves the date you created a title. Active interstate use does the same thing. I would advise that you do not register your title. I have never heard of any editor stealing a title from a free lance column submitted.

Let's move on to copyright. You cannot copyright a manuscript unless you submit two *printed* copies of it with $6.00 to the Registrar of Copyright, Library of Congress, Washington, D. C., and fill out the usual form. When your column has been built up to a point that you can afford $6.00 daily for the copyright, do it. Until then forget copyright and registration. Be sure, however, to submit your work only to papers covered by an overall copyright. Otherwise, "publication" could put your column in the public domain and you couldn't copyright them later, say, in a collection in a book. Responsible people don't steal literary material. They may do it in the movies and in the song business (in fact they do) but in newspaper and magazine work, it's unknown. Editors who have been in business fifty years and worked for 5 or 6 publishers would have a hard time recalling a single instance of actual editorial theft of copy from a free lance writer— out of millions of such words received.

The last point is the way you present the "head" or title for your column. You may get an artist friend to draw a neat little one column, one inch deep "head," illustrating your title, or you may simply write the words out and let the newpaper box it in type to suit themselves.

The chances are that amateur art will hurt the first impression the editor will get from your column. Even the fact that your artist would draw the column in anything but India ink would show professional unawareness.

If you can't secure a professional design, it is best to do without an illustrated head and simply title your column with the words in question. Stay away from illustrating your head with asterisks, dashes, exclamation marks, etc. All you need to separate your column's title from the beginning of the title is two inches of white space.

And all you need to get started, judging by a lot of columns I read, is gut. But you need that to do most anything well.

With 30 or more papers on your string, the bargaining position between you and a nationally established syndicate changes. You may write them a letter of this general order:

Editor

NEA Service, Inc.

Cleveland, Ohio

I am enclosing proof sheets of the last 12 days of my column "Let's Talk About Dogs" now appearing in 30 daily newspapers; also proof sheets of my weekly column, of the same title, which is used by 28 Sunday papers. In addition, I have 32 small town papers using my weekly column on their date of issue.

The monthly gross revenue is $1,500 and I would like to get out of the business end to concentrate on my column which is three years old today.

I note that among the 6 animal columns sold by various syndicates there are 3 about dogs but your syndicate does not handle one. I offer you photostats of 17 letters from editors commenting on the value of this column to them; also 100 photostats of letters from readers.

If you enjoy reading this column and believe that you can sell it successfully, please drop me a line and perhaps I can visit your office.

Jonathan Edwards

Such a letter sent to the 10 major syndicates, one after the other, would be likely to produce at least one desirable contract for you to consider. In selling a column, or anything else, the big thing is to have a *product*, a continually upgraded product. Thus, the syndicate's sales effort hangs upon the author's ability to create this. Syndicates will pay better for something ready to sell than for something they have to develop for a period of months before it can reveal its market value to them. The nationally established syndicates need columns. Without them, they do not exist. They need you, the author. Naturally, they prefer columns which indicate clearly that there is customer acceptance. If you go to the syndicate with 20 or 30 newspapers on your string, you are in a better position.

Then, There Is an Easier Way

Many writers sell columns without ever trying to create their own syndicate. Here, you simply send the syndicate 12 sample columns and a letter on this order:

> Editor
> **Smith National Syndicate**
> Cleveland, Ohio
>
> I am enclosing 12 sample columns on "Let's Talk About Dogs" and am able to produce this daily. For 6 years I was a dog handler on the dog show circuit and I judged 4 shows this year as shown by the attached programs. My father was a veterinarian, and, for years I helped him with small animals.
>
> If "Let's Talk About Dogs" interests you, please let me know.
>
> Jonathan Edwards

The editor of a national syndicate has a right to expect some experience background from you if you invade a technical field such as politics, dogs, weather, fashion, bridge or the like. However, when you start your own syndicate by offering your column free, you need not place so much emphasis on this. A national syndicate is not interested in free deals. They pay for what they use and get paid for what they sell.

The nice thing about a daily column is that you get paid for every day; $200 a day is not rare at all. (Your checks, either from your own client papers or from the syndicate, are probably delivered to you weekly or monthly). However, you have to write it.

Following are the names and addresses of 22 national syndicates. One hundred others are listed in the Editor and Publisher Syndicate Directory (see bottom, page 177), and this includes the kinds of columns each syndicate offers. If you can't secure this syndicate directory, write to the syndicates listed here and ask for a list of their syndicated columns and you'll get a general idea of which syndicate is closest to your field of interest.

AP Newsfeatures
50 Rockefeller Plaza
New York, N. Y. 10020

Authenticated News International
170 Fifth Ave.
New York, N. Y. 10010

Buddy Basch Syndicate
771 West End Ave.
New York, N. Y. 10025

Black Press Service
166 Madison Ave.
New York, N.Y. 10016

City Desk Features
310 E. 75th St.
New York, N.Y. 10021

Chicago Tribune—New York Times
Syndicate, Inc.
220 East 42 St.
New York, N. Y. 10017

Chronicle Features Syndicate
555 Sutter St.
San Francisco, Calif. 94102

General Features Corporation
Times Mirror Square
Los Angeles, Calif. 90053

Glanzer News Service
223 Coldstream Ave.
Toronto 12, Ont., Canada

King Features Syndicate
235 E. 45 St.
New York, N. Y. 10017

Los Angeles Times Syndicate
Times Mirror Square
Los Angeles, Calif. 90053

Mel Martin Enterprises
P.O. Box 22505
Houston, Texas 77027

Mid-Continent Feature Syndicate
Box 1662
Pittsburgh, PA

National Newspaper Syndicate
20 N. Wacker Dr.
Chicago, Ill. 60606

Newsco Press Features
P.O. Box 91
Blairville, Pa. 15717

North American Newspaper Alliance
230 W. 41 St.
New York, N. Y. 10036

Register and Tribune Syndicate
715 Locust St.
Des Moines, Iowa 50304

United Feature Syndicate, Inc.
220 E. 42 St.
New York, N. Y. 10017

United Press International
220 E. 42 St.
New York, N. Y. 10017

Women's News Service
230 W. 41 St.
New York, N. Y. 10036

Universal Science News
314 W. Commerce
Tomball, Texas 66365

World Union Press
507 Fifth Ave.
New York, N. Y. 10017

The Best Job On Earth

By Kirk Polking

Every morning for a year I have waked to a wonderful thought — this is my day. All mine. Is there any greater feeling?

This gleam of freedom, this chance to make the world over my own way, was the thought that urged me to take the chance.

For six years I was the circulation manager of *The Farm Quarterly*, a *Holiday* size magazine for the big farmer who earns $20,000 a year or more. I was one of only three women in similar executive positions in the country. I had the daily ego boost of a retinue of employees, the flattery and attention of salesmen who wanted my business. Each day someone would help me do my job.

An envelope salesman drops in and wants to know what I'm going to do for a Xmas mailing this year. An editor tells me some fact that reveals to me a little more clearly what makes the farmer buy. Gently prodding, they all help me think creatively about my job; force me to accomplish something each day. I was doing a good job. I was appreciated. But it wasn't enough. Honestly, hogs bored me.

Everyone wants the feeling of completeness about his work. In many jobs like the one I held, you are helped by many people whose own success depends partly on you. As a writer, your fate is yours alone. If you fail, no one else can be blamed. If you succeed, the glory's all yours.

But can you work if no one puts a nickel in your slot and jogs you along to your duty? Will you keep a working schedule with nothing but your own sense of discipline for help? Will you get despondent with a rash of rejections and no one to compliment you? Why give up security for so uncertain, so lonely a job?

You already know my answer.

What Do I Need?

Well, then, what qualifications do I have to be a free-lance writer? I have an inquisitiveness about the world and how it works. What makes a plant grow? How does a dam work? What makes a human being laugh? Where is the 20th Century's universal man?

Curiosity then, about things and an interest in ideas was a start. Next problem was whether I could write. For some magazines, yes. But not well enough for others. As a teen-ager, I had been crushed when my submissions to *The New Yorker* were returned with a speed beyond the wildest dreams of the Postmaster General. My metier became the Sunday school magazines and Sunday newspaper articles like "I am a Teen-Age Animal Tamer"!

From such beginnings then, to basically the same article on an adult level ("My Business is Going to Pot" — about a young man who built a successful business with artificial plants) I sold, on my spare time, articles to various trade journals and how-to-do-it-magazines. My income from these ventures over ten years had been a little over $2,000. I was confident that if I quit my job I could find ideas and places to sell twice that much a year!

Okay, then, let's get down to business. How much money will it take to indulge this private dream?

I shared a basement apartment with a friend; liked good food and drink. I wanted enough clothes to be dressed tastefully even if not in the latest fashion. I could count on local males for some entertainment; would have to buy some of my own. I needed my car for trips and local interviews.

My estimated expenses for 1 year of free-lancing:

Rent: (Half of a shared apartment) . . . . $ 540.00
Telephone (½) (exclud. special long distance) $ 40.00
Food (½) . . . . $ 720.00

Stamps . . . . $ 45.00
Newspaper, magazine subscriptions . . . . $ 75.00
Photo supplies . . . . $ 100.00
Clothes, miscellaneous . . . . $ 250.00
Entertainment . . . . $ 175.00
                                                    ‾‾‾‾‾‾‾‾
                                                    $2,355.00

Like most budgets, this one forgot a few things, too. My car, a 1961 Chevrolet my teen-age nephew calls "the green beetle", sprung a few gaskets, requiring some unexpected expenses that amounted to $89.93. I discovered I needed a better light over my desk. My roommate decided we needed some new drapes. I had a bout with the flu which meant a doctor and drug-store bill. After a busy career with people, I found that being alone all day every day made me want to entertain more in the evening. That meant the food and liquor bills went up. The microphone on my tape recorder went bad. I missed my estimate by some $232.00. So much for the left side of the ledger.

First Year Income

Since I had previously been successful in selling short bits to *Popular Mechanics* and *Mechanix Illustrated,* this field was naturally my first choice. The pay is a minimum of 10 cents a word — much better than two penny trade-journal markets. I watched the local newspapers, subscribed to the Sunday sections of the leading papers in two big cities nearby for leads of this type. Two examples of the one-pager articles I sold to *Popular Mechanics* are:

"T.V.M.D." a picture story about a steeplejack whose job it is to make repairs and adjustments at the tops of 1,000-ft TV towers. "Autoboat", the invention of a local Procter and Gamble executive. This is a catamaran that he can drive down the river or on a lake by hooking up to the driveshaft of his ancient but well-built Packard. When he's ready to come ashore, he beaches the craft, folds up the catamaran and drives away.

I drew on my business background to make some sales to *Management Methods*. One short article described a "Suggestive Selling" gimmick of nearby National Cash Register Company in Dayton, Ohio. Another showed the way various industries use aromatic chemicals to help sell their products ("Sell with Smell").

Because the area in which I live has a number of manufacturers in the porcelain enamel and pottery fields, I garnered news items, photos, and special product information from these firms for *Ceramic Industry*, a trade magazine of this field.

I learned how to sell everything but the pig's squeal from the same story idea. A pharmaceutical magazine which bought a story of mine about a pet cemetery used two out of a series of some 24 pictures I had made to illustrate the 1,800-word article. I put together a picture series with fat captions and sold it to the rotogravure magazine section of the local Sunday paper. A color transparency of the cemetery's overall view with carloads of Sunday visitors I submitted to the "Interesting Places" section of the Chevrolet magazine, *Friends*.

Now, as you can see, most of these ideas are strictly reporting jobs with a modest amount of creative thinking.

But I was thinking, too. In my new-found solitude away from a business office, I entered into a lot of reading that I had put off before. This sparked some article ideas and I spent a great deal of time reading background material, interviewing and then drafting what I thought were brilliant query letters. I don't know if the ideas were bad, or if I am just caught in a web of editorial circumstances. I'd like to name three of my queries which did not sell to a top magazine. What was wrong?

1. *"Are You Accident Prone?"* After interviewing two accident specialists, and reading the scientific papers of a dozen others, I constructed a popularly written, true-false quiz containing established facts on the subject.

2. *"What Makes a Successful President?"* If we grant that no president can at once be an able administrator and a manipulator

of men, a voice of the people and a man aware of his moral responsibilities, a leader of practical legislation and a world symbol; then which qualities *are* most important in the long run for the welfare of the nation and the world? Cornell University's Clinton Rossiter points out that Lincoln was a shabby administrator, but a great leader of public opinion; that Jackson was truculent and a demagogue, but a man who stamped the presidential office with a new independence and authority.

I proposed to ask 10 leaders in various fields for their opinion on the 2 or 3 qualities that they think are the most important for a president to have and to name the man they felt was our most successful president.*

‡3. *"The Loot They Leave Behind."* Each year a forgetful public leaves thousands of big, little, funny, and important personal items on trains, planes, busses, and in their respective terminals. One year, American Airlines alone picked up $1 million worth on its equipment. Most of it is claimed or returned without difficulty. In other cases, the human dramas make interesting anecdotes. I queried every major carrier for reference material for this article. The article would carry a thumbnail reference to the general rules most carriers have for how long they will hold merchandise, who gets it when it is unclaimed.

This effort for a $500 sale failed. No top magazine wanted these three articles. Wasted time: one month.

---

*The article editor for a syndicated newspaper magazine section, after reading three queries from Miss Polking, commented to us:
"Yes, her queries do make sense to me. We have used an article on lost and found — it is a pretty standard subject, I believe. We also ran a piece by Eugene Burdick, the sociologist, on what makes a successful President. I have seen queries on accident proneness, too, but never a good one.
"It bcomes evident that there are a good many more reasons for turning down a suggestion than the single one of not liking it. We have had something similar, or we may have, for example, just too many quizzes on hand."
Another editor, commenting on the same three queries says:
"I am sorry to tell you the queries by Kirk Polking all fall short: the first query falls short because the questionnaire simply establishes a fact and goes no further. The second poses a question that is merely academic, and the third, since the subject isn't basically exciting, would depend largely on the anecdotes which would have to be *excellent*. In this last case, the writer would have to offer more than simply a query."
† 1. This piece was sold eventually to *Science Digest*.
‡ 3. This was localized and sold to *The Cincinnati Enquirer*.

Grimly, I returned to the bread-and-butter markets. The local newspaper offered a lead.

I saw an announcement that a local hospital was going to have a Youth Day where 170 high-school boys and girls would help run the hospital for one day in a job of their choice. I spent the day there taking pictures; sold the story to a hospital magazine.

I spent hours going through the *Writer's Market, Writer's Year Book, Gebbie's House Organ Directory,* issues of *Writer's Digest,* just to keep myself aware of the large variety of magazines published and to spot possible markets for which I could quickly shoot off a query or send a short filler.

A Ford Motor Co. house organ said they were looking for pictures with fat captions of Ford trucks used for unusual purposes. I sent a photo of my veterinarian's Ford F-100 ½-ton truck which he had compartmentalized for his veterinary supplies and surgical equipment. I called local Ford dealers for leads on other unusual buyers of Ford trucks. Ditto Dodge and GMC.

My veterinarian had a Motorola short-wave radio communications set-up in his truck. I wrote to Motorola's house organ with a photo of the vet using his set; queried a local service agency for mobile communications equipment to learn if there were any other sets in town being used in a unique way.

Mundane?

Yes.

Four cents a word?

Yes. And, I kept telling myself, I am more adept with each sale.

There are other leads a new free-lancer can follow up. Although most of the fraternal organizations—Elks, Lions, Rotarians, Legionnaires—have a club secretary who sends local news to their national magazine editor, there are often hidden stories in individuals who happen incidentally to be an Elk and have accomplished something special. *If being an Elk* helped them, so much the better. A little digging will uncover these.

But I don't really want to work hard at that kind of article. I'll do it to learn; not as a career.

What Is My Goal?

I want to learn to write clearly, entertainingly and with honesty. There is a simple way to say everything. I want to find it. Reading is one of the few civilizing pleasures left. I don't want to help kill it by writing that forces readers elsewhere. But I don't want to turn a clever *Time*-like phrase at the expense of truth.

I would like to write fiction that would make the reader's heart beat a little faster, his understanding a little deeper, his faith in his own powers a little stronger. But this is beyond me. Desire and ability pass each other every day without ever meeting. I don't know how to tell a good, moving story.

Among the readers of this book I imagine, are many persons like myself who find no trouble hitting the medium markets but fall short of *Harper's* or *The New Yorker* or *Sports Illustrated*. Why?

I asked one of the editors who was paying me five cents a word for trade-paper interviews what he thought of my style. The answer, like vodka, left me breathless, and I pass it on. Perhaps you can apply it. He said:

"You're logical all right, and that's what you concentrate on. To the creative writer, the logic of the piece, the story line, if you please, flows easily out of him. But, as he sits at his typewriter, or lies on a couch thinking up his next sentence, his mind spins off to those unique words and expressions that always simmer within him, and now, find their way on to paper.

"There are a whole host of *writer's words*—words that in a million years would never appear in a letter from a reader of *Modern Romances* to Henry Malmgreen, or in the average office typist's letter if she were asked to do one herself.

"These words are part of all our reading vocabulary and we respond to them, but the point is these words are part of the *writing* vocabulary of a creative writer.

"I do not suggest that you can step up the octane rating of a story by substituting such words for routine ones after the story is written. Rather I mean that the creative writer is something like a baseball infielder with one runner on base and no one out. He constantly thinks about a double play. It's there, uppermost in his mind. So with the creative writer. The better word, the right word, is inside him all the time champing at the bit to be used. You know the words I mean, here are four:

indelible, seer, cunning, flotilla. Used in a fresh connotation, they spark an entire paragraph.

"The creative writer is a killer. He wants to knock the reader out and he doesn't care too much who suffers. It's not the reader he's after, but a character, a person or an idea. But there he is, club in hand, lurking for the kill."

I'm not sure yet if he told me off, or just told me.

Some of the Problems

With a year's experience as a free-lancer behind me I have learned some of my weakness. I don't work hard enough. A friend calls up and says, "since you're not working now, how about a game of tennis this afternoon."

That's all right. It's one of the reasons you quit a regular job. But unless you have an independent source of income, you can't do it long.

I had to make several rules to assure myself of an income exceeding my expense; and to develop as a writer as well as a person:

1. I will get up at 7:30 and be at work no later than 9:00.

2. Each day, something must go in the mail.

3. Each week I will write at least 1,000 words of observation or comment to improve my style and general awareness.

4. Because pictures are so important to many articles and they add to the writer's income I will improve my photography.

5. To organize my time, I will line up interviews on the same day, library research on another and telephone calls another, so I can write uninterruptedly for longer periods.

6. I will get some exercise each day to get a change of pace from mental work.

There is another bonus in my new job. I have become more womanly. As a business executive I acquired a clipped telephone voice. I gave orders and they were filled. Some of these traits slipped over into my social life. They are not ones that men appreciate.

As a free-lance writer working from home, I am more relaxed, have become a creative cook and in general a more simpatico companion. Every new good-looking guy I meet wants to come over and make love in the afternoon!

At the end of this first year, I am not so cocky but still confident. I sent out 182 article ideas to some 65 magazines; saw 19 accepted and paid for. After deducting my regular expenses and special traveling expenses, I had to take $616 from my savings. This is half the sum I'd been saving as a career girl while enjoying new clothes whenever I felt like it, cream in my coffee instead of half and half, and a basketful of minor luxuries that I took for granted. You don't become a career girl easily. You start as a typist. Form letters. Billing. When I started, $50 a week was good pay. By the time you double your original wage, you've learned there's another difference between men and women. In careers, men get five to ten thousand a year more for the same job, the same work. They have families, children, education to pay for. You are a career girl and the job itself is supposed to be part of the reward.

As a free-lance writer, you earn equal pay for equal work. Nobody cares how old you are, where you live, or a whit about your personal life. You are what you are because of what you produce. White or black, man or woman, it is the creativity you produce that fetches both buyer and price.

I now admit I am not ready for the $1,000 sale. I will have to spend a little more time in the lower pay markets; continue to dig ideas of national interest and learn to write well enough for the bigger magazines.

I know I can do it. Any salesman can tell you if you knock on enough doors you will be a success. Free-lance article writing is no different. I love that feeling of freedom I have when I wake up in the morning. I don't want to prove that John D. Rockefeller was right when he said most people don't know what to do with it. It takes most new businesses more than a year to get a good start. To me, that $616 loss for the first year is an inexpensive ticket to the most wonderful and exciting year of my life.

Writing and Selling Greeting Cards

By H. Joseph Chadwick

If you're looking for a "fun thing" to do between working in your garden and bowling on Wednesday nights, if you're looking for a hobby because you've got some extra time on your hands, if you need extra money and want something you can "dash off" in the evenings after your serious job, then don't try to write greeting cards. They're not for you.

But . . . if you are willing to spend the time, blood, sweat, and tears it takes to learn the craft of writing greeting cards, then you could corner a piece of one of the most lucrative writing markets there is.

The greeting card market is lucrative, all right; but it is also one of the toughest to sell. Greeting card companies pay out over $400,000 a year to freelance writers, at base rates of from 50c a line for general verse material to $50 for a single studio card gag. But when I was editor of a leading greeting card company, I received well over 1,000 ideas a week—and bought an average of less than 1 percent of them.

Almost without fail, however, I bought ideas from two to three new writers each month, writers who had never before sold me an idea, and who, in some cases, had never before sold anyone else anything either. They started, just like you, with a blank piece of paper on a desk or kitchen table. Now there is nothing more awesome, more fearful, more dreaded by any writer than a blank piece of paper. It conjures, teases, demands, and—more often than we like to think— just sits there and defies us. But if you keep trying, somewhere an idea begins to take shape in a dim, seldom-used brain cell that has been storing up bits of information for just this moment to release them.

You pull, you pray, you tease the words out one at a time, and timorously put them down. This time, the words come out right. So you revise them, type them, make a copy for your file, and then, along with several others that you have prayed into existence, you send the idea off to an editor who sits somewhere in Cardland playing

201

god with your brainchildren, deciding coldly which of them he will reject and which he will give life to. You wait and try not to think about how many days and hours and minutes it's been since you mailed your ideas to him. Then one day your return envelope comes back—the return envelope that all editors insist you send along with your submissions, and which always gives you the feeling of carrying the rope to your own hanging—and in the envelope, hidden among rejected ideas, is a short, terse note saying: *"I am buying your idea B-RTY for $35. Our check will be along in about a week."* You rejoice! All is right with your world! You love the editor and the mailman!

And how did you get from that blank piece of paper to the smiling check? Well, first of all, there were some things you had to know, because there are rules to this game as to any other.

Greeting cards. What are they? The dictionary on my desk defines a greeting as an "Expression of kindness or joy; salutation at meeting; a compliment from one absent." But to greeting card companies, a greeting is plainly and simply a "me-to-you-message."

Remember those four words: ME-TO-YOU-MESSAGE. They are the four most important words you'll ever see or hear in your greeting card writing career. Remember them and use them in every greeting card you write, and all your troubles will be checks. Forget them, and you'll be able to paper your house with rejection slips.

Let's take a look at the different types of greeting cards that you'll be meeting in your writing.

Greeting cards can be broken down into six basic types: *conventional, inspirational, informal, juvenile, humorous,* and *studio.* Conventional cards are also known as general cards, just as informals are sometimes called *cutes* and *studio* cards are often referred to as *contemporary* cards. But don't let the names confuse you, you'll soon learn to recognize the six basic types regardless of what they're called.

Conventional cards are the backbone of the greeting card industry. They put the meat and potatoes on the table. Recent figures indicate that over 10,000,000 conventional greeting cards are sold every day of the year. To satisfy this insatiable appetite, practically all greeting card companies that publish conventional cards are constantly in the market for good verses. For these, they pay anywhere from 50c to $3.00 a line, depending on the size of the company and the quality of the verse.

The types of verse used in conventional cards range from those on the highly formal cards that might say nothing more than *Happy Birthday and best wishes for the coming year,* to the extremely sentimental verse that might say:

TO MY WIFE

I love sharing Christmas
The way we do, Dear,
I love being with you
To start the New Year
I love you for doing
The sweet things you do
That make me so thankful
I share life with YOU!

Inspirational cards are usually highly poetical and almost Biblical in nature. There is a fine line between *good* inspirational verse that can send a thrill through you and *bad* inspirational verse that is overdramatic and corny. It takes an excellent writer to jump the line into truly inspirational verse, but on the average, inspirational verse will bring the writer more money per line than regular conventional verse. Here is an example of a well written inspirational by Helen Farries, Editor of Buzza-Cardozo:

I THOUGHT OF YOU AND SAID A LITTLE PRAYER

This morning when I wakened
And saw the sun above,
I softly said, "Good Morning, Lord,
Bless everyone I love!"

Right away I thought of you
And said a little prayer
That he would bless you specially
And keep you free from care . . .

I thought of all the happiness
A day could hold in store,
And wished it all for you because
No one deserves it more!

I felt so warm and good inside,
My heart was all aglow . . .
I know God heard my prayer for you,
He hears them all you know!

Informal cards, often called *cutes,* are softer in humor and more sentimental than studios. They are, in general, written in prose and follow basically the same humor formulas that studios do. In most cases, the rate of payment for informal ideas is about the same as for studio ideas, although it might be less in some instances if the informal idea is going to be used on a lower price card. When reading informal cards, look for the often used play-on-words, the tie-in with the illustration, and the soft humor. For example:

> (Cute toy horse on cover)
> Forget your birthday? . . .
> . . . NEIGH! Have a happy!

Juvenile cards are written to be sent *to children,* usually *by adults.* Some juveniles are nothing but a design and verse, while others are elaborate games and mechanical toys, and some are even complete story books. The pay for juvenile card ideas is as high as it is for studio ideas and is sometimes higher. Juvenile story books may earn the writer a $100 or more a book. In general, however, the pay for juvenile ideas will run from about $20 to $50, especially for the activity ideas, like this one:

> *Hi there! Merry Christmas!*
> No need to wait till Christmas,
> Start having fun right now.
> Play Santa's brand-new *bingo* game,
> Inside tells you how . . .
> (Inside the card is a spinner and a
> bingo game that uses toys instead
> of numbers.)

Humorous cards, like juveniles, range from simple design and verse to elaborate mechanicals. In general, the verse is tied tightly to the illustration, and the card gains its humor both from the verse and from the humorous illustration. Often, illustrations of animals are used to represent humans, just as is frequently done on juvenile cards. The pay for humorous cards is about the same as for juveniles and studio cards, depending, of course, on how elaborate the humorous card is. The humor in humorous cards is more often amusing than hilarious, more cute than contemporary. For example:

> I hope your day is happy,
> I hope your day is pleasant . . .
> And what is more, I also hope . . .
> . . . You didn't expect a present!

Studio cards are the thigh-slappers of the greeting card industry. If you were looking for a handle for the type of humor in studio cards, it would have to be contemporary humor, the *now* humor, humor that is happening, that is living and breathing every day. Studio cards are a direct reflection of what you and I are laughing at today.

> COVER: You're like a vintage wine . .
> you get nicer with age . . .
> INSIDE: . . . but your keg is starting to swell!
> HAPPY BIRTHDAY

The pay for such ideas ranges from $10 to $50, and it rises if you put something on your studio card idea or make something move.

Armed with this much general information, how do you apply it to writing your own cards? Here's what Chris Fitzgerald, former Gibson Editorial Director, has to say. "The best place to observe greeting card writing is, of course, in greeting cards. This seems so obvious that it's hardly worth mentioning, but many aspiring card writers have little patience with studying published cards. They look at a few superficially, but can hardly wait to write *much better verses of their own.* This is only natural, but if you really want to learn this business you have to read, read, and read greeting cards. It helps to be on friendly terms with the folks who run your local card shop. Buy a few cards once in a while, and hopefully they won't mind your doing research. I am not suggesting that you plagiarize existing cards. Read cards to observe idea content, verse pattern, writing style, rhyme schemes and the like; but when you sit down to write, come up with your own verse. Sometimes you can paraphrase an existing verse. Paraphrasing—saying the same thing in different words—is actually a good way for a beginner to learn technique.

"Let's imagine that you begin with a published verse that goes like this:

> Just a little passing thought
> To give your heart a lift:
> The joy of having friends like you
> Is life's most precious gift.

The basic idea is *the gift of friendship.* After some head-scratching and paper-scratching you come with this spin-off version:

> Among the finest gifts of life
> Is friendship, good and true—
> The kind of friendship I have found
> So nicely in you.

Pretty good for a new writer, but it does have its faults. The last line is rather short; it's missing a whole beat, or foot, in meter. The inverted word order in the second line—the adjectives "good and true" are placed behind the word they modify, "friendship"—is an unnatural usage in colloquial language and the language of everyday conversation is always best for greeting cards. Back to the writing board.

"After a few whacks at it, you take care of the first objection by changing the last two lines to read:

> The special kind of friendship
> That I value so in you.

The inversion is not objectionable in this case, so you could consider the verse finished, and you might even be able to sell it. Maybe. Then again, you might try a different tack and rewrite your lines something like these:

> Friendship is life's finest gift,
> And from my point of view
> No friendship could be nicer
> Than the one I share with you.

"Now you're getting somewhere. One idea leads to another. You start by paraphrasing, you sample ideas, and you accept or reject words and phrases on the basis of whether they fit or not. Finding ideas and words that fit is where craftsmanship comes in. Once you determine what you want to say, you must choose your words to do several things at the same time:

(1) Your idea must be expressed as a complete idea; it must have a beginning, a middle, and an end.

(2) There must be coherence in your verse. Every line must be linked logically and smoothly with its neighbors.

(3) Your expressions must be conversational. High-flown language rarely comes off successfully in greeting card writing.

(4) You must write with emphasis and enthusiasm. It's necessary to create interest in that all-important first line. From that point on, writing your verse is a matter of developing your idea and bringing it to a peak of emphasis in the last line. Occasionally you will find that you have shot your wad too early in the verse, and whatever you say after that point sounds like an afterthought.

(5) You must do all of the above and at the same time make everything come out right in the meter-and-rhyme department. The ability

to versify comes naturally to a few; for most of us, it is an acquired skill, and the only way to develop it is to keep working at it until you find yourself thinking in meter and anticipating rhymes."

In the funny card (*humorous*, *informal*, and *studio* cards), paraphrasing, or *switching* as it is called there, is one of the best techniques used to get ideas. Ideas seldom descend like doves on a writer. You have to prime the pump, and switching is your primer. Switching means taking an existing gag and altering it, rephrasing it, cleaning it up, or making it more risque, modernizing it, changing it in some manner so that it becomes a wholly new and different gag. Switching can provide you with more material than any other method. You should practice it constantly, with every gag you read. How is it done? Start with this published card:

> Happy Birthday, and don't worry about being ship-shape . . .
> . . . a little bulge in the bilge never hurt anyone!

Now take the basic lead-in and change the punchline:

> Happy Birthday, and don't wory about being ship-shape . . .
> . . . a few barnacles on your bottom doesn't mean you're ready
> for dry dock!

Take the basic punchline and change the lead-in:

> On your birthday, don't worry if you're beginning to look
> like a waterlogged ship . . .
> . . . a little bulge in the bilge never hurt anyone!

Retain the premise of the gag and write a new version of it:

> Have a Happy Birthday and don't worry if you can't run like
> an athlete . . .
> . . . a little jig when you jog won't hurt you!

Retaining the premise of a gag and writing a new version of it is probably the best method of switching. It will give your ideas more freshness and originality, and at the same time insure that you are not staying too close to the original gag. For instance:

Original gag:

> COMIC: I love the way those southern girls talk . . .
> by the time they tell you about their past,
> you're part of it.

Switched gag:

> COMIC: I love the slow way those southern girls talk . . .
> you ask one of them to say *yes*, and by the time
> she says *no*, it's too late!

Switched gag:

> GIRL: I've just got to learn to talk faster . . . the
> other night that salesman fellow asked me if I
> would, and by the time I said no, I had!

A lot of switchable material can be garnered from published greeting cards, magazine cartoons, advertising slogans and promotions, joke books, humorous dictionaries, and whatever word-of-mouth jokes may be popular. Of all these sources, published greeting cards are probably the best and most logical source of greeting card gags.

For *juveniles,* as for conventional and studio cards, there is no end of places to get ideas. Look at the world as a child does. There are dozens of ideas on the toy counters of the 5 & 10, waiting to be adapted to juvenile cards. Watch the children around you. Florence Bradley, a prolific juvenile card writer, sold a "penny saver" card when she saw her son working on his coin collection. She sold a card for children in bed to make shadow pictures on the wall. And watching children look for the golden egg in an Easter egg hunt resulted in a game card that sold to Hallmark.

Florence says: "Some juveniles are simply verse cards, but they have a special kind of verse that uses colorful words and is musically pleasing to the ear. If your verse is about a child, give him a name. If you're writing about an animal, give it a funny name—the funnier, the better. For instance:

> This is Blabbit the Rabbit,
> And he's come to say,
> Someone as nice as you deserves
> A happy Easter day!

Talk to children on their own level, and be up-to-date with your verse subjects. It used to be downy ducks and teddy bears—and still is for the very young children—but today's well-informed youngster goes for rocket ships and astronauts.

"You can sometimes help to sell a verse by suggesting it be made into a mechanical card. That is, it would have something moving in some way when the card is opened. Three to nine-year-olds love mechanicals. If you write a verse about a boy playing football, carry through on your idea, and as the card is opened, have his leg come up and kick the football. A juvenile verse about a cat will sell faster if you have the cat move in some way when the card is opened."

Studio cards? Here's what Bob Hammerquist, one of the best studio card writers, says about them. "There simply are no rules-to-write-studio-cards-by. At best, you have to have an innate sensitivity for the particular brand of lunacy. I wish there was a secret, but there isn't. Part of the idea-gathering process is simply keeping your eyes and ears open, and thinking greeting cards twenty-four hours a day. On some secondary level of awareness, you stay constantly awake to all audible and visual funny business. TV, radio, movies, theatre, chatter over cocktails and coffee breaks, popular phrases, customs, issues, attitudes and anxieties, morality, narcotics, living costs, etc.), articles and cartoons in magazines and newspapers and office jokes. These sources result in ideas such as these:

COVER: Happiness is me
INSIDE: . . . when I'm with you.

COVER: I like you . . you're so . . . so . . . so . . .
INSIDE: . . . .'phisticated.

COVER: (Cute neuter)
Psssst . . . Hey you . . .
INSIDE: . . . you is sexy!

COVER: Here's a nice birthday card for you, just to show how tolerant I am!
INSIDE: Why, some of my best friends are old! ! !

"If you plan to write studio cards, it doesn't hurt to appreciate as many styles and types of humor as possible. There are outlets for all of them. Risque ideas or slightly blue material can be outrageously funny or plain smut masquerading as humor. Satire and parody can be subtle and penetratingly funny. They can also be smug, bitter, self-righteous, and just plain dull. You'll find quite a variety in the types of studio cards being sold, from the more reserved to the more earthy. The essential ingredient in all of them is, however, sendability —the *reason for* a greeting card. It has to be sendable, it has to relate to a situation. Somebody's having a birthday. Or someone is sick, or is having an anniversary, or is going on a trip, or is a very special type of friend. The card buyer buys because of one of these or similar reasons. He wants to communicate with people he cares for. Your job is to offer a choice of messages for the communication."

Now can we submit? Certainly, if you know the form to use. For general verse material, use a 3 x 5 or 4 x 6 card or slip of paper or a card dummy. (A card dummy is a sheet of paper or heavier material cut and folded to studio or humorous card size.) Neatly print or type your idea on the dummy as it would appear on the card. If you can illustrate your idea, however roughly, do so, but don't waste time writing word-pictures unless the idea depends heavily on the proposed illustration. On the back of each dummy or card, type a code number of some sort. The code number makes it easier for the editor to refer to your idea when writing to you and helps you in keeping records. Always keep a file card of each idea. On the back of each file card, keep a record of where and when the idea was submitted. Submit from 10 to 15 ideas at a time (this makes up a batch). Be sure to include a stamped, self-addressed return envelope. Keep the file cards for each batch together until the ideas (those rejected) come back. For ideas you write that use attachments, try to get the actual attachment and put it on your dummy; if you cannot, suggest the attachment. For mechanical card ideas, you must make a workable mechanical dummy. Most companies will pay more for attachment and mechanical ideas.

If you discount the money, are all the hard work and tears worth it? Here's what happened to an idea you sold. After it had cleared a number of hurdles in production, your card arrived eventually at the card rack in a store. Just a few hours after the clerk put the cards up, a beautiful lady walked in, picked up your card, laughed, and said "This would be just *perfect* for Harriet. It's *her* all over!" She rushed to the counter, paid for your card, and hurried out the door to send it to Harriet who lived in California and would be 29 (she says) on Saturday.

The blank piece of paper you started with, the paper you put words, humor, and sentiment upon, those little bits and pieces of yourself, ultimately reaches its goal, bringing happiness, gladness, maybe a tear or a laugh to not only one, but thousands of people all over the world.

Through the medium of greeting cards, you, the writer, have

reached out from your desk or kitchen table and touched the heart, mind, and soul of another human being.

In so doing you have enriched his life, and yours.

Think about it.

It's kind of a nice talent to have.

A representative list of greeting card markets follows:

Allied Paper, Inc.
1151 W. Roscoe St.
Chicago, Ill. 60657

Amberley Greeting Card Co.
P.O. Box 37902
Cincinnati, Ohio 45237

American Greetings Corporation
10500 American Road
Cleveland, Ohio 44144

Barker Greeting Card Company
P.O. Box 9010
Cincinnati, Ohio 45209

Buzza-Cardozo Greeting Cards
1500 South Anaheim Blvd.
Anaheim, Calif. 92803

Charm Craft Publishers, Inc.
33 35th St.
Brooklyn, N. Y. 11232

Creative Soul Design Studio
P.O. Box 29101
Cincinnati, Ohio 45229

Curtis Circulation Co.
Card Dept.
Independence Square
Philadelphia, Pa. 19105

D. Forer and Co.
18 W. 18 St.
New York, N. Y. 10011

Fran Mar Greeting Cards, Ltd.
160 E. 3 St.
Mt. Vernon, N. Y. 10550

Gallant Greeting Corp.
2840 W. Fullerton St.
Chicago, Ill. 60647

Gibson Greeting Cards, Inc.
2100 Section Rd.
Cincinnati, Ohio 45237

Hallmark Cards, Inc.
Contemporary Dept.
25th & McGee
Kansas City, Mo. 64141

Hinz Publishing Co.
Creative and Editorial Depts.
1750 West Central Road
Mount Prospect, Ill. 60056

Keep 'n Touch
P.O. Box 212
Framingham, Mass. 01701

Little Eve Editions
Blackberry Lane
Morristown, N. J. 07960

Mister B. Greeting Card Co.
3500 NW 52 St.
Miami, Fla. 33142

Moderne Card Co., Inc.
3855 Lincoln
Chicago, Ill. 60613

The Paramount Line
400 Pine St.
Pawtucket, R. I. 02863

Reed Starline Card Co.
3331 Sunset Blvd.
Los Angeles, Calif. 90026

Roth Greeting Cards
6417 Selma Ave.
Hollywood, Calif. 90028

Rust Craft Greeting Cards, Inc.
Rust Craft Road
Dedham, Mass. 02026

Sholom Greeting Card Co., Inc.
26 South 6th Ave.
Mt. Vernon, N. Y. 10550

Sunshine Art Studios, Inc.
45 Warwick St.
Springfield, Mass. 01104

United Card Co.
1101 Carnege St.
Rolling Meadows, Ill. 60067

Vagabond Creations
2560 Vance Drive
Dayton, Ohio 45409

Vaughn Card Co.
6001 Canyonside
La Crescenta, Calif. 91214

Warner Press Publishers
(*Sunshine* and *Regent* lines)
Fifth at Chestnut St.
Anderson, Ind. 46011

Sangamon Co.
Route 48 West
Taylorville, Ill. 62568

[Cards mentioned through the courtesy of the following greeting card companies: Buzza-Cardozo Greeting Cards, Gibson Greeting Cards, Inc., Barker Greeting Card Company, Hallmark Cards, Inc., and Keep 'n Touch Greeting Cards, Inc.]

LETTER FROM THOMAS WOLFE

I am working from six to ten hours a day; Paris has no more interest for me than Sauk Center. I sleep till noon, go for a walk, buy an aperitif, lunch, go to a book store and buy a book, read for an hour, then back to my room and work from four or five o'clock until ten at night. Then out to eat and walk, back at midnight or one o'clock, and at work till three or four.

I suddenly decided that we spend too much of our lives looking for ideal conditions to work in, and that what we are after is an ideal condition of the soul which almost never comes. So I got tired and disgusted with myself, went to a little hotel — not very French, I'm afraid, but very touristy — and set to work.

The thing I have done is one of the cruelest forms of surgery in the world, but I knew that for me it was right. I can give you some idea of the way I have cut myself off from people I knew when I tell you that only once in the past six weeks have I seen anyone I knew.

I am writing a book so filled with the most unspeakable desire, longing, and love for my own country and ten thousands things in it, that I have to laugh at times to think what the Mencken crowd and all the other crowds are going to say about it. But I can't help it—if I have ever written anything with utter conviction it is this.

Finally, the best life I can now dream of for myself, the highest hope I have is this: that I believe in my work and know it is good and that somehow, in my own way, secretly and obscurely, I have power in me to get the books inside me out of me. I dream of a quiet modest life, but a life that is really high, secret, proud, and full of dignity for a writer in this country.

You ask again if I look upon writing as an escape from reality: in no sense of the word does it seem to me to be escape from reality; I should rather say that it is an attempt to approach and penetrate reality.—Thomas Wolfe

Call It Experience

Call It Experience

By Erskine Caldwell

As well as I can recollect, now that I am in my middle forties, I had no desire, no urge, no inclination to be a writer when I was growing up between the ages of twelve and sixteen. But evidently something did happen, about the time I was fifteen or sixteen, and when I got to be twenty-one or twenty-two, I realized I wanted to write more than do anything else in the world. Not long afterward I confidently made up my mind to make my way as an author, with no sidelines attached, to the end of life. The first goal I set out to reach was that of becoming a published fiction writer within ten years' time. It was an easy vow to make. I was able to acquire the necessary determination and stubbornness of mind, but the ability remained elusive for a long time.

I entered the University of Virginia in September, 1922. Within a short time I had a job, the hours being from six p.m. to midnight, six nights a week, working as clerk-cashier-janitor in a pool hall near the campus. The salary of six dollars a week which I received, together with the money supplied by my parents, enabled me to pay for my room, board, textbooks, and clothing.

The subjects that interested me most at Virginia were English and sociology. After field trips to state hospitals and county old-age homes and similar institutions, I began writing about what I had seen. At first I wrote strictly factual reports, much like the newspaper correspondence I had done, but gradually I began using the same material as the inspiration for sketches and brief stories. I was more interested in writing my impressions than I was in composing theme papers on such English course assignments as "What Wordsworth Means To Me."

Writing became such an absorbing interest that I began experimenting with many forms of it. I began submitting jokes, mostly of the he-and-she variety, to *The Virginia Reel*, the university humor magazine. Edward R. Stettinius, Jr., who was on the editorial board of the magazine, spent considerable time arguing about what constituted college humor. Probably because Arthur Hawkins was drawing for *The Virginia Reel*, he maintained that comic drawings should take up more than half the space in the *Reel*. Ed was on the editorial board and I was not, and the publication continued to appear with nearly twice as much space devoted to art work as went to literary content. The jokes that I could not get into the *Reel* were submitted to, and some were published in, humorous magazines with national circulation. The pay I received was usually a dollar for each joke published.

Several students at the university were writing books, but I hesitated to make the attempt. Charles Wertenbaker wrote a novel, and James Aswell wrote a book of poems. Gordon Lewis, who owned a bookshop near the campus, encouraged me by saying he would publish any book I wrote if, in his opinion, it had extraordinary merit and promising sales prospects.

In my desire to learn to write fiction, and to get it published by Gordon Lewis or by anyone else, I frequently changed courses and even dropped out of the university for long intervals while searching for the way to write. I knew how I wanted to write and what I wanted to write about. I wanted to write about the people I knew as they really lived, moved, and talked. During the four years that I was an in-and-out student at Virginia, only two years of which were actually spent in residence, I worked a milk delivery route for a while in Washington, D. C.

Finally, in the spring of 1925, I felt that I could wait no longer to start doing in earnest whatever I was going to do in life. Twenty-one years old, and still two years short of graduation, I left Charlottesville and went to Georgia and applied for a job on *The Atlanta Journal*. I had no ambition to make journalism my lifework, but newspaper work was writing, and that was what I wanted to learn to do.

Hunter Bell, the *Journal* city editor, was not enthusiastic about employing anybody fresh from college, but he agreed to take me on as a cub reporter, on a trial basis, at a salary of twenty dollars a week.

I thanked Hunter gratefully for giving me a job and told him that I would be back in three or four days to go to work. I was half-way across the city room when he recovered enough to yell at me.

"Hey! Come back here!" he shouted. "What's this about coming to work three or four days from now?"

I told him I wanted to go back to Charlottesville to pack up my things and bring them to Atlanta.

"What things?" he asked interestedly.

"Well, I've got some books, and a few other—"

"Books! If I'd known you think more of some bologna-stuffed books than you do about a newspaper job, I'd never have hired you. I think I'll take that job back, anyway. I want a reporter—not a bookworm!"

"All right, Mr. Bell," I said meekly, "I'll stay and go to work right away."

"Yeh. That's more like it, Caldwell. Now find yourself a typewriter and call up all the undertakers in town and get some obits."

There was much to learn, and unlearn as well, about the writing of a simple news story. First of all I had to put aside the wordy way of writing I had got into while working as a string correspondent several years before, and then I had to acquire the skill to write what Hunter Bell considered a readable news item.

The city editor would begin his copy reading by whisking a soft-lead pencil over a three- or four-hundred-word story about a fire or a holdup or an accident until there were perhaps a dozen lines left, and then he would hand it back to me. This was a realistic course of instruction in writing, completely different from anything

I had learned in English courses anywhere, and from that time forward I was glad something had prompted me to go to work on a newspaper.

Margaret Mitchell was a feature writer at that time on the staff of the *Journal's* Sunday magazine and her desk was on another floor of the building. Hunter used various means to try to persuade Peggy to write special stories for him and, although he rarely succeeded, he refused to stop trying, because he considered Peggy to be the best writer of human-interest stories on the paper. Frank Daniel, a reporter, whose desk was next to mine, told me that Peggy was going to resign and leave newspaper work to write a novel she had planned for many years. Hunter refused to believe it until she did not come to work one morning. All he would say then was that writing books was a fly-by-night occupation and he hoped nobody else on the *Journal* would ever make the same mistake.

It was during this time, the fall and winter of 1925-26, that I had actively engaged in the profession of fiction writing. I had been deeply impressed by a book, *The Short Story's Mutations,* that Frances Newman had edited the year before, and now almost every day Frank Daniel, who was a close friend of hers, brought to the *Journal* city room, over a period of several months, a typescript page of the novel Frances was working on. Each page was a complete day's work on *The Hard-Boiled Virgin.* The finished page, so neatly typed and without corrections, always looked as if it had been written with ease and without laborious revision, but Frank assured me that it was the final result of a full day's rewriting.

I would go home in the evening and write short stories and mail them to magazine editors in New York. The stories, no matter how many times I rewrote them, were always returned, usually without comment, with unfailing promptness. I received so many rejection slips, and such an interesting variety, that I pasted them neatly in a stamp collector's album. The only consolation I ever got out of them for many years was in visualizing how big a celebration bonfire I could make with them when I had my first short story accepted and published in a magazine.

Before the end of 1925 I wrote to a number of newspapers in Alabama, Georgia, and the Carolinas saying I would like to write reviews for their book sections. Only one reply was received. This was a prompt, enthusiastic letter from Cora Harris, the editor of the Sunday book page of *The Charlotte Observer*.

Cora said she had been looking for somebody to help her with reviews for a long time, that she would be delighted to send me some books for review, and, in fact, was mailing half a dozen that same day. She expressed regret that she would not be able to offer payment for the reviews, but added, however, that I could keep the books.

I was having trouble holding on to enough of my salary to pay the rent, among other things, and I had hoped to be able to earn a few dollars a week in addition to my salary of twenty dollars. Frank Daniel told me that I would probably be able to sell any of the review copies I did not wish to keep, and I agreed to contribute reviews to the *Observer*. Within a short time I was writing notices of a dozen or more books a week, and I found that the more reviews I wrote, and the quicker I mailed them to Charlotte, the more books I received. I sold a few of the mystery stories and some of the esoteric novels at a second-hand bookshop on Forsyth Street, usually for a quarter each, but kept the greater portion of them. At the end of three or four months I had several hundred volumes of novels, poetry, biography, anthologies, and how-to books on practically all conceivable subjects.

It was pleasing to receive, early in 1926, a letter from Cora Harris, informing me that the reviews I was writing were now appearing each Sunday in *The Houston Post*, in addition to *The Charlotte Observer*, and saying that I could look forward to receiving even more books for review in the future. I felt sure now that the reviews were being syndicated that I would begin receiving some payment any day. Soon books began arriving from Charlotte by the score several times a week. My room was stacked to the ceiling with them. Still looking forward hopefully to the day when I would receive at least token payment for my reviews, I read more rapidly than ever or looked more closely at the jacket of the book, and wrote briefer notices. But still no payment came.

Writing as many reviews as I was doing, an additional two or three was no strain, and I began contributing to the *Journal's* Sunday book-review page. I was paid two dollars each for the reviews printed in the *Journal*.

After six months on the *Journal* I was given a five-dollar-a-week raise in salary by Hunter Bell and initiated into the local brotherhood of reporters.

In the midyear of 1926 I decided my next step should be to give up my job and leave Atlanta. I had worked on the *Journal* for a year, I had written perhaps forty or fifty short stories, not one of which had been published, and I had about two thousand volumes of fiction and non-fiction I had been given in lieu of pay for reviewing. Besides, I had saved almost two hundred dollars.

All wisdom and human experience aside, I was going to quit my job and devote full and exclusive time to the writing of short stories and novels. I promised myself that any occupation, other than writing, that I engaged in would be temporary and solely for the purpose of staying alive, keeping a roof over my head, and being adequately clothed. I put aside the next five years in which to accomplish my ambition, with the reservation that I would take an additional five years, if necessary. I had no idea how I would support myself and fulfill personal obligations until I could learn to write fiction that editors would pay for, but that did not seem important at the time. I was confident that I would find a way when the need came.

After coming to the decision, and after making up my mind not to let anyone talk me into changing it, I then set out to choose some place in which to live. Except for several months spent in Pennsylvania, I had lived all my life in the South, and I wanted to be where I would find a new and different perspective. I intended to write about Southern life as I knew it and it seemed to me that I could best view it from a distance. Going abroad did not appeal to me; I wanted to live somewhere in the United States. In addition to the promise of inexpensive living costs, the State of Maine seemed to be a faraway place on the map. I decided to go Down East.

I began packing my books in wooden boxes for shipment by freight. I did not know what I was going to do with nearly two thousand review copies, especially since I had already read the ones that interested me, but they represented my only material possessions and were too valuable to give away or sell cheaply.

Frank Daniel, even if he had misgivings, gave no indication that he thought I was taking a misguided and foolhardy step. He even went so far as to say that if he thought he had the ability to write fiction successfully, he hoped he would have the courage to do what I was about to undertake. He had already made up his mind to continue his newspaper career.

On the other hand, Hunter Bell tried to forewarn me of what I could expect if I insisted upon going recklessly ahead. He described a miserable future for those unfortunates in life who expected to live, eat, and walk the earth without the security of a job. After I had given two weeks' notice, Hunter still tried to get me to change my mind. He gave me several assignments seemingly calculated to show me what I would miss if I left the paper.

"See there, Erskine?" he said earnestly. "You're too smart to want to take a chance writing books. Everybody knows it's a fly-by-night thing. Broke most of the time, and friends afraid to trust you for a few dollars until pay day. Even the loan-sharks are scared of it. If you stay here on the *Journal*, you know I'll give you a chit to the cashier for an advance against a week's salary anytime you need it." He stopped talking for a moment and watched me closely. "Now, do you still want to throw it all away?"

I told him I did.

He puffed on his cigar for a while, at the same time rolling it over and over in his mouth with his fingers. He continued to look directly at me, his expression unchanged.

"Yeh?" he said after several moments. "Well, so long, Erskine. Hope you don't have it too hard from now on, but you can always count on me to feel sorry for you."

Hunter then got up and walked away.

At the end of the week I left Atlanta for the State of Maine.

(After a summer and winter in Maine, Caldwell decided to head South again.)

Restlessness, wanderlust, and an unconquerable urge to go somewhere had always kept me from being content for long at a time. When we were living in Prosperity, South Carolina, and I was six,

I left home for the first time, running away to spend a day and part of a night in a livery stable before my parents could find me. When I was nine and selling afternoon papers in Staunton, Virginia, I got on a Chesapeake & Ohio passenger train with an armful of papers one night instead of going home; the train was stopped and I was told by the conductor never to ride on it again to Cincinnati in order to sell my papers. As I grew older, and I was now twenty-four years old, it became more difficult for me to stay in one place long at a time. Often I would find myself wondering what people might be doing at that moment elsewhere in America, in hundreds of villages and small towns across the country, in such cities as Denver, Grand Rapids, Spokane, Toledo, Shreveport, Des Moines, and I would want to leave right away to find out.

The fact that we had exhausted our supply of potatoes and fire-wood was to me not a misfortune; I now had good reason to go somewhere and the five-year-old second-hand Ford which I had bought with my savings in Atlanta had always been capable of one more trip. One of the reasons I so quickly gave up my job on the *Journal*, I suppose, was because I had to have freedom to travel whenever I could make the opportunity. And the occupation of writing, it seemed to me, was not one that required a settled existence.

I first went to Charlottesville and then to Augusta. For several weeks I lived in a one-room cabin in the piney woods near Morgana, Edgefield County, South Carolina, eating a can of pork-and-beans three times a day and writing for sixteen or eighteen hours at a time. After a while I went to Baltimore and lived on lentils and wrote short stories in a room on Charles Street. When money gave out, it was spring. I returned to Maine.

This time, early in June, endlessly fighting black flies in the woodlot, I began cutting rock maple, sawing it into heater chunks, and seasoning it in the sun and wind. I would cut wood during the day and hoe potatoes in the long purple twilight, and, when night came, I would sit down and work on a short story. At that time of the year, in that latitude, it was broad daylight at three o'clock in the morning when I went to sleep for a few hours. Time seemed to go so swiftly and there was so much to do that some nights I would stop the clock or turn the hour hand backward while I was at the typewriter.

I had written dozens of short stories during the past twelve months, in Mount Vernon, Augusta, Morgana, Baltimore, and I had the feeling that they were getting better, or at least more readable, all the time. For one thing, I was beginning to be able to form and shape imaginary incidents and events into the kind of story that produced the effect I wanted it to have on me as a reader. I tried to write with only myself in mind as the reader, just as if no one else would ever read it, believing that a writer himself must be pleased with a story before others could be. I had no faith in my ability to analyze fiction as a critic, and I would have been mistrustful of my own findings, but instead I looked for intensity of feeling in a story, weighing its emotional effect on some inner balance. If a story I had written appealed strongly to me, regardless of lack of conformity to the style of traditional fiction, I was amply satisfied with the result. The time would come, I hoped, when others too, not excluding editors, would accept it as being the only possible way that that particular story could have been written, either by me or by anyone else, to produce the sensation it gave.

Equally important to me was my belief that the contents of a story was of greater importance, for enduring effectiveness in fiction, than the style in which it was written. Content was the basic material of fiction—the things in life that one told about, the thought and aspiration of men and women everywhere, the true-to-nature quality of fictitious characters who never once lived on earth but who gave the reader the illusion of being real people.

I was not writing about real people, then, but about the acts and desires of imaginary ones who, in a successful story or novel, were so convincingly depicted that they should seem more like actual persons than living people would be. Naturally, all fictional personages are to some extent created from the recollection or observation of living people by the author, for otherwise people in novels and short stories would have slight resemblance to human beings. In my way of writing, I strove to take directly from life those qualities and attributes in men and women that would, under the circumstances I was about to invent, produce in a telling way the ideal characters for the story I wanted to create. Rarely, if ever, was any such fictional character not a composite one.

It was during this period, the year 1927, that I began getting with some frequency short notes from editors instead of printed rejection slips. Even though no magazine accepted a story, at least now and then an editor would reject my work with comment.

There was always something, however, that prevented the story from being published; it was too long, too brief, too informally written, too grotesque for readers of the particular publication, too realistic in presentation for the tastes of the editorial board. It was surprising how many reasons, logical and far-fetched, could be found for not accepting a story.

In addition to these terse editorial rejections, I sometimes received advice. I was not adverse to advice in principle, as long as it conformed in the main to what I was going ahead and do anyway, but it always seemed to me that the advice I received was surely intended for somebody else and had been directed to me in error.

One editor's advice was to make a careful study of the type of fiction that was published in his magazine and try to write as nearly like it as I could. Another said there was a good future in writing articles on assignment for certain trade publications on such subjects as home decoration, floor coverings, and furniture styling. One editor went to the trouble to write a fairly lengthy letter advising me to give up trying to write short stories, saying that in his opinion I would never be able to make a go of it and that the heartache of doggedly persisting would make my ultimate failure more difficult to bear.

All this was interesting correspondence and it gave me something to look forward to receiving in the mail, but it was neither rewarding nor promising. In order to keep several dozen short stories continuously making the rounds of editorial offices, a quantity of postage was necessary. There were certain semi-necessities of life, too, such as sugar and salt and shoes, which I felt I did not wish to do without. When money was needed the only thing to do was to pack two suitcases with copies of books I had received for review, take a bus to Boston, and visit second-hand bookshops. I may not have originated the twenty-five cent book business in America, but I believe I helped it get off to a good start in Boston.

During the early part of 1929, a little more than six years after I first began trying to write fiction at the University of Virginia, I received the first letter of its kind I had ever found in the mail.

The letter was from Alfred Kreymborg and it said that he and the other two editors of *The New American Caravan*, Lewis Mumford and Poul Rosenfield, were accepting for publication in October a short story I had submitted. The title was *Midsummer Passion* and it was a story with a Maine setting about a brief but violent incident having to do with a farmer who was passing a neighbor's house one summer afternoon. *Midsummer Passion* had been written the year before in Mount Vernon and it had been submitted to ten or twelve experimental magazines within the past twelve months. I did not discover until much later in the year that one of these little magazines, *transition*, edited and issued in France, had retained a copy and published the same story, and, without my knowledge, had changed the title of the story to *July*.

The New American Caravan was an anthology that appeared once a year and it was not a magazine. The amount to be paid for the story was less than twenty-five dollars, but to me that was of little matter; what was of prime importance was the fact that somebody somewhere had at last accepted one of the short stories I had written. The accumulated disappointment of many years was suddenly and completely erased from memory.

As the result of the good news from Alfred Kreymborg, I began submitting stories to magazines in batches of six and seven at a time. Within six months, stories were accepted for publication in *transition*, *Blues*, *The Hound and Horn*, *Nativity*, and *Pagany*. All of these were so-called little magazines without general circulation, and payment, if any, was even smaller than that offered by *The New American Caravan*. The total amount I received that year for these first six published short stories, as I recollect, was less than a hundred dollars. I would gladly have let them be published for nothing at all, because such experimental magazines constituted the only workshop I had access to. My foremost aim in life, still, was to become an accomplished writer; if I could approach that, I felt confident that any rewards coming to me would take care of themselves.

When I recovered to some extent from the excitement brought on by the letter from Alfred Kreymborg, I filled a suitcase with as many manuscripts as I could carry and took a bus to New York. I had twelve dollars, a round-trip bus ticket, and a copy of the first edition of *Sister Carrie*, by Theodore Dreiser, when I left Portland. I had hopefully saved the book, for which I had paid thirty-five cents in a second-hand bookshop in Atlanta and which was said to have a value several times its original published price, for just such an occasion, and I planned to sell it to help pay my expenses to New York.

With the affluence of an about-to-be-published author, I registered at the Manger Hotel (later the Taft) on Seventh Avenue at Fifty-first Street. The daily rate for my type of accommodation was two dollars, and I had enough money to stay four nights, even if I did not sell *Sister Carrie*, provided I limited the cost of meals and cigarettes to a dollar a day.

After the first full day in New York I had spent more than a dollar for food alone, and so I took the book to a dealer in first editions on East Fifty-ninth Street. The dealer inspected the copy and immediately declared that it had value, but just how much he was not ready to say. He suggested that I leave the book with him until the next day, and that in the meantime he would show it to a customer who lived on Long Island. I left it with the understanding that I was to come back the following morning to receive the current price.

My suitcase contained a little of everything in literary categories. I had several novelettes, portions of unfinished novels, poetry, jokes, essays and dozens of short stories. I had no plan of disposing of these wares, but I hoped in some way to get them published. However, after several unsuccessful attempts to get into editorial offices, I realized that it was more difficult to secure the attention of an editor in person than it was by mail.

I was not familiar with the characteristic functions of authors' agents, but it seemed to me then that it would be wise to make the acquaintance of one. Selecting an agent at random from the telephone book, I made an appointment to see him in his office. When I got there with my suitcase of manuscripts, the agent, whose name I have forgotten, took a long hard look at the contents and told me that I would have to leave everything for him to read at a later date. The later date was so indefinite that I decided that it was not something I wished to do. As I was leaving the office, the agent again asked me what my name was. When I told him, he remarked that there was at least one matter we would not have to worry about; he assured me that I had as good a name as any for literary purposes and it would not be necessary to change it to something else.

The next morning I went to Fifty-ninth Street to keep the appointment with the dealer in first editions, optimistically hopeful of receiving ten or twelve dollars for the book. As soon as I spoke to him, he disclaimed any knowledge of me or of what I was talking about. Furthermore, the dealer said that he had never seen me before in his life. I reminded him of the conversation we had had the day before, I described the book I had left with him, and I even remembered well enough the tie he had been wearing to describe that, too. He angrily claimed that I was trying to make trouble of some sort and threatened to call the police if I did not leave immediately. I had no way of proving my story, and there was nothing I could do but go. I remained slightly hungry the remainder of the time in New York.

Alfred Kreymborg heard by some means that I had brought a suitcase full of unpublished manuscripts to town and he suggested that I let a publisher read several of the longer stories or novelettes. I gave one of the novelettes to Erich Posselt, an energetic, dapper young man, who was the editor of a publishing concern called The Heron Press.

It seemed to me, although I could have been wrong, that Erich had no office at all, but conducted his affairs in a taxicab. I met Erich by appointment several times, and on each occasion I recall meeting him at a specified time at a designated corner on Madison Avenue. He would drive up in a taxi, ask me to hop in, and we would ride slowly up and down Madison Avenue in the vicinity of Murray Hill for half an hour or longer while he talked and I listened. After two such meetings with Erich, I was psychologically prepared to accept his offer, on his terms, to publish the novelette I had given him to read. I was so excited by the prospect of having a book published that, if Erich had made the request, I probably would have signed over to him my rights to the whole suitcaseful of manuscripts.

When the contract was signed for the novelette, it was then that Erich let it be known that he was going to publish the book under the title of *The Bastard*. It seemed to me to be an unusual title for a book of fiction, but I assumed that Erich knew the business of publishing far better than I.

In October, shortly after the publication of *The New American Caravan*, the novelette appeared in a costly limited edition of eleven hundred numbered copies with full-page illustrations by Ty Mahon. A few weeks later in Portland I received word from a county official that, although he made no claim to being a literary critic, he did know what he saw when he looked at pictures, and consequently considered it his duty to declare that the book should not be offered for sale in Portland.

In the foggy gray autumn at Cape Elizabeth I received one morning a briefly worded letter from Maxwell Perkins, the editor-in-chief of Charles Scribner's Sons, in which he said that he had read one or two of my stories in small publications and that he would like me to let *Scribner's Magazine* see some of the unpublished stories I might have on hand. This was the first time anyone had invited me to submit manuscripts for consideration and, since *Scribner's Magazine* could undoubtedly be classified as a commercial magazine of general circulation, to me it meant an even longer step forward than the actual printing of my work in *The New American Caravan* and the little magazines.

The letter touched off a three-month orgy of writing, the intensity of which had never before been reached and which I never equaled afterward.

To begin with, I sent Max Perkins a short story a day for a week. Each story was promptly declined by return mail, but I was in no mood to accept discouragement. After that, I settled down to a strictly enforced routine of completing two short stories a week.

As fast as Max Perkins rejected a story I sent it elsewhere. Most of these stories were accepted by *This Quarter*, *Pagany*, *Hound and Horn*, *Clay*, and other little magazines. By the end of February I thought I detected in Max's letter of rejection a decided softening of attitude toward my work. Stories were being returned less promptly, which I took to mean that he was giving them more consideration, and besides he seemed to have exhausted his stock of reasons for rejection. It may have been that he had become fatigued by my dogged persistence, but, nevertheless, his letters were increasingly less formal and more friendly and encouraging.

Erich Posselt asked me to send him another novelette, and I promptly did so. By the time it was published later in the year, Alex Hillman, who had been one of the principal owners of The Heron Press, had for some reason taken over Erich's duties as editor. Alex formed a new publishing company and brought out the novelette, which was called *Poor Fool*, under the imprint of The Rariora Press and in a limited edition with illustrations by Alexander Couard. Alex had an office—located in a conventional building and not in a Madison Avenue taxicab—for the transaction of business; but, nevertheless, either because of the efficiency of his organization, or of the lack of it, a misunderstanding arose and I never received a copy of the book.

But at that time I was too engrossed with other matters to worry about the business details connected with the publication of a novelette. During that period the main objective in life as far as I was concerned was to break down the editorial resistance of *Scribner's Magazine*.

Week after week I wrote a new story and immediately mailed it to Max Perkins. Some of the stories had New England settings, others had Southern background. My mind seemed to find an inexhaustible supply of things to write about; the difficulty was in finding time enough in which to write as much as I wanted to during such a relatively short period as twenty-four hours had come to be. For a while I stopped winding the only clock in the house, but as even the sight of it was discomforting, I finally came to the practice of keeping it stored out of sight. As fast as a story was returned, I sent it elsewhere until it was accepted. Postage became a greater item of expense than food and cigarettes.

It was shortly before the March thaw when I received a letter from Max Perkins bringing word that my three-month campaign gave promise of ending in success. Max said that he had decided to accept one of my stories for publication in the magazine. One was to be taken, it was explained, but at that writing he had not made up his mind which one it would be.

By looking at the chart I kept, which traced the travels of stories from one magazine to the next, I could see that Max was holding five stories from which to make the selection. My immediate fear was that he might change his mind—that the already tottering economic structure of the nation might crumble—that anything could happen before he actually printed one of my stories in the magazine. I went to work at dusk that evening to supply him with enough material to enable him to make his choice without further delay.

After two nights and a day I had completed three new stories. These, together with three additional ones which I selected from the stack on my table, made a total of eleven stories for him to consider. And this time, instead of hurriedly getting the new stories into the mail, I thought it would be wiser to take them to New York in person. There was, I reasoned, the possibility of a train being wrecked, causing a serious delay in the delivery of the mail.

During the overnight bus trip from Portland to New York, I was kept wide awake with forebodings of misfortune. By the time the bus had passed through Hartford, not long after midnight, confident aggressiveness had become a dubious asset, and I was questioning the wisdom of what I was doing. I had never seen Maxwell Perkins, my only contact with him having been through correspondence, and by daybreak I was beginning to visualize him as a fearsome person who would angrily resent the intrusion and become prejudiced against my work.

Clutching the envelope of manuscripts, I spent the time walking up and down Fifth Avenue in front of the Scribner Building from about eight until shortly after ten o'clock in the morning. For two hours I tried to think of a reasonable excuse to offer for presenting myself without invitation, but nothing would come to mind that sounded persuasive and effective. When ten o'clock passed, I crossed the street, feeling that what little remaining courage I had was rapidly vanishing, and took the elevator to the editorial offices.

A pleasant young woman immediately asked me what I wanted. Uneasy in the surroundings and by then thoroughly unnerved, I told her merely that I wished to leave an envelope of manuscripts for Maxwell Perkins. She asked if I would like to see him, and I hastily said I did not. As I was turning to go, she asked if I would like to leave a message with the envelope. I spelled out my name and said that I was going to be at the Manger Hotel for the next two days. Then I hurriedly took the elevator down.

When I got to the hotel, I went to my room and sat down to wait. Reason told me that it was foolish to be waiting, but nevertheless I could not admit to myself that the trip had been in vain, and I hoped that Max Perkins would phone me there instead of writing a note to me at Mount Vernon. I left the room only long enough to hurry down to the street and eat a sandwich and buy several newspapers, and at nightfall I went to bed and lay tensely awake until past midnight trying to find the necessary courage to phone Max Perkins if he should fail to call me before I left town.

At six-thirty I was up the next morning. I had eaten breakfast, bought more newspapers, and was back in my room waiting again by eight o'clock. It was midmorning when the phone rang. The sound was startling at first, but it was so pleasing to hear that I let the phone ring twice before answering it; I was certain there was only one person in all of New York who would be calling me.

As I remember it, the conversation was like this:

Perkins: Caldwell? Erskine Caldwell, from Mount Vernon, Maine?
Caldwell: Yes.
Perkins: Well, how are you, Caldwell? It's Perkins. Max Perkins. Scribner.
Caldwell: I'm all right, I guess.
Perkins: I got your new manuscripts yesterday, the ones you left at the office. I wish you had asked for me when you were here.
Caldwell: Well—you did?
Perkins: By the way, I've read all your stories on hand now, including the new ones you brought yesterday, and I don't think I need to see any more for a while.
Caldwell: (Silence).
Perkins: I think I wrote you some time ago that we want to publish one of your stories in *Scribner's Magazine*.
Caldwell: I received the letter. You haven't changed your mind, have you? I mean, about taking a story.
Perkins: Changed my mind? No. Not at all. The fact is, we're all

in agreement here at the office about your things. I guess so much so that we've decided now to take two stories, instead of one, and run them both in the magazine at the same time. We'd like to schedule them for the June issue. One of them is called *The Mating Of Marjorie* and the other one is *A Very Late Spring*. They're both good Northern New England stories. There's something about them that appeals strongly to me. There's a good feeling about them. It's something I like to find in fiction. So many writers master form and technique, but get so little feeling into their work. I think that's important.

Caldwell: I'm sure glad you like them—both of them.

Perkins: You're going to keep on, aren't you? Writing, I mean. You'll keep it up, won't you? We want to see some more of your work, later.

Caldwell: I'm going to keep on writing—I'm not going to stop.

Perkins: That's good to hear.

Caldwell: (Silence).

Perkins: Now about these two stories. As I said, we want to buy them both. How much do you want for the two together? We always have to talk about money sooner or later. There's no way of getting around that, is there?

Caldwell: Well, I don't know exactly. I mean, about the money. I hadn't thought much about it.

Perkins: Would two-fifty be all right? For both of them.

Caldwell: Two-fifty? I don't know. I thought maybe I'd receive a little more than that.

Perkins: You did? Well, what would you say to three-fifty then? That's about as much as we can pay, for both of them. In these times magazine circulation is not climbing the way it was, and we have to watch our costs. I don't think times will get any better soon, and maybe worse yet. Economic life isn't very healthy now. That's why we have to figure our costs closely at a time like this.

Caldwell: I guess that'll be all right. I'd thought I'd get a little more than three dollars and a half, though, for both of them.

Perkins: Three dollars and fifty cents? Oh, no! I must have given you the wrong impression, Caldwell. Not three dollars and a half. No. I meant three hundred and fifty dollars.

Caldwell: You did! Well, that's sure different. It sure is. Three hundred and fifty dollars is just fine. I didn't expect that much.

After the Fourth of July, 1930, I moved to a small cottage on Parker Lake where I would be able to go swimming between chores of writing and physical labor. I had been so engrossed in writing and submitting manuscripts during the past several years that I had not stopped to go back and re-read what I had written during that time. Now I gathered all the manuscripts which included novels and novelettes as well as other material, and took them to the cottage to read. There were nearly three suitcases full of manuscripts of unpublished work, but after a night of sampling of it, I was so dissatisfied with my past work that the next morning I carried everything down to the shore of the lake and burned it. The poetry, jokes, and essays were the first to go into the fire.

And while I was about it, and for good measure, I added to the bonfire the complete collection of rejection slips I had accumulated during the past seven years.

A few weeks after burning the manuscripts I received a letter from Max Perkins in which he said that he had been thinking about the stories I had submitted recently and that he now thought it would be a good idea to bring out a collection of them in book form after the first of the year. He suggested that I get together a sufficient number of stories, previously published in magazines and unpublished ones as well, to make a book of two hundred and fifty or three hundred pages.

Fifteen stories had either been published or accepted for publication in various magazines. One of these was *Story*, the most recently founded and most promising of the little magazines. It was ably edited by Whit Burnett and Martha Foley. To these fifteen I added ten new stories. It so happened that about half of the stories had New England settings and the other half had Southern background. After thinking about it for several days I decided I wanted to call the book *American Earth*.

The typing and revising of the manuscript, which was approximately two hundred and seventy-five pages in length, required three weeks or more, and it was late summer when I went to Boston and took the Eastern Steamship Line night boat to New York.

This time I did not hesitate to call on Max Perkins. He greeted me cordially in his sparsely furnished office when I went in and handed him the manuscript of *American Earth*. Wearing a hat with a turned-up brim, which appeared to be at least half a size too small for him, he sat down at his desk and slowly turned the pages of the manuscript for a quarter of an hour. No word was spoken while he sat there. At the end of that time he got up smiling a little and moved stiffly around his office in new bright-tan shoes, occasionally looking out his window at the traffic below, while he told of several incidents he recalled about life in Vermont when he was a youth.

After nearly an hour of reminiscing, sometimes seriously and often humorously, he mentioned for the first time the manuscript I had brought. All he said then was that Scribner's would want to publish it, probably in the spring of the following year, 1931, and that he would want to choose perhaps two of the unpublished stories to run in the magazine prior to publication in book form.

As I was getting ready to leave, he mentioned the matter of a contract for the book and asked if I had any suggestions to make concerning it. I told him I had none, except that I needed a little money to live on and that I would appreciate an advance royalty payment. First he cautioned me not to expect any large sale of a book of short stories, saying that the book-buying public preferred novels and that the royalty would do well to amount to two hundred and fifty dollars, and then he promised to have a small advance payment made, saying that the check would be sent with the contract when it was ready for my signature about the first of October. I was pleased with the prospect of receiving as much as two hundred and fifty dollars, and after leaving the office, I went down to the Providence Line pier and bought a ticket on the night boat.

The contract for *American Earth* and the check for the advance royalty payment were sent to me promptly, and as soon as I received the money I began making plans to take a trip somewhere. I had had little opportunity to travel recently, except between Maine and New York by bus or boat, and now I wanted to go on a trip to the Pacific Coast. I had never been west of the Mississippi River and I had been looking forward to seeing other regions of

America for a long time. After making a barrel of cider and storing it in the cellar, I was ready to leave. Early in October, taking my Corona portable typewriter, a Target cigarette-making machine, and a suitcase, I left Maine on a bus for California.

(*Caldwell's urge to write was stronger than his desire to see the sights in Hollywood; so he was rarely out of his hotel room for more than an hour at a time.*)

After six weeks at the Warwick Hotel, it became clear in my mind that I was dissatisfied with the progress I was making. It was during this time in October and November that I had gradually come to realize that I would not be completely satisfied with any of my work until I had written a full-length novel and, moreover, that it was inevitable that the novel was to be concerned with the tenant farmers and sharecropping families I had known in East Georgia.

Even though I had been away from Wrens and Jefferson County for a long time, I felt that I would never be able to write successfully about other people in other places until first I had written the story of the landless and poverty-stricken families living on East Georgia sand hills and tobacco roads. The novels I had read as a reviewer seemed even more remote from life now than they had at the time I read them; in retrospect they seemed more concerned with contrived situations and artificial events than with reality.

I wanted to tell the story of the people I knew in the manner in which they actually lived their lives from day to day and year to year, and to tell it without regard for fashions in writing and traditional plots. It seemed to me that the most authentic and enduring materials of fiction were the people themselves, not crafty plots and counterplots designed to manipulate the speech and actions of human beings. My mind was made up. I packed my suitcase and, traveling through Arizona, New Mexico, and Texas, went back to Georgia.

It was December when I arrived at my parents' home in Wrens. The weather had turned damp and cold and the cotton fields were brown and the dogwood hedges dormant.

Within a few miles from town, families on tenant farms were huddled around fireplaces in drafty hovels. Most of them were despondent. Some were hungry as usual; others were ill and without medical attention. Food and clothing were scarce, and in some instances nonexistent; jobs were rarely to be found. It was not a pleasant sight, more dispiriting to look upon now than it had been several years before. I could not keep from recalling Max Perkins's observation that the economic life of the nation was not healthy and would perhaps not improve for a long time; economic life on tenant and sharecropping farms in East Georgia had not been healthy for a long, long time.

Day after day I went into the country, becoming more depressed by what I saw as I traveled farther and farther from settlements and highways. I could not become accustomed to the sight of children's stomachs bloated from hunger and seeing the ill and aged too weak to walk to the fields to search for something to eat. In the evenings I wrote about what I had seen during the day, but nothing I put down on paper succeeded in conveying the full meaning of poverty and hopelessness and degradation as I had observed it. The more I traveled through Burke, Jefferson, and Richmond Counties, the less satisfied I became with what I wrote. In my mind, there was a foreordained story to be told, and it had to be related as the people themselves knew it. Finally, knowing it was something I was impelled to do before I could ever write about anything else, I left Wrens and went to New York. The perspective I gained by going there was what I had been seeking.

I rented a hall bedroom on the fourth floor of a brownstone house between Fifth and Sixth Avenues on the present site of Rockefeller Center. The room was small, there being only enough space for a narrow bed, a lamp table, and a chair, but it had a view of the brownstone fronts across the street.

The buildings in the locality were to be torn down to make way for the skyscrapers of Radio City, and rents in the meantime were low. The rent for my room was three dollars and a half weekly. I was able to live on fifty cents a day for food, chiefly by buying a loaf of rye bread and a pound of dairy cheese and eating it in my room. Once a day, usually in the late afternoon, I went to a nearby restaurant on Sixth Avenue, later renamed The Avenue of the Americas, and paid ten cents for a bowl of lentil soup and a nickel for a cup of coffee. By spending only seven dollars a week for room and food, five dollars a week less than I had spent in California, I had sufficient money to live there during the winter months from January to April.

To begin with I had spent fifty cents for a new typewriter ribbon, a quarter for a water-stained ream of yellow second sheets, and a nickel for two pencils. Then I destroyed everything I had written while I was in Georgia. When I was ready to start writing, I typed the title I had decided upon while riding on the bus to New York. There was only one possible title for the novel; it was to be called *Tobacco Road*. The term tobacco road had originally been applied to thoroughfares that had been made by rolling heavy hogsheads of tobacco along high ridges from East Georgia farms to the Savannah River, but when such roads were no longer used for that purpose, they reverted to landowners who did not keep them in repair.

There was never any doubt in my mind about the outcome of the novel from that time until I finished the first draft of it three months later. My daily habit, seven days a week, was to get up before noon, eat bread and cheese, and start writing. The story I wanted to tell was so vivid in my mind that I did not take the time to go back and read what I had written the day before. I usually stopped writing for an hour in the late afternoon to eat soup and take a walk along one of the streets in the Fifties, and then came back and wrote and rewrote until three or four o'clock in the morning. As soon as a chapter was finished, I revised it until I was satisfied with the way it read, and then began the next chapter. When the stack of second sheets began to dwindle, I used the reverse side of them in order to conserve paper.

I felt no loneliness during that period early in 1931, probably because I was so deeply absorbed in what I was doing, and I had occasion to meet only a few persons connected with writing and publishing, even refraining from phoning or going to see Max Perkins. I spent one evening talking to Raymond Everitt and Charles A. Pearce, both of whom were editors at the publishing house of Harcourt, Brace and Company, and late in March I attended a cocktail party at the offices of The Macaulay Company, publishers of *The American Caravan*.

There were two chief attractions, as far as I was concerned, at this party. One of these was a well-provisioned buffet table that provided the only full meal I had had in nearly three months, and the other attraction was Mae West. Fully fed and having gazed to my heart's content upon Mae West, my mind was then able to retain the experience of meeting some of the other guests, among them being Laurence Stallings, Robert Cantwell, Mike Gold, Edwin Seaver, Georges Schreiber, Dawn Powell, Lewis Mumford, John Chamberlain, Georgia O'Keeffe, and Edmund Wilson.

It was at this same gathering that I met Maxim Lieber, who had been an editor at the publishing house of Brentano's, and who was founding an author's literary agency. Max Lieber was the first agent to invite me to become a client, and the offer was such a surprise to me that I was unable to believe it was a genuine one. I told Max that I thought I should consider it for a while. I was afraid that he was making merely a friendly social gesture and that the offer would soon be forgotten, but a few months later Max wrote and asked me what decision I had come to. I quickly wrote in reply that I wanted to become associated with him, if he were still so minded, and from that time forward Max Lieber handled all my domestic and foreign contracts and negotiations for books and short stories.

The first draft of *Tobacco Road,* which was about two hundred pages in length, was finished the first week in April, 1931, and I had just enough money left to buy a bus ticket to Mount Vernon. *American Earth* was published later in the same month, I received three hundred and fifty dollars from *Scribner's Magazine* for two stories published that spring, and Max Perkins, after publication of the book of short stories, wrote to ask how I felt about writing a novel. I did not tell him that I had already finished the first draft of one, but I did say that I hoped to be able to send him the completed manuscript of a novel before the end of summer.

The newspaper and magazine reviews of *American Earth* were of a so-called mixed nature. That is to say, some of the reviews were favorable and sympathetic; the larger portion were not. I had not expected an avalanche of unstinted praise for this volume of short stories, because I was well aware of some of its shortcomings, but I was unprepared for the large proportion of unfavorable criticism.

My own experience as a reviewer had kept me from anticipating nothing but praise, but it was a revelation to find that the majority of reviewers, when not unconsciously demonstrating an ignorance of their calling, were often contemptuous or sadistic in their appraisal of a book of fiction. The notices of my book were not unique in this respect. I found by reading reviews of other authors' books that supercilious treatment was a common pattern. There seemed to be reasonable evidence, after all, that there might be some truth in the belief that a good many reviewers and critics were impotent lovers or unsuccessful authors.

With the exception of Gorham Munson, Horace Gregory, William Soskin, James Gray, and Harry Emerson Wildes, as well as several others who wrote perceptive notices, the reviewers for the most part looked upon *American Earth* with disdain. Beyond that point the majority of them appeared to be blind to their critical obligation to tell their readers something concerning the contents of the book and in what manner and to what degree the author had failed or succeeded in his attempt to write interesting fiction. The book, not necessarily because of the reviews, had a sale of less than a thousand copies.

After reading a sizable batch of these reviews from many parts of the nation, I no longer had respect for the profession of reviewing, and day by day my regard for it diminished. As a result of this, I became convinced that the average book-review column, page, and supplement was a pitiful stepchild of American journalism, grievously mistreated year after year, by impassive editors and psychopathic reviewers alike.

Following the experience of reading the reviews of *American Earth,* I went to work on the second draft of *Tobacco Road* with a better understanding of what I wished to accomplish. Until this time I had been apprehensive of the reception of my work by the critics, foolishly believing that a writer's success depended to a large degree upon his ability to win the favor of those who wrote reviews of his books. Now I had no such handicap. And at the same time I had learned a valuable lesson. It was now my conviction that a writer's obligation was to himself and to his readers, and that all his effort should be directed toward those two. Thereafter, in my credo, reviewers could look elsewhere for bootlicking; readers were to be the ones to pass final judgment on my books.

There was wood to be cut that spring and summer, and potatoes to be grown. I found that the most profitable division of time during this period was to devote eight hours a day to sleep, eight hours to writing, and eight hours to physical labor. By the end of July the second and final draft of *Tobacco Road* had been finished, the wood-shed was filled with sawn beech and maple, and the garden was free of potato bugs.

Less than two weeks after the manuscript had been sent away, I received a briefly worded note from Max Perkins in which he said that *Tobacco Road* was being accepted and would be published in book form by Charles Scribner's Sons early the following year. He wrote, further, that the manuscript needed no editing before sending it to the printer, and that consequently it was not necessary to suggest any changes or revisions.

I felt that I could safely count on receiving an advance royalty payment when I asked for it, and so I got ready to leave Mount Vernon. I had been there this time for almost five months, and that was a long time for me to stay in one place. Carrying my suitcase and typewriter, and not forgetting the cigarette-making machine, I left for New York after Labor Day.

The Pure And Simple Writer

By William Saroyan

My last batch of stories, all eleven of them, were written in the hope of being sold to magazines for big money because a writer's got to live, but only two of them got big money, though I'll never know why: "The Cocktail Party," $5,000, "The Pheasant Hunter," $3,000.

I mean I'll never know why they got so much and the others so little or nothing. Less was offered for each of them than I got, but as I had no agent to speak up for me I spoke up for myself. It was awkward to express the opinion that the stories were worth more, or to talk about the matter at all, especially since the editors had offered so much in the first place, but I had been out of touch with such things a good many years and it seemed to me that I ought to put as high a price on my product as possible.

The cost of living had gone up since I had been a whiz in the short story game back in 1934-1939, selling stories left and right for anywhere from $15 to $125. Even in those days it wasn't fame alone I was after, it was fame with honor, so to speak.

At that time, an editor of a new and tremendously successful magazine, himself a whiz, offered my agent $250 for one of my short stories. The tradition then was for writers to accept all such offers with gladness and a snappy letter of thanks to the editor, most of which would appear free of charge on the page about contributors: "I used to wash dishes, I used to steal money out of cash registers, I used to read Tolstoy, but now I write short stories and sell them. I like to fish and hunt, and one time at a movie when I saw Garbo take off her coat I felt pretty good, quiet-like, I mean, because I knew I had it."

The tradition was also for the boy to send the editor a snapshot of himself and be grateful to the editor for making him famous. The editor and the boys got along fine, the editor picking up stories for $75 or $100 or $150, and the boys picking up their fame every other year from where it had fallen, getting glad and masculine all over again.

So here was an offer that looked like a pretty good one: $250 for one little old measly short story, written in one day.

I picked up the latest issue of the magazine off the floor of my workroom and went through it from cover to cover, examining the advertisements. There were a lot of them. Then I found the place in the magazine that said how many subscribers the magazine had. There were a lot of subscribers, too. There were a lot of newsstand buyers. Then I counted the number of contributors to the magazine and I allowed each of them $250 per item, and the total came to a very small sum, about what two full-page advertisements in the magazine would cost Chesterfield or Coca-Cola. Then I went over my record with the magazine and discovered that my agent had offered the editor about a dozen different short stories over a period of a year and a half, all of which the editor had rejected.

I wrote to the agent and went over these facts and told him to write to the editor and tell him that according to my figures the short story was worth a minimum of $500 and that if he didn't want to pay that much, to send the story back, as I couldn't afford to let him have it for less. The agent wrote something or other to the editor and the editor wrote to me. He pointed out that he had paid a little more for each of my short stories he had accepted, three in all over a period of several years, and that his offer for the present story was $100 more than he had paid for the last one. I wrote back and told him I was aware of the progression involved, but that under the circumstances I still couldn't afford to let him have the story for less than $500. I pointed out that as the circulation of the magazine increased, the advertising rates also increased, and advertisers were not permitted to pay less than the new rate simply because they had advertised before at lower rates. I also told the editor that if he did not pay $500 for the story I wouldn't be interested in offering him any more. He wrote back and suggested that I see a psychiatrist, but in those days medical men weren't going in much for psychiatry and the best I could do was tell my story to a priest at a cocktail party.

He said I was all right.

The agent in the meantime urged me not to put him in bad with the editor insofar as his other writers were concerned and to please let the editor have the story for $250. The editor, it seems, had scheduled the story for a future issue and it would be difficult for him to change that issue. I told the agent to let the editor have the story with my compliments. The agent said he couldn't tell the editor that, so I wrote the editor and told him.

Several months later the editor sent a check for $250 to the agent, the agent deducted 10% and sent me a check for $225, which I spent in riotous living.

"The Assyrian" was started in the hope of having something irresistible to offer to an editor, for I was in Paris at the time and flat broke, and if the story turned out to be about 25,000 words long as well as irresistible, as I hoped it would, I knew I might be paid anywhere from $15,000 to $25,000 for it. The longer I worked on it, however, the more hopeless the possibility of this financial coup became, for the writing would not be cheerful, would not be amusing, would not be something hundreds of thousands of friendly, normal, cheerful people might find in a magazine and know would be nice.

But only three months earlier I had gone to the trouble of writing something nice and cheerful, "The Poet at Home," but this had not proved irresistible, either.

It isn't dishonorable for a writer to write something nice and clean and cheerful. It isn't dishonorable to try to write for money, either, or to try to write something that will appeal to magazine readers.

But if a writer knows he can't write a certain kind of story (not necessarily in itself worthless) but insists on trying to do so because he needs money badly, and then fails, that is foolish.

I have not often written anything *deliberately*. I was generally *impelled* to write, and whatever it turned out to be, it was O.K. as far as I was concerned because it was what I had been helpless not to write. If I saw that it seemed to be something an editor might want, I felt pleased and sent it along.

In other words, a writer's best chance of getting work done and making a living at the same time is apt to be in doing work he can't help doing, no matter how easily it may seem to be resisted by magazine editors.

To do good writing is the easiest thing in the world for a writer provided he can get located in himself and among his fellows, but the more a man grows, the more he tries to grow, the more he accepts the responsibility of trying to grow, the less located he becomes and the more difficult it becomes for him to do work that satisfies him. To do good writing is always easy if a writer is willing or able to stay firmly located, or in other words to play safe. Playing safe a whole lifetime can make a writer's reputation. It is a good thing to do if you don't know any better. If you know better, it is still a good thing to do, but a little on the careful side. A man can always go after the tough stuff — the stuff that's so hard to put into the form of the short story or the novel — in his letters to the people he loves, or in his autobiography, or in his private journal. He can easily make a case at the last minute for the way he worked, making known that he knew what he was doing all the time, knew it wasn't much, certainly not enough, certainly a little too skillful and safe, but did it because it was the best he could do effectively with what was left of his will at the time. A man can always go after the tough stuff in his private life, work at it as long as he lives, get nearer and nearer to an understanding of it, and never go after it in his writing, never take a chance on it.

During my apprentice years I must have written five hundred short stories, or a mean average of one hundred per annum. Most of them weren't actually short stories of course, but not one of them was written for money, either, so that whatever the hell they were in terms of literary form, they were certainly aloof at least, and they made my name, such as it is.

I wrote a lot of them because I enjoyed writing and always wanted to know, "What next?" For I always felt that I was apt to write something fine every time as not, and I believed that what I was trying to prove, what I was by way of demonstrating, was that when it comes to the matter of using words, anything can happen, should be permitted to happen, should be encouraged to happen. I believe I also meant to establish a tradition of carelessness, for it seemed to me from the years of my apprenticeship that the thing that blocked creation was carefulness.

What it came to was that either I wrote freely and easily or didn't write at all, and since I had after the age of twenty recognized that I was by nature unfit for any other trade, occupation or profession, I had to make up my mind to write freely and easily and at the same time make whatever I happened to write fairly acceptable, on a percentage basis. That is, one out of ten, one out of five, or one out of two.

The short story form, as such, never appealed to me especially and for years I couldn't do a thing with it. A bore was always involved in a boring problem and getting out of it in a boring way, and who wanted to be bothered? I just wanted to say the same words I was saying when I talked.

I didn't want to describe a room or a house or a city or a street or a sky or a hill or a valley or anything else. I wanted to say something about myself, and something about the effect people I happened to run into, including my family, had on me. I wasn't educated enough to write essays like the ones Max Beerbohm or Logan Pearsall Smith or George Santayana wrote, although I hadn't read any of their essays in those days, and besides I didn't like the way essays seemed to go, either. You are supposed to be in possession of certain facts, generally about something so tiresome I couldn't imagine caring to go into the matter at all, and then you are supposed to arrange them nicely and have something written that ought to be nice for an old lady sitting in a rocking-chair on the porch of the Old People's Home to read.

Everything I wrote seemed hopeless, though, because I couldn't get out of the habit of comparing it with something in a newspaper, a magazine, or a book, and no matter how bad the thing was that I compared my writing with, my writing seemed worse.

At last I decided that either I myself was the beginning and end of the matter, or there was no matter at all. I was interesting or I wasn't. The way I stayed alive was interesting or it wasn't. I just didn't have any other way of solving the problem of literature and getting to work.

I had always felt that I was the beginning and end of any matter, and that I was interesting, but I had been ashamed to make anything of it, for I knew it was the same with everybody else.

At the age of twenty when I stopped trying to make a living at work that bored me and openly declared that I was either a writer or a bum, my family agreed that there was no doubt about it, and pretty much let the matter go at that. This was a great achievement, for I was not obliged after that to prove every day that I was doing my share. I no longer had any share to do. If I worked one day a week or two days a month, the five or ten dollars I earned was spent on paper, clips, postage, envelopes, cigarettes and anything else a writer might need: typewriter ribbons. I had owned a typewriter since August, 1928, from the time I had first gone to New York to make my fame and fortune but had come back to San Francisco, homesick and broke, after six months.

The other thing I achieved was resignation to the loneliness a writer knows all the time; and the capacity not to need anything irrelevant: not to need good clothes, a fine house with a fine workroom in it in which to work, a big car in which to travel around, a lot of money, or a girl to sit at my feet and sigh because I had just written the word *beautiful* on the typewriter and permitted her to read it.

That is, I achieved *partial* resignation to this loneliness, for total resignation to it does not seem possible for me. I have heard that after years of such resignation, the loneliness that one has been resigned to ceases to be loneliness at all; but only now and then, for a week or two, have I found this to be the case with me.

I am the best company I know, but only because I *remember* other company. Kids are the best company of all of course, but they grow up, and even before they do you can't spend much time with them because it bores them. They are in fact the only aristocracy of the human race, and after them come those who fail or refuse to wholly relinquish the aristocracy they acquired at birth; that is, the better poets and scientists and other creatively alive people, for the one thing all childhood has in common, as everyone by now knows, is creativeness. And the one thing all adulthood has in common is literalness: the great block to any real achievement of growth. Thus, the so-called adult is for the most part a case of blocked growth, of failure to live all of life at once, from birth to death.

The American writer's preoccupation with earning, with being paid (underpaid or overpaid) for his work, is understandable, for it is simply a fact that unless a writer can count on earning at least a little money, he cannot expect to continue in his profession with comfort, or without embarrassment or bitterness; and these feelings, if they persist long enough, will do something to his work that is not necessarily good, for the cult of failure is as damaging as the cult of success.

Every writer knows that writing of all kinds earns good money for writers of all kinds at all times, including depressions and wars.

The writer who is only a writer is a rare bird these days, most writers having taken posts at universities, gone into the government on a full or part-time basis, or into publishing, play producing, moving picture directing, radio, medicine, agriculture, lecturing, acting, advertising, travel and adventure (to obtain exclusive material), book reviewing, article or interview writing on assignment, or journalism. A number of writers are lawyers or business men.

Pure and simple writing, it would seem, does not pay. The pure and simple writer must get help from the Guggenheim Foundation or from one or another of the annual prize awards, or from friends.

The profession of pure and simple writing is apt to become a dull one when a writer himself is dull or preoccupied with something else. Consequently, it is in order for the writer, unpublished or famous, to take stock of himself every year or two in order to find out what the score is. For the truth is that if a man is fit for the profession of writing at all, the profession's potential for expansion, enlargement, extension and variety is greater than the potential of any other profession, so that if it *has* become a dull profession, the writer may be sure that it is he himself who has become dull. It is desirable to avoid this, hence a few words on how to do so.

Rules for writers are the same as rules for anybody else whose basic intention is to live creatively: that is, as pleasantly as possible under the circumstances, with honor, integrity, intelligence, humor, decent pride and decent humility. And the making of rules is solely a personal thing, sure to be inadequate for others, or meaningless or incomplete. Even so, I would put it thus:

A writer should never stop work on the job of creating his own character. He should work at this job every day. It is the best if not the only work he can do for himself as a person, as a writer, and as a social being. No one has yet succeeded in making out a fair case against this seemingly selfish or even self-centered and lifetime task, and there is no evidence that it is not finally the best means by which a writer, or anybody else, may be helpful to others, or useful to society and the world. The creation of character is apt to be even more important than the creation of art, even though it is not likely that a writer will create his own character and not also create works of art.

In the nature of things this is a job that is never finished, for no man may believe he has created his character once and for all and is now free to live off of it, as he might say he has made his fortune and is now free to sit on it and live off the interest.

The following would appear to be the means, or some of them, by which the writer may work at the creation of his character:

1. Self-knowledge
2. Health
3. Intelligence
4. Imagination, intuition, collective unconscious
5. Social responsibility
6. Technical skill

The man who does not need to know about himself is not apt to be a writer in the first place, hence we may presume that a writer has self-knowledge to begin with, that in all probability having self-knowledge impelled him to start writing, and that if he is to have self-knowledge at all, the more he has of it the better it will be for him and for his work. The self is not static, therefore must be re-discovered and understood continuously.

The Creative Writer

A writer in order to live and work (in order to achieve self-knowledge and to create his character) ought to look after his health. His body should be exercised, his appetites satisfied, his lusts frequently disciplined and denied (if doing so does not impair his health: that is, do more harm than good). A writer should bathe as often as he is in need of a bath. He should shave (unless he prefers having a beard) as often as he needs a shave, unless he needs a shave twice a day, in which case once a day will do: in the morning when he gets up, as a clean face frequently improves a writer's work.

A writer should think, should be intelligent, but should not throw his intelligence around, as it is bad manners. In company he should be cheerful, courteous, considerate, well-mannered, sincere, affectionate, warm-hearted, but not intelligent in the classic sense, for if he were intelligent in the classic sense he could not be the other things, and if he could not be the other things he ought not to be in company. He should tell jokes, sing, dance, make fun for himself, take part in games, have a good time. If everybody is drinking, he should drink. He should not be above the minor social pleasures, but he should not remain in company which praises Russia and criticizes America, or criticizes Russia and praises America. He should leave such company and go home, as such criticizing and praising is neither intelligent nor a social pleasure. He should not despise people who do it, though. He should kill them on the spot or let them live and enjoy themselves the way they must. If he can convert somebody he happens to like to intelligence and is able to do so quietly, he should do so. He should not try to convert anybody he doesn't like. He is most apt to get along with all kinds of people and to do good work if he doesn't try to convert anybody at all, but if he must try, the best beginning he can make (if it is somebody he likes) is to say cheerfully, "Shut up, just shut up." He should never strike a woman for getting her sexual hunger identified with some cause, like socialized medicine, and he should not leap to conclusions about socialized medicine because of this identification. He should think about everything. He should think all the time. He should be intelligent all the time, which means that when it is intelligent not to be intelligent he should not be intelligent. He should be zealous about any conclusions he may reach by the exercise of intelligence, for that is the beginning of the betrayal of intelligence, the transformation of it into something else. He should never argue, except with children, and only in order to please them, and he should always lose such arguments as a matter of principle. He should sharpen and warm intelligence (and his skill as a writer) by observing carefully the intelligence and economic self-expression of children. If he happens to have children, he should spank them if they ask for it, and never apologize for having done so, for doing so is a second punishment, and one they certainly do not deserve.

As for his social responsibility, a writer should meet it at all times and under all circumstances, or at any rate try to do so. If doing so or trying to do so makes his responsibility to himself difficult, he may be sure that he has not yet been responsible enough to himself and that he is not yet ready for full social responsibility. A half-baked man being socially responsible is actually being socially mischievous. A writer should try to avoid this. Being half-baked and socially responsible may be fun for him but at the same time it may cause a lot of agony to a lot of strangers. A writer should not run for public office or permit himself to be appointed to any post in which he is not answerable solely to his conscience, regardless of trends, pressures, expediency. As this is inconceivable, he must not accept any such appointment unless he has decided to abandon the profession of writing and the hope of a creative life. A writer should have as many kinds of friends or acquaintances as possible, the more kinds the better. But he should also have available at all times an inviolable privacy, not for work alone but for meditation, recuperation, restoration. He should have enemies and he should be grateful for them, for if he had none, it would in all probability mean that his writing was basically indifferent.

And finally a writer should keep after his skill. He should try to avoid relaxing about it, being satisfied with it, believing it is as developed as he can make it. He should try to avoid imitating himself or repeating himself and should look upon each new work as a new problem to be worked out in a new and perhaps better way. He should write letters, for out of the directness of letter-writing frequently comes a freshening of skill, for in the end every form of writing is essentially a letter to friends, enemies, and strangers. Some of the heaviness of many novels by good writers appears to be the result of their having forgotten what they were doing. A writer should try to remember that anything he writes may have a relatively long life and be read in many different languages by many different races of people. He should recognize this as the greater part of his social responsibility. He should write accordingly. He should think well of himself, so that he may be able to think well of others. He should believe in himself, in his decency, in his devotion to the hope of truth, in his contempt for purposeful, deliberate crudity, vulgarity, crookedness, arrogance, deception, and the degradation, humiliation or corruption of man. He should find it impossible not to love honor and aspire to it at all times.

He should never permit humor to disappear out of his life or writing, for humor is the natural and necessary companion of survival, and there cannot be any survival (of anything) without it. He must survive. He should try to survive pleasantly, meaningfully, productively, and honorably, but if this proves difficult or impossible under his own circumstances, and if it also proves difficult or impossible for him to change his own circumstances because they are so much a part of circumstances in general, then he must try to survive anyway, without these things, or with as much of them as he is able to manage. A writer ought to try to keep himself away from the compulsion (at last) to commit suicide or murder, or to engage in prostitution, or to give false witness, or in any way to befoul or belittle life in any form, or the potential of any form of life to survive.

A writer should also avoid being, or trying to be, or always allowing others to make him seem to be a messiah, for messiahs are without humor, incapable of it, and they invariably make mischief and impel killing, hysteria, cruelty, mobbishness, and a rejection of intelligence. The only leading that is ever in order for a writer is the leading of his own children when he teaches them to walk and talk, and that would also appear to be the only kind of leadership the human race itself ought to be willing to put up with. The myth of leaders is an unholy one.

The question comes up every year or so (largely among writers themselves) as to whether or not writers are necessary. It has been coming up for many hundreds of years and many good writers have asked it and tried to answer it. Writers are not as necessary for man's body as farmers and physicians are; they are not as necessary for the easy entertainment of his soul, even, as movies, the stage, radio, television, magazines and newspapers are; and they are not as comforting to *all* of him as the church, baseball, or the horse races are.

Is there, then, any need for serious writers any longer? Any need, that is, for poets?

Language is needed obviously: print is needed, presses are needed, books are needed, magazines and newspapers are needed, writing is needed. But is the poet needed? The statesman must write his memoirs; the scientist must report his findings; the anthropologist, the biologist, the architect, the engineer, the mathematician, the inventor, the astronomer, the soldier, the sailor, the aviator, the explorer, the judge, the lawyer, the millionaire, the manufacturer, the banker and dozens of others must turn in their reports as memoirs, theory, history or general information, but is there any need for the poet, for the writer to turn in his report?

The question seems silly. It would be insulting were it not that poets themselves ask it. This would suggest that the profession is frequently inadequately rewarding, for even Tolstoy gave it up and took up the writing of propaganda, and almost every other great writer finally gave it up, or thought of doing so, and for all any of us knows soon afterwards died, perhaps as a direct result of finding the profession unsatisfying.

Henry James said at last something about his one regret being that he wrote life instead of living it. What did he believe life was? Where had his own, which he had lived with so much quiet style, failed him?

Only a man's own writing may be unnecessary, and it may be unnecessary only when he himself has doubts about its necessity. But every man sooner or later seems to come to the time when he feels his writing is not necessary, and he does not mean the writing he is presently doing or trying to do, he means all of it, the writing he did long ago, that he has probably forgotten how he did.

This does not seem to be a mysterious thing, as I see it. It is something that probably happens to all people and is not so noticeable in them only because they are not writers. This thing that happens is death: that is, death as it happens in the living before they stop altogether. It is exhaustion, or the beginning of it. It is weariness. It is overwhelming indifference about one's self, one's own life, about the whole business of life. It is a natural thing, I suspect. Its natural purpose is to enable men to die, to stop altogether, and thereby to make room for others. Every man sooner or later asks of himself if he is necessary, and soon afterwards knows that he isn't. And he forgets that he has been quite necessary, especially to himself.

Nothing is more necessary than writing, no one is more necessary than the poet as long as the writing and the poet are coming, so to say. When the writer and the poet are going, it is probably true that they are no longer very necessary, if at all. By going one must understand that *going dead* is meant and by coming *coming alive* is meant, for a writer, or any human being, may have been *going* physically for years, may have been literally dying of an organic disease, for instance, and still have been coming alive all the time.

Now, the question comes up, can a writer get all the work done that he feels he ought to get done and at the same time not get too tired and therefore in the prime of life find himself unbearably weary and sick of his profession? The answer is no, he can't. If he could he would.

What does this suggest? It suggests that writers will do what they must, but it also suggests that if it pleases them to do so they *may* evolve a procedure of living and working that will get *enough* work done and still not make them too tired.

I am interested in looking into the second half of this suggestion.

Anxiety at work is what tires a writer most. Anxiety to do the best it is possible for him to do, anxiety to get it done before his powers fail him, anxiety about size, texture, quality. If a different art of writing comes into being as a result of writing *without* anxiety, it does not necessarily follow that this art will be a lesser art or that it will appeal even less to readers than writing achieved with anxiety. There is no telling. Writing without anxiety is certain to do the writer himself good; which takes me back to what it was I had hoped to achieve for myself when I wrote so many short stories in 1934-1939. I felt that it was right to just write them and turn them loose and not take myself or the stories too seriously. I had hoped to achieve an easier way for a man to write: that is, a more natural way. I believe that this was a worthwhile thing to go after. I believe writing achieved in pain and torture is not necessarily better than writing gladly achieved.

If anxiety, then, is the thing for the writer to get rid of at his work, it follows that the way to get rid of it is for the writer to have implicit faith in himself, in his character, and in what he is apt to write. He must believe that it is not necessary for him to be careful if being careful makes him anxious and tired. He must believe that it is possible for him to achieve writing as good as he might ever achieve anyway by working easily, swiftly and with gladness. This means that he must have something to say, that he is experienced enough not to need to brood about how to say it, and experienced enough as a human being to know what the sum of what he is to say is to be.

In short, if a writer's character is all right, how can anything he writes not be the best he *ought* to write?

There is, in short, no exact and final way in which a writer may write, and if one way achieves great art it may not necessarily be great art *solely* because of the way in which it was achieved, it may be great art in *spite* of the way in which it was achieved, it may be great art because the writer had character, and it may finally be that he got tired because he did not get to his character in the simplest or most natural manner.

This writer believes that even the masterpieces of writing frequently have too much art in them, for instance. Too much art of a kind, that is. *All* is art of course, a matter of degree. The question is, then, Can writing be good art and still be gladly achieved?

I think it can.

It may be that the flaw in the lives of the great writers who got tired was that they were too much writers and too little human beings. Too little, that is, men like all others, men not living only the literary life but living the whole one.

Anybody *cannot* learn to write, cannot learn to create life or a sense of life through writing. But if a man is a writer, he definitely can learn to write, and this will be learned, as I have said, by creating his character, by working at it all the time.

Editor, French Underground

By Roger Massip

In this story of my experiences as an editor with the French Underground and a member of the secret press during the German occupation of France, I want to name several French journalists who refused to collaborate. These patriots refused to bow before the fait-accompli of 1940 and had only one thought and one wish — to buy back, at the sacrifice of their life if necessary, the honor of French journalism and to blot out the shame of the press which sold out to Vichy.

Following the Capitulation, these men, just as I did, put aside their pens and refused all the offers which were made to them. Emmanuel d'Astier, Pascal Capeau, Maurice Negre, Christian Ozanne, Louis Martin-Chauffier (the last three escaped from Buchenwald and Belsen) will forgive me for naming them here. Others who worked with us will never return from Germany.

In 1939 when the war broke out, I was directing the foreign news service of the *Petit Parisen*. The triumph of Germany left me with no illusions. To me any collaboration was treason, and when in

September of 1940 I saw some of my colleagues leave the unoccupied zone to return to Paris, pretending that they could exercise
their profession in freedom and dignity, I knew they were dupes.

I went to Lyon, the large city of provincial France, situated in
the unoccupied zone, the center for passage or for residence for all
those who left Paris in the hope of seeing better days.

In the summer of 1942, I found one of my friends in Lyon, Pascal
Capeau, the son of Jacques Capeau, a director in the contemporary
French theatre. We had been friends since 1939 and he knew my
ideas and I knew his. We agreed that we should start something to
cooking. The resistance movements, "Liberation", "Combat" and
"Franc-Tireur", were not advertising their wares on the market
place and new members were presented only by a trusted friend.

Capeau, I learned, was already a member of "Liberation". He
wished to share his fortune with me and offered to present me to
the "Liberation" group and entrusted to me the work he had been
doing for many weeks, the editing and printing of the clandestine
newspaper "Liberation". I accepted with profound joy. The road
was finally opened which would enable me to work for a sacred
cause and the honor and dignity of the press.

I shall not forget the day when I made my way for the first time,
guided by Capeau, into the subterranean world of the French Resistance. We squeezed into the nameless crowd on a street-car and
left the center of Lyon for the suburbs. Capeau was absent-
mindedly smoking his pipe and was unconscious of my deep
emotion. Calmly, as though it were a question of an ordinary walk
in a park, or a visit to a friend, he guided me through the streets
of the old town. He pointed out possible dangers en route. "Here
you must be sure to turn around. The street takes a sharp turn and
you can easily see if you are being followed. Over there the street
splits. You can take either road. Here is a cross street which comes
in handy to throw a follower off your track . . ." I thought I was
a character in a murder story. I was.

The editor's office was an apartment on the second floor of an
elderly house in an out-of-the-way suburb of Lyon. It consisted of
two large rooms and a kitchen. One of the rooms contained a few
tables, a clothes press of white wood, a typewriter, a mimeograph
and some suitcases filled with pamphlets and documents. In the

other room was a cupboard containing some arms, one machine gun, pistols and ammunition.

There we were, cut off from life. From behind the door we could hear sounds of ordinary living, tenants going up and down the stairs, children playing in the street — noises which were reassuring and annoying at the same time; annoying because it was sometimes difficult to distinguish, in the too familiar noises, the unexpected noise which we all awaited more or less unconsciously every hour of the day or night.

Each day I met a few comrades, the secret team of the newspaper; those who were responsible for communication with the printer, the stenographer, the contact man; those who guaranteed the relations between the newspaper team and the head of the underground, and the courier who twice a week made the trip to Vichy to bring back intelligence. Sometimes the comrade who had charge of distributing our paper came to see us.

These men circulated in the town with the greatest of caution, avoiding anything which might render them conspicuous. They taught me, who became their chief, the traits without which any secret work would have been impossible — the most extreme prudence, discretion and patience. Patience in particular was very necessary for those who wished to publish and distribute a clandestine newspaper.

The rhythm of publishing was very slow, an issue every three weeks, but this schedule was often interrupted. First we had to get our material. There were three sources: the Allied radio for bonafide news of the war; our organization at Vichy for French information; our local provincial centers for news of the Resistance (sabotages, uprisings, etc.) and the secret activities of our resistance movement.

We listened to the radio regularly and received mimeographed digests from an allied intelligence service specializing in this kind of work.

At Vichy we had many friends and supporters in the official organizations, in the ministries, and in the official French agency. Information from these sources was collected by one of our agents and twice a week our courier from Lyon went to Vichy and returned with envelopes bulging with papers: Laval's confidential memoranda, minutes of secret meetings of the cabinet, and military dispositions and dispatches were leaked to us.

Precious information came to us also from the provincial headquarters, from Marseille, Toulouse, Montpellier, Limoges, Clermont. This information was turned in to the central headquarters of the Movement at Lyon and from there was transmitted to us by a special service entrusted only with the inter-Lyon messages.

This service functioned as follows: An office was established in Lyon, the location of which was unknown even to the head of the Movement. This office had numerous scouts who spent the entire day going about in the city, making contact in predetermined locations which were changed several times a month with other scouts from various services — newspaper, sabotage, free-groups, etc. The scout from the newspaper office, for example, met one of the messenger scouts from the office twice a day. The newspaper scout was the only person knowing the identity of the messenger and received from his hand the papers destined for the editors, and he in turn handed over the papers to be delivered to the central office or to the provincial offices. In this manner each service was isolated from all the others, assuring a maximum of security for all in case of imprisonment and torture of one.

At the moment when I had in my possession all the essential information, and our articles were written and edited, we got word to the printer. One of us (and one of us only knew the printer) was entrusted with getting the material to him. Each piece of copy was carefully sized in advance, so proofs would not have to go back and forth. I always sent a dummy in order to facilitate the actual printing. The type had to be set up by hand, letter by letter. For each of our four page issues, the lone printer had to manipulate about 40,000 letters. It took a week to finish the composition. The printer ran one proof on glazed paper, which was photographed. From these an engraver from the newspaper *"Le Progrès de Lyon"* made us zinc plates. Thanks to these plates we were able to print the paper in other provinces and enlarge the distribution. We printed 50,000 copies in Lyon, and with the same zinc plates 25,000 at Toulouse, 25,000 at Toulon and 15,000 at Limoges.

Our engraver, after working two years for us at Lyons, was finally arrested by the Gestapo and shot.

Each month volunteers carried the heavy zinc plates from Lyon to Toulouse, Limoges, and Toulon, and in spite of the heavy surveillance, no one of them was ever caught.

At the end of three weeks the printing of each issue was finished and the distribution began; little postal packages to the smaller cities, distribution in the mail boxes in the large cities and in public places, cinemas, street cars, etc. The work was dangerous and men lost their lives.

Each month brought its own reward: first, the very human satisfaction of putting one over on the Germans and the Vichy police, and then the richer joy of having enabled thousands of Frenchmen to read something besides the lies and treachery printed in the Vichy controlled press.

In 1942 the work became much more difficult and infinitely more dangerous, especially after the Germans overran the non-occupied zone, following the Allied landings in Africa. The Gestapo, which up to this time had concentrated on Paris and the occupied zone, extended its efforts to the large cities of the center and south of France. We had to redouble our precautions and reinforce our system of security, but in spite of all our efforts, many of us were arrested.

In the meantime our relations with London were growing. We received from London some photographic plates of the landings in Sicily and Africa and in September of 1943 we published an issue containing these photos, pictures of the atrocities at Kharkov, and a document procurred by one of our free groups: the photo of a German military locomotive lying on its side on an embankment following the attack by a group of Maquis.

At the end of 1943 the chiefs of the various movements in non-occupied France moved to Paris for security, as well as political reasons. However, we left some teams in Lyon to continue the newspaper, while new teams were formed in Paris. We decided to have the original composition of the newspaper made up in Paris, as well as the printing of 50,000 copies, the rest to be printed in the south from the zinc plates.

I was chosen to direct the complete organization from Paris. This change could not have come at a more opportune moment because the entire group at Lyon was seriously threatened following an incident: One of our printing presses was located at Montelimar in the Rhone Valley and the other at Auch in the southwest of France. The same printer was in charge of both. Both presses were honored on the same day by a visit from the Gestapo. The issue then on press was seized, the paper stacks burned, and the printers arrested. Our suspicions soon were turned toward one of our men whom we knew as Bernard. Several months before he had been recommended to us by one of our friends in the Resistance at St. Etienne, near Lyon, and it was very difficult, in spite of everything, for us to admit that this man who had become our comrade and an ardent worker could have betrayed us.

We decided, in order to be perfectly sure, to set a trap. We had friends among the police at Lyon and they agreed to arrest him on the serious charges of dealing in Black Market goods. As soon as he was taken to the police station Bernard showed his Gestapo card, made out to a lieutenant in the Himmler police. To the police who had let him go, of course, he said he was just about to put his fingers on the whole "Liberation" organization. He went so far as to say he knew Capeau and myself under our real names. As soon as we were warned we took the greatest care and left at once for Paris. We left behind us a team whom Bernard didn't know at all and who did its best never to cross the path of this contemptible person.

In January of 1944 I settled in Paris and began an extraordinary life. I lived in the apartment of a friend who was then a prisoner in Germany. Consequently, I did not have to register with the police, but I was forced, because of my work, to give my address to a few friends. It was unfortunate because our rule was for no one person to know the address of the others. Our only contact was through meetings in the city or at the office. Unfortunately there were cases where knowing too much was fatal. One of my friends who knew my address was arrested. I had the greatest confidence in him and I learned later he never gave a word of information to his torturers. We exercised the greatest caution. I stopped sleeping at home and, until The Liberation, passed the nights with different friends. When one of these friends had reason to fear for his own safety, I moved out. I lived in every quarter of the city, and, like my comrades, led the life of a homeless tramp. But in this way only could we escape the dangers which came with the darkness.

The daytime risks remained great, however. Paris was infested with stool-pigeons and German police, and the cafes, subway stations, public squares, churches, even the peaceful banks of the Seine became more and more dangerous.

My underground existence culminated in a spectacular adventure in March, an adventure which almost cost my life as well as my liberty. I escaped only by a miracle. It was a beautiful spring day, so beautiful and clear that we were treated to a visit from American bombers. When my brother, who worked with me, and I came out of our office about three o'clock, we found a large crowd in front of the subway station awaiting the end of the "Alerte". We were to take some proofs to the engraver. My brother had folded the papers into a tiny bundle and a few minutes before leaving the office he had the bundle in his hand. We had scarcely reached the street, undecided as to whether we should walk or wait the end of the raid and go by subway, when I noticed three characters who seemed very much interested in what we were doing.

I knew intuitively that the Gestapo was about to focus on us and I signaled my discovery to my brother. He refused to be convinced and dragged me along to the boulevard. When I turned again, the agents were on our heels. It was at this moment that my brother, feeling his pockets, he whispered, "I have forgotten the papers". As we hesitated, the three, joined by a fourth whom I hadn't seen, rushed at us and one jammed his revolver against my breast, saying, "German police. Don't move!"

We both raised our arms while they searched us for guns. Then they took us to two automobiles parked nearby and we went to one of the Gestapo stations on the Avenue Foch, in the beautiful Etoile quarter. My brother's forgetfulness was our life. The discovery of that bundle would have meant horrible torture, for its possession would have shown we knew both the engraver and the printer, information for which the Germans would have paid dearly and made us pay even more dearly. I had no other papers on me and I knew my brother wasn't in the habit of walking around with compromising addresses or notices of meetings. However, I did know that after the Bernard affair a short time previously, we were hunted by the Gestapo under our real names, and the identity cards we carried now were completely authentic.

Handcuffed we were taken to the third floor of the Gestapo building and of course, they questioned us separately. The room faced the main avenue and a brilliant sun shone through the windows. I had the curious impression, in this room filled with tables and filing cabinets, that I was doing some administrative job. We had to wait a while. In one corner a young girl was typing — a German girl with blond hair and light blue eyes. Next to her an open cupboard revealed clubs, revolvers, a machine gun. This innocent looking creature must have been present at some shocking scenes of cruelty and savagery. However, she displayed a disconcerting tenderness . . . she searched her purse for a tiny piece of sugar and then from among the revolvers she took out a tiny cage containing a baby white mouse. To this tiny creature she fed the sugar bit by bit.

This idyllic scene was interrupted by the arrival of a police agent accompanied by a clerk wearing a gray military blouse. First they searched me very methodically. The clerk proved to be quite expert in searching for fountain pens and the cases of watches. He was also very clever in taking off socks and feeling the lining of jackets. All my papers were examined one by one. They read my letters. I no longer belonged to myself. I was simply an object — a field for research.

My identity card they examined with the greatest care and the gray blouse made careful notes and typed triplicate lists of my possessions. Never have I been so lucid, but at the same time frightened in my life. Apparently my name didn't grace the Paris Gestapo lists. I was not surprised, inasmuch as we had suspected that there were air-tight partitions between the Paris Gestapo and the Gestapo of the provinces. The clerk did not know that his friends in Lyon were looking for me. But this brought up a new difficulty. The German agents, out of sorts at finding no incriminating evidence, pretended that our identity cards were false. This was not true. But to verify they had to get in touch with Lyon because the cards had been issued by the Lyon police. We ran the risk of returning to our first problem. At this moment I remembered that I had paid the tax collector that very morning. Consequently,

I had a receipt in my name. I hoped this agreement of name would convince the Gestapo. I asked for my brief case and showed them the tax receipt. This convinced them. They returned our papers and our money and let us go. This incident took up three hours, but they had passed like a flash.

Before leaving I took the liberty of protesting against our arrest and demanding an explanation. Very pleasantly they excused themselves and informed us that when we came out at three o'clock we had run right into the arms of the Gestapo, who were searching the corridors of the Metro station for suspected meetings. Our indecision when we came into the street had attracted their attention. Having given my address to the Gestapo, I moved that evening. The Germans might deal one of two ways with a Resistance editor: shoot him, or torture, cripple and release him as an object lesson.

In April of 1944 the difficulties became much greater. Electricity was rationed. Each day the current was cut for several hours. We managed to operate by having the copy set up on the linotype machines of a Paris newspaper printer. Some of his workers were our sympathizers and did our work in secret, but the current being cut off stopped them. We got the idea of using a foot-pedal machine which produced 8,000 to 10,000 copies a day. As far as the actual composition was concerned, we again had to do it by hand, letter by letter, and I am an editor, not a typesetter.

In May the bombings in preparation for the Allied landings had made communication between Paris and the large southern cities very difficult. We gave each region its autonomy. From that time on we worked in Paris without directing the work of our comrades in Toulouse and Lyon. They relied on themselves alone.

Our efforts met with success. In spite of the mounting difficulties, technical and material, and in the face of the redoubled efforts of the police, "Liberation" continued to appear until August of 1944. It was precisely at the moment when there was electricity only on Sunday afternoon, and weekdays for half an hour in the evening, that we broke all our records for speed and produced 50,000 copies of our July 14 issue in less than five days.

One of our group got the idea of composing our newspaper on the typewriter, typing out the text on space three times as wide as the width of a newspaper column. He suggested using a good grade of glazed paper. Then we would have the text photographed, reducing it by one-third, and obtain a zinc plate to be used in the actual printing. This process saved us the time of putting the text together by hand, which was a lengthy process, and enabled us to maintain a substantial text, although shorter than usual. The actual printing problem was handled by a comrade who put us in touch with a curé whom he knew who had an electric printing press hidden in his church. The experiment was a success. In three days we had our zinc plates. The plans were completed and the following Sunday, taking advantage of the afternoon electric current, the printer-priest printed 50,000 copies. On the 14th of July, Bastille Day, everything was ready and we began distribution on time.

We were able to use this method only twice. The author of the whole plan was arrested late in July and the Gestapo found several copies of his newspaper on his person. They tortured him for 44 hours, but he died without revealing a bit of information. His disappearance forced us to return to our earlier method, and when the Paris Insurrection began on the 19th of August, our 54th secret edition was in preparation. This number never actually appeared, but in its place, on the 21st of August, while German vehicles were still circulating in Paris and the fighting continued in the barricades, Edition No. 1 of the newspaper "Liberation" appeared, and this took the place, in the broad daylight of liberty, of our humble secret newspaper.

These 53 issues, which marked the time between July 1941 and August 1944, cost the lives of four of my colleagues. A dozen others were arrested and doubtless died in extermination camps.

Such is the balance sheet of our efforts during three years. Other resistance newspapers, *"Combat"*, *"Franc-Tireur"*, *"Defense de la France"*, suffered similar losses. We produced as many as 175,000 copies an issue. Other secret newspapers produced even more. The Resistance groups together poured into France 1,000,000 copies of free newspapers each month.

It is fortunate that French journalists emerged who chose to turn a deaf ear to proposals of collaboration, who met torture with silence, and chose clandestine action rather than enslavement. Those who died did not die in vain. They wiped out the shame, inflicted by a handful of traitors, to the tradition of the Free Press.

The Fruit Of The Bittersweet

By Ken Purdy

During the twenty years from 1935 to 1955 I worked as a reporter on three newspapers and as editor of one; as associate editor of three magazines and managing editor of one; as editorial consultant to two magazines and as editor-in-chief of four. During this time, too, I sold short stories and articles to 20-odd major magazines and published two books. I cite this only to demonstrate my right to my prejudices. I have viewed the battlefield from both sides and I have the wound-stripes and the hatchet-scars to prove it.

The relationship between editor and writer is, now and then, a happy one. Now and then, indeed. A warm, pleasant, long-standing relationship between an editor and a writer is a rarity. By the very nature of things it must be. These two people, the editor and the writer, do not begin to understand each other. I know, because I have been both editor and writer, and, if you want more, both simultaneously. Let me sketch the width of the chasm separating the two. Let me show you what they think of each other.

The writer sees the editor as a secure, well-paid executive, surrounded by eager and competent seconds-in-command who do all the work and let him have all the credit; buffered from harsh reality by a pretty secretary, or a pair of them, intent only on keeping him happy, bringing him his coffee in the morning, reminding him of his appointments with his masseur, ministering to his creature comfort in every way — or almost every way. Somebody else pays the rent for his office, somebody else meets his phone bill, and his lunches and his cocktail dates go on the expense account.

The editor's working day? In the writer's view, it's an eight-hour vacation. In the morning he looks at his mail, not all of it, naturally, his secretary has screened it thoroughly, keeping from him anything unworthy of his attention, or anything that might upset him. He dictates a few answers, or, more likely, scribbles notes on the letter: "Anne, tell him no." "Anne, ask Mike fix this." "Anne, if this legit. complain, let me know otherwise you tk. care."

Now the Art Director brings in a few layouts, the editor runs a blasé eye over them. OK's some, makes suggestions for minor alterations. He reads three or four manuscripts, all of them previously read and evaluated by associate editors. Nine times in ten he accepts their judgment. By now it's time for lunch, a good lunch, preceded by two or three Martinis. He's back in the office by three. He has appointments with a couple of writers. One has an idea which he turns down after a minute's consideration. The other has an idea which he says just might possibly work out, he'd be delighted to see an outline. He makes a few phone calls, picks up his briefcase and leaves. He has to make an appearance at a cocktail party for Barbra Streisand, it's a bore, but he really must, and then off to catch the 6:02 to Connecticut, or Westchester, or Long Island where he can relax on his country estate and prepare himself for the rigors of the next day.

Is this the way it really is? Not quite. There are a couple of things missing. One thing in particular is missing: Pressure. The editor, you see, has a publisher. Or, if he's his own publisher, he has a board chairman, president, or whatever. This individual has not got where he is by being a nice fellow. He may be a nice fellow, but that isn't what made him publisher. He knows, or he wouldn't have the job, about the uses of Pressure. He knows, like a judo-player, how to keep his subordinates perpetually off-balance. He leans on them. The editor can never get off the treadmill. Supposing he pulls a brilliant coup of some kind and drives his circulation up 100,000. Fine. The publisher congratulates him. He is a fair-haired boy. He is a hero. Great. But after he has been hand-clasped, praised, drunk to, the needle goes in: 'Don't let it slide back, now. Be a pity to lose a nice chunk of circulation like that." For a few minutes the editor was thinking of that extra circulation as his own property. He pulled it in, it was all his. He has just received the message. He has just learned that it isn't his at all, it's the publisher's, and that if it drifts away in the next couple of months, the publisher's attitude will be that he, the editor, has stolen something.

Corollary to this the editor learns that the Basic Law of the little jungle in which he labors is that circulation must not be static; it must rise. Advertising revenue must rise, as well. And while increase in advertising revenue demonstrates only the brilliance of the head huckster, or advertising director, a drop in revenue proves conclusively that the editor is putting out an unattractive and ineffective magazine.

So the editor sits at his nice desk in his pretty office, and he rubs his head-bones hard together. I'd like to have a dollar for every hour I've spent at night in the various offices I can remember, sitting there with one light on, nobody else in the place, going through the magazine. You go through it page by page, front to back, back to front, then you do it over again. How could this title have been done better? Should this story have followed that one, or would it have been more effective farther back in the book? Is this a really funny cartoon? How in the name of God did our biggest competitor get onto the Dawes story before we did? Can't let that happen again. Can't, but how to prevent it? You turn off the light and look out the window and hope for an idea. It's August. What will be in the news in October? You must know what will make a good lead story for October. You read seven newspapers a day, 100 magazines a month, you try to know what's going on because that's the only way in which you can project a trend two or three months ahead. You've got to think of something, but you can't, not that night, anyway.

That's how it is with an editor — a good one; the others don't matter. What's going to be in the October book? That's what keeps him awake at night, that's what makes him seem, often, distant, rude, inconsiderate, hurried. He's doing a little work, too, on the side. If he's a good editor, he has read every word in the magazine three times over before the presses start to roll. Harold Ross of *The New Yorker* would stop the presses and pull an entire plate in order to change a comma.

The man is making $25,000 to $75,000 or more a year if he's top man on an important book. He's earning it. He knows the meaning of the old Spanish proverb: "In this life, take what you want — but pay for it." Even if he's a fraud, and I could name a couple, even if he's getting by on charm, guts and the brains of a brilliant and selfless subordinate, still he's sweating for it, like a tightrope walker sweats for it. Nobody gives anything away.

A bleak, harassed existence? Certainly not. There are great satisfactions. Editing a magazine is a creative enterprise, after all, and all the satisfactions of creation can be taken from it. But, looking in from the outside, the writer cannot correctly evaluate either the satisfaction or the penalties.

How does the writer look to the editor? As we talked about top-bracket editors, we must talk about top-bracket writers. There are about as many in the one category as the other. Usually the editor is as envious of the writer as the writer is of him. It's a cliché, but it's true as true: most editors are frustrated writers. The editor sees in a writer a man, or a woman, who's making almost as much money as the editor is, sometimes more, and doing it, the editor thinks, much more easily. He has no boss and his time is his own. The pressure that is the bane of the editor's existence cannot be put on the writer. All right, the writer has to pay the butcher and meet the mortgage, but so does the editor. The editor sees in front of him a guy who gets up at 10 in the morning if he feels like it, and runs for nobody's commuting train. He can spend a couple of days in the library, write a historical piece and get $1,500 for it. He can visit some alleged celebrity for a few hours and write an article that will get him another $1,500. So now he's made a month's pay and he can sit in his back yard and think big thoughts for a week or so. If he has any enterprise at all, it's easy for him to get a free trip, everything paid, to almost anywhere in the world. Airlines, tourist bureaus, industrial outfits will be happy to freight him around while he picks up stories for which he will be well paid. The chances are he's better-known than the editor. Why shouldn't he be? If Editor Zilch buys a piece from Writer Zounds, Zounds' name will be displayed with ten times the prominence of Zilch's in that issue. For every interesting or worthwhile contact that the editor can make, the writer, if he knows his business, can make five. And if the writer does fiction as well as non-fiction, the editor sees two more enviable facets of his profession: He can write where he pleases, he is tied to no one locality by the necessity of showing up at an office at 9:30 every morning, and, second, he may at any time hit the jackpot: a $100,000 movie sale, for instance, or a big book. It happens every week.

The editor sees in the writer somebody who wants to take something from him: money out of his budget, and space out of his magazine. He doesn't believe that the writer understands the importance of either of these items. He doesn't believe that the writer knows that there is, somewhere in the building, a gimlet-eyed treasurer-accountant type with the imagination of a gibbon ape who thinks that writing-off an article that turned out badly is plainly and simply a criminal act. The editor doesn't believe that the writer knows that every page in the magazine must carry its own weight, must somehow contribute to the easing of the pressure that dogs him. He looks at the writer almost as he looks at a job applicant, saying to himself, "Wouldn't it be wonderful if one of these jerks, instead of trying to get something from me, would offer to help me?" His pride is in the way, though, and usually he won't say to the writer, "Look, things are tough all over. I've got to have a hot story for October. Think for a minute. I need help, boy."

He rarely says it. He must maintain his facade, or he thinks he must. So he sits there, not paying as much attention to his visitor as he ought to, and maybe they get together on an assignment anyway. The writer leaves and the editor says to himself, "I hope he pulls it off." And in the back of his head he's thinking what an easy thing it is for the writer to do: research and write one story, turn it in and be paid for it. He'd like to settle for one problem like that, instead of the fifty that are hounding him.

Is that the way it really is with the writer? Again, yes, in part. It's true that he has no boss—excepting himself, the toughest boss of all.

For, being his own boss he is responsible for his own success, and if he fails he fails twice. It's true that he's working for himself and that nobody can write him an office memo with three carbons, pointing out his deficiencies in detail. He doesn't need it. He has a little book in which he keeps track of his income. If he has a bad week, it's a very bad week — he doesn't make any money. No ideas, no out-put, no money. The editor can have a sterile stretch in which not a single idea of any consequence occurs to him, but he'll be paid anyway. It's true that the writer has in his own hands the free disposition of his time, but he's likely to put in more hours than any 9-to-5 wage slave he knows. When the wage-slave's bell rings for freedom at five o'clock, he is legally and morally entitled to relax. The writer doesn't feel that similar privileges are his. The editor can spend an hour listening to a bore and convince himself that he's working, because, after all, something good may come of it. If a writer does the same thing he's cheating himself.

Strictly speaking, save only researching and the peddling of ideas, everything the non-fiction writer does that is not done at the typewriter is a waste of time. This realization is the slave who beats him, this is the monkey he carries on his back. If he steals time, he steals it from himself, and that hurts.

What else? If you're going to be a writer, you're going to be lonely. There's no way out of that one. Writing is like dying — you have to do it yourself.

Shall we provide the up-beat ending so dear to editors and so necessary to the financial well-being of writers?

Well, then, was I happy as an editor? But yes. As a writer? Certainly. More as one than the other? Yes. I'd rather be a writer than anything else. If I couldn't be a writer I'd rather be an editor than anything else.

Advice? Counsel? Surely.

How to Be an Editor:

1. Having read everything and written much, having worked on small-town newspapers and bush-league magazines, you have been hired. You look at the magazine. You know it well, of course, because you've read it for a long time, as you have all other magazines of any consequence. You consider first how it can be improved typographically, how the layouts can be bettered, how it can

be modernized and made brighter. This is easiest, so you do it first. There are ways to force the reader to look at a page, there are ways to force him to look at a certain part of the page first, another part later. You learned this years ago, it is one of the two or three secrets you have. You never tell anyone else.

2. You have an hour's talk with every member of the staff. You are trying to separate sheep from goats, men from boys. You watch them all for two weeks. You will find one, two, or three people who are phonies and/or deadweights. You get rid of them at once, not by firing them, but by telling them that, alas, you will not be able to get on together, and urging them to find other jobs, which you will help them to do. Stubborn cases you tell, Go now, before I find out so much about you that I cannot in good conscience help you find another job. When you are sure you know the good ones you promise them that you will assume all responsibility for every mistake they ever make, and that you will personally deliver to your own superior credit for every good thing they ever do. This is an honest promise and you keep it to the letter from that day onward.

3. You look for, and find, stories with a high publicity potential. This is hard. Having published them, you personally see to it that the publicity is obtained. This is very hard.

4. You crawl into your readers' minds. You find out what they want, what they like, what they want in your magazine that they do not want in another. This is terribly hard. It is possible to learn how to do this, but no one ever learned it in less than 15 years, and some people could not learn it in 50. But without it you cannot be a good editor, although you can be a successful one.

5. You flog yourself until you automatically think about the magazine as soon as you wake up in the morning, and you think about it the last thing at night. This is hard, and burdensome, but unless you do it your mind will not produce ideas in volume.

Do these things and you can improve almost any magazine in the world, increase its circulation, add to its advertising. You can maintain this pace for about three years. After that you must slack off for a while, vacation, or accept a nervous breakdown. The choice depends on your temperament.

How to Be A Writer:

1. This is uncomplicated. Having read everything and written much, having studied techniques and methods, you cast off and declare yourself a writer. You need no legal permission. It is a unilateral action. You then resolve to write for eight hours a day. This is brutal, harder than anything else you have ever done. At first you will have to spend 16 hours a day to write for eight. Ultimately you will find that you produce a useful volume of work in five or six consecutive, not scattered, hours per day, six days a week. You have arrived. You have made it. You are a writer.

What shall you write about? If you have to ask that question, do not, for the love of God, try at all, because you'll never succeed. Find a good job somewhere, and be happy.

The Summing Up

By Somerset Maugham

I have never kept a diary. I wish now that during the year that followed my first success as a dramatist I had done so, for I met then many persons of consequence and it might have proved an interesting document. At that period the confidence of the people in the aristocracy and the landed gentry had been shattered by the muddle they had made of things in South Africa, but the aristocracy and the landed gentry had not realized this and they preserved their old self-confidence. At certain political houses I frequented they still talked as though to run the British Empire were their private business. It gave me a peculiar sensation to hear, when a general election was in the air, whether Tom should have the Home Office and whether Dick would be satisfied with Ireland.

During this period I met persons who by their rank, fame or position might very well have thought themselves destined to become historical figures. I did not find them as brilliant as my fancy had painted them. The English are a political nation and I was often asked to houses where politics were the ruling interest. I could not discover in the eminent statesmen I met there any marked capacity. I concluded, perhaps rashly, that no great degree of intelligence was needed to rule a nation. Since then I have known in various countries a good many politicians who have attained high office. I have continued to be puzzled by what seemed to me the mediocrity of their minds. I have found them ill-informed upon the ordinary affairs of life and I have not often discovered in them either subtlety of intellect or liveliness of imagination. At one time I was inclined to think that they owed their illustrious position only to their gift of speech, for it must be next door to impossible to rise to power in a democratic community unless you can catch the ears of the public; and the gift of speech, as we know, is not often accompanied by the power of thought. But since I have seen statesmen, who did not seem to me very clever, conduct public affairs with reasonable success I cannot but think I was wrong: it must be that to govern a nation you need a specific talent and that this may very well exist without general ability. In the same way I have known men of affairs who have made great fortunes and brought vast enterprises to prosperity, but in everything unconcerned with their business appear to be devoid even of common sense.

I have been called cynical. I have been accused of making men out worse than they are. I do not think I have done this. All I have done is to bring into prominence certain traits that many writers shut their eyes to. I think what has chiefly struck me in human beings is their lack of consistency. I have never seen people all of a piece. It has amazed me that the most incongruous traits should exist in the same person and for all that yield a plausible harmony. I have often asked myself how characteristics, seemingly irreconcilable, can exist in the same person. I have known crooks who were capable of self-sacrifice, sneak-thieves who were sweet-natured and harlots for whom it was a point of honor to give good value for money. The only explanation I can offer is that so instinctive is each one's conviction that he is unique in the world, and privileged, that he feels that, however wrong it might be for others, what he for his part does, if not natural and right, is at least venial.

The contrast that I have found in people has interested me, but I do not think I have unduly emphasized it. The censure that has from time to time been passed on me is due perhaps to the fact that I have not expressly condemned what was bad in the characters of my invention and praised what was good. I am not gravely shocked at the sins of others unless they personally affect me, and even when they do I have learnt at last generally to excuse them. It is meet not to expect too much of others. You should be grateful when they treat you well, but unperturbed when they treat you ill. "For every one of us," as the Athenian Stranger said, "is made pretty much what he is by the bent of his desires and the nature of his soul." It is want of imagination that prevents people from seeing things from any point of view but their own, and it is unreasonable to be angry with them because they lack this faculty.

I think I could be justly blamed if I saw only people's faults and were blind to their virtues. I am not conscious that this is the case. There is nothing more beautiful than goodness and it has pleased me very often to show how much of it there is in persons who by common standards would be relentlessly condemned. I have shown it because I have seen it. It has seemed to me sometimes to shine more brightly in them because it was surrounded by the darkness of sin. I take the goodness of the good for granted and I am amused when I discover their defects or their vices; I am touched when I see the goodness of the wicked and I am willing enough to shrug a tolerant shoulder at their wickedness. I am not my brother's keeper. I cannot bring myself to judge my fellows; I am content to observe them. My observation has led me to believe that, all in all, there is not so much difference between the good and the bad as the moralists would have us believe.

I do not know a better training for a writer than to spend some years in the medical profession. I suppose that you can learn a good deal about human nature in a solicitor's office; but there on the whole you have to deal with men in full control of themselves. They lie perhaps as much as they lie to the doctor, but they lie more consistently, and it may be that for the solicitor it is not so necessary to know the truth. He sees human nature from a specialized standpoint. But the doctor, especially the hospital doctor, sees it bare. Reticences can generally be undermined; very often there are none. Fear for the most part will shatter every defense; even vanity is unnerved by it. Most people have a furious itch to talk about themselves and are restrained only by the disinclination of others to listen. Reserve is an artificial quality that is developed in most of us as the result of innumerable rebuffs. The doctor is discreet. It is his business to listen and no details are too intimate for his ears.

I do not particularly want to talk and I am very willing to listen. I have no desire to impart any knowledge I have to others nor do I feel the need to correct them if they are wrong. You can get a great deal of entertainment out of tedious people if you keep your head. I remember being taken for a drive in a foreign country by a kind lady who wanted to show me around. Her conversation was composed entirely of truisms and she had so large a vocabulary of hackneyed phrases that I despaired of remembering them. But one remark she made has struck in my memory as have few witticisms; we passed a row of little houses by the sea and she said to me: "Those are week-end bungalows, if you understand what I mean; in other words they're bungalows that people go to on Saturdays and leave on Mondays." I should have been sorry to miss that.

I would not claim for a moment that those years I spent in St. Thomas's Hospital gave me a complete knowledge of human nature. I do not suppose anyone can hope to have that. I have been studying it, consciously and subconsciously, for forty years and I still find men unaccountable; people I know intimately can surprise me by some action of which I never thought them capable or by the discovery of some trait exhibit a side of themselves that I never even suspected. It is possible that my training gave me a warped view.

I have no natural trust in others. I am more inclined to expect them to do ill than to do good. This is the price one has to pay for having a sense of humor. A sense of humor leads you to take pleasure in the discrepancies of human nature; it leads you to mistrust great professions and look for the unworthy motive that they conceal; the disparity between appearance and reality diverts you and you are apt, when you cannot find it, to create it. You tend to close your eyes to truth, beauty and goodness because they give no scope to your sense of the ridiculous.

The humorist has a quick eye for the humbug; he does not always recognize the saint. But if to see men one-sidedly is a heavy price to pay for a sense of humor there is a compensation that has a value too. Humor teaches tolerance, and the humorist, with a smile and perhaps a sigh, is more likely to shrug his shoulders than to condemn. He does not moralize, he is content to understand; and it is true that to understand is to pity and forgive.

I have seen men through my own idiosyncrasies. A buoyant, optimistic, healthy and sentimental person would have seen the same people quite differently. I can only claim to have seen them coherently. Many writers seem not to observe at all, but to create their characters in stock sizes from images in their own fancy. They are like draughtsmen who draw their figures from recollections of the antique and have never attempted to draw from the living model.

I have always worked from the living model. I remember that once in the dissecting room when I was going over my "part" with the demonstrator, he asked me what some nerve was and I did not know. He told me; whereupon I remonstrated, for it was in the wrong place. Nevertheless he insisted that it was the nerve I had been in vain looking for. I complained of the abnormality and he, smiling, said that in anatomy it was the normal that was uncommon. The remark sank into my mind and since then it has been forced upon me that it was true of man as well as of anatomy. The normal is what you find but rarely. The normal is an ideal. It is a picture that one fabricates of the average characteristics of men, and to find them all in a single man is hardly to be expected. It is this false picture that the writers I have spoken of take as their model and it is because they describe what is so exceptional that they seldom achieve the effect of life. Selfishness and kindliness, idealism and sensuality, vanity, shyness, disinterestedness, courage, laziness, nervousness, obstinacy, and diffidence, they can all exist in a single person and form a plausible harmony. It has taken a long time to persuade readers of the truth of this.

When novelists began to disclose the diversity that they had found in themselves or seen in others they were accused of maligning the human race. So far as I know the first novelist who did this with deliberate intention was Stendhal in "Le Rouge et le Noir." Contemporary criticism was outraged. Even Sainte-Beuve, who needed only to look into his own heart to discover that contrary qualities could exist side by side in some kind of harmony, took him to task. Julien Sorel is one of the most interesting characters that a novelist has ever created. For the first three quarters of the novel he is perfectly consistent. Sometimes he fills you with horror; sometimes he is entirely sympathetic; but he has an inner coherence, so that though you often shudder you accept.

It was a long time before Stendhal's example bore fruit. Balzac, with all his genius, drew his characters after the old models. He gave them his own immense vitality so that you accept them as real. His people are unforgettable, but they are seen from the standpoint of the ruling passion that affected those with whom they were brought in contact. It is evidently less trouble to make up one's mind about a man one way or the other and dismiss suspense with the phrase, he's one of the best or he's a dirty dog. It is disconcerting to find that the savior of his country may be stingy or that the poet who has opened new horizons to our consciousness may be a snob. Our natural egoism leads us to judge people by their relations to ourselves. We want them to be certain things to us, and for us that is what they are; because the rest of them is no good to us, we ignore it.

These reasons perhaps explain why there is so great a disinclination to accept the attempts to portray man with his incongruous and diverse qualities and why people turn away with dismay when candid biographies reveal the truth about famous persons. It is distressing to think that the composer of the quintet in the *Meistersinger* was dishonest in money matters and treacherous to those who had benefited him. But it may be that he could not have had great qualities if he had not also had great failings. I do not believe they are right who say that the defects of famous men should be ignored; I think it is better that we should know them. Then, though we are conscious of having faults as glaring as theirs, we can believe that that is no hindrance to our achieving also something of their virtues.

For me the race now is nearly run and it would ill become me to conceal the truth. Let those who like me take me as I am and let the rest leave me. I have more character than brains and more brains than specific gifts.

I am told that there are natural singers and made singers. The made singer owes the better part of his accomplishments to training; with taste and musical ability he can eke out the relative poverty of his organ and his singing can afford a great deal of pleasure, especially to the connoisseur; but he will never move you as you are moved to ecstasy by the pure, birdlike notes of the natural singer. The natural singer may be inadequately trained, he may have neither tact nor knowledge, he may outrage all the canons of art, but such is the magic of his voice that you are captivated. You forgive the liberties he takes, his vulgarities, his appeals to obvious emotion, when those heavenly sounds enchant your ear. I am a made writer.

But it would be vanity if I thought that such results as I have achieved on myself were due to a design that I deliberately carried out. I was drawn to various courses by very simple motives and it is only on looking back that I discover myself subconsciously working to a certain end. The end was to develop my character and so make up for the deficiencies in my natural gifts.

I have often heard writers complain that they wanted to write but had nothing to write about, and I remember one distinguished author telling me that she was reading through some books in which were epitomized all the plots that had ever been used in order to find a theme. I have never found myself in such a predicament. Swift, as we know, claimed that he could write on any subject whatever, and when challenged to write a discourse on a broomstick, he acquitted himself very creditably. I am almost inclined to say that I could not spend an hour in anyone's company without getting the material to write at least a readable story about him.

Reverie is the groundwork of creative imagination; it is the privilege of the artist that with him it is not as with other men an escape from reality, but the means by which he accedes to it. His reverie is purposeful. It affords him a delight in comparison with which the pleasures of sense are pale and it affords him the assurance of his freedom.

In my youth, when my instinctive feeling about a book differed from that of authoritative critics I did not hesitate to conclude that I was wrong. I did not know how often critics accept the conventional view and it never occurred to me that they could talk with assurance of what they did not know very much about. It was long before I realized that the only thing that mattered to me in a work of art was what I thought about it.

The only important thing in a book is the meaning it has for you; it may have other and much more profound meanings for the critic, but at second hand they can be of small service to you. I do not read a book for the book's sake, but for my own. It is not my business to judge it, but to absorb what I can of it, as the amoeba absorbs a particle of a foreign body, and what I cannot assimilate has nothing to do with me. I am not a scholar, a student or a critic; I am a professional writer and now I read only what is useful to me professionally.

Anyone can write a book that will revolutionize the ideas that have been held for centuries on the Ptolemies and I shall contentedly leave it unread; he can describe an incredibly adventurous journey in the heart of Patagonia and I shall remain ignorant of it. There is no need for the writer of fiction to be an expert on any subject but his own; on the contrary, it is hurtful to him, since, human nature being weak, he is hard put to it to resist the temptation of inappositely using his special knowledge. The novelist is ill-advised to be too technical. The practice, which came into fashion in the nineties, of using a multitude of cant terms is tiresome. It should be possible to give verisimilitude without that, and atmosphere is dearly bought at the price of tediousness.

The novelist should know something about the great issues that occupy men, who are his topics, but it is generally enough if he knows a little. He must avoid pedantry at all costs. But even at that the field is vast and I have tried to limit myself to such works as were significant to my purpose. You can never know enough about your characters. Biographies and reminiscences, technical works, will give you often an intimate detail, a telling truth, a revealing hint, that you might never have got from a living model. People are hard to know. It is a slow business to induct them to tell you the particular things about themselves that can be of use to you. They have the disadvantage that often you cannot look at them and put them aside, as you can a book, and you have to read the whole volume, as it were, only to learn that it had nothing much to tell.

Persons, who are anxious to write, sometimes pay me the compliment of asking me to tell them of certain books necessary for them to read. I do. They seldom read them, for they seem to have little curiosity. They do not care what their predecessors have done. English writers think they know everything that it is necessary to know of the art of fiction when they have read two or three novels by Mrs. Woolf, one by E. M. Forster, several by D. H. Lawrence and, oddly enough, the *Forsyte Saga*.

The writer can only be fertile if he renews himself and he can only renew himself if his soul is constantly enriched by fresh experience. There is no more fruitful source of this than the enchanting exploration of the great literatures of the past.

For the production of a work of art is not the result of a miracle. It requires preparation. The soil, be it ever so rich, must be fed. By taking thought; by deliberate effort, the artist must enlarge, deepen and diversify his personality. Then the soil must lie fallow. Like the bride of Christ, the artist waits for the illumination that shall bring forth a new spiritual life. He goes about his ordinary avocations with patience; the subconscious does its mysterious business; and then, suddenly springing, you might think from nowhere, the idea is produced. But like the corn that was sown on stony ground it may easily wither away; it must be tended with anxious care. All the power of the artist's mind must be set to work on it.

But I am not impatient with the young when, only at their request, I insist, I advise them to read Shakespeare and Swift, and they tell me that they read "Gulliver's Travels" in their nursery and "Henry IV" at school; and if they find "Vanity Fair" unendurable and "Anna Karenina" footling it is their own affair. No reading is worth while unless you enjoy it.

The artist, the writer especially, in the solitariness of his own mind constructs a world that is different from other men's; the idiosyncrasy that makes him a writer separates him from them and the paradox emerges that though his aim is to describe them truthfully his gift prevents him from knowing them as they really are. It is as though he wanted urgently to see a certain thing and by the act of looking at it drew before it a veil that obscured it. The writer stands outside the very action he is engaged in. He is the comedian who never quite loses himself in the part, for he is at the same time spectator and actor. It may be that the writers of the present day, who seem to be so much nearer to their raw material, ordinary men among ordinary men, rather than artists in an alien crowd, may break down the barrier and come nearer to the plain truth than has ever been done before. But then you have to make up your mind about the relations between truth and art.

II

I had my full share of the intellectual's arrogance and if, as I hope, I have lost it, I must ascribe it not to my own virtue or wisdom but to the chance that made me more of a traveller than most writers. I am attached to England, but I have never felt myself very much at home there. I have always been shy with English people. To me England has been a country where I had obligations that I did not want to fulfill and responsibilities that irked me. I have never felt entirely myself until I have put at least the Channel between my native country and me. Some fortunate persons find freedom in their own minds; I, with less spiritual power than they, find it in travel.

The first real journey I made was to Italy. I went primed with much reading of Walter Pater, Ruskin and John Addington Symonds. I had the six weeks of the Easter vacation at my disposal and twenty pounds in my pocket. After going to Genoa and Pisa, where I trudged the interminable distance to sit for a while in the pine wood in which Shelley read Sophocles and wrote verses on a guitar, I settled down for the inside of a month in Florence in the house of a widow lady, with whose daughter I read the "Purgatorio," and spent laborious days, Ruskin in hand, visiting the sights. I admired everything that Ruskin told me to admire (even that horrible tower of Giotto) and turned away in disgust from what he condemned. Never can he have had a more ardent disciple. After that I went to Venice, Verona and Milan. I returned to England very much pleased with myself and actively contemptuous of anyone who did not share my views (and Ruskin's) of Botticelli and Bellini. I was twenty.

A year later I went to Italy again and discovered Capri. It was the most enchanting spot I had ever seen and the following summer I spent the whole of my vacation there. Capri was then little known. There was no funicular from the beach to the town. Few people went there in summer and you could get board and lodging, with wine included, and from your bedroom window a view of Vesuvius, for four shillings a day. There was a poet there then, a Belgian composer, my friend from Heidelberg, Brown, a painter or two, a sculptor (Harvard Thomas) and an American colonel who had fought on the Southern side in the Civil War. I listened with transport to conversations, up at Anacapri at the colonel's house, or at Morgano's, the wine shop just off the Piazza, when they talked of art and beauty, literature and Roman history. I saw two men fly at one another's throats because they disagreed over the poetic merit of Heredia's sonnets. I thought it all grand. Art, art for art's sake, was the only thing that mattered in the world; and the artist alone gave this ridiculous world significance. Politics, commerce, the learned professions—what did they amount to from the standpoint of the Absolute? They might disagree, these friends of mine, about the value of a sonnet or the excellence of a Greek bas-relief (Greek, my eye! I tell you it's a Roman copy and if I tell you a thing it is so); but they were all agreed about this, that they burned with a hard, gem-like flame. I was too shy to tell them that I had written a novel and was halfway through another and it was a great mortification to me, burning as I was too with a hard, gem-like flame, to be treated as a philistine who cared for nothing but dissecting dead bodies and would seize an unguarded moment to give his best friend an enema.

Presently I was qualified. I had already published a novel and it had had an unexpected success. I thought my fortune was made, and, abandoning medicine to become a writer, I went to Spain. I was then twenty-three. I was much more ignorant than are, it seems to me, young men of that age at the present day. I settled down in Seville. I grew a moustache, smoked Filipino cigars, learnt the guitar, bought a broad-brimmed hat with a flat crown, in which I swaggered down the Sierpes, and hankered for a flowing cape, lined with green and red velvet. But on account of the expense I did not buy it.

I rode about the countryside on a horse lent me by a friend. Life was too pleasant to allow me to give an undivided attention to literature. My plan was to spend a year there till I had learnt Spanish, then go to Rome which I knew only as a tripper and perfect my superficial knowledge of Italian, follow that up with a journey to Greece where I intended to learn the vernacular as an approach to ancient Greek, and finally go to Cairo and learn Arabic. It was an ambitious programme, but I am glad now that I did not carry it out. I duly went to Rome (where I wrote my first play) but then I went back to Spain; for something had occurred that I had not anticipated. I fell in love with Seville and the life one led there and incidentally with a young thing with green eyes and a gay smile (but I got over that) and I could not resist its lure. I returned year after year. I wandered through the white and silent streets and strolled along the Guadalquivir, I dawdled about the Cathedral, I went to bullfights and made light love to pretty little creatures whose demands on me were no more than my exiguous means could satisfy. It was heavenly to live in Seville in the flower of one's youth. I postponed my education to a more convenient moment. The result is that I have never read the "Odyssey" but in English and I have never achieved my abition to read "A Thousand Nights and a Night" in Arabic.

It is hard enough for us to know our own people; we deceive ourselves, we English especially, if we think we can know those of other lands. The sea-girt isle sets us apart and the link that a common religion gave, which once mitigated our insularity, was snapped with the Reformation. I think then it is merely waste of time to learn more than a smattering of foreign tongues. The only exception I would make to this is French. For French is the common language of educated men. It has great literature; other countries, with the exception of England, have great writers, rather than a great literature; and its influence on the rest of the world has, till the last twenty years, been profound. There are limits, however, to the excellence with which you should allow yourself to speak it. As a matter of practice it is good to be on your guard against an Englishman who speaks French perfectly; he is very likely to be a card-sharper or an attaché in the diplomatic service.

It is very seldom that life provides the writer with a ready-made story. Facts indeed are often very tiresome. They will give a suggestion that excites the imagination, but then are apt to exercise an authority that is only pernicious. The classic example of this is to be found in "Le Rouge et le Noir." This is a very great novel, but it is generally acknowledged that the end is unsatisfactory. The reason is not hard to find. Stendhal got the idea for it from an incident that at that time made a great stir: a young seminarist killed his mistress, was tried and guillotined. But Stendhal put into Julien Sorel, his hero, not only a great deal of himself, but much more of what he would have liked to be and was miserably conscious that he was not; he created one of the most interesting personages of fiction and for fully three quarters of his book made him behave with coherence and probability; but then he found himself forced to return to the facts that had been his inspiration. He could only do this by causing his hero to act incongruously with his character and his intelligence. The shock is so great that you no longer believe, and when you do not believe in a novel you are no longer held. The moral is that you must have the courage to throw your facts overboard if they fail to comply with the logic of your character. I do not know how Stendhal could have ended his novel; but I think it would have been hard to find a more unsatisfactory end than the one he chose.

I have been blamed because I have drawn my characters from living persons, and from criticisms that I have read one might suppose that nobody had ever done this before. That is nonsense. It is the universal custom. From the beginning of literature authors have had originals for their creations. But we know very little even of the persons we know most intimately; we do not know them well enough to transfer them to the pages of a book and make human beings out of them. People are too elusive, too shadowy, to be copied; and they are also too incoherent and contradictory. The writer does not copy his originals; he takes what he wants from them, a few traits that have caught his attention, a turn of mind that has fired his imagination, and therefrom constructs his character. He is not concerned whether it is a truthful likeness; he is concerned only to create a plausible harmony convenient for his own purposes. So different may be the finished product from the original that it must be a common experience of authors to be accused of having drawn a lifelike portrait of a certain person when they had in mind someone quite different.

It is often enough for him to have caught a glimpse of someone in a tea-shop or chatted with him for a quarter of an hour in a ship's smoking-room. All he needs is that tiny, fertile substratum which he can then build up by means of his experience of life, his knowledge of human nature and his native intuition.

III

I have never been a propagandist. The reading public has enormously increased during the last thirty years and there is a large mass of ignorant people who want knowledge that can be acquired with little labor. They have thought that they were learning something when they read novels in which the characters delivered their views on the burning topics of the day. A bit of love-making thrown in here and there made the information they were given sufficiently palatable. The novel was regarded as a convenient pulpit for the dissemination of ideas and a good many novelists were willing enough to look upon themselves as leaders of thought. The novels they wrote were journalism rather than fiction. They had a news value. Their disadvantage was that after a little while they were as unreadable as last week's paper. But the demand of this great new public for knowledge has of late given rise to the production of a number of books in which subjects of common interest, science, education, social welfare and I know not what, are treated in nontechnical language. Their success has been very great and has killed the propaganda novel.

I look upon it as very natural then that the world of letters should have attached no great importance to my work. In the drama I have found myself at home in the traditional moulds. As a writer of fiction I go back, through innumerable generations, to the teller of tales round the fire in the cavern that sheltered neolithic men. I have had some sort of story to tell and it has interested me to tell it. To me it has been a sufficient object in itself. It has been my misfortune that for some time now a story has been despised by the intelligent. I have read a good many books on the art of fiction and all ascribe very small value to the plot. From these books you would judge that it is only a hindrance to the intelligent author and a concession that he makes to the stupid demands of the public. Indeed, sometimes you might think that the best novelist is the essayist, and that the only perfect short stories have been written by Charles Lamb and Hazlitt.

But the delight in listening to stories is as natural to human nature as the delight in looking at the dancing and miming out of which drama arose. That it exists unimpaired is shown by the vogue of the detective novel. The most intellectual persons read them, with condescension of course, but they read them, and why, if not because the psychological, the pedagogic, the psycho-analytic novels which alone their minds approve do not give them the satisfaction of this particular need? There are a number of clever writers who, with all sorts of good things in their heads to say and a gift for creating living people, do not know what on earth to do with them when they have created them. They cannot invent a plausible story. Like all writers (and in all writers there is a certain amount of humbug) they make a merit of their limitations and either tell the reader that he can imagine for himself what happens or else berate him for wanting to know. They claim that in life stories are not finished, situations are not rounded off and loose ends are left hanging.

It is a natural desire in the reader to want to know what happens to the people in whom his interest has been aroused and the plot is the means by which you gratify this desire. A good story is obviously a difficult thing to invent, but its difficulty is a poor reason for despising it. It should have coherence and sufficient probability for the needs of the theme; it should be of a nature to display the development of character, which is the chief concern of fiction at the present day, and it should have completeness, so that when it is finally unfolded no more questions can be asked about the persons who took part in it. It should have like Aristotle's tragedy a beginning, a middle and an end.

How important is criticism to the author? In my twenties the critics said I was brutal, in my thirties they said I was flippant, in my forties they said I was cynical, in my fifties they said I was competent. Now in my sixties they say I am superficial. I have gone my way, following the course I had mapped out for myself, and trying with my works to fill out the pattern I looked for. I think authors are unwise who do not read criticisms. It is salutary to train oneself to be no more affected by censure than by praise; for of course it is easy to shrug one's shoulders when one finds oneself described as a genius, but not so easy to be unconcerned when one is treated as a nincompoop. The history of criticism is there to show that contemporary criticism is fallible. It is a nice point to decide how far the author should consider it and how far ignore it. And such is the diversity of opinion that it is very difficult for an author to arrive at any conclusion about his merit. In England there is a natural tendency to despise the novel. The autobiography of an insignificant politician, the life of a royal courtesan will receive serious critical consideration, whereas half-a-dozen novels will be reviewed in a bunch by a reviewer who is concerned only too often to be amusing at their expense. The fact is simply that the English are more interested in works of information than in works of art. This makes it difficult for the novelist to get from criticisms of his work anything that will be useful to his own development.

Writers benefit by a critic who is gravely concerned with literature; even if they resent him they may be incited by antagonism to a clearer definition of their own aims. He can provoke in them an excitement that calls them to more conscious effort and his example urges them to take their art with a more intense seriousness.

In one of his dialogues Plato seemingly has tried to show the impossibility of criticism; but in fact he has only shown to what extravagance the Socratic method may sometimes lead. There is one sort of criticism that is evidently futile. This is that which is written by the critic to compensate himself for humiliations he has suffered in his early youth. Criticism affords him a means of regaining his self-esteem. Because at school, unable to adapt himself to the standards of that narrow world, he has been kicked and cuffed, he will when grown up cuff and kick in his turn in order to assuage his wounded feelings. His interest is in his reaction to the work he is considering, not in the reaction it has to him.

There can seldom have been a greater need than now of a critic of authority, for the arts are at sixes and sevens. We see composers telling stories, painters philosophizing, and novelists preaching sermons; we see poets impatient with their own harmony trying to fit with their verse the other harmony of prose, and we see the writers of prose trying to force on it the rhythms of verse. Someone is badly wanted to define once more the characters peculiar to the several arts and to point out to those who go astray that their experiments can lead only to their own confusion. It is too much to expect that anyone may be found who can speak with equal competence in all the arts; but, the demand producing the supply, we may still hope that one of these days a critic will arise to ascend the throne once occupied by Sainte-Beuve and Matthew Arnold. He can do much.

Criticism to my mind is a personal matter, but there is nothing against that if the critic has a great personality. It is dangerous for him to look upon his activity as creative. His business is to guide, to appraise, and to point to new avenues of creation, but if he looks upon himself as creative he will be more occupied with creation, the most enthralling of human activities, than with the functions proper to him. It is perhaps well for him to have written a play, a novel and some verse, for thus as in no other way can he acquire the technique of letters; but he cannot be a great critic unless he has realized that to create is not his affair. One of the reasons why current criticism is so useless is that it is done as a side-issue by creative writers.

The great critic should have a sympathy as wide as his knowledge is universal. It should be grounded not on a general indifference, such as makes men tolerant of things they care nothing about, but on an active delight in diversity. He must be familiar not only with the literature of his native land, but with standards founded on the literature of the past, and studious of contemporary literature in other countries, he will see clearly the trend that literature in its evolution is pursuing and so be enabled profitably to direct that of his own countrymen. He must support himself on tradition, for tradition is the expression of the inevitable idiosyncrasies of a nation's literature, but he must do everything he can to encourage its development in its natural direction. Tradition is a guide and not a jailer. He must have patience, firmness and enthusiasm. Each book he reads should be a new and thrilling adventure; he judges it by the universality of his knowledge and the strength of his character. In fact the great critic must be a great man.

He must be great enough to recognize with good-humored resignation that his work, though so important, can have but an ephemeral value; for his merit is that he responds to the needs of, and points the way to, his own generation. A new generation arises with other needs, a new way stretches before it; he has nothing more to say and is thrown with all his works into the dust-heap.

To spend his life to such an end can only be worth his while if he thinks literature one of the most important of human pursuits.

The artist's egoism is outrageous: it must be; he is by nature a solipsist and the world exists only for him to exercise upon it his powers of creation. He partakes of life only with part of him and never feels the common emotions of men with his whole being, for however urgent the necessity he is an observer as well as an actor. It often makes him seem heartless. Women with their shrewd sense are on their guard against him; they are attracted by him, but instinctively feel that they can never completely dominate him, which is their desire, for they know that somehow he escapes them. Has not Goethe, that great lover, himself told us how he composed verses in the arms of his beloved and with singing fingers softly tapped the beat of his hexameters on her shapely back? The artist is ill to live with. He can be perfectly sincere in his creative emotion and yet there is someone else within him who is capable of cocking a snook at its exercise. He is not dependable.

But the gods never make any of their gifts without adding to it a drawback. This multiplicity of the writer that enables him, like the gods, to create human beings prevents him from achieving perfect truth in their creation. Realism is relative. The most realistic writer by the direction of his interest falsifies his creatures. He sees them through his own eyes. He makes them more self-conscious than they really are. He makes them more reflective and more complicated. He throws himself into them, trying to make them ordinary men, but he never quite succeeds; for the peculiarity that gives him his talent and makes him a writer forever prevents him from knowing exactly what ordinary men are. It is not truth he attains, but merely a transposition of his own personality. And the greater his talent, the more powerful his individuality, the more fantastic is the picture of life he draws.

I have never been able to persuade myself that anything except learning to write well mattered. Notwithstanding, when men in millions are living on the border-line of starvation, when freedom in great parts of the inhabited globe is dying or dead, when a terrible war has been succeeded by another during which happiness has been out of reach of the great mass of the human race, when men are distraught because they can see no value in life and the hopes that had enabled them for so many centuries to support its misery seem illusory; it is hard not to ask oneself whether it is anything but futility to write plays and stories and novels. The only answer I can think of is that some of us are so made that there is nothing else we can do. We do not write because we want to; we write because we must. There may be other things in the world that more pressingly want doing; we must liberate our souls of the burden of creation. We must go on though Rome burns. Others may despise us because we do not lend a hand with a bucket of water; we cannot help it; we do not know how to handle a bucket. The conflagration thrills us and charges our mind with phrases.

IV

I was introduced to philosophy by Kuno Fischer whose lectures I attended when I was at Heidelberg. He had a reputation there and he was giving that winter a course of lectures on Schopenhauer. They were crowded and one had to queue up early in order to get a good seat. He was a dapper, short, stoutish man, neat in his dress, with a bullet head, white hair *en brosse* and a red face. His little eyes were quick and shining. He had a funny, flattened snub nose that looked as if it had been bashed in, and you would have been much more likely to take him for an old prize-fighter than for a philosopher. He was a humorist; he had indeed written a book on wit which I read at the time, but which I have completely forgotten, and every now and then a great guffaw broke from his audience of students as he made a joke. His voice was powerful and he was a vivid, impressive and exciting speaker. I was too young and too ignorant to understand much of what he said, but I got a very clear impression of Schopenhauer's odd and original personality and a confused feeling of the dramatic value and the romantic quality of his system. I hesitate to make any statement after so many years, but I have a notion that Kuno Fischer treated it as a work of art rather than as a serious contribution to metaphysics.

Since then I have read a great deal of philosophy. I have found it very good reading. Indeed, of the various great subjects that afford reading matter to the person for whom reading is a need and a delight it is the most varied, the most copious and the most satisfying. Ancient Greece is thrilling, but from this point of view there is not enough in it; a time comes when you have read the little that remains of its literature and all of significance that has been written about it. The Italian Renaissance is fascinating too, but the subject, comparatively, is small; the ideas that informed it were few, and you get tired of its art which has been long since drained of its creative value so that you are left only with grace, charm and symmetry (qualities of which you can have enough) and you get tired of its men, whose versatility falls into too uniform a pattern. You can go on reading about the Italian Renaissance forever, but your interest fails before the material is exhausted. The French Revolution is another subject that may well engage the attention and it has the advantage that its significance is actual. It is close to us in point of time so that with a very small effort of imagination we can put ourselves into the men who made it. They are almost contemporaries. And what they did and what they thought affect the lives we lead today; after a fashion we are all descendants of the French Revolution. And the material is abundant. The documents that relate to it are countless and the last thing has never been said about it. You can always find something fresh and interesting to read. But it does not satisfy. The art and literature it directly produced are negligible so that you are driven to the study of the men who made it, and the more you read about them the more are you dismayed by their pettiness and vulgarity. The actors in one of the greatest dramas in the world's history were pitifully inadequate to their parts. You turn away from the subject at last with a faint disgust.

But metaphysics never lets you down. You can never come to the end of it. It is as various as the soul of man. It has greatness, for it deals with nothing less than the whole of knowledge. It treats of the universe, of God and immortality, of the properties of human reason and the end and purpose of life, of the power and limitations of man; and if it cannot answer the questions that assail him on his journey through this dark and mysterious world it persuades him to support his ignorance with good humor. It teaches resignation and inculcates courage. It appeals to the imagination as well as to the intelligence; and to the amateur, much more, I suppose, than to the professional it affords matter for that reverie which is the most delicious pleasure with which man can beguile his idleness.

Since, inspired by Kuno Fischer's lectures, I began to read Schopenhauer I have read pretty well all the most important works of the great classical philosophers. Though there is in them a great deal that I did not understand, and perhaps I did not even understand as much as I thought, I read them with passionate interest.

I felt a wonderful exhilaration when I dizzily followed Plotonius in his flight from the alone to the alone, and though I have learnt since that Descartes drew preposterous conclusions from his effective premiss I was entranced by the lucidity of his expression. To read him was like swimming in a lake so clear that you could see the bottom; that crystalline water was wonderfully refreshing. I look upon my first reading of Spinoza as one of the signal experiences of my life. It filled me with just that feeling of majesty and exulting power that one has at the sight of a great mountain range.

And when I came to the English philosophers, with perhaps a slight prejudice, for it had been impressed upon me in Germany that, with the possible exception of Hume, they were quite negligible and Hume's only importance was that Kant had demolished him, I found that besides being philosophers they were uncommonly good writers. And though they might not be very great thinkers, of this I could not presume to judge, they were certainly very curious men. I should think that few could read Hobbes' *Leviathan* without being taken by the gruff, downright John Bullishness of his personality, and surely no one could read Berkeley's *Dialogues* without being ravished by the charm of that delightful bishop. And though it may be true that Kant made hay of Hume's theories, it would be impossible, I think, to write philosophy with more elegance, urbanity and clearness. They all, and Locke too for the matter of that, wrote English that the student of style could do much worse than study. Before I start writing a novel I read *Candide* over again so that I may have in the back of my mind the touchstone of that lucidity, grace and wit; I have a notion that it would not hurt the English philosophers of our own day if before they set about a work they submitted themselves to the discipline of reading Hume's *Inquiry Concerning the Human Understanding*.

The old woman who first said, "It's no good crying over spilt milk," was a philosopher in her way. For what did she mean by this except that regret was useless? A complete system of philosophy is implied. The determinist thinks that you cannot take a step in life that is not motivated by what you are at the moment; and you are not only your muscles, your nerves, your entrails and your brain; you are your habits, your opinions and your ideas. However little you may be aware of them, however contradictory, unreasonable and prejudiced they may be, they are there, influencing your actions and reactions. Even if you have never put them into words they are your philosophy. Perhaps it is well enough that most people should leave this unformulated. It is hardly thoughts they have, at least not conscious thoughts, it is a kind of vague feeling, a sort of experience like that muscular sense that the physiologists not so long ago discovered, which they have absorbed from the notions current in the society in which they live and which they faintly modified by their own experience. They lead their ordered lives and this confused body of ideas and feelings is enough. Since it includes something of the wisdom of the ages, it is adequate for the ordinary purposes of the ordinary life.

From an early age I wanted to make up my mind whether I had to consider only this life or a life to come; I wanted to discover whether I was a free agent or whether my feeling that I could mold myself according to my will was an illusion; I wanted to know whether life had any meaning or whether it was I that must strive to give it one. So in a desultory way I began to read.

The first subject that attracted my attention was religion. For it seemed to me of the greatest importance to decide whether this world I lived in was the only one I had to reckon with or whether I must look upon it as no more than a place of trial which was to prepare me for a life to come. When I wrote *Of Human Bondage* I gave a chapter to my hero's loss of the faith in which he had been brought up. The book was read in typescript by a very clever woman who at that time was good enough to be interested in me. She told me that this chapter was inadequate. I rewrote it; but I do not think I much improved it. For it described my own experience and I have no doubt that my reasons for coming to the conclusion I came to were inadequate. They were the reasons of an ignorant boy. They were of the heart rather than of the head. When my parents died I went to live with my uncle who was a clergyman. He was a childless man of fifty, and I am sure that it was a great nuisance to have the charge of a small boy thrust upon him. He read prayers morning and evening, and we went to church twice on Sundays. Sunday was the busy day. My uncle always said that he was the only man in his parish who worked seven days a week. In point of fact he was incredibly idle and left the work of his parish to his curate and his churchwardens. But I was impressionable and soon became very religious. I accepted what I was taught, both in my uncle's vicarage and afterwards at school, with unquestioning trust.

There was one point that immediately affected me. I had not been long at school before I discovered, through the ridicule to which I was exposed and the humiliations I suffered, how great a misfortune it was to me that I stammered; and I had read in the Bible that if you had faith you could move mountains. My uncle assured me that it was a literal fact. One night, when I was going back to school next day, I prayed to God with all my might that he would take away my impediment; and, such was my faith, I went to sleep quite certain that when I awoke next morning I should be able to speak like everybody else. I pictured to myself the surprise of the boys (I was still at a preparatory school) when they found that I no longer stammered. I woke full of exultation and it was a real, a terrible shock, when I discovered that I stammered as badly as ever.

I grew older. I went to the King's School. I was taught that we lived in the presence of God and that the chief business of man was to save his soul. I could not help seeing that none of these clergymen practiced what they preached. Fervent though my faith was, I had been terribly bored by all the church-going that was forced upon me, both at home and at school, and on going to Germany I welcomed the freedom that enabled me to stay away. But two or three times out of curiosity I went to High Mass at the Jesuit Church in Heidelberg. Though my uncle had a natural sympathy for Catholics (he was a High Churchman and at election time they painted on the garden fence, "This way to Rome"), he had no doubt they would frizzle in hell. He believed implicitly in eternal punishment. He hated the dissenters in his parish and indeed thought it a monstrous thing that the state tolerated them. His consolation was that they too would suffer eternal damnation. Heaven was reserved for the members of the Church of England. I accepted it as a great mercy of God that I had been bred in that communion. It was as wonderful as being born an Englishman.

But when I went to Germany I discovered that the Germans were just as proud of being Germans as I was proud of being English. I heard them say that the English did not understand music and that Shakespeare was only appreciated in Germany. They spoke of the English as a nation of shopkeepers and had no doubt in their minds that as artists, men of science and philosophers they were greatly superior. It shook me. And now at High Mass in Heidelberg I could not but notice that the students, who filled the church to its doors, seemed very devout. They had, indeed, all the appearance of believing in their religion as sincerely as I believed in mine. It was queer that they could, for of course I knew that theirs was false and mine was true.

It struck me that I might very well have been born in South Germany, and then I should naturally have been brought up as a Catholic. Thus through no fault of my own I should have been condemned to everlasting torment. My ingenuous nature revolted at the injustice. The next step was easy; I came to the conclusion that it could not matter a row of pins what one believed; God could not condemn people just because they were Spaniards or Hottentots. The whole horrible structure, based not on the love of God but on the fear of Hell, tumbled down like a house of cards.

With my mind at all events I ceased to believe in God; I felt the exhilaration of a new freedom. But we do not believe only with our minds; in some deep recess of my soul there lingered still the old dread of hell-fire, and for long my exultation was tempered by the shadow of that ancestral anxiety. I no longer believed in God; I still, in my bones, believed in the Devil.

It was this fear that I sought to banish when, becoming a medical student, I entered a new world. I read a great many books. They told me that man was a machine subject to mechanical laws; and when the machine ran down that was the end of him. I saw men die at the hospital and my startled sensibilities confirmed what my books had taught me. I was satisfied that religion and the idea of God were constructions that the human race had evolved as a convenience for living, and represented something that had at one time, and for all I was prepared to say still had, value for the survival of the species, but that must be historically explained and corresponded to nothing real. I called myself an agnostic, but in my blood and my bones I looked upon God as a hypothesis that a reasonable man must reject.

I waded conscientiously through many formidable tomes. I came to the conclusion that man aimed at nothing but his own pleasure and that when he sacrificed himself to others it was only an illusion that led him to believe that he was seeking anything but his own gratification. And since the future was uncertain it was only common sense to seize every pleasure that the moment offered. I decided that right and wrong were merely words and that the rules of conduct were no more than conventions that men had set up to serve their own selfish purposes. The free man had no reason to follow them except in so far as they suited his convenience. Having then an epigrammatic turn, and epigrams being the fashion, I put my conviction into a phrase and said to myself: follow your inclinations with due regard to the policeman round the corner. By the time I was twenty-four I had constructed a complete system of philosophy. It rested on two principles: The Relativity of Things and The Circumferentiality of Man. I have learnt since that the first of these was not a very original discovery. It may be that the other was profound, but though I have racked my brains I cannot for the life of me remember what on earth it meant.

I sought a book that would answer once for all the questions that puzzled me, so that, everything being settled for good and all, I could pursue the pattern of my life without let or hindrance. I read and read. From the classical philosophers I turned to the moderns, thinking that among them, perhaps, I should find what I wanted, but I could not discover much agreement among them.

When I read that Fichte had said that the kind of philosophy a man adopts depends on the kind of man he is, it occurred to me that perhaps I was looking for something that could not be found. It seemed to me then that if there was in philosophy no universal truth that agreed with the personality of the individual, the only thing for me was to narrow my search and look for some philosopher whose system suited me because I was the same sort of man that he was. The answers that he could provide to the questions that puzzled me must satisfy me because they would be the only possible answers to fit my humor.

For some time I was much attracted by the pragmatists. I had not got as much profit as I expected from the metaphysical writings of the dons at the great English universities. They seemed to me too gentlemanlike to be very good philosophers and I could not resist the suspicion that sometimes they failed to pursue an argument to its logical conclusion for fear of offending the susceptibilities of colleagues with whom they were in social relations. The pragmatists had vigor. They were very much alive. The most important of them wrote well, and they gave an appearance of simplicity to problems which I had not been able to make head or tail of. But much as I should have liked to I could not bring myself to believe, as they did, that truth is fashioned by us to meet our practical needs. The sense-datum, on which I thought all knowledge was based, seemed to me something given, which had to be accepted whether it suited the convenience or not. Nor did I feel comfortable with the argument that God existed if it consoled me to believe that he did. The pragmatists ceased to interest me so much. I found Bergson good to read, but singularly unconvincing; nor did I find in Benedetto Croce anything to my purpose. On the other hand, in Bertrand Russell I discovered a writer who greatly pleased me; he was easy to understand and his English was good. I read him with admiration.

I was very willing to accept him as the guide I sought. He had wordly wisdom and common sense. He was tolerant of human weakness. But I discovered in time that he was a guide none too certain of the way. His mind was restless. He was like an architect who, when you want a house to live in, having persuaded you to build it of brick, then sets before you good reasons why it should be built of stone; but when you have agreed to this produces reasons just as good to prove that the only material to use is reinforced concrete. Meanwhile you have not a roof to your head. I was looking for a system of philosophy as coherent and self-contained as Bradley's, in which one part hung necessarily on another, so that nothing could be altered without the whole fabric falling to pieces. This Bertrand Russell could not give me.

At last I came to the conclusion that I could never find the one, complete and satisfying book I sought, because that book could only be an expression of myself. So with more courage than discretion I made up my mind that I must write it for myself. I found out what were the books set for the undergraduate to read in order to take a philosophical degree and laboriously perused them. I thought I should thus have at least a foundation for my own work. It seemed to me that with this, the knowledge of the world I had acquired during the forty years of my life (for I was forty when I conceived this idea) and the industrious study of philosophical literature to which I was prepared to devote some years, I should be competent to write such a book as I had in mind. I meant to make a system that would be valid for me and enable me to pursue the course of my life.

But the more I read the more complicated the subject seemed to me and the more conscious I grew of my ignorance. I was peculiarly discouraged by the philosophical magazines in which I found topics discussed at great length which were evidently of importance but which seemed to me in my darkness very trivial. The authorities quoted proved to me that philosophy, at all events now, was a business for the experts to deal with between them. The layman could little hope to comprehend its subtleties. I should need twenty years to prepare myself to write the book I proposed and by the time it was done I might be on my death bed and to me at least the labor I had taken would no longer be of use.

I abandoned the idea and all I have to show for my efforts now are the few desultory notes that follow. I claim no originality for them, or even for the words in which I have put them. I am like a tramp who has rigged himself up as best he could with a pair of trousers from a charitable farmer's wife, a coat off a scarecrow, odd boots out of a dustbin, and a hat that he has found in the road. They are just shreds and patches, and, uncomely as they may be, he finds that they suit him well enough.

The problem presses when you come to consider whether God exists, and if he does, what nature must be ascribed to him. The time came when, like everybody else, I read the engaging works of the physicists. I was seized with awe at the contemplation of the immense distances that separated the stars and the stretches of time that light traversed in order to come from them to us. I was staggered by the unimaginable extent of the nebulae. If I understood aright what I read, I must suppose that at the beginning the two forces of cosmical attraction and repulsion balanced so that the universe remained for untold ages in a state of perfect equilibrium. Then at some moment this was disturbed and the universe, toppling off its balance, gave rise to the universe the astronomers tell us of and the little earth we know. But what caused the original act of creation and what upset the balance of equilibrium? I seemed inevitably drawn to the conception of a creator, and what could create this vast, this stupendous universe but a being all-powerful? But the evil of the world then forces on us the conclusion that this being cannot be all-powerful and all-good. A God who is all-powerful may be justly blamed for the evil of the world and it seems absurd to consider him with admiration or accord him worship. But mind and heart revolt against the conception of a God who is not all-good. We are forced then to accept the supposition of a God who is not all-powerful: such a God contains within himself no explanation of his own existence or of that of the universe he creates.

Men are passionate, men are weak, men are stupid, men are pitiful; to bring to bear on them anything so tremendous as the wrath of God seems strangely inept.

Every artist wishes to be believed in, but he is not angry with those who will not accept the communication he offers. God is not so reasonable. He craves so urgently to be believed in that you might think he needed your belief in order to reassure himself of his own existence. He promises rewards to those who believe in him and threatens with horrible punishment those who do not. For my part I cannot believe in a God who is angry with me because I do not believe in him. I cannot believe in a God who is less tolerant than I. I cannot believe in a God who has neither humor nor common sense. Plutarch long ago put the matter succinctly. "I would much rather," he writes, "have men say of me that there never was a Plutarch, nor is now, than to say that Plutarch is a man inconstant, fickle, easily moved to anger, revengeful for trifling provocations and vexed at small things."

But though men have ascribed to God imperfections that they would deplore in themselves, that does not prove that God does not exist. Arguments have been adduced to prove the existence of God, and I will ask the reader to have patience with me while I briefly consider them. One of them assumes that man has an idea of a perfect being; and since perfection includes existence a perfect being must exist. Another, the argument from design, which Kant said was the clearest, oldest and best suited to human reason, is thus stated by one of the characters in Hume's great dialogues: "the order and arrangement of nature, the curious adjustment of final causes, the plain use and intention of every part and organ; all these bespeak in the clearest language an intelligent cause or Author." But Kant showed conclusively that there was no more to be said in favor of this argument than in that of the other two. In their place he propounded another. In a few words, it is to the effect that without God there is no guarantee that the sense of duty, which presupposes a free and real self, is not an illusion and therefore that it is morally necessary to believe in God. This has been generally thought more creditable to Kant's amiable nature than to his subtle intelligence.

The argument which to me seems more persuasive than any of these is one that has now fallen out of favor. It is known as the proof *e consensu gentium*. It asserts that all men from the remotest origins have had some sort of belief in God and it is hard to think that a belief that has grown up with the human race, a belief that has been accepted by the wisest men, the sages of the East, the philosophers of Greece, the great Scholastics, should not have a foundation in fact. It has seemed to many instinctive and it may be (one can only say, it may be, for it is far from certain) that an instinct does not exist unless there is a possibility of its being satisfied. Experience has shown that the prevalence of a belief, no matter for how long it has been held, is no guarantee of its truth.

It appears, then, that none of the arguments for the existence of God is valid. But of course you do not disprove his existence because you cannot prove it. Awe remains, man's sense of helplessness, and his desire to attain harmony between himself and the universe at large. These, rather than the worship of nature or of ancestors, magic or morality, are the sources of religion. There is no reason to believe that what you desire exists, but it is a hard saying that you have no right to believe what you cannot prove; there is no reason why you should not believe so long as you are aware that your belief lacks proof.

I suppose that if your nature is such that you want comfort in your trials and a love that sustains and encourages you, you will neither ask for proofs nor have need of them. Your intuition suffices.

Faced with this, awed by the greatness of the universe and malcontent with what the philosophers told me, and what the saints said, I have sometimes gone back, beyond Mohammed, Jesus and Buddha, beyond the gods of Greece, Jehovah and Baal, to the Brahma of the Upanishads. That spirit, if spirit it may be called self-created and independent of all other existence, though all that exists, exists in it, the sole source of life in all that lives, has at least a grandeur that satisfies the imagination. But I have been busy with words too long not to be suspicious of them, and when I look at those I have just written I cannot but see that their meaning is tenuous. The only God that is of use is a being who is personal, supreme and good, and whose existence is as certain as that two and two make four. I cannot penetrate the mystery. I remain an agnostic, and the practical outcome of agnosticism is that you act as though God did not exist.

If then one puts aside the existence of God and the possibility of survival as too doubtful to have any effect on one's behavior, one has to make up one's mind what is the meaning and use of life. If death ends all, if I have neither to hope for good to come nor to fear evil, I must ask myself what I am here for and how in these circumstances I must conduct myself. Now the answer to one of these questions is plain, but it is so unpalatable that most men will not face it.

There is no reason for life and life has no meaning. We are here, inhabitants for a little while of a small planet, revolving round a minor star which in its turn is a member of one of unnumbered galaxies. And if the astronomer tells us truth this planet will eventually reach a condition when living things can no longer exist upon it and at long last the universe will attain that final stage of equilibrium when nothing more can happen. Aeons and aeons before this man will have disappeared. Is it possible to suppose that it will matter then that he ever existed? He will have been a chapter in the history of the universe as pointless as the chapter in which is written the life stories of the strange monsters that inhabited the primeval earth.

Most people think little. They accept their presence in the world; blind slaves of the striving which is their mainspring, they are driven this way and that to satisfy their natural impulses, and when it dwindles they go out like the light of a candle. Their lives are purely instinctive. It may be that theirs is the greater wisdom. But if your consciousness has so far developed that you find certain questions pressing upon you and you think the old answers wrong, what are you going to do? What answers will you give? To at least one of these questions two of the wisest men who ever lived have given their own answers. When you come to look at them they seem to mean pretty much the same thing and I am not so sure that that is very much. Aristotle has said that the end of human activity is right action, and Goethe that the secret of life is living.

I suppose that Goethe means that man makes the most of his life when he arrives at self-realization; he had small respect for a life governed by passing whims and uncontrolled instincts. That there is a singular delight in self-sacrifice few would deny, and in so far as it offers a new field for activity and the opportunity to develop a new side of the self, it has value in self-realization; but if you aim at self-realization only in so far as it interferes with no one else's attempts at the same thing you will not get very far. Such an aim demands a good deal of ruthlessness and an absorption in oneself which is offensive to others and thus often stultifies itself.

V

A question presents itself which I shirked. Now that I can avoid it no longer, I cannot but draw back. I am conscious that here and there I have taken free-will for granted; I have spoken as though I had power to mold my intentions and direct my actions as the whim took me. In other places I have spoken as though I accepted determinism. Such shilly-shallying would have been deplorable had I been writing a philosophical work. I make no such pretension.

But how can I, an amateur, be expected to settle a question which the philosophers have not yet ceased to argue?

It might seem only sensible to leave the matter alone, but it happens to be one in which the writer of fiction is peculiarly concerned. For as a writer, he finds himself compelled by his readers to rigid determination. I pointed out earlier in these pages how unwilling an audience is to accept impulse on the stage. Now an impulse is merely an urge to action of whose motive the agent is not conscious; it is analogous to an intuition, which is a judgment you make without being aware of its grounds.

But though an impulse has its motive, an audience, because it is not obvious, will not accept it. The spectators of a play and the readers of a book insist on knowing the reasons of action and they will not admit its probability unless the reasons are cogent. Each person must behave in character; that means that he must do what from their knowledge of him they expect him to do. Cunning must be exercised in order to persuade them to accept the coincidences and accidents which in real life they swallow without a second thought. They are determinists to a man and the writer who trifles with their obstinate prejudice is lost.

But when I look back upon my life I cannot but notice how much that vitally affected me has been due to circumstances that it is hard not to regard as pure chance. Determinism tells us that choice follows the line of least resistance or the strongest motive. I am not conscious that I have always followed the line of least resistance, and if I have followed the strongest motive, that motive has been an idea of myself that I have gradually evolved.

I do not think it unreasonable to hold the opinion that everything in the universe combines to cause every one of our actions, and this naturally includes all our opinions and desires; but whether an action, once performed, was inevitable from all eternity can only be decided when you have made up your mind whether or no there are events, the events that Dr. Broad calls casual progenitors, which are not completely determined. The physicists themselves tell us that physics is making such rapid progress that it is only possible to keep abreast of it by a close study of the periodical literature. It is surely rash to found a theory on principles suggested by a science that is so unstable. Schrödinger himself has stated that a final and comprehensive judgment on the matter is at present impossible. The plain man is justified in sitting on the fence, but perhaps he is prudent to keep his legs dangling on the side of determinism.

The life force is vigorous. The delight that accompanies it counterbalances all the pains and hardships that confront men. It makes life worth living, for it works from within and lights with its own bright flame each one's circumstances so that, however intolerable, they seem tolerable to him. Much pessimism is caused by ascribing to others the feelings you would feel if you were in their place. It is this (among much else) that makes novels so false. The novelist constructs a public world out of his own private world and gives to the characters of his fancy a sensitiveness, a power of reflection and an emotional capacity, which are peculiar to himself.

Most people have little imagination and they do not suffer from circumstances that to the imaginative would be unbearable. The lack of privacy, to take an instance, in which the very poor live seems frightful to us who value it; but it does not seem so to the very poor. They hate to be alone; it gives them a sense of security to live in company. No one who has dwelt among them can fail to have noticed how little they envy the well-to-do. The fact is that they do not want many of the things that to others of us appear essential. It is fortunate for the well-to-do. For he is blind who will not see that in the lives of the proletariat in the great cities all is misery and confusion. It is hard to reconcile oneself to the fact that work should be so dreary, that they should live, they, their wives and their children, on the edge of starvation, and in the end have nothing to look forward to but destitution. If only revolution can remedy this, then let revolution come and come quickly. When we see the cruelty with which men treat one another in countries that we have been in the habit of calling civilized, it would be rash to say that they are any better than they were.

One may reasonably hope that with the increase of knowledge, with the discarding of many cruel superstitions and outworn conventions, with a livelier sense of loving-kindness many of the evils from which men suffer will be removed. But many evils must continue to exist. We are the play-things of nature. Earthquakes will continue to wreak havoc, droughts to ruin crops and unforeseen floods to destroy the prudent constructions of men. Human folly, alas, will continue to devastate the nations with war. Men will continue to be born who are not fitted for life and life will be a burden to them. So long as some are strong and some are weak, the weak will be driven to the wall. So long as men are cursed with the sense of possession, and that I presume is as long as they exist, they will wrest what they can from those who are powerless to hold it. So long as they have the instinct of self-assertion, they will exercise it at the expense of others' happiness. In short, so long as man is man he must be prepared to face all the woes that he can bear.

There is no explanation for evil. It must be looked upon as a necessary part of the order of the universe. To ignore it is childish; to bewail it senseless. Spinoza called pity womanish; the epithet has a harsh sound on the lips of that tender and austere spirit. I suppose he thought that it was but waste of emotion to feel strongly about what you could not alter. I am not a pessimist. Indeed, it would be nonsensical of me to be so, for I have been one of the lucky ones. I have often wondered at my good fortune. An accident here, an accident there, might have changed everything and frustrated me as so many with talents equal to, or greater than, mine, with equal opportunities, have been frustrated. With all my limitations, physical and mental, I have been glad to live. I would not live my life over again. There would be no point in that. Nor would I care to pass again through the anguish I have suffered. It is one of the faults of my nature that I have suffered more from the pains, than I have enjoyed the pleasures of my life. But without my physical imperfections, with a stronger body and a better brain, I would not mind entering upon the world afresh. The years that now stretch immediately in front of us look as if they would be interesting.

The young enter upon life now with advantages that were denied to the young of my generation. They are hampered by fewer conventions and they have learnt how great is the value of youth. The world of my twenties was a middle-aged world and youth was something to be got through as quickly as possible so that maturity might be reached. The young things of the present day, at least in that middle class to which I belong, seem to me better prepared. They are taught now many things that are useful to them, whereas we had to pick them up as best we could. The relation between the sexes is more normal. Young women have learnt now to be the companions of young men. One of the difficulties that my generation had to face, the generation that saw the emancipation of women, was this: They were no longer housewives and had not yet learnt to be good fellows. There is no more pleasant spectacle for an elderly gentleman than that of the young girl of the present day, so competent and so self-assured, who can run an office and play a hard game of tennis, who is intelligently concerned with public affairs and can appreciate the arts, and, prepared to stand on her own feet, faces life with cool, shrewd and tolerant eyes.

It is clear that these young folk who are now taking the stage must look forward to economic changes that will transform civilization. They will not know the *douceur de vivre*. We live on the eve of great revolutions.

If I live I shall write other books, for my amusement and I hope for the amusement of my readers, but I do not think they will add anything essential to my design. The house is built. There will be additions, a terrace from which one has a pretty view, or an arbor in which to meditate in the heat of summer; but should death prevent me from producing them, the house, though the house-breakers may set to work on it the day after I am buried in an obituary notice, will have been built.

I look forward to old age without dismay. When Lawrence of Arabia was killed I read in an article contributed by a friend that it was his habit to ride his motor-bicycle at an excessive speed with the notion that an accident would end his life while he was still in full possession of his powers and so spare him the indignity of old age. If this is true it was a great weakness in that strange and somewhat theatrical character. It showed want of sense. For the complete life, the perfect pattern, includes old age as well as youth and maturity. The beauty of the morning and the radiance of noon are good, but it would be a very silly person who drew the curtains and turned on the light in order to shut out the tranquility of the evening. Old age has its pleasures, which, though different, are not less than the pleasures of youth. The philosophers have always told us that we are the slaves of our passions, and is it so small a thing to be liberated from their sway? The fool's old age will be foolish, but so was his youth. The young man turns away from it with horror because he thinks that when he reaches it, he will yearn for the things that give variety and gusto to his youth. He is mistaken. It is true that the old man will no longer be able to climb an Alp or tumble a pretty girl on a bed; it is true that he can no longer arouse the concupiscence of others. It is something to be free from the pangs of unrequited love and the torment of jealousy. It is something that envy, which so often poisons youth, should be assuaged by the extinction of desire.

But these are negative compensations; old age has positive compensations also. Paradoxical as it may sound it has more time. When I was young I was amazed at Plutarch's statement that the elder Cato began at the age of eighty to learn Greek. I am amazed no longer. Old age is ready to undertake tasks that youth shirked because they would take too long.

Spinoza says that a free man thinks of nothing less than of death. It is unnecssary to dwell upon it, but it is foolish, as so many do, to shrink from all consideration of it. It is well to make up one's mind about it. It is impossible to know till death is there facing one whether one will fear it. I have often tried to imagine what my feelings would be if a doctor told me I had a fatal disease and had no more than a little time to live. I have put them into the mouths of various characters of my invention, but I am aware how I should actually feel. I do not think I have a very strong instinctive hold on life. I have had a good many serious illnesses, but have only once known myself to be within measurable distance of death; then I was so tired that I could not fear, I only wanted to get done with the struggle. Death is inevitable and it does not much matter how one meets it. I do not think one can be blamed if one hopes that one will not be aware of its imminence and be fortunate enough to undergo it without pain.

I have always lived so much in the future that now, though the future is so short, I cannot get out of the habit and my mind looks forward with a certain complacency to the completion within an indefinite number of years of the pattern that I have tried to make. There are moments when I have so palpitating an eagerness for death that I could fly to it as to the arms of a lover. It gives me the same passionate thrill as years ago was given me by life. I am drunk with the thought of it. It seems to offer the final and absolute freedom. Notwithstanding, I am willing enough to go on living so long as the doctors can keep me in tolerable health; I enjoy the spectacle of the world and it interests me to see what is going to happen. The consummation of many lives that have run their course parallel with my own gives me continual food for reflection and sometimes for the confirmation of theories that I formed long ago. I shall be sorry to part from my friends. Having held a certain place in the world for a long time I am content that others soon should occupy it. After all the point of a pattern is that it should be completed. When nothing can be added without spoiling the design the artist leaves it.

For many years I thought that it was beauty alone that gave significance to life and that the only purpose that could be assigned to the teeming generations that succeed one another on the face of the earth was to produce now and then an artist. The work of art, I decided, was the crowning product of human activity, and the final justification for all the misery, the endless toil and the frustrated strivings of humanity. And though I modified this extravagance later by including the beautiful life among the works of art that alone gave a meaning to life, it was still beauty that I valued. All these notions I have long since abandoned.

In the first place I discovered that beauty was a full stop. When I considered beautiful things I found that there was nothing for me to do but to gaze and admire. The emotion they gave me was exquisite, but I could not preserve it, nor could I definitely repeat it; the most beautiful things in the world finished by boring me. I noticed that I got a more lasting satisfaction from works of a more tentative character. Because they had not achieved complete success they gave more scope for the activity of my imagination. In the greatest of all works of art everything had been realized. I could give nothing, and my restless mind tired of passive contemplation.

It seemed to me that beauty was like the summit of a mountain peak; when you had reached it there was nothing to do but to come down again. Perfection is a trifle dull. It is not the least of life's ironies that this, which we all aim at, is better not quite achieved.

One of the most curious things that has forced itself on my notice is that there is no permanence in the judgment of beauty. The museums are full of objects which the most cultivated taste of a period considered beautiful, but which seem to us now worthless; and in my lifetime I have seen the beauty evaporate from poems and pictures, exquisite not so long ago, like hoar frost before the morning sun. Vain as we may be we can hardly think our own judgment ultimate; what we think beautiful will doubtless be scorned in another generation, and what we have despised may be raised to honor. The only conclusion is that beauty is relative to the needs of a particular generation, and that to examine the things we consider beautiful for qualities of absolute beauty is futile. If beauty is one of the values that give life significance it is something that is constantly changing and thus cannot be analyzed, for we can as little feel the beauty our ancestors felt as we can smell the roses they smelt.

What exactly is one's reaction to a great work of art? What does one feel when for instance one looks at Titian's Entombment in the Louvre or listens to the quintet in the *Meistersinger?* I know what mine is. It is an excitement that gives me a sense of exhilaration, intellectual but suffused with sensuality, a feeling of well-being in which I seem to discern a sense of power and of liberation from human ties; at the same time I feel in myself a tenderness which is rich with human sympathy; I feel rested, at peace and yet spiritually aloof.

On occasion, looking at certain pictures or statues, listening to certain music, I have had an emotion so strong that I could only describe it in the same words as those the mystics use to describe the union with God. But I have asked myself what was the use of this emotion. Of course it is delightful and pleasure in itself is good, but what is there in it that makes it superior to any other pleasure, so superior that to speak of it as pleasure at all seems to depreciate it? The answer the mystics gave to this question was unequivocal. They said that rapture was worthless unless it strengthened the character and rendered man more capable of right action. The value of it lay in works.

If beauty is one of the great values of life, then it seems hard to believe that the aesthetic sense which enables men to appreciate it should be the privilege only of a class. It is not possible to maintain that a form of sensibility that is shared but by the elect can be a necessity of human life. Yet that is what the aesthetic claim. I must confess that in my foolish youth when I considered that art (in which I included the beauties of nature, for I was very much of opinion, as indeed I still am, that their beauty was constructed by men as definitely as they constructed pictures or symphonies) was the crown of human endeavor and the justification of man's existence, it gave me a peculiar satisfaction to think that it could be appreciated only by the chosen few. But this notion has long stuck in my gizzard. An art is only great and significant if it is one that all may enjoy. The art of a clique is but a plaything. I do not know why distinctions are made between ancient art and modern art. There is nothing but art. Art is living. To attempt to give an object of art life by dwelling on its historical, cultural, or archaeological associations is senseless. It does not matter whether a statue was hewn by an archaic Greek or a modern Frenchman. Its only importance is that it should give us here and now the aesthetic thrill and that this aesthetic thrill should move us to works.

And little as I like the deduction, I cannot but accept it; and this is that the work of art must be judged by its fruits, and if these are not good it is valueless. It is an odd fact, which must be accepted as in the nature of things and for which I know no explanation, that the artist achieves this effect only when he does not intend it. His sermon is most efficacious if he has no notion that he is preaching one.

Goodness is the only value that seems in this world of appearances to have any claim to be an end in itself. Virtue is its own reward. I am ashamed to have reached so commonplace a conclusion. With my instinct for effect I should have liked to end my book with some startling and paradoxical announcement or with a cynicism that my readers would have recognized with a chuckle as characteristic. It seems I have little more to say than can be read in any copybook or heard from any pulpit. I have gone a long way round to discover what everyone knew already.

I have little sense of reverence. There is a great deal too much of it in the world. It is claimed for many objects that do not deserve it. It is often no more than the conventional homage we pay to things in which we are not willing to take an active interest. The best homage we can pay to the great figures of the past, Dante, Titian, Shakespeare, Spinoza, is to treat them not with reverence, but with the familiarity we should exercise if they were our contemporaries. Thus we pay them the highest compliment we can; our familiarity acknowledges that they are alive for us. But when now and then I have come across real goodness I have found reverence rise naturally in my heart.

Plato, as we know, enjoined upon his wise men to abandon the serene life of contemplation for the turmoil of practical affairs and thereby set the claim of duty above the desire for happiness; and we have all of us, I suppose, on occasion adopted a course because we thought it right though we well knew that it could bring us happiness neither then nor in the future. What then is right action? For my own part the best answer I know is that given by Fray Luis de Leon. To follow it does not look so difficult that human weakness quails before it as beyond its strength. With it I can end my book. The beauty of life, he says, is nothing but this, that each should act in conformity with his nature and his business.

A Decade of American Poetry 1957—67

By Judson Jerome

No question: we were too genteel, if that's
the word for mentalities which gave
that '49 award to Pound, retreating
from human value, disregarding meaning.
Only professors could defend a point
by swallowing erudite ugliness—or those
Quartets without music—nor joy nor love nor light
but lots of certitude. As C. P. Snow
told us, the literary mind at best
was irresponsible, at worst pernicious,
most charming when most innocently effete.

Ten years ago our poets were coming back
from Fulbrights bearing sheafs of landscape poems
with colons in their titles, mincing, rare:
"Penzance: Bank Holiday," or "Twilight: Villa
de los Huesos Secos." Everyone was writing
poems about Bruegel. Rago was weary
of historical monologues about the Duchess
of Portsmouth explaining Original Sin to Rowley.
The Fisher King, like Mistah Kurtz, was dead;
Tiresias was a scholar. Jarrell pondered
fertility embodied in a girl
who dozed in a library. We all were dozing
in libraries; fertility flipped out
to demonstrate at lunch counters. Ciardi—
having assaulted Mrs. Lindbergh—said
the most probable word in *Poetry* was *improbable*,
"the improbable rose," "her improbable smile," that faint
bemused, impersonal irony we all
relished in our refinement. When Ginsberg
said poetry in *Hudson* in the Fifties
was simply unreadable, he was dead right.

314

Shapiro, back before he proclaimed himself
the Peck's Bad Boy of the Establishment,
said if he had one book on a desert island
he'd want the poems of Lawrence, that bristly daddy
of all the angry outs to ask for blood.
Shapiro talked of starting a magazine—
but not some little secretive emission
tolerated by friends, but one like LIFE
with pictures, color, sex—and circulation.
Was poetry an escape from emotion, or
a catalyst which occurred at the intersection
of Brooks and Warren? Ogden and Richards? Did
Hayakawa class it with advertising?
Let poetry burst through the bric-a-brac
and wave its stubby selfhood in the face
of the Committee on Explication. McCarthy
died, 1957, while *Howl* was heard
as a depraved moan in the ruins. Ciardi saw
it slouched on my couch with Dant in hand. I'd called
it unreadable—but Ciardi did not sneer.
He quoted, "in the total animal soup of time,"
and there pronounced, "If Whitman is poetry,
then that is poetry." (In those lost days
one quarreled whether things were poetry.)
But even he sought jewels in the lava flow.
That's how we all were taught to read—for phrases,
symbols, for art, at least for pattern, wit—
but if these qualities occurred at all
in the new torrent, they were rubble of
museums. You don't sit by and watch the madman
shaking his dead geranium in your face
and analyze his language. The tide was sweat—
and in it many drowned. Some learned to swim.

In *The New York Times* a buoyant Lowell hailed
the West Coast Renaissance, and promptly abandoned
pentameter and classical allusions,
began to sell fillets of tattered heart.
(Who touches his *Life Studies* touches a man.)
Somewhere were dug up Patchen and Rexroth, who
come out for revolutions like the green
of St. Patrick's. Poets read to jazz (remember

jazz?), stripped, smoked pot as Dad smoked cornsilk, cursed.
(Heroin was exotic—for musicians.)
Books were promoted by censorship and raids
while picture-spreads in LIFE at long last brought
poetry to the attention of commuters.
How innocent and distant seem those days
when refugees from Black Mountain were ranging
from Majorca to Albuquerque, sitting at
the feet of guru Rexroth in the West,
the feet of guru Williams in the East—
Levertov, Olson, Creeley, Blackburn, Goodman—
with lines of nervous breath, images of
profound simplicity. When Pound was freed—
that guru of White Citizens' Councils—he
removed the fascist stain from Whitman's vision.
Negro became the *lingua franca.* Values
reversed, as in a photo negative
where hot looks cool: achievement, wealth, success
were black (or, rather, white). One scoured for junk
to cherish: poverty, pain and slovenly dress,
sexual aberration, drugs, whatever
elders considered vulgar or obscene.
Negroes were used (why did they not resent it?)
as guides to degradation, as connections
to the cool world of grass and rock-and-roll.
This conscious search for sin was clearly also
a search for innocence, for sexlessness,
for endless puberty, release from mind,
a refusal to mature in the Western World,
a yearning for an Eastern sweet unreason . . . .

And how this product sold! For in a guilty
nation, nothing succeeds like defeat. Grove Press
and *Playboy* made it plain there's money in
rebellion. Corso sold like Yevtushenko.
Ferlinghetti sold like Ogden Nash.
(And New Directions seemed as staid as Knopf.)
Avant and pop were suddenly all the same!
Elvis, James Dean and Marilyn Monroe
made it in to be out. (Intellectual pets,
these shaggy little rock groups.) In ten years
mass media, once object of aversion,

became the great white hope in blinking lights
for the hipcult. Riesman predicted all:
McLuhan made it cool to be what we
are bound to become—other-directed, tribal.
And inarticulate poetry is at least
democratic; anyone can do it; all
can understand; ignorance is a kind
of primitive virtue. Poetry, which once
was too cerebral, now was oral (on
its way to becoming genital), and poets thrived
on records, in college readings, entertaining
at parties of the rich—the new jongleurs.

And all the publishing professors perished,
in word and influence if not in deed.
Wilbur's prophet cried in the wilderness;
Nemerov, Roethke, Kunitz, Simpson, Jarrell—
writing as much as ever, and as well,
gained something from the popularity
of poetry in general, but sensed they were
outmoded. Many began translating. They
wrote about Goya now—and race, and war—
attempted to limber up their lines, to find
a narrative mode, dramatic mode. Some followed
Lowell to booths of confessions; some followed Bly
to fish in the deep snow for images
which might unlock their hopelessly rational minds.
We looked to Snodgrass to teach us about how
to emerge from the self's swamp to social comment,
retaining the mind's music, a sense of shape,
and saw skill grow while his ambition faltered.
Dickey put on a good show, telling tales
of making a girl in an abandoned car,
a stewardess falling out of an airplane, or
the plight of sunburned lovers—a poet with
competence and no mission—like so many.
And older men wrote on: MacLeish and Frost,
Auden and Cummings. *J.B.* cried out the fate
of virtue, quality, in a world obsessed
with boils—a lean form speaking to the times,
his impact lost in the hurly-burly tide.
Auden was launching one book after another

317

with reason's keel and irony's tricky rudder,
archaic as justice—and as unexciting.
Alas that wit in Auden as in Adlai
was such a pin-point, though affirming, flame.
When Cummings died the hippies took no notice
of that bohemian dinosaur. Frost died,
dismissed by Lowell as a great "pre-modern,"
though he alone of modern poets took
true cognizance of current science and thought.
And Williams toppled, that other snowy giant,
as left of Frost as Yeats and Eliot
had been to his right—and no howl that I heard
bemoaned his passing. (Remember the elegies
for Dylan? Thomas, I mean.) I heard Ginsberg
explain to a college crowd why Williams failed
to measure up to the highest poetic standards:
"He never got laid enough," sad Allen said.
And who has sung for Eliot, who seemed
himself to have forgotten how to sing?

No question. The impulse of the decade was right:
to find a new engagement, an audience,
to find a cause, protest forms which held nothing,
to be human again—itchy of crotch and barefoot.
It even seemed a noble undertaking
to find a substitute for alcohol.
But what did we discover? All roads led
to that delicious word, laving us softly:
self, self, self, self, self, self, and again self.
How we prefer personalities to products,
poets to poems—not art, but the private man!
Commitment? To Love? To love of being flaccid—
for who needs poetry who can have acid?
To freedom? The passive freedom of the trance,
each one engaged in onanistic dance.
Negroes be damned: the demonstration's over,
Mother is properly shocked, the pot delivered.
If peace can be achieved by turning on
(or off, or out), why organize resistance?
And social justice, like art, requires an effort.
The only relevance is here and now
and you and me, and sometimes I wonder whether

you are as relevent as once you seemed.
The strobe lights flash, the music screams we're free,
Ginsberg records each Texaco marquee . . . .
Is this the revolution of which we dreamed?
Beneath the din the voice of reason drones
untiring with its necessary labor.
Depend on the professors to survive.
Hardly a campus now without its poet—
a tweedy type, articulate at meetings,
a station wagon, kids, a pretty wife,
insistent on his raises, gives good readings,
has half a heart for poetry, half for life.
By night he sharpens weapons. He learns, he learns.
You got to believe his heart in silence burns.
His anger builds, his focus narrows, his tools
lie ready in bright array. There'll come a day,
after the last great Happening, when he
will clear his throat and stand—with something to say.

Into Print

How to Get into
Book Publishing
As Editor or Publisher

*A transcript from a college workshop
on book publishing*

Q. *I want to be a book publisher. How do I start?*

A. One way is to publish an annual or some form of Americana.

Q. *Why these?*

A. An annual is rewarding. It blooms each year. Think of it this way: if you publish a work of fiction, you begin by buying a manuscript from an author, usually on royalty; you edit it, sell the book to stores and pretty soon you have to get yourself another book or another author because the sales on this one have worn off. Out of one hundred fiction titles, 80 will peter out one year after publication. But an annual goes on forever.

Q. *Eight fiction titles out of 10 are duds?*

A. Yes, in the sense their sales potential hasn't proved strong enough to justify continuous advertising. A book publisher is fortunate to break even with 8 fiction books out of 10. His profit comes from the two that are a good flash in the pan or, best of all, hold up for two or three years. When you publish adult fiction, your bet is that one, or maybe two books out of every ten will net you $20,000 or more on the title. The rest are also-rans.

Q. *Are annuals that much better?*

A. They usually are. The kind of annual we are talking about is sound editorially and has a market that grows with the country. An annual gives you a new edition to sell each year and meanwhile you learn how to improve it editorially.

Q. *Could you give us some examples?*

A. There are two main kinds of annuals. One is really just a directory. Some directories are in the trade field; others are for the consumer. There are hundreds of trade directories. I'll name three: *Gift and Tableware Directory* and its competitor, *Gift and Decorative Accessory Buyers Guide,* or Patterson's *American Education.*

Q. *Directories are just names and addresses then?*

A. More than that. The listings are categorized. The more information given in each listing, the more valuable the directory becomes to the purchaser and to the company that is listed. Here are two others: *World Aviation Directory* and *Hardware Age Directory.*

Q. *What trade directories are already published?*

A. All the directories that contain both advertising space and editorial listings appear in both the "Consumer and Farm Publications" and the "Business Publications" of *Standard Rate and Data,* 5201 Old Orchard Road, Skokie, Illinois, 60076. A single copy of each is $10.00. Most directories listed in *Standard Rate and Data* are paper bound. There are, however, numerous cloth-bound directories. One good example is *The American Library Directory.*

Q. *Do you publish a directory?*

A. Yes. *Writer's Market.* It is clothbound, 900 pages, 6x9, $9.95.

Q. *Do you sell more than 10,000 copies a year?*

A. Yes. We founded *Writer's Market* in 1930, priced it at $2.50, and printed 2,000 copies the first year. We secured an advance sale of 1,000 copies to Newspaper Institute of America, a home study course, at 90c each. Their $900.00 paid for the composition of the entire book and allowed us to buy our own 1,000 copies for around $1.00 a copy.

Q. *How come?*

A. The *fixed costs* of any book (composition, press make-ready, editorial expenses) remain the same whether you print one thousand or two thousand copies, or more. When you divide your fixed costs by 2,000 instead of by 1,000, the fixed costs per book are less. Take one fixed cost: composition. Pretend your book has 100 pages and the cost of setting the type and breaking it into pages comes to $10 per page. That's a total of $1,000 for composition (100 pages x $10 a page). If you print 1,000 books, the cost of the composition per book would be one dollar. If you printed 2,000 books, the cost for composition per book would be fifty cents. So, in this case, although we sold one thousand copies to Newspaper Institute of America at our cost price, the savings we made on the books we retained were considerable since we were able to divide our fixed costs by 2,000 instead of by 1,000.

Q. *So, if you publish a directory and believe you can sell only 1,000 copies and you could pre-sell 3,000 copies to someone else at the printer's price, or even a few pennies less, you would really be ahead because you would be able to buy your 1,000 copies for half as much as otherwise.*

A. You're talking like a publisher.

Q. *Have you founded any other directory?*

A. Yes. A small one called *Cartoonist's Market*. It's paper bound, sells for $2.50.

Q. *Do you sell 10,000 copies a year?*

A. Nothing like it. This is an annual we'll have to develop or kill. *Cartoonist's Market* contains 650 names and addresses of markets that buy cartoons and the details a cartoonist wants to know about each. Because the listings are relatively few and the number of pages in the book is so low, under 100, the most we can get is $2.50.

Q. *Why do you sell so few copies?*

A. The market is thin, spread out, hard to reach. We have no growth prospects and no margin for profit.

Q. *How can you get more than $2.50 a copy and increase your sale?*

A. Good for you. To charge more and also widen our audience we have to give more value. We are thinking of adding a 40 page instructive editorial section each year. The working title of the first one is "Styles in Cartooning and how to know when your thin black line is dated."

Q. *How would this widen your market? Your new editorial feature doesn't increase the number of cartoonists or make them easier to reach. What's the principle you're giving us?*

A. Let me describe the editorial feature. The way I see it right now, we could start off with Nast and move into the better cartoonists at the turn of the century. It's surprising the number of cartoonists who ape the heavy cartoon lines of 90 years ago. In a contest we ran for cartoonists, a lot of the work sent to us was quite dated—that's where I got the idea of offering an editorial section, in *Cartoonist's Market,* to help cartoonists improve their art.

Q. *Why should cartoonists do dated work?*

A. They never really draw a bead on what happened to the cartoonist's black line. It's become more and more of an economical line. More is suggested, less is documented. Cartoonists want to be aware of the mainstream of cartoon art and how it has moved forward. In this 40 page editorial section, I would treat different facets of this. Of course, next year's issue would require a different feature in its place.

Q. *Will cartoonists spend an extra $1.00 or $2.00 for these 40 pages?*

A. We can only find out by trying. However, I believe in this kind of editorial improvement. To get this kind of editorial feature, we'll have to find an informed cartoonist and then draw him out by tape. Usually, cartoonists can't write.

Q. *How about going to an art teacher instead?*

A. A good idea.

Q. *Will you be able to get an initial wholesale order from a home study cartoonist school?*

A. You've picked up our idea of expanding the market. Some of these schools are themselves dated in the examples of cartoons that their ads show. They might feel the kind of editorial feature I have been describing will prejudice their course. Other home study cartoon courses are progressive. High school courses in art might use this book for supplementary reading once it was removed from being a 100% market guide. If the high schools can use it for supplementary reading in art classes, we might develop a sale of 10 to 30 copies into each metropolitan school district.

Q. *Is that much?*

A. 300 districts might order a total 5,000 books a year for supplementary reading in art classes.

Q. *Would it still be called a directory?*

A. It would be a directory-plus, and naturally a more spirited job to edit. It might develop into a yearbook like our *Writer's Yearbook.*

An economical way to enter book publishing is to issue an annual. One technique for a publisher who thinks he may have an annual but isn't completely positive is to date the publication to cover a two-year period, e.g., 1971-72. This gives the publication a two-year life if it fails to move promptly. If it does sell, the publisher is all set to make it an annual.

Q. *What are some other yearbooks?*

A. Here are the yearbooks that one house issues: *Better Homes and Gardens Apartment Ideas, Better Homes and Gardens Home Furnishing Ideas, Better Homes and Gardens Kitchen and Family Room Ideas, Bettter Homes and Gardens Travel Ideas.*

Q. *Going back to directories, aren't they boring to edit?*

A. You start with the sweat work and the glamour comes later.

Q. *What glamour things did you do?*

A. I founded *Writer's Yearbook, Modern Photography* and *The Farm Quarterly.* However, if you produce an annual every year for five years and it ends up with a 15,000 annual sale, you'll know the publishing business and you are ready to ride your bike on any road.

Q. *Did all your annuals succeed?*

A. A good one got away.

Q. *What was the idea?*

A. A jazz annual. My son arranged music for Kenton, and then composed for "Second City" for 10 years so I was immersed in jazz during the years he was at home.

Q. *Did you publish a jazz annual?*

A. No. We issued a one-shot jazz picture book.

Q. *Why didn't you turn it into an annual? Wouldn't that still be a good idea?*

A. I agree. The only man we had who knew publishing and who knew jazz and had taste, couldn't tell time.

Q. *Couldn't tell time?*

A. He couldn't complete a job on time. We were unable to control him or replace him. So we lost out. A publisher lives off talent. Take away the talent and the publisher is dead.

Q. *Isn't the publisher talented, too?*

A. Mostly administratively. He can't also write, edit, shoot pix, draw, sell, and design with the best.

Q. *May I go back to the first question. I still want to be a book publisher and I still don't know how to begin.*

A. Let's say you are 25, out of college, and ready to go to work. Allow yourself some time to get professional training at the grass roots.

How to Enter Publishing

Q. *What is my first step?*

A. Get a job as a retail book clerk. Try to work in 2 or 3 stores over a period of a year. If you feel that you are actually learning something, and you can give yourself the time, you can do this over a year and a half.

Q. *Why should I be a clerk?*

A. The purpose is always the same. Think of yourself as an octopus, constantly putting out 100 feelers; touching, sensing, evaluating.

Q. *What are the things I am supposed to notice?*

A. You notice the kind of people that come into a book store. What brings them to the store? Do they come for a specific book or are they just browsing? If they want a specific book, and it will take too long for your store to order it, how do you turn the customer's interest to another title? Can you get the customer's name and address and some idea of his hobbies and interests so that, when a book comes in that will interest this customer, you will be able to send him a postcard and tell him about it?

Q. *Do book clerks do this?*

A. Successful owners of small "personal" book stores do this. This is their charm and makes them contributors to their community.

Q. *Do book clerks who are ordinary employees do this?*

A. A few score of book clerks in the nation may do this, and they turn into book sellers, not clerks. Mostly, a clerk is a clerk. He writes up an order and makes change.

Q. *Are you being sarcastic?*

A. For what?

Q. *Why is it necessary that I go through this?*

When my son was about 13 years old, Stan Kenton was at our home for dinner, and our son asked: "Stan, what do I have to do to be a band leader like you?" Stan answered: "You have to outplay, out-fight, and out—— the rest of the band." Now, this is one way of looking at the job of being a band leader or a book publisher, and it is a very good way. But there is another way, and if there is time we will come to it. Right now, I am following what, for want of a better phrase, is the Stan Kenton approach. It is not the only way but right now, it is the way that we are talking about.

Q. *Where should I work as a retail book clerk?*

A. The best stores are in the big city. One year and a half as a clerk asks a lot of human flesh. In the United States, there are 279,000 doctors, 253,000 lawyers, and 17,000 professors of engineering, and 300 general book publishers. Being a book publisher is something like being a ballet dancer. Dedication and energy won't take you the whole way. On the other hand, talent and grace and good looks go a long way, but they don't take you the whole way either. The whole darn truth is that in a tough field, like ballet dancing or book publishing, you need the energy, the dedication, the interior trade knowledge *and* the talent. You can run a gas station and do well on just the first two.

Q. *After a year and a half of being a retail clerk, how have I moved closer toward being a book publisher?*

A. All you have in this world is your personal attitude toward people, things, ideas, places, and events that confront you. You distinguish yourself by the style in which you implement your attitude. At the end of your tour as a retail clerk, you should begin to develop personal attitudes toward the method by which book dealers stock their shelves and dress their windows, toward the means by which publishers get their books into stores, and toward the means by which retailers sell their books. And, of course, you are constantly developing a personal attitude toward certain kinds of writing. You now start to think in terms of *implementing your personal attitude with your own style. It's your style that is you.*

Q. *Could you give me an example?*

A. You probably know that Richard Burton was a poor Welsh boy who worked the coal mines. Like the other Welsh kids, Burton played soccer and he was good at it. In *Vogue* for January 1971, Richard Burton writes a piece about going back to a small Welsh town and playing soccer with the hard-bitten locals. He wore old clothes, a skull cap, and came on incognito. They killed him.

Q. *And this article in* Vogue——?

A. Is all Burton's style. It shows so beautifully this man's attitude toward a thousand things. Here's a quote:

It was played against a village whose name is known

only to its inhabitants and crippled masochists drooling quietly in kitchen corners, a mining village with all the natural beauty of the valleys of the moon, and just as welcoming, with a team composed almost entirely of colliers. I hadn't played for four or five years but was fairly fit, I thought, and the opposition was bottom of the third class and reasonably beatable. Except, of course, on their home ground. I should have thought of that. I should have called to mind that this was the kind of team where, towards the end of the match, you kept your bus ticking over near the touch-line in case you won and had to run for your life.

I wasn't particularly nervous before the match until, though I was disguised with a skullcap and everyone had been sworn to secrecy, I heard a voice from the other team asking, "le ma'r blydi film star 'ma?" (Where's the bloody film star here?), as we were running onto the field. My cover, as they say in spy stories, was already blown . . .

Burton implements his attitude toward life (not just soccer) with his style. By selecting this article, the editor of *Vogue* has found a way to implement her own attitude. The article becomes *her* style just as much as Burton's. Ask yourself: what's my attitude toward thus-and-thus? How will the style of what I publish implement my own attitude? It is your answer to this question that makes you into the kind of publisher you will be.

Q. *Clerking will help me select the books I am going to publish?*

A. As a clerk, you are daily confronted by publishing tastes other than your own. This may not cause you to alter your tastes, but it should cause you to reconsider your attitude, or personal taste, toward any piece of copy. If you are going to be a publisher, you need to feel within yourself a rapport for other human beings; to feel a delight within yourself when you set up a little quiver in the other person by reaching him either spiritally, emotionally, intellectually. By communicating with people who come in to buy books, you develop this touch, this ability to be interested in the other human being and to respond to him.

Q. *Does this mean, if a Daughter of the Southern Confederacy comes in and asks for a particular kind of book, that I should work to develop her point of view within myself?*

A. It means that each human being offers you an opportunity of increasing your understanding of other human beings, and as this understanding occurs within you, your ability to satisfy any segment of the human market is improved.

Q. *Then, part of the reason I am being a book clerk is to learn the inner workings of the book store and part is to learn people's response to books and how I can communicate to that response.*

A. Exactly.

Next Stop: Holiday Inn

Q. *Where do I go from here?*

A. You get a job as a book salesman with a small territory. This gives you a chance to get to know the individual accounts. It doesn't really matter if you sell Bibles or encyclopedias or technical books or general trade books. You want to call on retailers with a line of books and understand what it takes to sell books to them. Some will welcome you; some won't see you; one or two will look at you and say: "Drop dead," and turn away.

Q. *How long should I do this?*

A. A year is a long time on the road, but it may have to stand you in good stead for a lifetime. If you are ever to hire book salesmen, and get them to respect you, you are going to have to understand what they go through.

Q. *Already that is 2½ years out of my life.*

A. If you are going to work for thirty years in book publishing and you love the profession, it doesn't matter what part of it you are in as long as you are in it and working as hard as you can to the best of your ability. With this attitude, your work as a clerk or a salesman is a delight.

Q. *Do you believe what you said?*

A. I am being as "for real" as I know how.

The Man With 10,000 Titles

Q. *Well, I am 27½ years old and I have finished my retail clerking and my year on the road; what do I do next?*

A. You get a job with a wholesaler as a road representative or an in-house promoter and you find out the difference between selling a single line of books for one publisher and working for a wholesaler.

Q. *What is this difference?*

A. It's like going into the men's room. You have to experience it or you will never know. A lot of sticks are thrown at the wholesaler. Publishers say that all he does is take orders and never does any selling. Retailers say they get a short discount and that every year the wholesaler increases the minimum order he will accept. The wholesaler is necessary to book publishing. When the time comes for you to negotiate terms with wholesalers, you will find yourself using words in the same sense and with the same meaning as the book wholesaler himself. Unless you can do this, you're an outlander and get sloughed off.

Q. *Who are the book wholesalers?*

A. Baker & Taylor, Bookazine, Raymar, American News Company, Richard Abel, Ingram, Bro-Dart. Each represents more than 100 book publishers, and each of these publishers has some 20 to 100 titles and some have many more.

Q. *How can the wholesaler's salesmen know the names of all these titles, let alone the sales story for each one?*

A. He cannot. Mostly, he nudges. He says: "Buy from one supplier; get a single bill; receive books promptly from our nearby warehouse. All this with practically the same discount."

Q. *Is the wholesaler really needed?*

A. Yes. The book dealer, particularly if he has a small store, is hard put to order from two hundred separate book publishers. It is too much bookkeeping, too many delays, too many incoming packages, too much paperwork. He would rather receive a slightly smaller discount from the wholesaler in exchange for one source of supply. As you work for a wholesaler, you learn realistically what he can be expected to do. When you know that, you can demand your rights and possibly can get them, because you know what goes on. For instance, most wholesalers issue a catalog that they send to all their retail prospects. If you are a book publisher, what logic can you bring to bear to be featured in this catalog? Experience as a wholesaler's salesman will teach you.

G. *If I publish a book for $10.00 retail, what will I receive?*

A. The wholesaler usually buys the book from the publisher at about 50% off and sells them to the retail store at around 25% to 44%, depending upon the quantity of the order. However, when hardcover books are purchased in lots of 5 or 10, direct from the book publisher, the retailer receives around 40% off on the books. As the order size is increased, the discount increases.

Q. *If I am going to publish a book for $10.00, I will actually collect about $6.00 per book, average?*

A. In that area. You will sell some books for $5.00 and you will sell some books for $7.50. You will also have some consumer sales that come to you direct for $10.00. On the retail price of $10.00, you will collect around $6.00 per book. Usually you can add the postage to your bill.

Q. *If the publisher collects $6.00 on a $10.00 book, does the author get his royalty from the $6.00 or the $10.00?*

A. This depends upon the need the publisher has for the book, the amount of the royalty, the reputation of the author, the bargaining ability of the literary agent, the general condition of business, and whether it is a mail order, text or trade book.

Q. *What kind of contract would be good for the author?*

A. 15% royalty of the retail. That means the author receives $1.50 royalty on a clothbound book selling for $10.00, regardless of how much the publisher receives for the book. In a favorable contract, the author also receives several thousand dollars royalty in advance of publication.

Q. *What kind of contract would be less favorable to the author?*

A. The unfavorable ones come in all colors and sizes. For instance, 10% royalty on the first 10,000 copies sold; then 15%. Or, worse yet, 5% of the money that the publisher collects, and with no advance. However, this kind of contract would not be unfavorable to the author if it were for an elementary textbook (grades 1-8) where the sales can run to 200,000 a year. Textbook editorial costs to the publisher are almost always over $50,000 per title, as no textbook comes to the publisher ready to print.

Fourth Stop: the Mail Order Publisher

Q. *After a year working for a wholesaler—where next?*

A. Well, you are now 3½ years into being a book publisher, and you have great expectations. The next job, the ideal one, is to work for a mail-order publisher for about a year.

Q. *What is a mail-order publisher?*

A. This fellow sells his books by mail to libraries, institutions, schools, organizations, individuals, companies, and the armed services. He may even sprout a small book club.

Q. *Would you give us an example?*

A. Let's say that you are publishing a farm magazine, and you have a circulation of 500,000 in the Midwest. You publish a book called "Everything You Always Wanted To Know About Growing Grain," and the book follows a clear logic line with no skips, is easy to read, and illustrated in a step-by-step manner. That would be some book. May God deliver it to me. Let's say it runs about 400 pages, and you are able to buy the book from the printer in lots of 30,000 for $2.00 a copy, and, therefore, you price it at $8. If you are a mail-order publisher, you sell the book through the following channels:

1. A display ad in your own farm magazine.

2. When mailing letters to your subscribers soliciting their renewal subscription, you enclose a circular on this book.

3. There are four thousand farm schools in the Midwest that are interested in this kind of book and their names and addresses are available to you. These would be agriculture colleges, farm vocational schools at the high school level, as well as farm organizations who might want to offer your book piggy-back in their own letters to their members, or included as part of the cost of belonging to the organization.

4. You might find a book club with some special interest in farming that could use this book as a bonus or even as a selection.

5. You might combine the book with several others so that you could go for a sale price of $19.95, or something like that, and rent lists of high-income farmers. There are about 400,000 such names in the Midwest, and they rent for $25.00 a thousand.

Q. *Do magazine publishers issue books and sell them by mail?*

A. Yes. It has become a good source of revenue for them without great additional sales cost. If *Look* magazine had enjoyed *Life* magazine's book revenues, they might have been able to continue.

Q. *What kind of job should I try to get with the mail-order publisher?*

A. You're now ready to try your hand at publishing with the other fellow taking the risks. Your first job is to create mail campaigns that will sell books the publisher already has issued. And you will work with costs all the way. The second job is to find the talent that will create an outline and several sample chapters of a book that can be sold by mail.

Q. *What happens to my tastes?*

A. They will improve. You will learn that there are no bad subjects, no bad fields. There are great opportunitties for quality books in every field of endeavor. Bad publishers congregate in certain fields. That makes it easier for you to distinguish yourself in that very field.

Q. *What main fact will I learn from working for a mail-order publisher?*

A. You will learn the incredible, sky-is-the-limit market for books sold by mail to individuals, libraries, schools, organizations, firms, and outlet houses.

Q. *What is an outlet house?*

A. You know what a scrap dealer is.

Q. *He buys what's left over?*

A. Yes. The outlet house is the dumping ground for books that fail to sell at their original retail price. Almost every run of books, even the press runs of the best sellers, leave several thousand or more books unsold. The outlet house buys them for 5 to 20 cents on the dollar and sells them for 10 to 30 cents on the dollar.

Q. *What else will I learn from my mail-order publisher experience?*

A. Your mail-order experience will show you that the average mail campaign costs about 9c to 12c a letter, when sent third class mail. Today, 10c is a fair average. A mail-order publisher creates both the books *and* the mail campaign to sell them. You need campaigns that will fish 3 to 4 orders from every 100 letters that you mail. You will learn the thousands of sources for prospects. As a result, if someone comes to you with a remainder—something he couldn't move—you may be able to create a plan to sell it. Or, with access to the right kind of large list, you may develop a book for it.

Q. *But this isn't publishing, this is selling.*

A. A good wife is part of a lot of things, and so is a good book publisher.

Q. *Am I ready to go into book publishing after:*

    1½ years of retail clerking
    1   year as a book publisher's "rep"
    1   year wholesale representative
    1   year mail-order publisher
    ———
    4½ years shot

A. The years are not shot. They are learning years. Your talent grows because of them. You are not yet ready to go into book publishing as a publisher. You have one more stop.

Last Stop: Head for Home

Q. *An editorial or sales job with a book publisher?*

A. Yes. Work for a small publisher who will give you a shot at both desks. One year watching the unrush mail . . .

Q. *What?*

A. Unsolicited manuscripts. Working with a small publisher, issuing 10 to 20 titles a year, allows you to be all over the place and contribute weekends and nights in order to try your hand at every avenue in book publishing.

Q. *Will they pay overtime?*

A. You should be paying them.

Q. *How long should I be with the small book publisher before going off on my own as a book publisher?*

A. Three years. This gives you a seven-year apprenticeship.

Q. *Why a small publisher? Won't I learn more from the big boys?*

A. The large publisher is tightly departmentalized. If you are an editorial worker, they'll never let you into the accounting department. Many of the larger book publishers are owned by conglomerates, and their managers are no longer the owners. They are more interested in early retirement at half pay than, let us say, was Alfred Knopf in his prime. Knopf was willing to publish a book because he loved its style or what it said. He was willing to accept a loss. Today, the large publisher is run by an accounting syndrome.

They figure this way: we lay out a given number of dollars every day for rent, light, clerks, bookkeepers and other overhead. Therefore, to keep afloat, we must have a gross annual income of "X" dollars. This means we must publish 100 or 200 titles a year, or however the figures work out. We are paying a weekly draw to 40 road salesmen and these men must have new titles to sell. Therefore, each month we have to publish 20 new titles. Now, multiply that times the 20 large publishers. There aren't that many titles worth publishing. So the large companies issue a lot of "non-books." They don't have enough of a staff to give hard nosed editing and sock-sock-sock selling to each title. Charlie Oviatt of McGraw-Hill told me, "A title that is going to stay alive with McGraw-Hill has to have someone in the sales office or some editor who loves that book and will always push it." In a big company, the titles are so numerous, and the devoted creative people are so few, that a lot of titles get one hard shove, a pat on the back and that's it. When a house issues 100 titles a year, you can expect many to be mediocre. If you are the editor of a large book publishing company, you couldn't possibly know the names of all the titles you publish, let alone read them. You are dependent on your help. Great editorial help and devoted hard-slugging sales help are scarce.

Q. *Why is this so?*

A. I asked this of Ken McCormick while he was chief operational officer at Doubleday, and he said: "Not too many book publishing employees put all they have into their work. They hire themselves out to us, we find out about them and let some of them go, and they drift over to another publisher. How many great editors and great sales people who slug at every title they touch do you think we have? Fifteen? Eight? Ten?"

Q. *Doesn't the small publisher have mediocre titles, too?*

A. Yes, but for different reasons. He doesn't have to publish to support a 40-man road staff. If he has a relatively low fixed overhead, he isn't forced to issue even a title a month. He can take his sweet time and work a book up until it sings and then sell it till the cows come home.

Q. *Are all small book publisher titles good ones?*

A. No. Authors don't give them first pick. Often the small book

LOST CAUSE PRESS
MICROCARD/MICROFICHE

THE PLAINS AND THE ROCKIES

L OST Cause Press has published, on Microcard, every item we have been able to find from the Wagner-Camp bibliography *Plains and Rockies*. We continue to search.

Abbey, James. California. A trip across the plains, in the spring of 1850, being a daily record of incidents of the trip . . . and containing valuable information to emigrants . . . New Albany, Ind., Kent & Norman, and J. R. Nunemacher, 1850. No. 178.

Adams, James Capen. The hair-breadth escapes and adventures of "Grizzly Adams," in catching and conquering the wild animals included in his California menagerie. Written by himself. New York, 1860. No. 347.

Belisle, David W. The American Family Robinson; or, The Adventures of a Family Lost in the Great Desert of the West. Philadelphia, W. P. Hazard, 1854. No. 236.

Bennett, Emerson. The Prairie Flower; or, Adventures in the Far West. Cincinnati and St. Louis, Stratton & Barnard, 1849. No. 162.

Bennett, Emerson. The Trapper's Bride; or, Spirit of Adventure. Cincinnati, Stratton and Barnard, 1848. No. 145.

Bennett, Emerson. Wild Scenes on the Frontiers. Philadelphia, Hamelin, 1859. No. 317a.

Benton, Thomas Hart. Discourse of Mr. Benton, of Missouri before the Boston Mercantile Library Association, on the physical geography of the country between the states of Missouri and California, with a view to show its adaptation to settlement, and to the construction of a railroad. Delivered at Boston, 1854.

Benton, Thomas Hart. Letter from Col. Benton to the people of Missouri. Central national highway from the Mississippi River to the Pacific. Washington, 1853. No. 221.

Berkeley, George Charles Grantley. Fitzhardinge. The English sportsman in the western prairies. London, Hurst & Blackett, 1861. No. 368.

Beschke, William. The Dreadful Sufferings and Thrilling Adventures of an Overland Party of Emigrants to California. Compiled from the journal of Mr. George Adam, one of the adventurers, by Prof. Wm. Beschke. St. Louis, Mo., published by Barclay & Co., 1850. No. 179.

Bidwell, John. Journal of a trip to California in 1841. Weston, Mo., 1844. No. 88.

Bigelow, John. Memoir of the Life and Public Services of John Charles Fremont. New York, Derby & Jackson; Cincinnati, H. W. Derby & Co., 1856. No. 271a.

Bliss, Edward. A Brief History of the New Gold Regions of Colorado Territory, together with hints and suggestions to intending emigrants. New York, J. W. Amerman, printer, 1864. No. 397.

Blue, Daniel. Thrilling Narrative of the Adventures, Sufferings and Starvation of Pike's Peak Gold Seekers on the Plains of the West in the Winter and Spring of 1859. By one of the survivors. Chicago, Evening Journal Steam Print, 1860. No. 350b.

A page of Americana from the Lost Cause Press catalogue

publisher lacks taste and skill, because talent is so rare and hard to come by, and because his own intellectual attainments are limited.

Q. *You said that before. There is so little talent, so little devotion, so few people willing to give all of themselves.*

A. Yep.

Q. *Then what chance is there for me?*

A. Talent alone won't do it for the ballet dancer or for you. You need the dedication, the energy, the intellectuality *and* the talent. That's why there are relatively few book publishers and even fewer whose books matter.

Q. *Are the rewards worth it?*

A. Sure.

Q. *What are they?*

A. The usual: privilege and power. It's nice to have both of these and the money to go with it. Being a book publisher gives this to you. You earn it and you deserve it.

What Is Americana?

Q. *You said the two types of books that are easiest to create, buy, edit and sell were annuals and Americana. Why Americana?*

A. It never goes out of style.

Q. *Where are some samples of Americana that are out of copyright and that I could publish?*

A. That's good thinking. A young book publisher with an interest in Americana has a ready made gold mine in *The Lost Cause Press*, at 1140 Starks Building, Louisville, Kentucky 40202. The owner, Mr. Charles Farnsley, put thousands of early manuscripts, letters, pamphlets, privately printed books on microfilm. This includes the entire Civil War slave literature from the library at Oberlin College. The microfilm card file of Lost Cause Press sells for around $75,000. You could ask them for the name and address of the closest library to you that owns a complete set. About 30 libraries have the full set of microfilm cards. Plan a week's visit to that library. In advance, however, order a set of catalogs from The Lost Cause Press. Mr. Farnsley will let you have a set for $5.00 if a professor of a recognized university will approve your letter to him. By studying these catalogs in advance, you can figure out the material you want to see. Otherwise, you'll be lost in a sea of Americana. One of the strange things about book publishing is that this unused material sits there like a sitting duck for energetic creative young minds who have the taste and style to know what to splice together.

Q. *Have you published any Americana?*

A. Yes, one book, *The Good Old Days*. It is about farming from the turn of the century to around 1920. It's a large, illustrated, cloth bound ten dollar book that we brought out in 1960.

Q. *What was your investment to start it off?*

A. A good question. We hesitated to print more than 10,000 copies. How could we know they would sell? And 10,000 copies cost $40,000 to print, or $4 a copy because there are 20 color plates in the book. We estimated our sales cost at $2 a book, so that meant we were "in" for $6 on each book. Since the net income to the publisher for a $10 book is $6, we had to buy the book for under $4 a copy to break even on an initial press of 10,000. I got in touch with Harper and they agreed to take over all the book store sales while we would handle the mail order sales. Harper took 10,000 copies and we agreed to buy them back if Harper failed to sell them to the book stores in two years. We also took 10,000 copies and that brought our price per copy down to $2.75 on the first printing. Harper also paid us a small royalty; I think 8%. Ten years later, in 1971, in spite of 40% higher prices, our cost per copy is down to $2.50 because we no longer have to figure in the cost of the plates or composition.

Q. *Did Harper keep on selling the book to book stores?*

A. No. After three years, they were moving under 400 copies a year and their figures showed they couldn't afford to handle a title that slow so they gave us back the rights to sell to book stores.

Q. *Did they make a charge to give you back the book store rights?*

A. No. It was just a publisher's courtesy. And we were grateful.

Q. *Is there any other way to move into book publishing besides Americana, a directory or an annual?*

A. There are two minor ways, and both are esoteric. Let's say you happen to know a lot about the tactics and interests of one specialized group—a union, a national association or a corporation. Then you could dummy up and create an outline for a book that would serve their interests and sell it to them on the basis of the outline and a few chapters. This is rare and possible.

Q. *What would be some examples?*

A. Here's one: The working title is "How To Keep Busy, Be Sought After by Attractive Women and Make Money as a Contractor." Interview an educated, able contractor, and with him create a three-page editorial outline. Show the outline to 20 literate people who might buy the book and learn from them what ideas they have for improving the outline. Re-do the outline. Interview your contractor in considerable depth and with him write three chapters. Show the three chapters and the outline to a large building supply house. They might finance it with their name as publisher as a promotional venture to be sent to their prospects and customers. You can apply this idea forty ways from Sunday to any field that you know and like. The idea is to cut your publishing eye teeth and let the other fellow make the investment. If you net a few dollars, plus the experience, you've done well. Incidentally, the author should receive a sum equal to yours. If this book is well done, it will also have a national paperback newsstand sale. You could sell the rights to this to a paperback book publisher who has the know-how to turn out a professionally looking paperback and the newsstand distribution to go with it.

Q. *What is the other minor way to get into book publishing?*

A. Pornography. A camel has entered our tent. This is the Trans Media type book store selling straight pornography. In Cincinnati, for instance, there are 9 regular book stores or department stores with book departments, and 6 X-rated "book" stores. Until you read one, you cannot imagine how poorly written such books are. In my opinion, a well written, well constructed, well plotted novella with honest character development that is in the X-rated area will attract a large audience. "Large" is hardly the word.

Q. *Is anything like this published now?*

A. The only well written thing I've seen is *The Story of O*. The opening six pages are practically an innovative style. The book received a beautiful *New York Times* review and sold over one million copies.

Q. *Where can you get a manuscript like this?*

A. I don't know. Get to the kind of writer you admire and you believe in and get him to do it. To advertise for material, however, is impossible as what you would get will reduce you to tears. Every agent who advertised for this type of material in *Writer's Digest* backed out of the field because they couldn't stand a diet of such horrible incoming manuscripts.

Q. *How would you sell a book like this?*

A. Through the jobbers who sell the X-rated book stores. You get their names by getting to know some of the local operators. Investment would be low, under $8,000 for a paperback test. I can't understand why books in this field are not only so awfully bad but so worse than awfully bad.

Q. *Would you advise giving this kind of book a trial effort?*

A. No.

Q. *Then why did you suggest it?*

A. You asked me a professional question and I answered it. I would not advise you to do it.

Q. *Why?*

A. After you've had the background we discussed, you could consider it as one alternative. Otherwise, you're picking up the stick at the wrong end.

Q. *What are some of the amenities of book publishing?*

A. Long after you stop eating at "21" because that kind of fine food is too much and long after you have made your 25th talk to graduating students at some journalism college and long after you stopped pasting things in a personal scrap book, one thing holds you to it.

Q. *What?*

A. The joy of work.

Q. *You have an attitude that the publisher "makes" the book. I thought the author wrote the book and the publisher published it.*

A. That's an interesting point of view. How real is it? A book publisher buys a manuscript, converts it to a book and sells it. Nonfiction book manuscripts that are sent to publishers usually have not first been submitted to a dozen literate, knowledgeable, prospective buyers of that book in order to secure their comments on the discipline of its logic line as well as what's missing, what's boring. Fiction manuscripts are often too long for the weight of their story line; or the characters are not developed to life size.

Q. *Says who?*

A. The book publisher is the objective reader. The author may either agree to his reasoning or go elsewhere.

Q. *But the big name authors, do they submit to this sort of thing?*

A. When Harold Latham used our office to interview talent in Cincinnati, he had the *Gone With the Wind* manuscript with him. The original script was 50% longer than the published book and every page of the original had been edited, in addition to being cut. Latham's other contribution to this book was his decision to publish it as one book instead of two volumes. This was a large financial risk and he was willing to put his job on the line. It meant he would have to print 50,000 copies of the first edition to come out because, otherwise, the cost per copy would be too high due to the wordage.

Q. *Do novels by new writers usually need this much changing?*

A. Experience in reading the unrush mail will give you an editor's eye. Take Hemingway's second novel, *The Sun Also Rises.* In its original submission, before Maxwell Perkins got to work on it, that marvelous economy of style that became the hallmark of Hemingway was not so much in evidence. The correspondence between Perkins and Hemingway is, in my judgment, a put-on by Perkins to take away from the heavy editing and re-write requests he was making. Perkins helped Hemingway discover his style. If you want to read what Hemingway could do without that kind of editing, try his book *Across the River and Into the Trees.*

Q. *And without Perkins . . .*

A. Hemingway would have been a good writer but his economical style might not have come about so quickly nor developed as well.

Q. *Does the author have to go along with the changes the editor wants?*

A. He doesn't have to. He can go elsewhere. It is the book publisher's attitude that sets, for him, the style of books he wants to publish. Naturally, some book publishers can muck up a writer. The writer needs to have faith in himself as well as being open to reason.

Ideas
For A Writer's Conference

Each year, some sixty writer's conferences play host to 10,000 writers. These literary work-sessions last from 3 to 30 days and a list of them appears in *Saturday Review* and *Writer's Digest* during the month of May. The conferences are held mostly in June and July. After questioning many writers who have attended these conferences, we offer these suggestions to conference secretaries:

1. When asking for enrollments, give the writer a chance to say what particular help he needs. For instance, a questionnaire with room for the writer to check the areas which he would like discussed, gives the conference a track on which to run.

    Do any of these points on novels interest you?
    ☐ Flashbacks
    ☐ Royalties paid on usual contracts
    ☐ How book clubs choose a novel
    ☐ How can I tell if it's dated?

2. Speakers may then be assigned subjects with a direct interest to a large percentage of the writers who will attend. By securing an advance outline from the speaker, you nail him to a given subject and prevent him from playing the part of the wandering raconteur.

3. When the outline is received, the conference director should show it to a dozen writers who have signed up for the conference. Does this cover what they want to know about the subject? The comments of the writers should go to the speaker in order that his talk is more fruitful and beamed to them.

"Could we see an outline of a non-fiction book that was contracted for on the basis of the outline?" one writer will ask. "May I see some query letters from free-lance article writers that led to an editorial OK?" requests another writer. "Read us the opening chapter of a novel you just bought and tell us what is good and what is bad about it," says a third.

A writer will travel 500 miles and go home with a smile on his face for this, but a diet of "what I said to Bennett Cerf at the Plaza" can weigh him down.

4. "Name" speakers are not needed. The thunderheads know they will be misunderstood if they speak candidly and without reserve. "Name" speakers at writer's conferences usually tell funny stories and then sit down. An assistant non-fiction editor of *Harper's Magazine* will do a better job at a writer's conference than the publisher of *Newsweek*, as far as writers are concerned. He may know less about policy, little or nothing about the functioning of the other departments of the magazine but he will know how *Harper's* looks at non-fiction and he won't be afraid to discuss it for fear some idling half-listening reporter will misquote him. (No reporter will pay any attention to him unless the reporter is a writer. Then he'll be all ears.)

5. Speakers should be changed from year to year. A carry-over of four speakers out of ten can be too many. The golden roar of last year's lion rarely sounds the same twice.

6. Provide a tutorial system whereby, after each lecture, small groups of writers may gather around conference leaders and have a question and answer session about the talk just given.

7. Some people get lit from a lecture; others require a personal and private moment. This is what most conferences deny their members. Yet, it is the spark that can light a fire. An hour of personal attention from an urbane, good humored editor, who loves to teach, is a transfusion.

Man Against White Space

by Aron M. Mathieu

The successful publisher marries art and logic at a profit. Always, his first consideration is the reader. Should he tamper with either the art or the logic, merely for the sake of greater profit, his undoing has begun. In these four chapters, the inter-relationship of a magazine's departments, with regard to its art and logic, are fully stated.

Man Against White Space

Part 1 Editorial

Within pretty wide limits, a magazine rises or falls on the aptitude of one man: the editor-in-chief.

The essential difference between the editor and his circulation manager, advertising manager, and mechanical superintendent is that the editor is presumptively not only a professional at editing, but also is culturally aware. The reason the editor normally cannot get advice at his own shop is that his *vis-a-vis* departmental chiefs are good pros at their given work, but culturally are relatively less informed.

When sales fall, the newsstand sales manager generally has one piece of advice to offer the editor: "Put red on the cover!"

The mechanical superintendent can be counted on to say: "If you make your schedule a day *ahead* of time we will give you a good clean book," and the circulation manager, who perhaps is weak in certain States, will come up with a resonant plea for more stories about the Rocky Mountains so that he can get some good licks in that area.

The advertising manager, when his advice is solicited, will produce a copy of a certain article published two years back. It was this article that the President of "Chuckles Nut Bar" liked so well he ordered 4,000 reprints for all his dealers and followed this with an advertising contract. Placing the reprint on the editor's desk, and leaning forward for emphasis, he says: "Now *that's* what we need more of."

The staff, on the editor's same executive level, put most of their time into being experts in printing, circulation, advertising, or management; and very little of their time into studying the history of ideas. Lacking this experience, they are often trite in the editorial concepts they offer because they cannot relate their ideas to the significant ideas of the past.

The editor's mind is splashed with names of authorities who can be reached and who are articulate. This knowledge, plus his own point of view, enables him to take any situation and integrate it into a concept with contempory meaning.

For instance, if the circulation manager is shown a copy of Edward Steichen's picture of J. P. Morgan, made in 1910, he is pleased in being able to say, "Oh, that's J. P. Morgan, isn't it?" But the editor sees more than the familiar face. He recognizes that the picture of this man, with eyes like locomotive headlights, seated and gripping the arm of the chair, as though it were a dagger about to be plunged into you, is one of those singular photographs which set up the entire attitude of a generation of magazine photographers who followed Steichen. He knows the history, development and present status of photographic attitudes and in *accepting, changing,* or *rejecting* this photographic-attitude the editor shows himself.

Thirty years later, Walker Evans published in a chastely laid out volume a group of pictures that synthesized what great photographers had learned. Then, twenty-five years later, Truman Capote and Richard Avedon teamed up in a punchy visual kick picture book, the comment of a later day. A great editor needs first to be familiar with all this, and this part is simply a matter of diligence. But second, he shows his greatness in his reaction. "Bill," he tells his photographer, "let's sit down and criticize these Avedon pictures. I want to offer you a new point of view." If the editor is fortunate, the photographer not only fields the idea, but makes a double play by adding his own interpretation to the editor's. Behind any great magazine is the "flash" concept of its editor. Usually he is something of a missionary, a reformer, a zealot. He speaks his piece with an intense belief that what he has to say is worth hearing.

When Beatrice Gould came back from Russia and said the attitude of the Russian people toward the Americans, and toward their own leaders, would be radically changed if everyone of them could read a copy of the *Ladies' Home Journal* for a year, she wasn't kidding. She meant what she said with her whole heart and soul.

Lesser magazines are edited by lesser editors who have nothing to say for the simple reason that ideas are not the thing that matter most to them. They are interested in making deadlines and in making money; in their own recreation, or family, or security—*ideas* and *influencing others* aren't the consuming interest in their lives. These people should not be editors, and when they become editors they are invariably lesser editors, and their publications come down to their level. An editor is part messiah, and, since he needs to have a lot of people dancing his tune, he is part a honky-tonk guy, because crowds don't follow straight Bach. Mostly, individuals who are all these things cannot stay in the high seat decade after decade. The world changes, but individuals do not. For every Mary Wollman Chase, who successfully headed up *Vogue* for almost 50 years, there are a score of Frank Vizatellis of *Literary Digest*, who appeared to pass their heyday, but remained in the saddle till death did them part.

How Do We Get Dated?

It's no disgrace to become dated. This happens to all of us. It just about has to happen as, if we are writers, we cannot be creative forever, and at one point of our life we stop being creative and for the rest of our lives simply try to reaffirm the credos and conditions that previously brought us success and recognition. Some of us get dated a little earlier than others. But few editors can expect to go into their 60s, and remain good editors. The thing that happens to them is that they lose their enthusiasm for volunteering new ideas. Already, because of their years of experience they know the new idea won't work.

As an example, a young editor of 30 might suggest a great new agricultural program that will take America out of its market glut. But a 60-year-old editor already knows there is no hope for a farm solution. He knows it is too complex for any solution. He knows that through technology the farmers are producing too much and that through political log rolling, the Congress is going to vote some kind of a high-price support program to farmers, even though farmers already are producing food for which there is no market. He knows that any approach to reducing the farm surplus without consideration of the farm vote is foolish, so to him the problem is too intricate, and, through years of living with it, he is mute. But the thirty-year-older hasn't been hit by 75 ideas that were mutilated under selfish political appraisal, so he comes up with something that may be screwy, but at least it's new and fresh, and in the long run he shoves the 60-year-old editor out of his seat. That is not to say the 60-year-older was at fault; but it is to say that the public is willing to bite at new suggestions and the 30-year-older had them, while the 60-year-older knows too well that they won't work.

It is interesting to see that *Life*, come what may, is always ready with an editorial solution answering the burning question of the day. If you are not sure of what to do, or where to go, or how to think or where to turn, at least one week out of three, *Life's* editorial page gives you a packaged answer. Years ago in *Life*, Ambassador Bullitt treated China like a hard-boiled egg, peeled it down, and said we should consume it. Now! Before the Russians completed what even then only a few people suspected as their goal. He gave the costs, the risks, the rewards. A blue print. "Take over China," he said. "Now." Sometimes nationalistic, sometimes idealistic, *Life* puts down a step-by-step solution to big-time problems as fast as they rise.

Will Mr. Luce's successor find these ready solutions within himself 20 years from today, when, looking back over the years and reading his previous programs, he can savor the sting of hindsight?

Will a coma settle over him? If so, Luce, himself, prophesied what will happen. Speaking to a journalism class, he once said: "I have no fear of competitors who imitate us as closely as they can. They don't have what we have, and they can never out-copy us. The man who is going to put *Life* out of business is in a journalism

Two or three days before going to bed, the editor hangs out the wash, as some shops call it, and the staff comes in to inspect the show. Stories and articles are re-arranged to give pace and permit the book to give off a "feeling of expanding" as the reader pages through it. Some stories are cut because, in seeing the line-up, the editor gets a feeling of lag and he hastens to insert a quickening of interest. By viewing the book as a whole, rather than outlined on a single sheet of paper, the editor hopes better to spot repetitious material in layout as well as subject matter. In the center, Lynne Ellinwood, studies some photostats of laid out pages that are available for the current issue of Writer's Digest. Kirk Polking, holding pad, takes notes on her remarks. Other staff members study the pages tacked on the wall.

school today, and he's picking up our magazine and saying: 'My God, what a bore this is!' Then he is going to put out something that doesn't bore him, and if it has the same effect on millions of other people, we are through." It was Mr. Luce himself, who, through the invention of *Time*, put *Literary Digest* out of business, because when Mr. Luce was in journalism school, *Literary Digest* relentlessly bored him to tears.

No editor is afraid of a slavish imitator. The only man he needs fear is the editor who picks up his book and is bored by it, and as a result of his boredom creates something so new and fresh and wonderful that it counteracts all the ideas and layouts, and pages, and captions, and points of view that he found so deadly dull. Mr. Luce was once young and had nothing, and he enjoyed the wisdom of knowing that probably the only man who will ever overtake *Time, Inc.* is a person who is now as he once was, rather than some manufacturer who merely tries to copy him.

Why Do Editors Edit?

The motor that drives the editor is the message he wants to get over to people, and his utilization of communicative techniques that to him, at least, are not boring. That means the editor must have a more sensitive and impulsive reaction to each and every little thing than anyone else. If you feel, he feels 10 times as much. If you hurt, he hurts 100 times as much. If your eyes moisten, he is bathed in tears. This is figurative, of course, but it is the editor's acute awareness that makes him struggle to make each word, and each paragraph and each spot on a page a fraction better than it otherwise would be.

The placid nature of most magazines comes from the fact that their editors have no clear firm message and are ignorant of all but the editorial side of the publishing business. It is interesting to recall that William Randolph Hearst picked Herb Mayes to edit *Good Housekeeping* because he was young, tough, ambitious, had done a good job with *The American Druggist* and, as Hearst added, "was experienced in advertising, circulation, and merchandising." That, plus having a message, is what it takes to run a big book. When Herb Mayes left *Good Housekeeping* and went to *McCall's*, he produced the excitement in the magazine publishing business in the early sixties. Editorially, he said little significantly different from what Otis Wiese of *McCall's* had said before him. But he said it with an ornamental fireworks visual kick which in itself had such enormous freshness and vigor that it passed for a new statement.

For a while, a brilliant flashpan treatment will suffice in lieu of a new or more significant editorial comment.

However, the other major magazines competing with *McCall's* do not stand still while this struggle goes on. Their editors will invent a flash treatment of their own or create a deeper, more significant editorial purpose. Of the two methods, the latter is the most difficult and dangerous and the most rewarding.

The pay for magazine editors on small books runs from about $6,000 a year to $15,000. An experienced professional editor knows which cartoonists to call upon for children's pieces; who can write tenderly of women past sixty ("My God, Joe, there's 18 million women over sixty. They all got two bits. Let's go after 'em"); where to get stone rubbings of ancient Mexican friezes, and what writer can meet a given personality on his own level and impale his significance on a sheet of paper. The editor has a thousand strings out to all kinds of talent that he can call upon to fill a given space.

But when, in addition, this is laced together with a message this editor has to give to people, he has pushed himself into the salary realm where he is equal to the President of the United States—and he earns it, too.

Often publishers ask, "How do you pick an editor?" There is no test to guide the publisher, no outline of mistakes not to make. For the truth is, on a great book, someone has The Word, and passes it down the line where it is picked up, echoed, resounded, and implemented. But The Word is always there, clear and bright and loud to every ear, like a trumpet soaring over a band. And who gives The Word? It could be either the publisher or editor-in-chief or both. But without it, one is a manufacturer who is about to lose a lot of money and the other is a pedestrian set loose on a race track.

A lot of magazines, for instance, are edited for business and professional people. One of these is *U. S. News and World Report* with David Lawrence as editor and publisher. And David has The Word. He picks, and often writes those incredibly timely front cover headlines and assigns them to writers who grasp the Lawrence idea.

What is The Word that Mr. Lawrence gave his staff? He puts it this way:

> "I wanted a point of communication between the government and people—where the people could learn what their government was up to. And also a two-way street that would let the government know what the people were doing. We want to give the consequences of events that will flow from them. In a tax law, we tell whom it affects; in a treaty, we tell its consequences in relieving or exerting tension."

When a publisher relays The Word for public relations consumption it never is the same as when he sits in a little room with his editors and angles out a story. The one is bland; the other is barbed.

If you seriously want to study publishing, ask your library to give you *U. S. News and World Report* of 1948. Then catch every 12th issue thereafter for a few years. Break it down into The Word itself and the editorial techniques by which it is implemented. No school, no book does that for any editor. In fact, he hasn't even a trade journal to call his own. You can do it for yourself and be the gainer.

Would you like another example of The Word. This time as applied to art and layout rather than editorial policy? Conde Nast hired Dr. M. F. Agha, who was working for the German *Vogue*, to come to America and take over the art direction of the American *Vogue*. Why? Mr. Nast felt Dr. Agha had The Word.

Dr. Agha knew and loved the asymmetrical abstracts of Pietre Mondrian and the modern ideas of Paul Klee, Walter Gropius, and Herbert Bayer—artists, architects, typographers who attended Germany's Bauhaus, a school for creative people. From them, Agha imbibed The Word. He simply wanted to apply this Bauhaus revelation to magazine layout. Want to see it happen before your very eyes? Ask your librarian to give you *Vogue* for 1919. Then ask for a book of Mondrian's abstracts—especially a slim little volume that came out around 1920. This book doomed symmetrical layouts, the kind that look like pictures hung over a 1910 mantle; and it set Agha afire. Now get yourself 10 years of *Vogue*, 1928-1938, and flip the pages. The change did not come all at once, nor in a straight line. Agha had obstacles. But by the time 10 years passed, *Vogue* had it; the rest were forced to become tardy imitators.

The buoys that set the course of magazine publishing are established by editors who have The Word.

When Arnold Gingrich took over *Esquire* in 1952, there occurred one of those astonishing reversals of editorial appeal.

What did Mr. Gingrich do?

"I got rid of the mysteries and westerns and brought fashion out of its eclipse. Our layouts were like a road company of *Cosmopolitan*. The big garish spreads were killed."

What he actually did and how he did it will never be put into words for these are the dearest of all trade secrets. But you can gauge it yourself by a study of *Esquire* for the year 1950 against the last 6 issues of 1960.

Lucky is the editor who has a "pusher," an assistant of wit and energy who tries to lead rather than follow him. Good editorial staffs are rife with intellectual feuds (*never* personal grudges) that tear apart the issue of the day so the editor may better make a

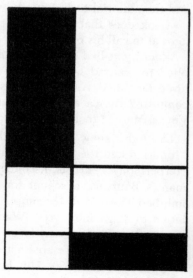

In 1918 (left), Vogue's pictures were set symmetrically, one over the other. Shortly after, Dr. M. F. Agha became art director of Vogue and searched for attractive balance through asymmetrical design. He was influenced by Pietre Mondrian, (right below). It took 20 years (final illustration, Vogue, 1940) for this revolution to be in effect on every illustrated page in Vogue. It took another ten years to reach the majority of the better known magazines. This revolution

decision. Editorial decisions are not made by jury, unless the editor feels it is politic to do so. He makes *all* judgments and suffers *all* consequences of *every* published word. When he dodges this fact, the publisher, if he knows publishing, goes editor-hunting.

Since, in truth, most magazines say very little, the avenue for a job on a publication is to analyze what the publication has said in the last six issues. Has it vacillated? Can you put down what it *did* say? Was it mute while its competition gave tongue? Are its readers aware of what it stands for? And finally, what *should* it say and *how* should this be implemented? A job application along this line equates you on the level of deepest conviction with anyone reading your letter who is anxious for the magazine to succeed.

Any editor is on the World Stage. His is a knock-out game played for keeps. The prospective reader sits in a chair about to read but he has a stomach ache from something he ate, outside a dog is

in design backed and filled, rested and started, even in the pages of Vogue itself. It is not necessary to imitate Mondrian but it is necessary to know what he stood for and to possess your own fresh and original attitude toward this. Equally important, in changing magazine design, was Harper's Bazaar under Alexis Brodovitch, 1933-1958.

barking, and next door the T.V. drills a commercial into his ear. The reader picks up the editor's magazine and challenges him, "Entertain me if you can!"

Mostly, printed matter is thrown away, but sometimes odd things happen. An idea of yours can cause more change than a thousand earthquakes. All editors, large or small, have a pot shot at humanity with each issue. It is ideas, not the passage of time or the rising or lowering of seas that cause real changes. Ideas come mostly from the printed word and so it is given to editors to have the greatest power of man: to change man himself.

Will They Read It?

Writers often want to know if the material they send to a magazine is read. Disallowing the occasional one-man inefficient operations, it is the law of competition (rather than any sense of fair play or cordiality to an unknown) that assures each writer a hearing. At each editorial shop are article editors, fiction editors, etc., each with their staff of two or three assistants. The first reader has one way to keep his job and to advance. He needs to discover in the morning mail a manuscript, sell it to his own editor, who in turn has to sell it to the editor-in-chief. If the published manuscript pulls fan mail, if it is quoted and reprinted, and generally pushes the magazine ahead, then the assistant who found the manuscript, goes up the line; assuming he does this with some regularity. He is not unlike a baseball talent scout. Find talent or get a new job, are his standing orders. The American way of competition and the editorial staff assistant assure every manuscript not only of a hearing, but of a prejudiced hearing; prejudiced insofar as your first reader is rooting to find something to stake his judgment on.

Being dated is the suicidal act of many writers. Essentially, a writer needs to know the works of only a few of the well-known writers from the Greeks till now—perhaps two hundred are plenty. But it is required that he understand the significance of these writers. Are they has-beens? Are they frauds of another day; or are they alive and kicking? Merely to know the originators of the Great Ideas of the past is a pedant's toil. A given number of hours a week and it's done. But what makes a writer (or an editor or a pro in any field) is having this background knowledge *plus* a refreshing, original attitude of his own toward each one of these Ideas.

For instance, to repeat the point of view of Thomas Mann, unrefreshed by the changes in the world's thinking, is to do what he did in his later books: whip a dead horse.

Styles, just like point of view, date you.

Can we be more precise about this? Take Ulysses. As a writer, you naturally need be aware of the catalytic influence of James Joyce's style. Now, you can deny Joyce and create your style in the very act of denying him, or you can alter your style by accepting some of his techniques and practicing them with alterations of your own. But *not to know* the significance and effect of his techniques is to be unaware and therefore dated.

We speak of Hemingway as a great writer. Hemingway's historical significance is his contribution to American style. This appears primarily in his book, "The Sun Also Rises." Copy out one thousand words and try to edit, change, and rewrite it. That's one way of savouring the other man's style and making it part of you. You can love, hate or be bored by "The Sun Also Rises" but not to take a position on it at all, and not to have your own literary style affected by your position is to be dated.

In the personal act of accepting or rejecting parts of the styles of other writers, you create your own. Most scripts that editors read are dated; that is, the author simply isn't responsive to the 100-odd ideas that have mattered in the past 5,000 years and the succession of literary styles that have put them over.

For writers and editors, the business of not being dated, of being truly *au courant*, and being able to express your message in the idiom of the day, is the elusive art.

Man Against White Space

Part 2 Circulation

There are few circulation managers in the business who call themselves successful. This is because the demands made upon them are so great that their goals are out of reach. The publisher wants complete coverage in his field. His competition already claim they possess it. Only the circulation manager is aware that complete paid circulation coverage in any field means that you have sold nearly everybody, and its accomplishment is impossible. General Motors, with only three competitors, sells 47% of its market. To beat that is nice going. But circulation managers are supposed to have 70, 80, even 85 percent coverage of their field. This is beyond human flesh and pushes them into deceit.

The beginner in magazine publishing thinks of circulation as something you sell. The fact is, circulation is something that you buy. Paid-mail circulation, almost without exception, is secured at a direct loss; that is, the cost of securing four dollars for a one-year subscription is greater than the four dollars the individual pays. To this loss must be added the cost of printing and delivering the magazine. Within the several implications of this fact is the first key to understanding magazine publishing.

The net loss of securing one paid-mail subscriber may run as little as 5c to as high as $1.00. The cost of printing and delivering the actual magazine is from 12c to 40c a copy for most publications. Thus, each subscriber represents a net loss for the publisher of about $2.00 a year for printing and delivering the magazine, plus a loss of 5c to $1.00 to secure the subscription. On a magazine of one million circulation, this means that about $2,000,000 must be picked up some other way to meet the loss of the circulation department. On a successful magazine, this loss is met through the sale of advertising, plus occasionally, the sale of books, patterns, or services the subscriber wants.

Here are some usual methods by which circulation is secured.

Catalogue Agencies

A catalogue agency is a clearing house for thousands of part-time, subscription salesmen. They receive a printed catalogue from an agency (from whence it derives the name catalogue agency). In the catalogue is an alphabetical list of perhaps 500 different magazines, along with the subscription price of each one, and the commission paid to the sales person for selling a subscription. On collecting $3.00 from a subscriber, the salesman pockets 75c for himself and sends the remaining 2.25 to the catalogue agency. The catalogue agency keeps approximately 75c and sends $1.50 to the publisher. This is one type of circulation, for which the publisher expends little effort and the money he receives is greater than his selling cost.

Subscriptions sold by catalogue agencies take care of up to 5% of the total paid-mail list of major magazines. The people who work for the catalogue agencies are housewives, handicapped people, shut-ins, or retired folks who call up their friends and say: "When you renew your subscription to your favorite magazine, please send me the money. It won't cost you any more, and I will make a little commission." The selling pitch, of course, could be more forceful and informative, but usually is as flat as the example given.

The catalogue agency does not generate much new circulation but, from the circulation manager's point of view, it does deliver another little peck at the stone.

A few of the large magazine publishers own and operate their own catalogue agency. The catalogues they distribute push their own books in various attractive combinations with other magazines, and also offer subscriptions to several hundred other publications. Any bright young man desirous of getting into publishing need only establish his own catalogue agency, run it well for two or three years, and dump perhaps a thousand or fifteen hundred subscriptions into the lap of the publisher whose employment he covets. Then, with this record and experience, ask for a job.

A young man with this kind of push would start for $6,500 as assistant catalogue manager and be welcomed like Lindbergh in Paris. A catalogue agency is one of the few remaining businesses that can be started on small capital, and either continued as a business or used as an "in" to get a job on the big book.

It seldom occurs to a job seeker in publishing to learn the nuts and bolts of the trade first, and then reward his prospective employer with a little concrete testimonial.

Direct Mail

When 100,000 letters, soliciting a subscription to a magazine, are dropped in the mail, the cost of the envelopes, stationery, order blank, postage, printing, addressing, inserting is $9,000. If a magazine sells for $3.50 a year, the publsher can expect between 1,000 and 3,000 orders from a 100,000 mailing. Thus if he mails 100,000 letters, sells 2,000 subscriptions, collects $7,000, and the entire operation costs him $9,000, he loses $2,000 or a net loss of $1 for each subscription that he sold plus, of course, the cost of printing and fulfilling the 12 issues to each subscriber.

Once in a while a subscription letter to a "cold" list closes better than 2%. There are instances where direct mail letters sent to small, highly selected lists, close 7 or 8 per cent. On the average today, a mailing sent to a cold list, offering a magazine at $4.00 a year, "pulls" a 1.5% return; i.e., 1,500 orders from a 100,000 mailing.

Every specialized publisher is hungry to circularize lists that contain high income subscribers who will buy heavily from his advertisers because they *need* the products. A young man who would beat the bushes in his home state and locate 20 or 30 such lists which a single specialized publisher could use, and then lay on the publisher's desk the name and address of the list owner, the cost of renting the list ($20.00 to $30.00 a thousand), a strip list sample of the first 50 names on each list and a description of the list itself would be regarded as a sharp-as-a-tack young operator and grabbed vigorously by the neck before anyone else got him. This inside track approach has as its competitor, "I have an M.A. at Southern Idaho Teachers' and will start as a proofreader."

Renewal Subscriptions

Circulation managers send from 5 to 12 letters to individuals whose subscriptions expire. These letters begin 3 months before the subscription expires and continue to be mailed at a rate that varies from every ten days to every 6 weeks, until the series is completed.

The first letter, mailed 90 days prior to the subscription expiration, will produce from 3% to 6% return (i.e., from 3,000 to 6,000 cash orders come back to the publisher for every 100,000 letters mailed to "pre-expires") and show a profit on the actual cost of the mailing.

The "renewal letter" which comes to the subscriber a few days before he receives the last issue of his magazine subscription will close from 6% to 20%. This is the only letter in the whole series of "renewal letters" that shows a real profit. With the next letter, the returns drop sharply to around 3%. Starting with the fifth and succeeding letters, the redoubtable circulation manager offers premiums, cut rates and deals. If the series of renewal letters were stopped with the third letter, there would be a tidy profit for the publisher. However, to acquire the desired amount of circulation, these letters soliciting renewals are continued for a series up to 12, and their total cost is usually about 10% to 20% under the total income.

Some magazines back up their renewal letters, especially in big cities, with "telephone campaigns" to expired subscribers. This increases the number of renewals but the added cost of telephoning is not equalled by increased revenue. The *increase* in the per cent of renewals is passed along to advertisers as evidence of the strong desire on the subscriber's part to want the magazine.

Today, a consumer magazine would do well to renew 25% using only three letters and no deals. A mass circulating farm paper, with its reader interest spread between town and country, would be excellent at 20% on the same arrangement while a trade paper should do 30% before having to bear down.

The methods, as well as the number of times they are employed by the circulation manager on the same subscriber, to secure his renewal is revealed so casually by the publisher to the advertiser that the advertiser never grasps the difference between a high renewal rate under pressure and a high renewal rate. Thus, with a few outstanding exceptions, like *The New Yorker,* a high renewal rate reflects more credit on the skill of the circulation manager than on the reader interest which advertisers hope will be showered on their printed message.

Does this amiable illusion matter? It matters to all publishers, especially trade paper publishers, as paid advertising is placed in one magazine over another because of 30 or 40 factors of which a high renewal per cent is one.

A good magazine will renew between 35 and 60 per cent of its subscribers. Thus, if a publication has one million readers, each of whom subscribes for one year, and half of them renew, then the circulation manager must sell a half million new subscriptions a year to run in place. Picking up 10,000 new subscriptions a week is a feat for the most skilled circulation expert.

What if the same subscribers bought the magazine for a two year period, and the subscriptions are evenly spaced? Now the circulation manager needs sell only 5,000 a week to hold his ground. It has occurred to many hard pressed circulation men that if they sold 10 year subscriptions, and if they were properly spaced, it would require only one-tenth the effort to stay even and any extra effort could go into growth. If it costs money to sell a subscription, why not cut the price and sell it for as long a term as you can?

There is another side of the ledger. Can the advertiser be sure that 10 years from now the subscriber will have the same interests he has today? Will the reader's tastes change, his interests cool?

Long term subscriptions (10, 15 and 20 year terms) are a sweet balance pole for the circulation manager but of dubious value to the advertiser. The shorter the term, the more sure the advertiser can be of the subscriber's immediate interest in the magazine and its subject matter; the longer the term, the less likely.

A young person seeking a job with the Circulation Department of a magazine could do no better than painstakingly interview 100 subscribers of a given publication and then submit, on the basis of this research, a series of 12 letters showing the kind of efforts he could produce to secure renewal subscriptions for that magazine. Along with his series of 12 letters, the job applicant would also show the circulation manager a typed copy of each of his 100 interviews.

This calculated initiative is as foreign to job seekers in the publishing business as it is today to see a man going West with a wife, a mule, an ax and a bag of beans. Yet a young man with this approach would be hired enthusiastically, and way made for him to move directly into management level.

Inserts

Circulation managers make arrangements with department stores, mail order, seed and other catalogue distributors, for the inclusion of a card offering a subscription to their magazine that rides along in a mailing produced by the department store or other company. The commission exacted by the department store, and the cost of producing the card, are generally in excess of the income received for such subscriptions.

The charm of such inserts is that they may give the publisher access to the particular kind of reader his advertisers are seeking because of the selectivity employed by the catalogue distributor; as for instance, a catalogue of architect's supplies would be a perfect carrier for a subscription insert from *Architectural Forum*.

Is there, in your city, a big commercial printer of catalogues? Can you marry the interests of a specialized publisher to a manufacturer issuing a catalogue? Going to the publisher with an envelope of ideas like this in your hand may give him a heart attack but his heirs will hire you.

Combinations

Publishers of daily newspapers have found that they can increase their own carrier sales by offering the choice of a magazine along with the newspaper. Such circulation is known in the trade as "no net." The newspaper reader pays a few cents a week more and gets a magazine (at a cut price) in addition to his daily newspaper. The magazine publisher receives nothing for the magazine and, of course, has to pay to print and deliver it. The extra weekly pennies paid by the newspaper reader are split between the newspaper (which gets the least) and the magazine subscription company that originated the deal and provides the promotion. The advertiser has the assurance that the new reader, in his own good time, in his own home, chose the magazine voluntarily. Weighted against this is the fact that the order was secured via cut price and weekly installment payment. An individual reader secured this way may be excellent; but can ten thousand such circulation compare to ten thousand subscribers who plunk down the full price for a short term (1 or 2 year) subscription without any inducement? Can you alter this newspaper promotion idea so as to retain the good features and build out the bad ones?

Field Sold Subscriptions

There are a number of organizations in the country who specialize in hiring crews that travel door-to-door and town-to-town selling magazine subscriptions. After selling a subscription, the "field sellers" keep the money; the publishers receive none. When a publisher has made a guarantee to his advertisers for a given amount of circulation and is at a loss to secure it, or when he seeks to "bury" a competitor, he may offer "field selling" organizations 5%, 10% or 15% bonus for every subscription sold. On such "bonus deals," the publisher receives no money whatsoever, and lays out from 15c to 75c *per subscription*. This is paid to the crew members as a special bonus to push one particular magazine.

Here's how it's done.

To capture the attention of the door-to-door salesman who may have 100 magazines on his list (but rarely carries copies of them) the publisher offers "points" in addition to the regular commission. These "points" are the bonus which the salesman receives for pushing one particular magazine over all others. "Points" given to crew salesmen are paid off by way of an expense-paid trip to Florida, a portable T.V. set, a suit of clothes, etc. The publisher is not required (i.e., forced) to state what percent, if any, of his circulation is secured in this manner.

The following quote is from Warren Brubaker, known jokingly

but respectfully in the trade as "Honest Bru, the farmer's friend." Mr. Brubaker heads up Globe Reader's Service, a volatile and vibrant group of crew managers and crew salesmen who solicit magazine subscriptions door-to-door in small towns and farms.

(Mr. Brubaker is speaking:)

"No, I never dictate a letter. My wife does all that for me. Hell, I can't write. I sell. You take down what I say.

"We travel from 50 to 125 at a time. We go by private car, 4 to 5 sales people in a car. We have men crews and girls crews.

"So we hit a town like Cincinnati. We'll put up at the Metropole. I'll pay maybe $9 for a room and we sleep 4 to a room. We all eat breakfast together at 7:30 A.M. There's a prize for the best song on how to sell one of our magazines. Maybe that morning we offer $10 for the best song. After breakfast we break into car crews and each car has a Captain. The Captain works under an Assistant Crew Manager who watches 5 cars. Each car works a territory.

"Each Captain briefs his crew on the books to sell and checks their sales pitch. I mean, he says, 'all right now, boy give it to me.' He lets it come to him; then tones it up if he can. Every man and woman checks in at noon so we know where they are. We meet again for dinner at 6:30. Anyone in the bar is fined 50c. Anyone collecting under $30 for the day's work goes to evening session on magazine selling.

"Twice a week I take the gang to a movie treat. About once a week we have a steak and beans on the side banquet. Bed check is at 11:30. Anyone missing is fined 50c. The fines are used for prizes.

"I stake a new member to meals and room to get him started. If he fails on the job, I give him a bus ticket back to the town where I found him. College kids don't go the job. Too lazy. A good man or woman will make themselves $300 a week over and above all expenses. A bum won't last a day with me. Bonuses from publishers for pushing their book give my people paid vacations, travel bags, portable TV sets.

"Assistant Crew Managers easily make $150 a week. Crew Managers, however, make money. Everything is commission. Me, too."

I have been a publisher for 40 years. I have never met a literate, educated, civilized young man or woman who cared enough about publishing to spend a year with a pro like Warren Brubaker and then seek out a job with a publisher. What Warren knows and doesn't tell (his business isn't educating publishers) would be welcomed with genuine tears of joy in any magazine shop.

At each magazine shop are people who deal with those organizations headed up by men like Warren Brubaker. But often the men holding down such jobs have no real personal understanding of the task faced by the crew manager. Therefore the field selling boss, in facing up to the publisher for all the irregularities that come up, slips readily into amiable double talk as the simplest way of answering and yet not answering.

Here is a morsel of conversation between the publisher of an automotive trade paper and Jack Martin, one of the founding fathers of "field sold subs" in the trade field:

Publisher: "Jack, how many men do you have now selling *Service Digest?*"

Martin: "Never had so many as we have today."

Publisher: "Jack, how about that premium we printed for you? Are you selling it or giving it away?"

Martin: "We're doing wonders with it."

People who know and love Jack Martin would not call him evasive. His amiable patter is part and parcel of the way many field selling representatives talk. It's their way. Few of these people came to field selling from publishing. They came up through door-to-door selling, car captaincy, assistant crew managers, crew managers and, finally, owners of field selling set-ups themselves.

It is a rare one among field salesmen who fits into the cultural background of editorial Ivy Leaguers, with their gentle irony and tweed sport coats or advertising executives with their grey flannel.

When a publisher wants to find a person to head up his field selling department, he seeks someone with *both* practical experience and the manner of speech, so to put it, that fits into his own organization. Usually, all he can find is a man who has written a lot of letters to field selling organizations, but who, himself has never written up an order. Any person (young or old) understanding this *need,* who will join up with a firm like Martin's or Brubaker's for a year or two and learn the trade, and then possessing the cultural and educational background to work on a national magazine, has himself a good job.

Robert Haig, formerly with Hearst, used to head up a group of 300 men who sold trade magazine subscriptions to owners of hardware stores, feed and hay dealers, drug stores, printing plants, etc. Bob puts it this way:

> "We have 300 mature men selling trade subscriptions for trade journal publishers and about 100 of these men do 90% of our business. In the trade field, we find a man over 35 does the best job because he seems to get more respect from the businessmen on whom he calls. Our men all operate on a commission basis and a man who works has no difficulty in netting $250 a week. Our problem is in finding men. My best method is to go to one of my 100 key salesmen and offer them an override on the first $10,000 worth of business sold by a new man. Afterwards, naturally, they tell them to beat it out of their territory.
>
> "The colleges feed every profession: law, medicine, architecture, insurance selling, etc. But we have no talent pool flowing into field selling. I hope some college, perhaps a night college, specializing in adult education, will work with an established field selling organization to get teachers and offer training courses in trade sub selling."

The Audit Bureau of Circulation, Chicago, Illinois, will supply the addresses of reliable field selling companies in both the trade and consumer field to any institution of learning. Should they receive such a request it could well be their first.

Any fraternal, social or religious organization that desires to make money by selling magazine subscriptions can do so. Usually the organization is permitted to retain a minimum of 35% of the money it collects, but prizes, premiums and bonuses may carry that up to 80%. The cost of locating an organization and then communicating to it the job to be done, when added to the commissions given to the organization, result in all such subscriptions being sold at a loss of 5 to 15 cents per subscription.

Let's say you want to get into the publishing business and happen to be friendly with a few garden clubs in your area. By lining up these garden clubs as a subscription sales organization, and then contacting one of the publishers in either the garden or shelter field, you can receive a quick reply to a query sent a publisher asking if you can sell subscriptions for him using the garden club members as agents. If you can deliver to *Better Homes & Gardens, House and Garden,* or *Popular Gardening,* 500 subscriptions sold by the local garden club (in which you would make perhaps $250 and the garden clubs $1,000), you will capture such favorable attention from the publisher that you'll feel like a 10-0 college pitcher with Los Angeles and New York ball teams on the trail.

Which Way Is Up?

Generally speaking, the lay public, as well as people in the magazine business themselves, do not understand that circulation is dead loss. Publishers themselves hold back on the subject. They rightly feel it undercuts the sales story of their advertising staff to have it known that their circulation has been pushed to the point where every new subscriber added means either an added penny of cost to the advertiser or a loss in net to the publisher. Whenever added circulation reflects readers who genuinely want the magazine, who have faith and interest in it, this burden of cost can well be paid by the advertiser. But when the additional circulation goes to individuals who are induced to buy the magazine by a device, whether it be cut price, a premium or a keyed-up bonus salesman calling door-to-door, then the added burden of cost may give the advertiser doubtful value. Such readers bring less than genuine personal affection to the publication and glance at it with but casual interest when it comes into their home.

Thus it becomes readily apparent that as publishers fight to be top dog in their field, and push their circulation beyond the point where people have deep-rooted desires to read it, that the advertiser is asked to pay for circulation, a growing part of which is of decreasing value.

If advertisers understood this, they would not encourage publishers to vie so frantically with each other for increased circulation, as this increase in circulation eventually reflects numbers rather than devoted readers. The advertiser profits best when his message is given time and consideration in the home of the reader who needs his product.

Who cares?

You care!

Not only as a writer, but as a citizen. For the closer a magazine publisher is to the red, in his business operation, the more iron goes out of his spine, the more likely he is to yield to every pretext to publish editorial copy that ties in with the advertiser's desires, regardless of merit, citizenship or integrity. Publishers are people. Pushed hard enough, they give. Not all — of course, but enough to muddle our American free press.

A kept press comes about when it is profitless press to the owner. Demands for increases in circulation, beyond the point of gain to the publisher, are a force that harms.

A.B.C. — The Cop

Guardian over most circulation managers is an organization of publishers and advertisers called Audit Bureau of Circulation.

Once a year an independent auditor comes into the publisher's office and lifts, at random, out of the circulation files, the names of approximately one-half of one per cent of the net-paid subscriptions. It is then the job of the circulation manager to show that each and every one of these names qualify as net-paid subscribers. He must produce the original paid orders.

The Audit Bureau of Circulation is naturally willing to accept a modest few subscriptions that do not qualify as paid, because of clerical errors, etc., but if the subscriptions that do not qualify run over a dozen, then the auditor may deduct from a magazine's circulation the per cent of the whole that does not qualify in the random test. The publisher must then refund percentage-wise to the advertisers the money he received if, after this deduction is made, his total net paid subscribers are under the amount of paid circulation he guaranteed. The A.B.C. auditors, to a man, are honorable, accurate and objective.

The unfortunate part about the Audit Bureau of Circulation is that the advertisers who are a member of this group, are individuals who are international successes at making soap, or perfume, or motor cars, but know little about the magazine publishing business. The publishers, who are important committee members of the Audit Bureau of Circulation, know the publishing business thoroughly and are very much aware of the conditions and directions of the rules that are adopted. As a result of this, the publisher's own know-how tends to overwhelm the representatives of the various advertisers, so that an Audit Bureau of Circulation statement is 100% correct on quantity, but with each passing year the quality is a little more unknown than it was before.

For instance, it follows that if a magazine sells long-term subscriptions, say a twenty-year subscription for $15.00, a number of its readers who bought the magazine in 1955 might no longer voluntarily go out and buy the magazine today. In spite of this, in some divisions of Audit Bureau of Circulation, the publishers have managed to "simplify" the Audit Bureau of Circulation statement so that long-term subscriptions are grouped under one umbrella heading: "Subscriptions received for 5 years or more." That the advertiser failed to grasp why this was being done to him is routinely accepted by publishers because the advertiser is an outlander. Although he may know the hotel business better than anybody else in the world, he is no match for a publisher when it comes to trading points on publishing. Here and there talk is heard today that the entire publishing business would be helped were the Audit Bureau of Circulation to include as part of its goal the surveying and reporting of the quality of the magazine's subscriptions list as well as its precise and exact quantity.

How Much Do You Get Paid For This?

The average rate of pay for a circulation manager runs from $5,000 to $20,000 with three dozen individuals getting up to three times that. The job is underpaid only because the current demands made upon the circulation manager are greater than he can fulfill. Every time he adds circulation he comes closer to, if not passing, the point of diminishing returns. Each new 10,000 subscribers bring him nearer the area of readers who really don't *need* the magazine; and so to secure a profitable rate of renewal from them becomes impossible rather than difficult.

Who Dares But Go Higher?

In his own field, the advertiser is very much aware that he can never hope to sell half of his prospects. Most businessmen would consider themselves next to immortal if they sold 25% of their prospects. The same businessman, however, is willing to believe that the publisher, though made of the same flesh and blood as he, is able to sell 80%, 90%, or even 100% of his total market. Thus, in a field in which there are 50,000 bona fide prospects within a given state, the publisher comes up with 50,000 circulation and claims that he had complete coverage of all the prospects. The advertiser will accept this, even though common sense should tell him that no one can sell his entire market, and few people have ever sold one-half of it. In most cases, where there are 50,000 prospects in a given area and the publisher claims 50,000 circulation, or complete coverage of all those prospects, he may actually have 20,000 of the prospects as subscribers and the other 30,000 are also-rans who paid their money and get the magazine, but are not the prospects the advertiser thinks they are.

And does this matter? Yes. Because this is the cross on which the publishing field rests today. By forcing its circulation beyond the point where it is profitable to take it and then, by surveys, attempting to prove that all of the circulation is exactly what the advertiser desires, the publisher has boxed himself in. He has no place to go but up, and every step up is more costly than the income he can get from it. Magazine publishers make a net profit, national average of 3%. If a publisher takes in $20,000 a week or $1,000,000 a year, his net is $30,000. Thirty years ago the same publisher was making $80,000 and the dollars bought more. Five years from now the publisher may be making 1-1/2% or 2% if he continues the same way. Should the national average drop to 1-1/2% or 2%, this means that some magazines will be losing money and folding.

Bold magazine thinking suggests double crossing the field by flat-footed honesty in setting up circulation goals. That is, make no claim for impossible "coverage," and credit the advertiser with being a reasonable man. A few magazines sought out this fantastic principle and stuck by it. *The New Yorker* is one. Their average profits, in recent years, were over 10%.

If *The New Yorker's* circulation goal was 2 million instead of a half million, and if their advertising rate increased in reasonable proportion, I suspect advertisers would get less return per dollar spent because a *New Yorker* reader, as it is now, is neither secured nor held under pressure. Readers of this character are more responsive to advertisers. In addition, the editor of *The New Yorker* does not have to fan out his editorial appeal, doling pages to factions of reader interest in order to win their support (one mass magazine's theory is that sufficient reader response can be had in exchange for the money the reader pays if the reader will read 3 major articles out of 10). When a magazine aims at its natural level of circulation, the reader actually gets more reading matter aimed directly at him and spends more time with the magazine.

A less ingenious but easier way of circumventing circulation problems is "controlled circulation," that is, free circulation. You, the publisher, select the list and mail your magazine to it. Then you spend the rest of your life proving to advertisers that your list is bona fide. Trade books with five to over one hundred thousand readers accomplish this, and the auditing organization that reports as advertisers on whether they do precisely as they say is called C.C.A. (Controlled Circulation Audit). The idea of free circulation gives an easier access to enter publishing for individuals with a small trade book in mind.

Newsstand

Some 110,000 stores have newsstands and sell magazines. To arrive at its final destination on one of these newsstands, slightly ruffled from travel and 1/3 covered up by several non-related publications, a magazine goes through many hands. First, there is the national distributor. This company, (such as Macfadden, Hearst, Dell, Fawcett, Kable, etc.) usually owns a string of its own periodicals. Then, having created a distributing organization, it feels six can eat at a table set for five without anybody getting up hungry. Sometimes the distributing company itself prospers better than the publishing venture and the personnel at the head of it become primarily interested in selling magazines. Except for a publisher who owns his distributing organization, and there are barely a dozen in the country, the others shift uneasily from one foot to the other when they eye the newsstand looking for their books.

Macfadden, for instance, distributes its own eleven publications along with an equal number from other publishers. One of these is *Writer's Digest*. Here is exactly how the distribution works.

We set our own "newsstand press run" which is a hope, a prayer and a guess. In our case, we know there are about 600 magazine wholesalers of consequence in the country, and, of these about 200 are in areas where *Writer's Digest* is least likely to succeed on the basis of educational and literary statistics we can secure. That leaves 400 wholesalers in areas where we might sell copies. In each of these areas, we secure information on the newsstand sale of magazines that are relatively competitive to *Writer's Digest,* or are in an allied field. We pay special attention to University towns, writers' colonies and publishing centers. From this data we guess the number of copies of *Writer's Digest* these 400 wholesalers could use. This figure is transmitted to Macfadden who in turn sends our printer a list of some 400 independent newsstand wholesalers throughout the United States. Alongside the name and address of each wholesaler is a recommended order, supplied by Macfadden. This represents the copies of *Writer's Digest* to be shipped that wholesaler for a given issue.

The copies go prepaid and the magazine wholesaler at Peoria or Portland opens them up and then decides which newsstands in his territory will receive *Writer's Digest*. In this work he is helped by the Macfadden local representative who has cased the town and knows which neighborhoods may sell this magazine better than another.

A check-up is made within the first two weeks after it is placed on sale and stands that are sold out are given more copies and stands that have moved no magazines at all are relieved of their copies which are shipped off to other stands.

As often happens, many key persons in any spread out distribution idea, are individuals whose name the publisher never knows. These people, in most cases, are not on intimate terms with the magazine itself. One such key person is the wholesaler's "periodical superintendent." He will personally supervise the distribution of the big magazines, listing with his own pencil, on long galley strips, the number of copies of Big Magazine A that will go to each and every newsstand at his wholesale branch.

But how about Little Magazine Z?

How about it?

The periodical superintendent's assistant does this. There may be no incentive system, no close supervision based on an intimate understanding of the magazine's personality, the people it attracts, where they might live. Yet it is the assistant who writes down the fatal numbers: Butch's News Shop, 8; Cater's Drug, 2; Abe's Shine Parlor, 3. On that pencil a fortune rides.

Hand in hand with this assistant's happenchance acquaintance with Little Magazine Z is the hard fact that in each town there is one magazine wholesaler; not two, not three. Just one. Don't you like him? Doesn't he like you? Patch and make up for there is only one. The clutch of competition is not fast upon him. Here is where the young and ambitious may enter publishing. By the honest ingenuity that has made the American way famous, a capable young man might get hold of the local newsstand distribution list of some small quality journal such as *Railroad Magazine*. If in this town there are a half dozen spots where such a journal might be placed, with some common sense hope for sale, a letter to the publisher explaining this would be like a thunderbolt. Such a letter would itemize the stands, quote the wholesaler, name the personalities who would do the copy shifting, reveal by accurate and diligent reporting the whereabouts of *Railroad Magazine* as of today and where it should be tomorrow. It would cause the publisher, in this case Harry Steeger, to creep quietly to his penthouse where he could pull the letter out of his pocket and slowly stare at each word. Receiving such a letter from an applicant for a job in publishing has been the night time fantasy of several publishers of Small Magazine Z, who find this a more engaging thought than what you might think, at the lonely quiet hour between awake and sleeping.

For a monthly magazine that sells for 50c, the publisher receives between 27c and 30c a copy depending on the importance of his magazine. "Importance" has nothing to do with its literary value but only with its net sale on the newsstand and frequency of issue. Since a news dealer has only so many square feet to display his wares, a weekly is thirteen times more important to him than a quarterly. The news dealer buys the 50c magazine for 40 to 42 cents. The publishers get about 28c. The 10 to 12 cent spread between what the publisher gets and what the newsstand dealer pays is split up by the national distributor and the local wholesaler. All magazines are shipped on a consignment basis.

Few magazines sell more than 75% of their newsstand print order; i.e., if a magazine gives their national newsstand distributor 100,000 copies on a consignment basis, it is fortunate if 75,000 are sold.

Magazines *do* sell over 75%, and a few whip out a sale in excess of 90%. This, however, is accomplished at great cost to the publisher. By newspaper advertising, he asks the public to go to the newsstands. He may back this up with TV or radio advertising. Third, he sends a paid employee, called a newsstand supervisor, into each major town. The job of the newsstand supervisor is to distribute and display his magazine on the kind of newsstands where it will move best.

Publishers take a dim view of some magazine wholesalers. For every good one there is another who, granted 300 newsstands in his area and 300 copies of a given magazine to distribute, will place ten copies on thirty stands and call it a day. Some of those stands should in truth receive only two copies, and some should receive twenty.

It has never occurred to a vocational school that magazine wholesalers need talent. A young man who would do two weeks' leg work and present a magazine wholesaler with a list of 200 newsstands and specific reasons for adding or taking off various titles would be investigated first as a Russian spy, and, after the wonderment died, hired. Probably the wholesaler would take out adoption papers. It is the job of the publisher's newsstand supervisor to ferret out which stand will sell his magazine best. Newsstand supervisors receive from $4,000 to $9,000 a year plus expenses. Macfadden has 60 such newsstand supervisors. Triangle (*TV Guide, Seventeen,* etc.) has 130.

When a publisher of a 35c magazine sells half of them, and the wholesaler pays him 20c for every copy that sells, he will end up getting 20c a copy for those that he sells and nothing for those that do not sell, or an average of 10c for each copy distributed.

If 75% of his magazines sell on the newsstands and he receives 20c a copy for each sold, he winds up with 15c for each copy distributed.

It is generally believed in the trade that newsstand sales are superior circulation, since each sale is voluntary. The reader buys the magazine in open choice with 200 other books. Nobody pressures him. He walks in with his 35c and walks out with a magazine. The Fawcett organization has built a great deal of its success by proving to advertisers that most of their sales come in this voluntary, low-pressure way.

An indication of a magazine's level of popular acceptance can often be seen from its newsstand sale as compared to its competitors.

Occasionally an individual field will flourish into an uproar overnight, led by some spectacular single success. In this case, both the leader and the followers make money on newsstand sales alone, since the public's appetite for this field is so keen that for a limited time a high price (50c) and a thin book (48 to 64 pages) do not beat down the sale. Examples are the *Confidential* wave in 1954 and the *Playboy* torrent in 1956.

The Game Is Played for Keeps

The life-or-death earnestness in the historic race for circulation by *Life, Look* and the *Post* was revealed in a statement made by Lester Suhler, then circulation director of *Look*, who said: "If the *Post* drops a million and we pick it up, they're through."

In other words, more than 150 years of consecutive publishing and high reputation is no antidote for being a bad third in the field of three. If they are close together they may all live. If one falls far behind, he is through.

The game is played for keeps and the stakes are very high. In almost every field of American manufacturing from book publishing to steel, and in all the professions, the leaders get together, if not to hold up prices, at least to maintain a truce. In big-time magazine publishing the stakes are Life and Death and there is no truce between the leaders. Publishers do not "get together" to help keep each other alive and well.

Lots of Room at the Top

We are now in front of the gate marked "Magazine Publisher" and want in.

A flesh-eating dragon in front of the gate offers us a free pass. All we need have in exchange for our pass is an idea for a 50c retail book that will sell 50% on the newsstands and be printed for 12c.

And there is yet another door, also with a dragon handing out free passes or taking a mouthful (of you) instead. This one asks for an idea for a 75c retail book that will sell 50% and can be printed for 18c.

Only books like the above can prosper without advertising.

The tranquilizing thought that a new publication without advertising, newsstand supervisors, or wide national publicity can sell over 50% is dreamy. A new publication may go over 50% on newsstand sale and reach 70 or 75%, but this is effected only when the publisher's budget is enlarged to include the cost of letting the public know that it is there waiting for them.

In the next ten years, if the past is to judge, we can anticipate a dozen publishers to originate a field for themselves wherein they will make a profit on newsstand sales alone. Around their publications will circle imitating satellites.

It should follow that the man or woman who pioneers one of these fields and breaks in with a new book should be a person of solid and sober judgment, blessed with years of experience in publishing who has figured out the whole matter in dollars and cents. If the future follows the past, this won't be so. The books will be founded by kids out of school who know little about costs, and have more credit than they do dollars, and are more full of the love of publishing than a desire to make money. It is this lambent, human and statistic-defying quality that is continually beating down the manufacturers who come into the field and try to convert paper and ink into a publication in order to make a profit. In this day of fast communication, magazine publishing offers world recognition to individuals who believe in what they have to say and intend to say it because communication is their very being.

In any brief discussion of a segment of the publishing business, there must of necessity be a limiting group of examples, and a superficial touching on hard nut problems. This, surely, is the case here. One purpose prompted this series, and if it is effective, we shall be grateful. To date, very little has been published about the innards of magazine publishing. *Advertising Age* or *Marketing/Communications,* for instance, are hell on wheels when it comes to ferreting out news of one executive leaving a company to go with another. Perhaps their able editors will be stimulated to publishing critical, interpretative probings into publishing methods so that young publishers have a library of research to consult. Communication between departments of major magazines is thin. Ideas that could flow from one to the other are never born because the people in one department don't really know how the other lives.

Our company issues a small string of magazines and prints fourteen different magazines for other publishers. Now and then, publishing ideas are placed on our desk by newcomers. Usually, such an entrepreneur has no working knowledge, even the scant bare bones given here, about publishing management. This is a contributing cause to the short and upsy-downy life of many new books.

Our second reason for this series is that it gives free lance writers a whiff of the matters with which publishing people contend. With one part of their minds they read the manuscript in front of them, and with the other they weigh the nuances of its total effect on their business.

Man Against White Space

Part 3 Advertising

Of the five departments of the magazine publishing business, one of them, advertising, is profitable. The others spend more than they take in. Operating in the red are Editorial, Production, Administration, and usually, Circulation. How can one department carry four?

The chief difference between selling space and almost any other product is that advertising is an intangible. The advertiser buys a given amount of white space in a periodical that is distributed to a given number of people. He wants to know: *one*, who are the people who will read my ad?; *two*, do these people respect this magazine, or do they merely break the wrapper, glance at it, and throw it away?; *three*, what interest, if any, do these people have in my product and can they afford it?

The charm of selling advertising is that *none* of these questions may be answered factually. The only question that can be answered to the decimal point is the actual ABC* circulation of the magazine. Balanced against these 3 points, the manufacturer needs answer 6 other questions to himself: Is my product good or am I just kidding myself? Is it competitive in quality and price? Does my dealer organization follow the general pattern of the magazine circulation that I'm thinking about buying? Does the magazine have any plus values, such as dealer and jobber influence? Is it read by influential people generally—that is, people influential to the success of my product? Are there merchandising tie-ups offered me whose value and effect I can check?

Who Sells Space?

The job of selling white space has attracted two kinds of minds and both have had success. The one is cagey, full of guile, trigger quick, always punching, never retreating, alert to every opportunity to seek out the manufacturer's needs, whims, or ambitions and illustrate how the publication in question fulfills them. Such a mind is inventive with figures to prove the publication's story and disprove its competitors'—all of this being bedded down with a personality that is warm, social, and convincing.

The other type of mind in the advertising business has all of these qualities in varying degrees, but due to the responsibilities, commitments, and dignities that go with big business, it is more thorough, careful and serious in its approach. It is pervaded by a compulsion to understand the manufacturer's problems, his product and his market, and soberly to work with him to solve them through

---

*Practically all national magazines of every sort and description are members of the Audit Bureau of Circulation. An independent, qualified auditor, employed by the Bureau, whose expenses are paid by national advertisers as well as by all publishers, so that the auditor is responsible not only to the advertiser but also to the competitors of the publisher, analyzes and reports on the circulation of each magazine annually. These audits are sober, precise, and unqualifiedly accurate. An error of ½ of 1% is almost unknown. The auditors explore the paper, postage, and printing bills and the total circulation files. Their reports, however, and this is the weakness of the Audit Bureau of Circulation, reflect only upon the numerical content of the magazine's circulation and have little to do with its quality. The nature of the magazine's circulation is so wound around and etiolated in the ABC report that its true quality, even to a competitive circulation manager himself, is not easy to ascertain. To someone not actively engaged in day to day circulation work, the quality of the magazine's readers as seen through an A.B.C. report alone, is a relatively unknown factor. Generally speaking, individuals who are responsible for buying advertising space are unaware of this significance. This is the hole in the sale of advertising space in which the white rabbits live.

the use of the publication's white space.

Both kinds of mind work on almost every magazine, but the bigger books tend to attract to themselves more men of the latter type because, although conjuring often accompanies the sale of an intangible, the sober desire to give the other people a fair and square run for their money is the real quality that differentiates between the footloose peddler and the superior salesman.

Magazine advertising men who perform best range themselves among the country's largest salaried executives. A page in *Life* in black and white sells for $38,650. Let's say you are The Man, its publisher. At your desk is a guy named Joe who, because of his ability to sell an intangible, is able to add to your publication one page an issue that you otherwise wouldn't have; a net annual additional billing of $1,700,000. How much would you be willing to pay such a man?

Ladies' Home Journal sells one page in black and white for $27,760. Being a monthly, it is fatter than a weekly, having more time to build up pages for each issue. If you were advertising director of the *Journal*, how much would you pay a man who was able to add four pages a month that you otherwise wouldn't sell?

Granted two publications of the same size and quality, with page rates of approximately $5,000 for black and white, the difference between an annual gross advertising billing of $4,000,000 and $6,000,000 is the difference between the advertising manager, the merchandising manager and the two top space salesmen on the publication. Two million dollars in additional billing hangs on the talents of four men. If these men would normally earn $25,000 a year, how much more would you be willing to pay each of them to get that extra $2,000,000? Income taxes being what they are, publishers cannot buy advertising talent. First, the talent isn't available; second, the men are held in place more by the respect and dignity of their job, by fringe benefits, retirement plans, friendship, courtesies, and affection than by an offer down the street for an additional $300 a week more.

How Do I Get In?

A young man seeking entry into the publication business might well pick up a magazine of his choice and analyze the advertising in each issue for the last two years, noting the category of advertisers in the book (car, food, perfume, etc.) and the advertisers under each category. Then he would do the same thing with the magazine's competitors. This lays bare what a rare few in the trade know—the categories in which the publication is strong, the categories in which it is weak, and the big basic advertisers in each category which this publisher does not have and which all or some of its competitors do have.

This chore-boy research lifts this young man from the welter of practically everybody else seeking a job in the advertising business. Having done this, and no more, a young man or woman could gain a job on the magazine's research department. But bigger things are to be had. The next step is to outline to the publisher exactly what he ought to do to land contracts from those big basic advertisers not now using the publisher's pages. Young men with this kind of mind are sought after with such terrifying earnestness that their appearance by the method described in any publisher's office would be met with a hush followed by a swoop and the young man would be gobbled, hobbled and had.

To understand the enthusiasm a publisher has for this type of approach you need merely see the applicants who walk in for a job in the Advertising Department, whose bachelor of arts degree is equal to something handed out by the University of Indiana and whose conformity is best understood by their opening sentence which is: "I would like a career in Advertising."

What Do They Earn?

The man in the single-breasted grey flannel suit, wearing a blue shirt, a quiet tie, and carrying an attaché case, is the ten-pin humorously known in the trade as the Space Cadet, Space Pilot, Space Salesman, or more dignifiedly, as the publisher's representative. On the smaller books with page rates ranging around $300, he receives 20% of all the money the publisher collects for the white space that he sells. Out of this he has to pay all of his expenses—automobile, train, plane, hotel, motel, tips, laundry, pressing, secretarial, postage, telephone, wires—and make a profit if there is anything left. In the lower reaches of publishing such a space salesman will be fortunate to sell $50,000 worth of space a year out of which he will receive $10,000 and be lucky to make himself $90 a week. Such jobs are stepping stones.

On monthlies with page rates ranging up to $1500 and perhaps even $2000 for one page, the space salesman has the same arrangement, but his commission is 15%. Here, a good man moves $150,000 worth of space a year and receives $22,500 gross of which he will generally keep about $12,000.

In publications with page rates of $1500 and up, space salesmen will frequently be on a salary, plus expenses, plus a bonus for all net paid advertising sold over a given amount. Thus, a space salesman working for a monthly magazine with a $4,000 page rate might receive a salary of $250 a week, plus all of his expenses, plus 4% of the net business that he sells over $400,000 a year, and 8% of the net paid business that he sells over $750,000 a year. Such a man would make a bonus of perhaps $1,500 a month from September through March, and scrape by on his salary from May through August, unless the publication has a special issue during the warm weather months.

"Scrape by" may sound odd to writers earning $125 a week, but space salesmen lead a tense, driving life and are often under compulsion to "live high" just to get rid of the irritations heaped on them. On a Monday morning, he poketh his head into the open office door. The incumbent, seeing him standing there, stares coolly. "Drop dead or go away." Having traveled by plane and bus and taxi, 716 miles for this reception, the space salesman finds a feast on vanilla ice cream calmeth him down not.

Most publications divide up the country into territories; each salesman's territory gives him from 100 to 250 accounts. These may be located in one state, or, in the west, 15 states. On some publications, men are assigned types of accounts. Thus, one man will handle all food accounts regardless of where they are located. He becomes a specialist in the food business.

The T.O.

Heading up the Advertising Department of a big book is the advertising director. Under him are three assistant advertising managers, each in charge of certain product categories. One assistant will handle all new cars, trucks, gasoline, oil, and car tools, while another assistant advertising manager might specialize in drug accounts. Working with the three assistant advertising managers is a promotion manager and an artist who create literature proving the value of the publication. On the same level as the promotion manager is a merchandise manager who thinks up techniques to hold wavering accounts in the book, or to attract to the publication accounts that are not readily sold.

The merchandise manager offers ideas to all advertisers in the publication, but the heat is naturally turned on the more difficult accounts, i.e., "difficult" to sell or "difficult" to hold. Let's say you are a manufacturer of a light meter and about to enter the photographic field. Of all the varied consumer photographic books, you select one. The others hammered at your door to no avail. "No!" you said.

The merchandise manager of one of the magazines you turned down digs in his heels and tries to turn you around. Let's peek in at this merchandising manager at work. Here is his offer as stated in his letter to you:

Dear Mr. Light Meter Manufacturer:

As you know, light meters in the early days of photography were hand held and apart from the camera. Up to 1950 only two cameras (both imported) had a built-in light meter. Today, buyers of middle and upper price cameras believe the light meter should be an integral part of the camera itself. Therefore, one of your biggest markets for light meters are the camera manufacturers themselves who can purchase your equipment in large wholesale orders and make it an integral part of their camera. We know this is part of your sales plan and that you, yourself, as well as your salesmen are now calling on camera manufacturers.

When you send your order to us for six pages in *Camera Corner* we will send a copy of the magazine (*Camera Corner*) containing your advertisement to 67 camera manufacturers with a letter from us outlining the 32 advantages that your advertising has for them in this publication when they use *your* light meter as part of their camera. These 32 advantages are listed on a separate sheet.

As a separate part of your light meter selling program, your salesmen call on jobbers. Today, there are 116 jobbers in the United States whose agents sell light meters to camera stores. When you contract for six pages in *Camera Corner*, we will send a copy of *Camera Corner* to the salesmen who work for each of these jobbers with a step-by-step outline of 27 advantages that your meter has for them because of the fact that you are now using *Camera Corner* as an advertising media.

Although there are over 5000 retail outlets for light meters in the country, you will know from your own research, that 85% of the light meter business is really done by 635 retail camera stores. We will send to each of these 635 stores, when you order six pages in *Camera Corner*, a copy of *Camera Corner* containing your advertisement and a list of 14 reasons why this advertising of your light meter in *Camera Corner* makes it advantageous for them to order your meter, to display it on their counters, and to put one in the window.

Last, we will equip all of your salesmen with plastic-covered copies of *Camera Corner* to show the trade when they call. As you know, *Camera Corner* sells for 35c a copy on newsstands. We will pay all of the costs of the above merchandising and bill you only for 50% of the retail price of the magazines used and will pay the postage, addressing, letter writing, inserting, mailing, sealing and stuffing charges of this three-star one-package deal.

We have asked our publisher's representative, Johnny Jones, to see you this Monday at 11 o'clock in the morning and hope you will have your order ready for him for six pages in *Camera Corner*.

This is a typical sally exerted by a merchandise manager. It is one drum in his orchestra. It is something that he does with his left hand and his eyes shut and without thinking. He is capable of a hundred ideas like this and he is the kind of a man who has only to point an arm and ideas run out of all fingers. The manufacturer gets ideas like this from other publications. They are not new; but whenever you talk about *him,* he listens.

Now, the merchandise manager needs help. It isn't that he hasn't ideas—it is that he runs out of energy to dictate them, to push them around, to implement them. To put one idea like this into effect, once the light meter manufacturer is sold, is no tiddledy-winks job. He looks each day for the bright young man who can come to him and say: "I noticed that in 1955 you carried 24 pages of General Electric; in 1956 you carried 18 pages; in 1957 you carried 12 pages and one four-page insert. My figures show you are not quite holding your own with the rest of the books in the field, in regard to General Electric. Surely, there are special reasons for this of which I know nothing. However, I have created four merchandising programs for GE tying in with a specific GE product and with their dealers, salesmen and their service stations. Here is my plan."

Such a program given to a merchandising manager evokes from him the sigh that is reserved for the fulfillment of desire. He might not be so quick to hire you as assistant promotion manager, but he would be likely to let you try implementing the ideas already on his desk; such as the one the light meter man may have bought.

The Promotion Manager

The promotion manager in the Advertising Department office has the most fun. After the editor has built up reader loyalty; after the circulation manager secures subscriptions from all The People Who Matter, the promotion manager's job is *to prove it.* To do this, he summons art, culture, surveys, statistics, sex, gimmicks, wit and the black arts.

The big books don't push hot and heavy for this kind of promotion as they rely more on their space salesmen; they have them in depth. They can call on an account five, even six times a year, and make a full-dress presentation. The smaller books lack the manpower to do this because their page rate is too low to justify hiring enough help.

The middle-size books, running from 200,000 to perhaps 500,000 circulation, are the ones that produce peppy fanfare. Let's look up a specific example of what one publication did. We have selected *The Farm Quarterly* because it was founded in our shop and we can detail the following matter factually.

Here's what *Farm Quarterly* did promotionwise in a single three-month period:

(1) Sent its prospective advertisers, and their agencies an advance editorial outline of what will appear in the next issue.

(2) Sent the same group a little box of soybean seeds that the Madison Avenue Fraternity could plant in a cigar box next to some sunny window and watch the beans sprout and then cut them at about 3 or 4 inches height and use in a green salad. The beans were grown by a *Farm Quarterly* reader who was particularly proud of his certified soybean seed crop. The letter that the prospective advertiser received from *Farm Quarterly* detailed the farm interests of this particular typical reader, his equipment, his acreage, his income, *and his ability to buy from the advertiser.*

(3) The next promotion consisted of a half dozen leaves of the Lemon Verbena plant. A short letter tied in the fragrance of these delicate lemon-scented leaves with the pleasant manner in which advertising returns from *Farm Quarterly* hang on and on to the advertisers who grace its pages.

(4) A folder of statistics secured from the Agricultural Census Department in Washington, D. C., detailed, year by year, the number of farms since 1900 (6,000,000 in 1900; 2,000,000 today);
the dollar value of all crops sold each year and the continuing increase in revenue secured by one numerically small group of farmers who, because of their annual increase in production, are the prime prospects for farm manufacturers. A letter accompanying the booklet then made clear that the circulation of *Farm Quarterly* paralleled this particular group of farmers.

(5) A cow bell with a little Happy New Year card attached to it cheerfully related that the New Year of the farmer comes early in spring when he sprays liquid fertilizer on the pastures, cuts his first furrow, and repairs his fences against the nuzzling of the new born. A tie-in was made of the fact that the Spring

issue of the *Farm Quarterly* came to farmers on February 20th, just when the farmer's "New Year" begins and the farmer starts to buy equipment.

(6) A list of *Farm Quarterly* subscribers in the farm town closest to the advertiser was enclosed with a short letter, suggesting that he personally inspect the readership of this magazine and, in this first-hand way, recognize the buying power of its readers in regard to farm equipment.

Do such high jinks sell space? Here is an actual letter from an advertiser:

> "Sir:
>
> Well now, I am but human. After soybeans, verbena leaves, lists of well-to-do farmers who subscribe to *Farm Quarterly* in Boone County, Oklahoma, statistics, the plaintive note of a cow bell, which still haunts my ears, we are going to give you a third of a page for_____in your Spring issue. Small indeed, but a beginning. If_____gets enough inquiries and sales, you will get a contract for the rest of the year. From then on it's up to you."

A few minutes back we asked a question: "Does mail promotion really sell space?" Actually, no letter, telegram, gimmick, statistic, or the like gets an order. The order is secured by the space salesman who calls on the advertiser and by dint of hard labor rattles the order loose.

The promotion helps. Charles Anderson, one of the better space salesmen in the Midwest says, "Every good promotion piece that comes into my territory is a free call. I'm lucky to make 100 calls a month. The promotion piece calls on 1,000 people I can't see."

How can a young man or woman get a job in the promotion division of the Advertising Department? First, it is important where you apply. The big books already are filled up and have a standing line. The small "break-even" books can't afford you. They may pay your salary but they are not willing to make the long-term investment that mail promotion requires before it pays off. In addition, the small books don't have enough space salesmen on the road to get the benefit of the warm-up that the promotion awakens in the mind of the prospect. So, as a job applicant, the book you want to choose is one that appears prosperous, but perhaps is not getting its full share of space. Try the No. 2 book in a good field. Or, select a fat trade journal in a field of three fat magazines, so that the publisher needs be relentless to get every order or the other books will scrape it up and there won't even be a grease spot left.

Select a trade paper with at least 50% of its pages filled with advertising and one that you respect editorially because nothing beats good editorial content. Try for a book with a relatively higher rate per page per thousand readers than the other books in the field because it shows the publisher is realistic. Call on five advertisers and see how they feel about the book. Call on five non-advertisers that are in the competing books but not in this one, and get their reaction. Call on five advertising agencies who are placing space in the book and get their viewpoint. Only with independent exhaustive research can there be a real foundation to what you will do. If you have a promotion mind, and the time and willingness to do research, and put on the publisher's desk a complete package of four promotion mailings and an envelope containing your research, he will hire you if someone gives him some smelling salts first, to recover. You must remember that you have been preceded by 360 applicants who said: "The employment agency said you didn't need anybody, but I thought I would come over anyway."

Who's for Research?

One of the most interesting divisions of the Advertising Department is Research. Save for a few great big books, most publishers have no idea what people think of them. They know this is a tremendous hole in their makeup, but truly, they have never found the time, opportunity, personnel, and the energy to get into it seriously. You may ask, how can it be that a going business, operating for perhaps fifty years, doesn't really know what the public thinks of them.

Well, take yourself.

If twenty people who know you would fill three 8 1/2 x 11 sheets of paper giving an honest analysis of YOU and someone read these twenty reports, they would likely think it was written about twenty different people. If YOU read them you would be amazed. Most of all, you might be shocked by the unfairness, the injustice, the rank prejudices, without facts and true understanding, that would be presented by your friends and acquaintances.

Magazines are just like people. To individuals, working with magazines all their lives, magazines *are* people. They have quarrels, hates, loves, bickerings, good luck, bad luck, windy moments, spurts, temperamental days and moments of wild genius but the publisher, editor, advertising manager, and the other departmental heads never really and truly get to know how the public has analyzed them.

The public doesn't go in for independent exhaustive research. As a result, the public's analysis of any magazine is as biased, unjust, naive, and uninformed about a magazine as they well might be about you. Yet, if the publisher knew precisely how his property was regarded, he would be better able to turn the public's attitude into the direction where he wanted it to go. He could do this first by changing the publication in certain areas; second, by directing his promotion at that segment of the public thinking which was biased or uninformed about his product.

Most research that the publisher sees is angled. The king cannot get away from his sycophants. Occasional research instituted by the magazine, that goes against the grain of what the executives on the magazine want to believe, is expostulated against and buried like an undeserved, uncomplimentary remark.

Most books in the half-million-or-less circulation field have no Research Department that honestly, and in depth, and in an unerring, unbiased way, tells them what the public is thinking about them. Only when this is truly known is the publisher able to deflect public thinking along the routes where *he* wants it to go. You are at the gateway of a wonderful opening for a competent person.

A job applicant could call upon a hundred people in the trade, using a Polaroid camera to take a picture of each. He could then paste each picture on an 8½x11 sheet of white paper, and alongside it type the person's comment on the publication. He would be recognized instantly as a young man or woman of rare perspicacity.

But this tidy little job needs be topped. The cherry is a page summary of what people said and step-by-step detailed program of how to alter and improve the public's attitude toward this publication. Publishers are extraordinarily sensitive as to what advertisers, agencies, dealers, jobbers, and wholesalers in their particular field think of their book. This is the kind of a job that a girl who takes dictation and has a sharp business mind can handle beautifully. If the publication were fifty years old and had never had a Research Department and the publisher was dead set, from the day he was born, against wasting money on a Research Department, the chances are such a presentation would spin him around like a top.

If it didn't, this same presentation could be shown to several other publishers as an example of what the job applicant can produce.

What Should a Page Cost?

On what are advertising rates based? There are as many ways to figure the rate a magazine should charge for a page of white space as there are publishers themselves. One method, unchallenged for its realism, is used by people who are in publishing not only as a way of life, but as a means of sustenance.

This method is simplicity itself.

On the left-hand side of a sheet of paper you list the total monthly loss of the Editorial Department. Since the Editorial Department, like the furnace of a steel mill, has no income whatsoever, all of its expenses are loss. On a monthly magazine of approximately 500,000 circulation this loss including copy, art, pix, engravings, travel, salaries, layout, and incidental editorial office expenses will come to about $20,000 in the east, perhaps less west of Chicago.

On the same left hand side of the paper, we list the Production Department which includes printing, paper, binding, and wrapping of 500,000 magazines a month. For a magazine between 96 and 112 pages, the production costs will come to about 16c a copy or $80,000. *The Production Department takes in no money at all so this, too, is total loss.

So far, we have $100,000 a month shot.

Next, we list the Circulation Department which has income as well as expenses. Since our publication has a press run of approxi-

*Based on its size being 6½ x 9½ inches. Moving the book to 8½ x 11, adding 4 color and using coated stock doubles the price.

mately 500,000, we will assume that 200,000 copies go to the newsstands of which 140,000 are sold, the other 300,000 are net paid mail. After the total income of the Circulation Department is balanced against its expenses, its loss will be in the vicinity of $2,-000 to $5,000 a month, and we will arbitrarily fix it at $3,000. Perhaps this publication will build up a "house business" which will sell a book or maybe produce business movie films. This may make enough profit to offset the loss of the Circulation Department. At this time, the net of this future "house business" cannot be counted. So, we have $3,000 monthly loss.

Under the Administration Department we list all those expenses which cannot conveniently be allocated to any of the above departments without such intricate bookkeeping that it is simply cheaper and easier to set up one department called Administration and charge to it such items as rent, auditor, bookkeeper, PBX board, light, heat, publisher's salary, workman's compensation and social security taxes, legal fees, interest, air conditioning, etc. The administrative cost of a big magazine is in the vicinity of 3% to 6% of its gross income; the smaller books running 12% or even 15%. In this case we are going to figure the administration cost at $5,000 a month. The above, save for the cost of selling advertising, represents the total cost of issuing our monthly of 500,000 net paid circulation, a matter of $108,000 per month.

Now for the finite business of figuring what the advertising rate should be.

When publishing a magazine of approximately 100 pages the minimum number of net paid pages of advertising that should be carried are forty, the maximum is sixty. So the problem is really very simple. On 40 pages, the publisher should be able to break even; on 50 pages he should make a moderate profit.

To get the page rate, we simply divide 40 into the monthly expenses and that gives us a figure of $2700. To this figure we must add the cost of selling the advertising. In this case the publisher will need a staff of five men representing the East, Mid-Central, Mid-West, Far West, and South. These men with their expenses, plus an advertising director, merchandise manager, promotion manager, advertising artist and lay-out man, secretaries, stenographers, and incidental office expense, will come to approximately $12,500 a

HOW TO FIGURE THE PRICE OF ONE PAGE
OF ADVERTISING

When you are publishing a monthly magazine of 100 pages and you feel sufficiently secure to assume you will sell at least 40 pages of advertising, here is how to figure the price of 1 page.
First, estimate your expenses.

Expenses per month

Editorial _____$20,000
Production _____$80,000
Administration _____$ 5,000
(The above 3 departments have no income.)
Circulation _____$ 3,000

(This department does have income,
and, in this case, $3,000 is the monthly estimated net loss)

Monthly net loss of above four departments _____$108,000.
Since only the sale of advertising can make up this $108,000 loss per month, how much should one page cost, if we can sell 40 pages?
One page of advertising _____$2,700
(You arrive at this by dividing 40 into $108,000.)

Cost of selling one page of advertising _____$ 312
(You arrive at this figure by dividing 40 into $12,500. The latter figure is the estimated cost of maintaining an advertising department.)

Cost of one page including selling cost _____$3,012
Price of one page as it will appear on your rate card _____$3,540
(Advertising agencies charge 15% commission. Therefore this 15% needs to be added to your page cost.)

Cost of one page of advertising including all costs _____$3,540
(If 40 pages are sold the magazine will break-even. On 50 pages, it will show a profit.)

month. Forty into this equals $312. We add this figure to our basic rate of $2700 and now have $3012. But this is still not the final figure.

The advertising agency gets 15% of the business that it sends the publisher. If a black and white page costs $1000, the advertising agency sends the publisher $850, keeping $150 for their profit and expenses in sending that piece of business to the magazine. This 15% must now be added to the last figure we had of $3,012, and so we now come up with $3,540, which is the rate which this particular publication would have to charge for one page of black and white advertising on a publication of approximately 100 pages with a 500,000 net paid circulation, to break even when it sells and collects for 40 pages of advertising.

The next step is to look around and see what the other publications in this field charge. If they are charging half as much — whoa! You can't start. If they're charging twice as much, then maybe your figures are wrong. As the publication adds additional pages of paid advertising, the publisher naturally doesn't put it all in his back pocket. First, the advertising agency takes off 15%. Second, there are additional selling costs in getting more paid space. Third, some pages of text may have to be added or "the book will be top heavy." Finally, the supply wolves who live off the publisher are quick to notice the publication has moved from 40% advertising to 55%. As a result, they firm up their prices. Printer, compositor, labor unions, paper jobbers, photographic agencies — every big supplier keeps a finger on the publisher's pulse and as his magazine moves from 40% advertising to 55% or a shade over 55% advertising, all the suppliers crowd in for a bite. They don't need charts; they can smell it.

Let's watch a supplier try for an extra nibble. Bill Waters walks in. Bill had been making the four-color plates for this particular magazine. He lowers himself comfortably in a chair next to the publisher's desk, smiles gently and says:

"Jake, we've been working with you now at 35% off union scale since you fellows started a year and a half ago and I have been catching hell from the International. Our trade association stood me up at our meetings and lashed me. Jake, these engravings you send over mean a lot and I've stood by you, but the last raise of 5%

I had to give my men and the raise of 2 1/2% on copper and the last 3% raise on acid has knocked me out and I can't give you 35% off scale no more. We are prepared to let you have 23%, but, Jake, if I have to take it out of my commission, I'm going to try to sell the old man on giving you 26%."

All the above is, of course, complete double talk and Bill Waters knows it. The publisher knows it, and both know the other knows it. They settle at 32% off scale. But twenty settlements like that and the bloom is gone from moving a book from 40% advertising to 55%.

That is why the publisher at his next meeting with his advertising staff gets up and says:

"Fred, nobody here wants to raise page rates and even though you fellows get a little bigger bonus when we have higher advertising rates because your commissions are going to be a little bigger, I still don't want to raise rates. Our costs are terrible and we are going to have to do something. I think we will let the black and white alone, but just bump the color."

Which Book Should I Buy?

Why is one magazine bought over another? If you were to read the advertising story of some state farm paper that is issued on newsprint and sells for fifty cents a year, and compare that with the advertising story of *Fortune*, *Vogue*, or a fraternal magazine of some ancient order whose publication is included with the dues, and whose members number into the hundred of thousands, but whose actual readers can be counted by the dozen because the members simply throw the publication away on receipt — what would it say? The incredible thing is that the advertising story of these publications would read alike. They say the same thing.

They say: *one*, we have quality circulation; *two*, we have high-buying power per reader; *three*, we offer valuable trade interest; *four*, we have extraordinary reader interest; *five*, ours is an influential market; *six*, our prosperous readers demonstrably have great and immediate need of your product right now.

How can such varied and unlikely publications as the above claim the same thing? The answer is simple. The above six points are what the advertiser wants, so magazine salesmen simply lay claim to them. The technique in selling advertising space, therefore, is being able to prove to the advertiser that you actually have each of the above six points. Granted a reasonably good publication, an able advertising director can prove each of these points up to the very hilt and then a little bit more besides. This places the space buyer in one hell of a position. Whom is he to believe? Everybody tells him the same thing and everybody proves it. Yet even Coca Cola can't use the back cover of every magazine every month. Which one should they use? How often? The people who buy advertising space have many answers to this.

One gentleman by the name of Jack Martin of Martin Advertising Agency of Milwaukee, who certainly isn't the brainiest or even the best advertising man in the country, has a system which I have long respected. He puts it this way:

"You can't beat a space peddler at his own game — those guys stay up all night thinking things to tell me and they've got a whole staff of people to prepare charts to prove it. They come in my office with three or four assistants, they barrel me in, and they pour on statistics. I don't say I don't listen, but I got a system of my own. This is my system. All I do is take a magazine home and read it. If it entertains, instructs and educates me and animates me to want to do something then I feel it's got reader interest. If editorially it builds up in me a hospitable climate for a particular product or a particular class of products, and I got a product of that sort in the house, then I'm going to recommend to my clients to advertise in this magazine. That's all there is to it."

Edward Grauel was one of the advertising managers of Eastman Kodak, and bought thousands of pages for some thirty years. At one time he bought strictly mass circulation that offered him the cheapest rate per page per 1000 readers; then he bought on the basis of printing quality and general appearance; then he developed an abiding interest in surveys which showed him how one magazine's audience represented a disproportionately high market for camera equipment; and finally, out of it all, Ed Grauel evolved this theory in regard to all the 20 or 30 trade and consumer photographic publications. Here's Ed:

"Confidentially, I don't pay too much attention to a magazine's circulation or its advertising rates. If I read every issue of a photographic book for two years and at the end of that time I feel that this publication contributes to the good and welfare of photography, I recommend that Kodak be in it."

Stanley Wildrick, president of a large eastern advertising agency, has a rare method of his own by which he decides which publications he will recommend to his clients. Mr. Wildrick arrives unexpectedly at a magazine office and goes directly to the circulation manager. He introduces himself and asks permission to open the morning mail. This tears the circulation manager apart but there is nothing he can do about it.

Mr. Wildrick will sit at a desk in the circulation office for four straight hours opening one letter after another, analyzing the circulation mail received by a publication that day. He will note whether the subscriptions are paid for in stamps, coins, dollar bills, express orders, money orders or checks. He will note whether the checks are counter checks or printed. He looks at the stationery on which readers write, the envelopes they use. He scans the handwriting to indicate the age, as there is quite a difference between the handwriting of a group of people between 20 and 40 and a group between 60 and 80 years of age. He looks to see how many subscriptions are coming in "over the transom" (that is, unsolicited), how many come in from sheet writers, etc. Partly on this experience, Mr. Wildrick makes his judgments. It takes the circulation manager a week to recover from this operation, for, on the wrong Monday morning, Mr. Wildrick uncovers the devil's own brew.

There remains one last and intricate method to judge a publication. This is practiced by a Buffalo gentleman I know by the name of Morse Flagler. He inspects a magazine for the last five years and lists, issue by issue, all the 1", 2", 3", and 4" ads and also the one-column advertisers who use a coupon with a key (viz., 100-A 10th St., 100-B 10th St., etc. Thus, the answers to the ad reveal the media that evoked them). He charts the frequency with which these particular advertisers have used the publication. Whenever he finds any one magazine harboring the same group of keyed or coupon ads month after month and year after year in their pages, he is able truthfully to say: "For these advertisers, at least, this publication must pay out." He goes to his clients who have similar products and says with some justice, "I recommend this particular publication to you." Other advertising agencies also follow this system, which is not unique but merely tedious. It is easy to think the idea up, but a tremendous chore-boy job to implement.

Is It Worth It?

Among my acquaintances are people in various kinds of businesses and professions. I know a surgeon who loves to operate. He schedules operations for 8:00 A.M. because he rises happiest with nothing to do but go straight "to the cutting room." I know a well-fixed attorney who, having inherited great wealth, prefers his daily work. But everyone else I know, and I have asked most of my friends, are not in their line of work by both intellectual and emotional preference.

They don't like it. They want out.

The amenity of the publishing business is this: the people who are in it like it. You pit yourself against the ablest men and women —not in your state or city—but the ablest people *nationally*. Unlike local retailers or wholesalers, you will meet top-level executives almost exclusively. Some, of course, are culturally illiterate, but two or three times a week you come into contact with people of sensitivity and education who carry their job magnificently and with dignity. This doesn't happen often in other trades.

Were it not for advertising, there would be an entirely different kind of press; freer, no doubt, but poor pickings and with so little pay that talent would go elsewhere. Advertising keeps the press oiled with the money to buy literary, editorial and art talent. Without it, our press would be equal to the American ballet.

Man Against White Space

Part 4 Administration

Of a magazine's five departments, Administration, the command post, is the only one to which job applicants never apply.

The man who takes on the job of publisher stands alone in a little world that he has built. When he comes to work in the morning, the elevator man doesn't wait to fill the car; he shoots the boss right up. When the boss steps onto his main floor, by singular osmosis, six bright little heads pop up and speak aloud a cheery good morning but, if an hour later the same little heads are gathered around the water fountain and the boss comes over to take a drink, in ten seconds he is alone.

In a magazine of some forty employees, the administration department usually employs two people: the publisher and a bookkeeper. On minor magazines, the publisher also holds down one of the main departmental jobs. He is usually advertising manager or production manager. This is not because he is too cheap to hire one of these men, but because they are so hard to find. As a result, the small magazine publisher never finds time really to be a publisher, to inter-relate his departments, to stand on one foot and do nothing

The Creative Writer

but think. He is concerned by day with detail. At night he catches up on his trade reading. He dries up young for lack of time to develop his cultural depth. Should his company grow, add one or two magazines, and the number of employees swell to ninety, the administration department will fit nicely in a small room: the publisher, two bookkeepers and a part-time auditor.

Next step up is an administrative assistant for the publisher, while the final step adds a creative cost accountant.

In the mornings, as the departments begin to function, there is a great bustle and to-do, the cheerful amenities of intelligent people working together. The publisher partakes of this, for it is a succulent part of his life; but when he entereth his little cell, there is no one on whom he can call for advice. What are his problems?

They are few in number.

First, he has the personnel problems of any employer. Christmas comes on Thursday and everybody wants Friday off, too. Catherine, the best secretary the office ever had, does three letters to the other girls' one, but comes to work at 9:30, the other girls at 9. They say: "Why can't we all come to work at 9:30?"

Second, the publisher is the spark. He pulls out of himself the inspirations for his department chiefs when they are up against it, and leaves them alone with soft words of warm encouragement when they do well without him.

Let us watch the publisher in action.

TIME: 9 A.M.

PLACE: The circulation manager's office. Enter girl with a message off the Watts line.

Circulation Manager reads: "Ten day check-up of 1,100 newsstands shows our newsstand sales down 11%."

He crumples up the message and leaves.

CURTAIN

The circulation manager walks into the publisher's office to ask for advice.

"Good morning," he says. "Look at this message!"

The new issue is ready to go to press. Should we cut the newsstand press run, in the face of falling sales and thus surely sell

402

even less, or should we increase the press run and try to hold the sale at the expense of heavy returns? How about cutting the price per copy? 75c is a lot of money these days. How about 60c?

Instead of that, how about experimenting with a price change in one region of the country? Better still, back up the newsstand copies with newspaper advertising? Too expensive. Then, print fewer pages and more magazines? Or, the same magazine on thinner paper? Try a new kind of cover? What kind? Start a bright new serial? Where is it? Get a new editor! Who? Oh hell, let's ride out the storm. Maybe it will pass. How about a survey that will tell *why* the newsstand sales are down? How do you ask people who didn't buy a copy?

Wait a minute! Are the sales down only in one region? Should there be a regional edition? Damn it, we never *do* anything about the West Coast growing so much. Can't we just back up the newsstand with a TV program? To hell with the newsstand! Push the mail instead. Then they're ours.

These, the classic alternates, seldom vary. Only in applying them does the skill differ.

The publisher runs through them all in his mind. He has done this before and he knows them by heart. It isn't just one thing he tells himself; it's a combination of many. How much can he trust the circulation manager? If he sounds dismal, which is how he feels this minute, and lets it all come out, which is what he wants to do, will the circulation manager talk and upset the whole zoo? The publisher sighs and goes to his club to think.

He wishes he had someone besides himself who had sold space, written captions, cropped pictures, run a door-to-door crew, created a magazine, and had the courage to risk his own money.

Except that the department heads who come to him vary, and sometimes there is good news and sometimes there is bad, this is how he makes his bread.

There is Good News, Too

The good news takes less time to digest. In the afternoon, the editor-in-chief brings in the layouts of the issue to hit the stands in 3 months. They light up the office like a Christmas tree. The clean, white over-sized layout pages, with their big borders, make the color prints sparkle just like the layout editor thought they would. "Look," says the publisher, and lays his hand over one part of a picture. "If we blew up this one part would it be a cover?" The editor nods happily. By God, the Old Man came through.

The publisher remembers, in Hollywood, forty years ago, watching Shirley Temple go before the cameras. Her mother stood close by her and warmed the child's hand as she passed by. "Sparkle, Shirley, sparkle," she whispered.

Sparkle. God dammit that's what he has to do all day. And he can, too, and he will. And he loves it. He'll beat the socks off the world. What's one month's drop in newsstand sales with an issue like this coming up? The publisher makes a mental note to tell the layout man to use smaller layout sheets. Those big ones trick the eye.

The advertising manager rolls in. Rolls is the word. In his hand is a blue and white N. W. Ayer contract. An 8-page insert! A neat little $50,000 order. "Boss, it came right in over the transom. We work like hell, we fight and make calls and then this drops in and we never even knew they were considering us."

The publisher smiles. Now he is at his best. "You earned this, Fritz," he says. "Remember the presentation you made at Ayer two years ago? The one where you took 'em to 21 next night. They never forgot what you showed 'em. Remember that mile long pull-out you took there last year? I'll bet you taught it to them by heart. Why you've been at them for years. You did it, boy."

Fritz walks out happy. The boss understands.

The non-fiction editor strolls in with a manila folder showing 30 letters that came in from prominent, really famous people, all excited about a controversial article the magazine used two months ago. The publisher reads them, thanks the editor, calls the promotion manager.

"Manny, I got something for you."

Manny comes in, reads the letters, mentally makes a package out of it and is off and running. A wonderful tool to prove to a lot of stiffnecks that the people who read this magazine *really* matter. Fritz calls back and says the new package will help him a lot with the Ford account. "A great idea," says the publisher.

A Budget Gives Form to a Magazine

But there is a third job.

It is called budgeting and people who know nothing about it think it is tedious. Budgeting is as creative as editing. Sometimes, it is done this way.

In October, the publisher estimates his gross income for the coming year. He would like to net ten cents on the dollar *before* taxes which means not quite five cents after taxes. If he takes in one million dollars, he hopes $50,000 will be his, plus salary.

So his first step in creative budgeting is to come up with a reasonable estimate of his gross income for the next year.

Well, maybe it will be $1,300,000. No, that's too high. But wouldn't it be nice if it were true? He calls on his only two executives whose departments take in money—circulation and advertising. What do they think will be their gross income next year? They sigh. If they say low, they will get nothing to spend; if they say high, they practically have to hang up a world's record to keep from eating their own words. They fiddle. They faddle. They writhe and move in and out. In the end, they come clean and play it straight and lay down a figure, $1,000,000.

Next, the publisher takes each department and estimates how much he can give each one; but he holds back 10% of $1,000,000 to cover his net profit and his federal taxes. With a pencil, he gives the production department $450,000, editorial $140,000, advertising $110,000, circulation $150,000, administration (this covers the salaries of his bookkeeper, secretary, himself, and his own business travel expenses) $50,000.

His secretary puts each departmental figure, and its monthly expense breakdown for the last 12 months, into sealed envelopes and delivers them. She notes that the administration department is allotted $50,000, same as last year. That means no raise for her and this was the year she planned to move from $125 a week to a neat $150. She decides to bide her time until the Ford people see what Manny has to show them. Maybe that will pry them loose. Or, maybe that $50,000 net will come through and she can ask for a bonus. With a bonus, she could trade in her Plymouth on a good compact.

The editor looks at the $150,000 figure and knows he cannot

meet the pay raise requests he senses are coming from his staff before Christmas. And he must meet them or lose talent. Talent that he trained. He calls the production manager.

What if they could get some four-color forms up ahead and run them together. What would the savings be? Six thousand dollars will cover the increase he wants to give his staff.

The production manager, who wants to hire an assistant to do quality control, phones his paper supplier and they make a date for lunch. He puts through a half dozen long distance calls to other paper mills and begins a squeeze.

The circulation manager, who dearly wants a spot TV program to back his newsstand sales, calls Fritz. Had they underestimated advertising income? Fritz says, well if they got Ford, they can put the hammer to Chevrolet. The circulation manager asks how much it would help if he could add 2,000 Ford dealers as subscribers.

Together, as a working team, they give and take and create a budget.

One night, the publisher, and his staff run through it all, dollar for dollar. They examine the magazine that is their child. They admire it, they criticize it, they respect it. They go home agreed on a working budget.

The Publisher's Job Defined

Only at the very large companies does the publisher function purely as a publisher—a director of his five departments. Elsewhere, he remains a worker, doing a departmental job by day, and striving by night to inter-relate the workings of the magazine. Particularly, it is hard for the publisher who came up through accounting to release his hold on the Administrative department. You can spot this situation if you work there a day. The bookkeeper and pay clerk may be the sole employees of the Administrative department, and they will report directly to the publisher for so small an item as re-varnishing a desk.

Often, the man with editorial experience will tend to identify himself, as do Gingrich, Lawrence and Wallace, with the Editorial department; or McGraw with the Business department. I suspect the making of Richard Deems as a publisher came about when he left *Esquire* and went to Hearst. At *Esquire* he might have forever remained faithful to one department: Advertising.

In my own experience, I enjoyed selling advertising so much that I never relinquished this departmental job, so that although I was publisher in name, I did precious little thinking and a great deal of selling. Few can serve as both captain and general.

Here is Bernie Davis speaking on this subject:

"The publisher normally stands as an apex of the triangle, alone, with no special orientation to any of the key departments. Of course, some publishers rise through an editorial background (as did I), or through an advertising, circulation or finance background, in which case he would then have a special aptitude. Once he becomes a publisher, he must be responsible rather equally for coordinating each of the subsidiary departments.

"For example, how far should a publisher go in getting subscriptions? Do you stop at the highest income producing level which would mean accepting only subscriptions that come in over the transom at regular rates without any discount, or do you push harder and go after, in succession, catalog agencies, school plans, field selling, etc., where the discounts might vary from 40% to 100%, or even more?

"How tight do you hold your newsstand draw? You have either a choice of keeping it very tight to minimize returns, or shoot for the higher sales at the risk of taking exorbitant returns. The same thing applies on direct mail activities: are you so anxious to get the subscriptions that you will continue a mailing with 1 or 2% returns, or do you restrict the promotion to those lists or appeals which bring you 4 or 5%? Are you willing to carry on a direct mail campaign where you net zero, or do you require a sufficient income in direct mail to pay the *cost* of the subscription itself *plus* the cost of the mailing?

"Obviously, the circulation manager wants to show these big circulation increases, but the economic facts of life may not permit it. Or perhaps the advertising manager is convinced that he either doesn't need it, or he cannot get the sufficient advertising to pay the higher rate to compensate for it. Conversely, the advertising manager might demand higher and higher circulation figures. The cost of getting them might make the whole thing impractical.

"Similarly, the question of advertising rates creates some problems. Are you governed by the treasurer who demands a certain rate to meet his costs, or are you governed by competitive features? Do you raise your rates in anticipation of circulation growth, or should you have to obtain the circulation growth first and then raise your rates?

"In short, the publisher's function is to weigh all of these internal pressures and make the determination as to which decision is in the long run the most productive for the publication as a whole. If this orientation is directly tied in with that of his bookkeeper, he is no publisher and sooner or later he will cause the publication to dry up. Obviously, many calculated risks must be taken which any sound treasurer would have to resist and with good cause. In short, a good publisher spends half his time on adjusting his operation to conditions as they are at the moment, but the other half of his time must be devoted to expansion and long range operations which might be economically unjustified at the moment, but would put his publication at a higher level of income and volume a year or two hence."

Who's For Publishing?

The men who prefer publishing as a way of life, who wake up each morning with great relish and an abundance of wit and energy to turn into publishing, their life-long mistress, grow fewer by the year. Why is this so?

I think we all admit the quality that makes a man a good physician is the desire to cure other people, to help them become well and to get a bang out of it himself. The same is true, of course, of good cooks. They love to feed people.

Publishing is no different. For a magazine to command the love and respect of its audience, it requires a human being who has something to say and is going to keep on saying it via the printed word if he is in solitary in a county jail, or expelled to run a mimeograph machine in the print shop of a ball bearing factory.

The trouble about publishing is that individuals who feel this way are not collected together, encouraged, patted on the back, warmed and fed with the literature and companionship of their kind.

Let's pretend that you are a farmer and you want to know

whether you should plow your field deep or shallow, churn it with a rotary hoe or spike it and drop a seed in each hole. In each state is an agricultural college; each county has an agricultural high school and a county agent. Both state and federal governments spew out literally tens of thousands of booklets answering technical questions about farming. In esoteric fields, almost beyond the blue yonder of disbelief, the U. S. Government Printing Office has issued booklets on shad roe, prehistoric Indians and inverted atoms.

But, for magazine publishing there is nothing and we have nobody. Go to a library and ask if they have a book on how to be a magazine publisher. Write the Association of University Extension offices and ask if they have a course on how to learn the principles of magazine publishing. For us, there is nothing.

Publishers have no pool on which to draw.

As a result, many of the men who run our magazines today are not publishers at all. They are manufacturers who would just as soon be making furniture or glass buttons or garage doors if they could make a buck faster. This is not to say that they are dishonest or bad citizens, or that they deserve our censure. But, publishers who are in the business only for money, rather than as a way of life, produce publications that treat people as customers. Just what does this mean? A customer is someone you want to sell something to—all you ask is they should pay for it and get out. In its crudest sense that is a customer. But as we progress in business, we want to upgrade out product so a customer buys it, comes back for more and tells his friends to do the same thing.

In the professions, the situation again upgrades itself. The engineer doesn't want only to earn a fee and build a bridge. He wants to erect a thing of beauty that will reward the beholder just for the looking. He wants something fine and functional, that will transport great bodies of traffic from one area to another and do it cleanly with economy of line and economy of dollars and without any excrescence or pretense. To help the engineer reach this state of mind, there is a whole library dealing with the ethics of engineering; there is a great national body of professors of engineering who teach service to mankind through engineering. The same is true in law and medicine, architecture and in fine design. In publishing, no such body exists. No professors of publishing instill in young people the idea of a life-long career to produce a noble magazine that says something, that is a work of art and that is honest. If there are no schools, no professors, no libraries for publishers-to-be, how then does a man become a publisher, and how does this wayward state affect publishing?

The Boys Become Men, Laissez Faire Style

Let's examine three magazines on the newsstands that are issued from one chain. They are titled, with a slight revision on my part, *Titter-Up; Shocking Divorce Cases* and *Hammerhead Butch*. The man who heads this group of publications is a human being, even as you and I. When he was in the seventh grade he edited the seventh grade magazine and in the eighth grade, the eighth grade magazine. In college he worked his way through, as a newspaper stringer and as a trade journal correspondent. He took journalism. But he came under the influence of no one who proposed a code of artistry and ethics for magazine publishing. No great editors spoke to him; no great publishers came to counsel him; no profound and intellectual individuals, with mature feelings, for extending the civilities of mankind through magazines, kindled within his heart the flame of their own beliefs. The end result is about the same as if young doctors, dentists and lawyers would never own a code of conduct and ethics. *Titter-up* indeed. Why not?

Let's take the situation on a higher level. For years, the *Saturday Evening Post* rejected liquor advertising. Only the individuals at Curtis who laid down this dicta are able accurately to tell the reasons why. Perhaps, they felt that hard liquor creates problems rather than softens them. Whatever its reason, the *Post* refused liquor advertising. Meanwhile, when on certain occasions, a manufacturer selected *Life* over the *Post* as an advertising media, how much credit did they give to the management of the *Post* for upholding their version of the dignity of man by refusing to take part in the advertising of hard liquor? Did they give it a thought; did they even know that the *Post* didn't carry hard liquor advertising; did they care?

Whatever the answers were, the management of the *Post* decided in the middle of the year 1958 to accept liquor advertising. That day the stock of the Curtis Publishing Company went up 10% because, as one brokerage house stated it: "At an advertising page rate of $25,000 *Post* revenue should increase at once by two million dollars a year, while the costs will not go up by more than $200,000 a year. Thus, Curtis' net profit and dividends have better prospects."

Perhaps everything is a matter of degree. Is the negation of the life-long policy of publishing no hard liquor advertising a crime? Almost every publisher accepts liquor advertising; in addition, they fight like hell to get it. But here, at the *Post*, the difference was that an ideology had changed. It had spun around full circle.

Did this mean that *Post* editors changed their minds and now believe liquor should be advertised and sold more widely? Does it mean someone said: "We tried to do what we thought was right but it costs too much. We need the dough. Sell Schenley."

What was the reasoning? What were the ethics?

To us, the point of this whole thing is that no literature came forth from any publication; no lectures were offered to an assembled group of publishers; no monographs were written by university professors; no minutes of publishing trade meetings were circulated in which the ins and outs of this decision were discussed on an intellectual as well as on a business and ethical basis.

The thing just happened and that was that. Perhaps, the *Post* got fifty letters from the dry clique cancelling their subscriptions and fifty letters from their wet counterparts extending subscriptions. As a group, advertisers didn't know, didn't care and paid no nevermind.

Were the same thing to happen in medicine or law or politics an abundance of comment would instantly bubble up and the whole nation would be the better for it through being better informed. But publishing, although it deals with the subject of communication, does not communicate to itself and has no articulate, accepted, universal code of ethics that are respected.

Nothing substantial is being done to educate and stimulate creative people to become publishers. As a result, publishing jobs are being filled by manufacturers who wish to buy cheap and sell dear. They have no compulsion to communicate and they have nothing to say. Where is a young man or woman to learn a set of standards

411

by which the acceptance of advertising should be judged? Where is the aspiring young publisher to learn a set of rigorous standards by which the validity of a net paid subscriber may be judged? Are there any journalism teachers who can answer the question from experience?

Can Publishing Be Taught?

At the college level, no one is being taught that a magazine has five departments, that they are inter-related, that they *all* need talent, and, that to be great in one department you have to know the other four.

One summer day I was asked to lecture at one of the nation's oldest Universities; an ivy clad, red brick, highly regarded Eastern school. I spoke on publishing as I was asked to. At the end of three hours, and when I tell you this, believe me, it humiliates me to say it, the instructor in charge of the class vanished in a state of tears. Why? Because what I had said violated the gentle misinformation that had drifted into this hall of learning. I was humiliated because that misinformation came not from the teacher, who was a gracious soul, but from publishing shops themselves who had been asked to send representatives to this school, and, for the most part, had lectured to this teacher's class along the lines of bland promotion for their own companies. Unprepared by this background, I had made the mistake of leading green troops into battle.

Many times, I have heard knowledgeable publishing people speak to University groups and invariably they say nothing whatsoever and punctuate this with funny stories. They sound like Kodak publicity executives.

I heard Ed Miller tell 50 journalism deans that editors are people but people are not editors; that few people have the talent to create an editorial mix and that the consulting of readers for an opinion is useful but the editor's best guide is his own experience, intention and intuition. Valid! I suppose that's all you *can* say in 30 minutes. But what *I* wanted to hear was how Ed Miller ran *McCall's*. I would have sat all day bug-eyed listening. And then I would have paid $100 to listen for one more hour. But of this, he said not a word.

But, we in the publishing business don't come clean when we

talk to University groups. It's all chit-chat, amiable and funny stories; a neuterizing of all our experience. Why do we do this? For fear of being misunderstood, I suspect.

We need to correct our public appearances before the Universities and tell how we make our bread.

We have 120 Schools of Journalism dedicated to the theory that it takes 600 hours to teach a person how to write a news story. Birdie Tebbets, while a baseball manager, observed that a catcher is a roughneck who can hit. By the same token a newspaper man is a person with two legs who knows how to use them. Does one need to spend four years at a University to learn this?

Barry Bingham, publisher of the *Times* and *The Courier-Journal* of Louisville, said, "To a young man who wants to prepare for newspaper work, I would urge four years of the stiffest, best-rounded liberal arts college training he can possibly manage. I much prefer this to the vocational type of training. If he feels a need for academic courses in journalism, I would recommend that he wait and take them at a good graduate school."

I mention this so that it will be clear that the idea I have to offer is not brand new and that I am sure other people have touched on it, and, in their own words, said the same thing better.

To me, the name that you give something has importance. It is the customer's first introduction to what you have to offer. I suggest that the name "School of Journalism" be altered to "College of Publishing." George Kienzle, while at the journalism school at Ohio State University, said that according to his researches, the image that leads a student to enter a School of Journalism is the desire to write. Publishing is broader than this. The name, College of Publishing, would tend to attract students who wished to participate in communication through the printed word; not *only* to write it. This is so much broader than turning the whole thing on the point of a pin, that is, learning to be a newspaper reporter. Harold Ross was a superb editor for thirty years and it is almost impossible to find something that he wrote. What did Ted Patrick ever write? Or Mayes? Their contribution came not so much from the words they wrote as from the ideas they created and then helped implement.

In the College of Publishing, I suggest there be four years of arts and that it be the stiffest, most authentic, hardest course on Liberal Arts offered by that particular University of which a College of Publishing is part.

Then, when a man graduated from the College of Publishing he would be respected for his arts background. Today, this is less than true because the "arts" he receives have a Currents Events I flavor (prerequisite: Sociology I, Political Science II).

In the College of Publishing I would offer arts for four years with five hours of writing, dummying, news casting, editing, rewriting, creative photography, layout, publishing accounting, interviewing and production per week, depending upon the semester and the year. I would make these five hours optional and admit to the fifth year of the College of Publishing those students who had completed this optional work and secured a grade of B, average. In the single year of graduate work, I would invite departmental executives of magazine publishing houses to come to the various Colleges of Publishing for lecture purposes. I refer particularly to the departmental executives who, up to this time, have seldom been noticed by the Schools of Journalism. They are the ones who need the most help in employing new talent and it is upon the future of their departments that publishing rests.

In addition to asking publishing exectutives to give a week a year of their time to teaching the young, I would ask the heads of the whole cart and padoodle of the separate businesses that feed publishers, to give a week a year for the same purpose. And, how these men and women would love to do this! Their value to the industry would be recognized and their own great need of a talent pool would, for the first time, be appreciated.

In this latter group would be the heads of sheet writer's, catalogue, independent space sellers, picture agencies, literary agents, public relation counsels, syndicates, national newsstand wholesalers, advertising agency copy writers, full time free-lance non-fiction writers, typographers, direct mail letter specialists, paper, plate and printing managers and the scores of special services without which there would be no publishing.

As I see it, in the fifth year of this College of Publishing, such an individual would come to the College to lecture from 10 to 11 in the morning and from 2 to 3 in the afternoon, four days of one week. I admit that the first hour he would talk about himself and the second hour he would talk about his company, and the third hour he would tell all the stories he knew. Now, worn down to the stump, the time has come when he has to tell the students what his job consists of, how he does it, his schemes, his ideas, his practices, his hopes, his feelings, his plans, his ambitions, his problems, his guile, his solutions, his failures, his goals. This is terribly difficult. Who communicates well? Left to his own devices, the layout man won't be able to tell how he does his job. His skill is layouts. If he could marshall facts, expound, analyze, parade a sequence of events, he would doubtless be somebody else. Thus, a great challenge rests on the teacher's ability to sit down with the lecturer, *before* he talks to the students and work out a logical and truthful explanation of the man's job and special skills. The teacher would, of course, quickly learn to become selective of the people whom he invites and be better equipped to help them prepare an outline of their lectures. For, without these advance outlines, little will come of it.

Before me, in my mind's eye, I see one of these industry-executives, one of our proposed lecturers. By name he is Julius Cowan, whose $40 an hour fee is the cheapest thing our company buys. Julius is a short, stocky man, drives a Cadillac, has a picture of his wife and children on his desk, arrives at work on time, listens with a slight shortening of his breath should the conversation turn to Albert Camus, gave up hand painted neckties many years ago, and regardless of how he dresses, always looks as though he had on a double breasted suit. Awed by creative artists, he does not realize he is one himself. But with all his gifts, Julius is no lecturer. Take him away from his comptometer and he glances about unsurely, shifts from one foot to the other, sighs and comes slowly to a complete stop. By trade he is a tax consultant for publishers; in fine, he is a wizard. He can put certain publishing problems into elementary mathematics and is a devotee of paying only the taxes you owe.

How could you get a series of eight lectures out of Julius that would make students aware of the finesse of creative accounting? Half of the people who would come to lecture, under the plan I outlined, would be as mute as Julius before a class. But if journalism teachers have any ability at the reporting which they teach, they will quickly learn to prod, to pry, to uncover the vocational excitements of Julius and his kind.

When a student came out of a College of Publishing he would have four years of authentic arts and know, ideologically, from whence he came, for this is the purpose of liberal arts. Also, from the first four years he would have a smattering of publishing as a whole. In his fifth year he would run headlong against the incredible number of openings in the profession he hopes to enter. As a matter stands today, and, it is no different from when I went to Journalism School 40 years ago, if a journalism teacher asks a student to take a course in advertising, or circulation, or accounting it is the next thing to an insult. Like asking a literary man to clean up after a steer. The image that draws us to Journalism Schools is the image of the foreign correspondent, the night city editor, the by-line reporter. This image has remained unchanged for sixty years and it needs to be enlarged to the true and beautiful picture which it really is. Welcome to the student who comes to Journalism School to learn to partake of publishing.

This Way
To The Egress

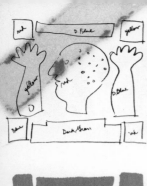